JOHN STUART MILL

Almost from his birth in 1806 John Stuart Mill
began one of the most extraordinary educations a
boy ever received. Mill's father, a renowned intellectual himself, decided he would act as his son's
teacher, and the precocious boy responded eagerly
and brilliantly to the challenge. He completed his
study of the classics before he was twelve. Following in his father's footsteps, Mill became a disciple
of Jeremy Bentham and founded a society for
young Benthamists. At twenty-one, however, he
suffered a severe depression which lasted for
several years. When he emerged he could no longer
share his father's doctrinaire beliefs; the result
was Mill's own restatement and refinement of
utilitarian philosophy which he describes in the
works included in this volume.

MAX LERNER

is Professor of American Civilization and World Politics at Brandeis University and a nationally known, syndicated newspaper columnist. He received his Ph.D. at the Robert Brookings Graduate School of Economics and Government, in Washington, D.C. He has taught political science at Williams College and was at one time Editor of **The Nation.** Professor Lerner is the author of **Ideas Are Weapons, The Mind and Faith of Justice Holmes, America As A Civilization,** and the editor of **The Portable Veblen.**

BANTAM MATRIX EDITIONS

essential works of john stuart mill

•

edited and with an introduction
by Max Lerner

•

BANTAM BOOKS
NEW YORK/TORONTO/LONDON

ESSENTIAL WORKS OF JOHN STUART MILL

Bantam Classic edition published August 1961
Bantam Matrix edition published February 1965
3rd printing

Bantam Books are published by Bantam Books, Inc., a subsidiary
of Grosset & Dunlap, Inc. Its trade-mark, consisting of the words
"Bantam Books" and the portrayal of a bantam, is registered in the
United States Patent Office and in other countries. Marca Registrada.
Bantam Books, Inc., 271 Madison Avenue, New York 16, New York.

PRINTED IN THE UNITED STATES OF AMERICA

CONTENTS

THERE are two kinds of successes in intellectual history—that of the thinker whose originality revives each time we read him, and that of the thinker whose influence spreads imperceptibly over the generations, so that his originality has become part of the intellectual air we breathe. John Stuart Mill belongs with the second kind of thinker. No figure in the history of Western liberal thought can match his impact and achievement, yet none has been more taken-for-granted as a good grey liberal, a slightly stuffy eminent Victorian, a man who had the right sentiments on the right occasions, a writer who seems to have written in classical quotations because we have warmed ourselves for generations on his glowing sentences and their luminousness has made them cosily familiar.

The fact is that Mill is a towering intellectual who is as fresh as tomorrow morning's newspaper and as relevant as the latest publicized crisis of our time. But it will take an effort of the imagination to think ourselves back into the issues and conditions of his time, out of which his thought grew. More than most great political and social theorists he was in the center of every melee of his age, as reformer and social radical, as anti-colonial fighter, as libertarian, as shaper and critic of democratic institutions, as a working social theorist. His was a many-faceted mind, any one of whose facets would have made the reputation of a lesser man.

Not the least interesting of his facets is the story of Mill's education—one of the strangest, most dramatic stories in the history of educational literature, at once exhilarating and tragic. The best source for it is in Mill's own *Autobiography* with which this volume of his essential works begins.

John Sterling, who had the rare distinction of being a friend both to Mill and to his bitter opponent, Thomas Carlyle, said of Mill that he was a "made or manufactured man." This expressed the consensus of the intellectual group in England which watched with fascination the experiment that James Mill carried on in the laboratory of his own home—the experiment of turning his son, John Mill, into a trained and disciplined genius. James Mill had aspired for the ministry, but he failed to get a post, and turned to the blandishments of philosophy and the rigors of radical social reform. Perhaps he carried into these pursuits something of the unsparing commitment which he might have invested in a religious vocation. As a tutor to a young Scottish noblewoman, and later as a divinity student, he had extended his reading and become a most learned young man. He became a magazine writer and newspaper editor in London, married a pretty girl whose mother (the proprietor of a house for lunatics) was able to give her a not negligible dowry, and settled down to raise a family and make a name for himself. His growing family had to be supported by the rather irregular income of a free-lance writer. But London was the center of an imperial cluster and —next to Paris—the focus of a bourgeoning intellectual life. James Mill placed himself deliberately at the center of it. He could discourse on psychology, philosophy, or politics, on the classical and modern authors, on revolution and reaction, on God and man, and he was able to transmit the flame of his intellectual excitement to others. He was a writer who didn't quite make the first-grade, but he had an almost matchless magnetic talent to attract young intellectuals from every rank and party, and to shed an incandescent glow in whatever areas his mind touched. The fact that he was utterly bored with his wife meant an increasing withdrawal into the life of the mind and the give and take of intellectual discussion. His *History of British India* made something of a reputation for him and got him a post with a regular income in the East India Company. He could devote the rest of his life to the not ignoble goal of absorbing all relevant knowledge, building it into a rational body of thought, and using that body of thought as an engine for reforming society and bringing "the greatest happiness to the greatest number." This phrase was used by his friend, Jeremy Bentham, whose chaotic flow of thought James Mill systematized.

His first-born child, John Stuart Mill, was scheduled both as test and instrument of the doctrine of the James Mill-Jeremy Bentham group. At the age of three, he had started his reading of the Greek classics; his father, sitting across the narrow table and working on his own writing, would stop occasionally to explain a Greek word or phrase, since no Greek-English dictionary was yet available. At eight, after having read a list of Greek works that would make the reputation of a classics instructor today, he started Latin. At the same time, he became the teacher of his younger sister, transmitting to her his father's instructions, hearing her recite the reading, and correcting and commending her as his father had corrected and commended him. It was a heavy burden to place on a child's shoulders, but Mill carried it—although I suspect this was one of the things for which he never forgave his father.

Beyond Greek and Latin lay mathematics, on which James Mill had started his son, but which John had to carry on for himself when he moved into its higher reaches, beyond his father's memory and competence. Along with the art of studying under his father, and that of acting as a teacher to his sister, John had to learn the art of teaching himself—charting out an unfamiliar subject, getting at its rudiments, exploring its nuances. As he had gone beyond his father in mathematics, so he went beyond him in logic as well. But his great delight lay in history. He picked up with ease most of the great classics of historical writing—Greek, Roman, and European. He even ventured into poetry and a bit of fiction, but these were trimmings, and their marginality came back to plague both pupil and teacher later.

Francis Place, one of the great leaders of the working class of his day, a self-educated master tailor who was involved in every reform movement of his time, visited the Mill family during one of the summers which they spent with Jeremy Bentham at Ford Abbey. John Mill was eleven, and the impression this half little-prodigy and half little-monster made on Place was startling. "John is truly a prodigy, a most wonderful fellow," Place wrote his wife, "and when his Logic, his Languages, his Mathematics, his Philosophy shall be combined with a general knowledge of mankind and the affairs of the world, he will be a truly astonishing man; but he will

probably be morose and selfish." It is clear from Place's reports to his wife that the young boy irritated the older man
by challenging and contradicting him and by always having
the right question, the right answer, and—what was worst of
all—the right logic and reasoning. It was at this period that
James Mill, the father, was working hardest, getting up at
four in the morning, capturing only a few hours sleep, and
working away at a series of articles for an English encyclo-
pedia. The eleven year old helped his father with the galleys
of the *History of British India*, adding to his regular chores
this rather delightful apprenticeship to a working writer.

Young Mill may have been something of a monster at the
time, and something of a prig, but when he came to write his
Autobiography he looked back at himself and gave the sober
verdict that he had been neither—only a boy whose natural
gifts had responded so well to his father's educational methods
that "I started, I may fairly say, with an advantage of a
quarter-century over my contemporaries." He was probably
accurate about the head start he was given, but over-modest
about what he started with. The boy clearly had the stuff of
genius in him. Yet while the potential was there as seed, the
soil and nourishment which it needed for flourishing were
furnished by that relation of tension between student and
teacher which we call an "education."

In our own day, when we are straining to rethink and re-
build our educational system, and recanvass the ingredients of
a viable educational theory for the so-called "gifted children,"
the carriers of promise in America, John Stuart Mill's education has a special relevance. One can draw from it several
clues to an educational theory for an intellectual elite. One
is to start the child young, while his learning impulses are
still utterly spontaneous, while he is open to every influence
and can absorb languages and literatures. Secondly, demand
the utmost. John Mill said that his father "demanded of me
not only the utmost that I could do, but much that I could
by no possibility have done." Francis Place's comment on
James Mill as teacher was that "his method is by far the best
I have ever witnessed, and is infinitely precise; but he is
excessively severe. No fault, however trivial, escapes his notice; none goes without any reprehension or punishment of
some sort." There were times when the younger children
were denied their dinner because they had not said their lessons well, and John suffered the same penalty because he had

allowed their mistakes to pass. His later judgment in his *Auto-biography*, as he looked back at these chastisements, was that "a pupil from whom nothing is ever demanded which he cannot do, never does all he can."

A more important principle is that of the milieu in which the teaching and learning are carried on. James Mill's household was indeed, to borrow Barzun's phrase, a "house of intellect." Ideas and events were constantly being discussed in it, theories analyzed, logic scrutinized, fallacies pointed out. There was a constant stream of writers, journalists, politicians, working-class leaders, reformers, both in James Mill's house and in Jeremy Bentham's, where the family spent a number of summers. When the life of the mind is taken for granted, when it is given part of the natural universe, there can be no need to cozen or seduce the child into commitment to it. The commitment comes as part of the growing up.

There are few, if any, families in American mass society which are like Mill's and Bentham's in this respect. But the school or college has the chance to create an intellectual community which can provide this sort of atmosphere—although unfortunately at a much later period, when other influences and images may already have become established. The experience of John Mill may suggest that the first duty of a college is the creation of an authentic intellectual community, within each classroom and on each campus, in which the things that are taken for granted are the things that count.

Then there is the question of the dialogue of the generations. American educational theory has been saddled, since John Dewey's day, with the notion that children learn best from their "peer groups," since the experience of one's peers is most easily transmitted. The fact about Mill was that he had no real peer group. He was from the start, except for his chores as a teacher of the younger children, in converse with older people. Aside from his father, he learned most from John Austin, a brilliant if somewhat neurotic legal theorist who founded the Analytical School of jurisprudence, and who seemed drawn to young Mill and taught him much of his own sharpness of analysis and discipline of mind. Charles Austin, his younger brother, was also an influence on Mill—a half-generation removed, and for that reason perhaps the more attractive as a kind of older brother. And Thomas Carlyle was for a time a shaping and disturbing force in Mill's development; but that came later when the young man had already astonished the intellectual world of England with his accomplishments. There has been considerable research recently to indicate that in a high percentage of the known historical instances of genius, the child in his mental growth responded far more to an older generation than to his own.

With this history of education, John Mill's success in the intellectual circles of his day was almost inevitable. He wrote letters to the editor which blossomed into regular newspaper contributions. He formed a fighting nucleus of young writers and thinkers, and the name he picked for their doctrine—"utilitarianism"—has been accepted as the designation of a whole era of English thought, starting with Jeremy Bentham. He formed a debating society and did brilliantly in it. He started a literary magazine for the new philosophical radicals, with the high hopes that it would serve as a counter-force to the organs of the Establishment. And all of this before he was twenty-one.

But he had to pay a heavy price for it, a price in anguish of mind and barrenness of spirit. The dialogue of the generations had evoked young Mill's intellectual promise, but had left him emotionally immature, with his aesthetic side almost wholly undeveloped, and without having developed the capacity of feeling for which secretly his spirit longed. The result was the breakdown that Mill describes in his *Autobiography*—probably the most important part of it, and certainly the most poignant and human. It was not a "nervous breakdown," in the sense in which that term is now used. Mill went on functioning in all his intellectual activities, and his friends scarcely noted the crisis through which he was passing—which is probably the final commentary on the sources of the crisis and the lack of intimacy in his friendships. As Mill expressed it, "If I had loved anyone sufficiently to make confiding my griefs a necessity, I should not have been in the condition I was."

But the sickness was none the less real, even if it was an ambulatory one. Mill diagnosed it well as an incapacity for feeling, and indeed for love itself. His "habit of analysis" had worn away his feeling, with a dissolving force that threatened to dissolve his whole being. He played with thoughts of suicide. What dismayed him was the knowledge that even if his dream of a perfected and rebuilt social system were to be achieved on the next day, it would be of no account to him. He was suffering from over-rationalism, a disease which his father had as surely communicated to him as the disease of tuberculosis, during those early days when they had sat across the narrow board table while the father wrote away at the *History of British India* and the son wrestled with Greek syntax. This was, Mill wrote later, "a perpetual worm at the root both of the passions and of the virtues." As for his father, Mill never gave him an inkling of what he was going through: "I saw no use in giving him the pain of thinking that his plans had failed, when the failure was probably irremediable."

Mill's crisis had its first resolution when he read a passage in Marmontel's *Memoirs*, where the author's father dies, and the boy has a rush of feeling and pictures himself as being everything to his family that his father had been. "A vivid conception of the scene and his feelings came over me, and I was moved to tears." A. W. Levi, writing in the *Psychoanalytic Review*, surmises that Mill's crisis was the result of a repressed death-wish toward his father, that he had harbored a hostility against him during the course of his training, that the unwillingness to recognize the death-wish led to an attrition of his whole feeling-capacity, and that the passage in Marmontel, by resolving his conflict, released his capacity for feeling as well as his fears. This is as good a clue as any. Mill was unable to love because his father had never loved him but had used him as a test of his educational ideas and an engine of his reformist zeal. In his search for the sources of feeling, Mill was characteristically methodical and turned to the reading of the English romantic poets. Byron proved unrewarding, but Wordsworth suited Mill's mood and his love for the natural scene, and in the reading of Wordsworth he found a second resolution of his mental crisis.

But I suspect that the real resolution came several years later, when at twenty-three, with a fluttering readiness for emotional experience, Mill was introduced to Mrs. Harriet Taylor, and thereby met his life's destiny and the greatest shaping force of his mind. Mill fails to connect his mental crisis with the completeness of his response to Mrs. Taylor, but the connection seems clear enough. She was young, married to a worthy man who had few intellectual interests, felt arid and starved for an outlet to her restless talent and some meaning to her life. Mill helped her to find new interests, and saw in her the fusion of beauty and grace, intellect and character, the answer to his longings. She in turn saw his greatness, and the possibility of developing a body of thought and writing unparalleled in intellectual history. She was a blue-stocking, but more; more also than an Aspasia to his Pericles. There is little doubt now, after the publication of the letters that passed between them until her death, that she was a woman of commanding intellect who furnished exactly the motive force and the critical sense that Mill needed for his books. For the next twenty years they were constantly to-gether, in her husband's household, and on trips through France and Italy. When, for any reason they were away from each other, they kept up a constant exchange of letters. Mill was married to her in all but name and fact. Spiritually and intellectually they were husband and wife, although Harriet felt bound to her own legal marriage, perhaps unwilling to hurt John Taylor too much, perhaps welcoming the frame he gave her for her real life with Mill. Those who have studied the letters and diaries most closely have concluded that Mill did not have any sexual intimacy with Mrs. Taylor during those twenty years. They both felt that there were "lower" and "higher" feelings and experiences, that sex definitely belonged with the lower, and that a creative relationship between a man and woman transmuted the baser impulses into something loftier. In short, Mill was a proper Victorian in his attitudes toward sex, and Harriet Taylor was in all probability a frigid woman. One might add, as Crane Brinton adds about her, that her frigidity was a matter of principle rather than of neurosis.

When Taylor died, the two platonic lovers who had defied public sentiment in order to be together while the husband was alive, now found themselves with freedom to marry but without much will to do so. They waited for several years, wore out each other's nerves and became thoroughly entan-gled in family feuds, and finally married. Mill testifies that their life during the seven years of marriage was Paradise. It was not Paradise for his mother or sisters or brother, with all of whom Mill broke relations because of fancied slights to-ward Mrs. Taylor. There is a ruthless quality in the way he treated his family—a ruthless quality not wholly unrelated to the strength he had shown in maintaining his unconventional relationship with Mrs. Taylor for twenty years.

His public testimony to her greatness is well known. The reader will find it in the pages of his *Autobiography* and in the dedication page to the essay *On Liberty*, Mill's greatest book, on which there is pretty good evidence that it was a

joint product. It will also be found on the tombstone that Mill
set up for his wife when she died, of tuberculosis which she
had probably caught from him. "Were there but a few hearts
and intellects like hers," Mill said on the tombstone, "this
earth would already become the hope for heaven." And in
the dedication of *On Liberty* he wrote, "were I but capable
of interpreting to the world one half of the great thoughts
and noble feelings which are buried in her grave, I should be
the medium of a greater benefit to it than is ever likely to
arise from anything that I can write, unprompted and unassisted by her all but unrivaled wisdom." Mill genuinely
believed that his was the inferior mind of the two. Certainly
hers was a mind he needed, whether for intellectual or emotional reasons. She lent his thought a quality of radicalism
which it had not had without her, a willingness to associate
itself with the new and daring experiments of the time, an
identification with revolutionary movements, and with the
new classes making a bid for power in Europe. Mill's basic
mental stance was one of balance; his mind was many-sided.
It was Mrs. Taylor who was responsible for the chapter "On
the Probable Future of the Laboring Classes" which he added
to the later editions of the *Principles of Political Economy*,
and in which he expressed his sympathy for Socialism and
his prophecy of its triumph.

Harriet was buried at Avignon, and Mill took a small house
nearby so as to be constantly near her, living out the remaining years of his life in the shadow of her memory and influence, and adopting her daughter, Helen Taylor, as his own.
Helen quickly assumed the role that her mother had filled, of
assistant and collaborator in Mill's work, and he transferred
to her much of the devotion and dependence he had felt for
Harriet. It is hard not to conclude that Mill's nature, for all
the independence of his thinking, was one which was incomplete without some complement. At the start it had been his
father, later Mrs. Taylor, still later Helen Taylor. In the case
of his father, Mill's estimate of him was at once affectionate
and judicious, as given in the *Autobiography*, although he
never overcame an underlying hostility. In the case of the two
women, however, he could not do without superlatives which
are today embarrassing to the reader. In a sense he required
a teacher all his life, even while he was himself the guide and
teacher of half of Europe. With all his own thin-lipped
strength of will, he required strength in another person, espe-

cially in a woman, on which he could lean, with an emotional urge which compelled him to realize from the relationship nothing less than a community of two loving people—that is to say, the beloved community.

Without quite knowing it, Mill was in search of the Beloved Community all his life. He gave it a number of names— "utilitarianism," "the greatest happiness of the greatest number," "liberty," "diversity"—but always he was driving his mind toward clarifying the conditions under which as many people as possible could find their fulfillment within a good society. He was (let the truth be told) what Justice Holmes used to call half-derisively an "onward and upward thinker." Which is to say that he was at once the product and in part the shaper of the eighteenth and nineteenth century conviction that men can mold their destiny by molding and remolding their society. The French *philosophes* were part of this movement, and the French and English Utopian socialists, and the "Philosophical Radicals" of the first half of the nineteenth century in England, with whom Mill belonged and whose ideas he brought to their clearest and most orderly form. Mill was in this sense a child of his age, and he suffered from the disease of his age—the gnawing doubt about whether the institutions that Western civilization had built would live or deserved to live, the sense of complicity in guilt for the great inequalities of distribution in a prosperous society, the question of what to do with the new wealth and new power which Europe had piled up, the bewilderment about how to reconcile the belief in education and democracy with the obvious fact that the former was linked with a minority and the latter based on a majority, and quite generally the anxiety about the new and somewhat barbarous classes who were knocking at the gate of history. (Remember how in the 1820's and 30's and 40's the flaring, fitful fires of libertarian revolutions swept across the face of Europe, from the Carbonari in Italy to the July days in Paris and the Chartists in England.)

I stress these doubts, guilts, bewilderments and anxieties because Mill's era has usually been described as one of optimism, and Mill as a High Priest not only of reason but of the complacencies. This misses the meaning both of Mill and his age. True, it was the century of the Great Hope, when the dream was of the perfectibility of man, when the foundations of the old religion were sapped and new religions of science and of humanity were being invoked. In Paris and London alike there were young men eager to reform the world, to resolve the problems of poverty, to organize thought into a single system. The middle class had come into its golden hour and was seeking some principle to cement its power—a principle whether of material progress or Reason or Liberty, which would enable it to rationalize its position by morality. And Mill was part of this current of history, the child of this era. But he was an anxious child of his time, and one whose dominant passion was not complacency but dissent, not dogma but the use of the critical intelligence for the benefit of man's condition.

One of the best ways to get at the quality of his vision is to note the enemies he fought. He waged a continuing smoldering war against all forms of authority that demanded unquestioning faith, and were not bolstered by man's independent mind. This meant a war with all supernatural religions and established Churches, with Natural Law, with Protestant morality, with intuitionism in philosophy, with mysticism of every kind in thought, with the arrogance of the male in subjecting woman to an inferior position, with the privileged power of the few and with the tyranny of the many in crushing dissent. His enemies were superstition, unreason, privilege, conformity. They were good enemies for a young man to have as he felt out his strength.

He went at them with a lusty vigor. Mill never became the kind of political thinker, like Hobbes or Machiavelli, who had a feeling for power and its ways and its location. Harold Laski, contrasting him with the masculine strength of Hobbes, was later to call him a "hermaphrodite" thinker. But he did have a feeling for intellectual power, and he knew how to fight the battles for the sovereignty of the little Republic of Ideas of which he became part. London in his day was compact, compassable, and somewhat insular. It was governed by a handful of literary magazines, newspapers, intellectual leaders. Mill set out to win over the newspaper editors to his cause, rounded up a new group of magazine contributors for his *London and Westminster Review*, assigned them books and subjects, read and criticized their copy; he invaded the two great Universities and sought out the most promising student leaders; he set up a correspondence with the Saint-Simonians, Comtists, and others of the intellectual avant-garde in Paris. Very quickly he became a force in the intellectual—and therefore the political—world.

But he was an independent force. The best instance of his independence is his break from Jeremy Bentham. The *London and Westminster Review* was the organ of the young Philosophical Radicals, such as Roebuck, the Grotes, Molesworth, who in turn were tied to Bentham's hedonic calculus and his "Table of the Springs of Action." It was a pretty sectarian affair, and Carlyle wrote Emerson that it was "Hide-bound Radicalism; a to me well-nigh insupportable thing! Open it not: a breath as of the Sahara and the Infinite Sterile comes from every page of it." Yet in the end Carlyle wrote for it, as did others who were anathema to the Radicals. Mill insisted on turning it into an organ of liberalism in politics and the broadest cultural interests. There was a saving quality in Mill which kept him from ever becoming a political sectarian, or a slavish disciple of any thinker. He broke from his father, from Bentham, from Carlyle, from the Saint-Simonians, from Comte, although each had eagerly hoped to use his talents. With Bentham, as with his father, Mill's objection was to the excessive rationalism which squeezed out everything else. The pure milk of Benthamism no longer held any nourishment for him. He saw Bentham as a man who, himself almost without experience, sought to generalize from his own poverty of experience and impose a rule of motivation and ethics upon mankind. "He never knew prosperity and adversity, passion nor satiety. . . . His own lot was cast in a generation of the leanest and barrenest men whom England has yet produced."

No, Mill was not content to be a sectarian politician nor a free-lance journalist nor a narrow rationalist reformer. He saw his own function as going down to the roots of thinking, and charting the domain of knowledge. In 1830, at twenty-four, he started his first important book, *System of Logic*, and he kept at it (with interruptions) for thirteen years. He saw it as a seminal work. "Good seed is never wasted," he told a French friend, "it takes root, and springs up somewhere. It will assist the general reconstruction of the ideas of the civilized world for which ours is but a period of preparation." He was fighting the forces of reaction, but he knew that their deepest fortifications were in the minds of men, in the things they took for granted and which they therefore held as a matter of faith or intuition. In his *Logic*, which is now read only by the specialists but was a sensation in its day, Mill attacked this citadel of unreason entrenched in the syllogism. He showed that deductive reasoning by the syllogism presented no new

truth that was not already contained in the major premise.
His principal target, Dr. Whewell, argued that there were
universal, necessary truths, as in the laws of geometry, which
went beyond experience. Mill answered that the principles of
geometry were useful assumptions, that there were no necessary truths, and that every general proposition—and therefore
every major premise in logic—is taken from experience. You
arrive at your major premise by induction, you apply your
minor premise and get your conclusion, and you then submit
the conclusion to verification by inductive experience again.
This was the method of science, and Mill classified the sciences by their reduction of experience to scientific method,
starting with mathematics and going down to the social and
moral studies. Even the latter, he hoped, would some day
become exact sciences—a hope which still persists today.

What is worth noting here is that Mill was a philosopher of
experience. The whole school of American pragmatists, from
Peirce through Dewey, rests on him. When William James
wrote his pathbreaking lectures on *Pragmatism,* he dedicated
the book to Mill, "whom my fancy likes to think of as our
leader, were he alive to-day." Bertrand Russell, in tracing his
own philosophical development, writes "I did not come across
any books, except Buckle . . . which seemed to me to possess
intellectual integrity . . . until I read Mill's *Logic.*" In fact,
if one were to seek a parallel to Mill in our own more recent
time, it would have to be a blend of William James, John
Dewey, John Maynard Keynes, and Bertrand Russell, with a
dash of Walter Lippmann thrown in. He had the open-mind-
edness and far-roaming interests that James later had, the
grounding in science and experience of Dewey, the interest
in logic and economics that Keynes had, the luminousness of
style and the moral clarity and gravity that Lippmann developed, and the anti-clerical rebelliousness and the feel for
unpopular causes of Russell. But note that it has taken a
whole platoon of thinkers to replace him.

He never limited his interests, and refused to be hedged in
behind the trim boundaries of particular disciplines, but
roamed through logic, metaphysics, ethics, psychology, economics, religion, politics, education. He was in the best sense
a generalist, not a particularist. He was a great name in the
history of each of the disciplines I have mentioned, exactly
because he refused to restrict himself to any one of them,
and was thus able to break down the boundaries between

them, and shed fresh light on each by focusing on it search-lights from the others. In a sense he was the Aristotle of the Victorian Age, as Aristotle was the Mill of the Alexandrian: in fact, Mill refers (in *On Liberty*, II) to the "judicious utili-tarianism" of Aristotle, thereby conscripting the Stagirite into his own little phalanx.

I don't mean to slight Mill's weaknesses. Although a good logician, and although he longed to be a master of meta-physics (hence his *Examination of Sir William Hamilton's Philosophy*, a long and today pretty dull piece), he lacked the metaphysical genius of Berkeley and Locke and Hume, as in politics he lacked the sense of the organic state and society one finds in Edmund Burke. He failed to go as deep as Bentham did into the meaning of meaning, and the distortions produced by language itself. While he took up Tocqueville's insights into the inner dangers of mass culture, it was he who followed the lead of the French thinker, rather than the other way around. He recognized the role of the irrational, yet did almost nothing to chart it, as Nietzsche and William James, Freud and Jung were to do. And while he knew the limits of science as a method and saw its barrenness as an exclusive way of life, he did not fight stubbornly against its sway, as he did against dangers about which he was clearer.

What he failed to see was that, once he had knocked out religion and natural law, intuition and mysticism and faith, as the underpinnings of men's conduct, he had nothing left ex-cept science and materialism. In his recoil from them, he was compelled to appeal from the "lower" to the "higher" sensi-tivities and tastes, but here again he had to fall back either upon subjectivism (a man's tastes are his tastes) or upon the authority of some intellectual and aesthetic elite in whose keeping would be the "religion of humanity." (Hence his dis-astrous, if short-lived, flirtation with August Comte's pedan-tocracy.) With the fluid movement of classes, and the *embour-geoisement* of Western society, the arbiters of taste, culture, and morals had vanished. The middle-class which was to be guided to a proper appreciation of these values had become the arbiter of its own values.

I have run ahead of my story, since Mill was not yet aware —when he published his first book, the *Logic*—of the depths and whirlpools he was getting into. He was enjoying his new-found power. It was good to have some sport with Dr. Whewell's history of the sciences and his deductive logic, especially when—in Book V of his *Logic*, "On Fallacies"—he could illustrate the various species of fallacious reasoning by examples from Whewell and his other targets. He was later to have the same kind of fun with Sir William Hamilton. The task of being a working social thinker was not all lugubriousness: there was a joyousness in it, and Mill let it shine through his grave historical excursions and his rolling periods.

Nor was economics for him the dismal science it had been for his predecessors. The success of his *Logic* emboldened Mill to put out as a volume a group of articles he had earlier written in his spare hours as a functionary in India House, just as he had written his *Logic* there, since he spent only three or four hours of the day on his official work. These appeared as *Essays on Some Unsettled Questions of Political Economy* in 1844, the year after the *Logic*. This led Mill to attempt the bigger task of setting down, in the wake of Adam Smith, Ricardo, McCulloch, and Nassau Senior, his own *Principles of Political Economy*. There is a legend, unfortunately picked up by some recent popularizations of the history of economic thought, that Mill wrote the book in six weeks. But he did it fast enough: over a period of eighteen months he spent only ten months at it, and then took nine months to rewrite his first draft. It was as if he had been waiting all his life for the chance to survey the whole realm of economics. The sentences came tumbling out of his well-stocked memory, mainly in recall of the conversations of the Ricardo group when he was still a stripling, and the discussions at the Debating Society, and all the books he had read then. They came tumbling out much too easily. For a decade or more Mill had not kept up with the new insights into economics. He came at the tail-end of the classical system of economics, giving the work of the earlier and more original thinkers a clarity and gloss they had never possessed from the start; he put it all into the seemingly rigorous frame of his theory of logic and scientific method; he dealt with production, distribution, and exchange, with value theory and profits, with wages and rent, with the theory of international trade. He thereby gave an appearance of finality to a system of thought which he himself recognized as belonging to a specific historical period, rather than as part of the eternal laws of society—gave it the appearance of finality exactly at the point when it was most sharply challenged by the rise of new classes within the system of capitalist production, and their claims for a new deal.

Thorstein Veblen, in his essays on "The Preconceptions of Economic Science," was later to lump Mill's economics with that of the rest of the classical school, as taking the same things for granted. And both in England and America, there were men who either wilfully or ignorantly misread Mill, and tried to use him to bolster both the status quo of economic power and the method of laissez-faire.

They were unjust on both scores. Mill shook rather than bolstered the structure of economic power and its buttressing theory. He distinguished between the realm of production on one hand, where the problem was the relation between man and the forces of Nature, and where therefore one could speak of fixed laws, and on the other hand the realm of distribution, where the problem was the relation of man to man and there were no fixed laws. "The things are there," he wrote. "Mankind, individually or collectively, can do with them as they please . . . The distribution of wealth therefore depends on the laws and customs of society." This left the door open for at least one brand of Socialism—the kind that sought distributive justice. In a famous passage Mill expressed his aesthetic as well as moral dislike of "the trampling, crushing, elbowing, and treading on each others' heels, which form the existing type of social life." But Mill was against revolution to change this. He thought that the struggle for riches kept the energies of most men better employed than if they rusted or stagnated. "While minds are coarse they require coarse stimuli, and let them have them." His hope was that in time the better minds would "succeed in educating the others into better things."

But Mrs. Mill, who had helped Mill all through the book, was scarcely satisfied with this brand of mildness. After the revolutions of 1848, which were a watershed for so many thinkers in England as throughout Europe, she pressed Mill to make revisions in the later editions of the *Principles*. Mill had ended with a group of chapters which he called "Of the Influence of Government," which were delicately balanced between laissez-faire and governmental intervention. Under Mrs. Mill's pressure he changed much, sharpened much, added a chapter (which she largely wrote) on the future of the laboring classes, and in general managed to push the book over from its original liberalism into a tract on the margin of Socialism. In fact, there was even a passage in Book II, Ch. I, "Of Property," which was inserted in 1852 and was much quoted by the Left-wing group of Mill's disciples, starting "If therefore the choice were to be made between Communism with all its chances, and the present (1852) state of society with all its sufferings and injustices . . ." and ending ". . . all the difficulties, great or small, of Communism would be but as dust in the balance." It should be added, of course, that Mill used the terms "Communism" and "Socialism" interchangeably, that he knew next to nothing about Marx who was then working away in the British Museum, and that he had in mind chiefly the Utopian Socialisms of Fourier and the Saint-Simonians. Yet even with this caveat, it remains true that any effort to classify Mill as a traditional individualist liberal is very wide of the mark. True, much of this was due to the curious hypnotic effect of his wife upon his mind. Carlyle explained this effect in terms of "those great dark eyes, that were flashing unutterable things while he was discoursin' the utterable concernin' all sorts of high topics."

In 1854 Mill thought that he would die of tuberculosis. "The most disagreeable thing about dying is the intolerable ennui of it. There ought to be no slow deaths." When he recovered he re-planned his life and his writing career. His mood was similar to John Keats' "When I have fears that I may cease to be . . ." He wanted to make certain that the "full-ripened sheaves" of his thought would be gathered before he died. For five years, until after his wife's death in 1858, he published no books, but wrote steadily with her help, after drawing up a table early in 1854 of the subjects he wished to treat. They were to be essays—"on Love, Education of tastes . . . Foundation of Morals . . . Utility of Religion . . . Liberty," and a number of others. It will be seen that each of the essays grew into a book. The "Education of Tastes . . . and Foundation of Morals" became *Utilitarianism*. The "Utility of Religion," along with *Theism* and the essay he had just finished on Nature, were ultimately published as the *Three Essays on Religion*. "Liberty" became *On Liberty*. Work on the *Autobiography* was started immediately. The years between 1854 and 1861 were the incredible years in Mill's life. His six greatest and most readable books—the foundation and summary of his thought—were written in that period. It would be hard to point to any comparable period in the life of any of the great social thinkers of the modern age that could match it for sheer fertility and for the quality of the writing. Three of those six books (*Utilitarianism, On Liberty,* and the *Autobiography*), and two complete essays from the fourth (*Nature*, and *Utility of Religion*) are contained in this edition of Mill's Essential Works. Despite the changes that took place in his thinking in the course of his lifetime, the fact that these crucial books were all compressed within a brief seven years gives them a unity and an interrelationship, like panels on a central theme.

Utilitarianism was meant as an attempt to find a basis for the principles of moral behavior. By a rough formula, Mill's aim was *humanitarianism* (the Benthamite "greatest happiness of the greatest number"), his means was to be *reason*, his guide was *utility*, by which he meant well-being, or what we should today call *welfare*. It is an earnest and somewhat plodding book, welcome for its brevity and lucidity, admirable for its courage at the time in breaking morals away from the sanctions of religion. There was also something admirable about it in another sense. Mill sought nothing less than the regeneration of man. But instead of building it on the wishfulness of altruism, he insisted on appealing to every man's self-interest. This was to be, in a phrase William James was later to make current, a "tough-minded" approach to morality and the conduct of life. What Mill was driving at was that the justification of life was not to be found in the hereafter, nor in codes imposed from above by an aristocracy of power and privilege—by the Establishments of the day, but that the test of a good life was whether it was good for the man who lived it. And the test of the rightness or morality of any action is its consequences for mankind—whether it increases the sum of human happiness.

One can admire the boldness of this without concluding that Mill was able to bring it off. There were too many unsolved difficulties. There was the qualitative problem, and Mill answered the argument from hoggishness—that his system was that of "a hog from Epicurus' sty"—by saying that there are higher and lower forms of happiness, that it is a matter of training, that "men lose their high aspirations as they lose their intellectual tastes, because they have not time or opportunity for indulging them," and that with education and with equality of opportunity for all, the quality of welfare can be raised for all.

One must note here that Mill evades the question of objective standards for the quality of happiness, or utility. What is best, he says in effect, is what the best men practice. Fine,

but who decides who are the best men? His answer has a
Gertrude Stein quality in it: they are best because they are
best because they are best. The thinkers with an organic concept of society have the merit of assuming candidly that the
established arbiters of morals and taste, in the Establishments
of a society, are the best. Mill has discarded that, but is unwilling to follow skepticism or relativism all the way, and he
bases the principle of utility and happiness within man himself: a man knows when he is happy, and what it consists of.

A second difficulty lies with sanctions: what will keep men
in the path of their right conduct? If the penalties of society
are largely removed, what takes their place? Mill answers that
"this firm foundation is that of the social feelings of mankind;
the desire to be in unity with our fellow-creatures, which is
already a powerful principle in human nature, and happily one
of those which tend to become stronger." But alas, the experience with the totalitarians has shown us that this "desire to
be in unity with our fellow-creatures" can lead to a mystique
of submission, and in mass democracies it leads to a mystique
of conformity.

A third difficulty lies with Mill's basic optimism. He sees
quite rightly that the unhappiness of many people is due to
their being denied, by the injustices of society, the same life-
chances that the more fortunate have. This was linked with his
doctrine of liberty as requiring a base or frame of social action
—a theme strongly marked in *On Liberty* and also in his essay
On Social Freedom. But he goes further, and while disposing
of the pathetic in the human condition, seeks to dispose of the
tragic as well. "All the grand sources of human suffering," he
writes in Chapter II, "are in a great degree, many of them
almost entirely, conquerable by human care and effort; and
though their removal is grievously slow—though a long succession of generations will perish in the breach before the conquest is completed . . . yet every mind sufficiently intelligent
and generous . . . will draw a noble enjoyment from the contest itself." Thus, in the noblest terms, Mill manages to
squeeze the universe almost dry of the element of the tragic,
which is not man-made and cannot be man-unmade but is
part of the human predicament.

I do not say it is an easy universe, this universe of Mill's. It
involves ardors and rigors. But it is a curiously limited universe. The "pursuit of happiness," in the phrase that Jefferson
took over into the Declaration, becomes self-conscious in it

and almost obsessive; and the calculus is still there, although
Mill has moved from Bentham's rather crude pleasures and
pains to more refined standards of happiness.

Most of the pleasures turn out to be not very different from
the virtues of a middle-class society which the preachers of
Mill's day preached—without the theological trappings. True,
Mill was furious at the lack of sensitivity of many members
of the British middle-class, and Harriet and he were drawn
into a kind of *égoïsme à deux* in defying their stuffiness. Yet
when he set down his verities of the life of reason, they were
strangely those of the best of middle-class England. The
tragic and the irrational are squeezed out. The psychology is
shockingly weak. There is no hint of any inner nature of man,
because Mill rejects "innate ideas." The strain which Freud
cultivated as pessimist—the death-urge in man, and the extent to which society is itself organized repression of the
erotic drives—of that too there is no hint. Sex itself is treated
discreetly, but we know from the letters between Mill and
Mrs. Taylor that she was a frigid woman sexually, and that
she and Mill agreed that sexuality was something of the lower
order of values, something more than faintly disgusting. In
A History of Western Morals, Crane Brinton speaks of Mill
as "that ascetic hedonist, so incapable of anything you or I
could accept as *hedone*, or pleasure." And as for society, Mill
cannot go much farther than to define its happiness as the
sum of the individual happiness of its members. Thus, despite
Mill's references to "the desire to be in unity with our fellow-
creatures," his society is an atomized one. It was a mistake
that the conservative thinkers like Burke and Carlyle did not
make.

The key question about morality was not a question about
the intellectual and cultural elites, but about the big majority
of men and women. In an age of mass culture, of passive
spectator sports, of violence and dehumanization, how were
Mill's elites to teach them values, instruct them in the authentic character of happiness? The successive trial answers have
been given by the British welfare-state, from Keir Hardie
through Sidney Webb to Aneuran Bevan: to shape welfare
through social construction, so that the beneficiaries will have
an artificial identification of interests with the better groups,
and thus learn to appreciate life. The Communists have a
short-cut, in the indoctrination of the many by the Party elite
with Party-line truth. Much as he wished to spread happiness

among the many, Mill was too committed a believer in liberty to suffer any attempt at indoctrination.

It was his recoil from any betrayal of the method of Reason which also set the frame for his views on religion. In his approach to this problem, which no great thinker of the 19th century could leave alone, Mill was not wholly disinterested. He knew the extent to which the established supernatural religions fortified the established social institutions. He wrote his three essays to undercut the hold which religion had on men's attitude toward society. His first essay, *Nature*, is a devastating refutation of the idea of religion as based on natural law. To say that the universe is part of God's design, and that God reveals himself through Nature, is (says Mill) to ignore the cruelty and injustice of Nature. "In sober truth," he writes in a great and terrifying passage, "nearly all the things which men are hanged or imprisoned for doing to one another are nature's everyday performances . . ." And then comes a recital too long to quote and too powerful to summarize. But in throwing out the laws of Nature, Mill also throws out the whole cluster of the human instincts. His position is that of the extreme institutionalists: that everything about man is socially learned and socially conditioned, and just as there are no innate ideas there are no innate instincts.

In *Utility of Religion* Mill argues that religion is not a necessary base for morality, being capable of neither proof nor disproof. If he were cynical he might have taken the view of Edward Gibbon, that in the Roman Empire all religions were equally true and false and all religions were equally useful. Machiavelli held this view of religion, like Plato before him. But Mill's drive is different: he wants to extract the "essence" of religion from its supernatural trappings. The essence turns out to be, not so surprisingly, the religion of humanity—or, as it now tends to be called, humanist religion. As a young man Mill had been drawn far more than he knew to the Comtian religion of humanity. But Comte, who was one-third genius, one-third charlatan, and one-third madman, could not long hold Mill's respect. What his religion finally turned out to be, with all its rituals and trappings but without any sense of mystery and wonder, was (as someone put it) "Christianity without Christianity." Mill discards all the trappings, but he too ends without either wonder or worship—with something that is not much more than morality itself, but that casts a mystique of a sort around the body of moral principles.

Mill's true religion, one must conclude, was neither morality nor the religion of humanity, but quite simply the idea of freedom. I shall be discussing the ideas of *On Liberty* itself in the special Preface to that book. What must be noted here is the relation of his thinking about freedom to the general body of his thought. Here was something he could write about with passion, because it embodied his whole being and striving, and more than any other idea it was linked with his sense of identity. Liberty was for him (to paraphrase a sentence of Holmes's) not a duty, but only a necessity. Without it the growth of a person was unthinkable, since Mill defined liberty as essentially the frame of freedom needed for fulfillment of potentials. But it followed from this that without liberty a good society was also impossible, since without liberty there could be none of the benefits of the diffusion of the relatively true ideas, nor the deposit which even the relatively false ones have left on history, nor the balancing and competition of true and false, nor the diversity of personalities (each based on the freedom to select his truth, and to grow with it) which makes a rich culture.

Nothing as eloquent, weighty, luminous as this has ever been written in so sustained a way on freedom—not even, I venture to say, Milton's tract, the *Areopagitica*, while Acton's essays are fragmentary, and Holmes's decisions atomistic. For once Mill can dispense with much of his abracadabra about utility, since he is dealing with a value so fundamental to society and to meaningful life that he makes out of it almost a first principle. He handles the problem of negative and positive freedoms well. He is vulnerable, however, when discussing the limits of freedom and he is in danger of forgetting that there is more to the universe than individuals revolving in interstellar space.

But his real problem comes with the question of the tyranny of the majority. He had learned much from Tocqueville on this, especially from the second set of volumes of *Democracy in America*. If you give the majority the freedom to push others around, you have tryanny. But he would not adopt an iron attitude toward the majority, nor allow it to adopt an iron one toward minorities. As a result the book becomes a lonely, agonizing debate between the claims of a freely growing man to be free of state and majority and all, and the claims of the many to impose their will in order to have effective government, or perhaps only in order to give themselves the illusion of security. "It may be necessary," wrote Rousseau, "to compel a man to be free." Mill would be in violent disagreement. And so he stands, a lonely figure on the shores of the world, weighing the conflicting claims of the two principles, without knowing quite how to integrate them.

Let us leave him thus. He outlived his wife by fifteen years, working mostly in France, near her grave, sometimes in London. He came to be almost revered as a "saint of rationalism." He had, as a young man, been arrested for distributing birth control pamphlets. As an older man he still had his hand in almost every cause, whether it was women's suffrage, or the Northern side in the American Civil War, or proportional representation, or farmers' cooperatives. It was as a moralist, however, that he had his greatest impact. Intellectuals living under a tyranny as far away as Czarist Russia read his works, and caught from them a vision of a not impossible reconstruction of society and regeneration of man, and their minds were stirred by the controlled passion in his words.

Primarily he was a working thinker, intent on finding the best sources and conditions for his thought, reading books and conversing with their writers for the light they might shed on whatever problem he was tussling with. I do not say that he was a dehumanized thinking machine. No one who reads his *Autobiography* or his Letters could fail to see that, for all his apparatus of rationalism, he was a committed and incurable romantic. He saw everything in more than lifesize proportions, whether it was Mrs. Taylor or the idea of liberty or the blind malevolence of a Nature over which there could be no presiding Deity. But he had the same romantic dedication to his craft as a working thinker, a dedication which kept him going through all the years of illness and struggle, with an obstinacy of will which recognized no obstacle, and a passionate fire (on such issues as women's rights or anti-colonialism) which left his opponents incredulous at its intensity.

Here was no man, then, of gruel-water intellect and thin emotions, no sawdust-stuffed Victorian moralist, no prim and unctuous spokesman for a carefully ordered world. Here was rather a man of strong passions, large vision, tenacious will, powerful intellect, who used and fused all his qualities in the service of a vision of a better world for all his fellow men. This is what he meant by the principle of "utilitarianism," which can be redefined simply as social happiness and the good life for all.

I am by no means certain that Mill ranks with the really first-rate minds of world history—with Newton and Hume, with Burke, with Tocqueville, with Marx and Freud. The sum total of his books, especially those contained in the present volume which are the outstanding ones, give him however a rank in intellectual history almost equal to those I have named. It is possible to be a genius, and to use one's genius to the full, and yet not be among the great creative minds. It is hard to associate Mill with any very original theories, yet it is hard *not* to associate him with a powerful and comprehensive system of thought. His strength lay in extracting the implications of what was known, drawing the inferences, examining the proofs, and fitting everything together into a system of relation. His strength lay also not so much as an intellectual innovator, as in the world of values which he helped to shape and clarify. He was at once a moralist and a militant. He brought to its highest point of perfection the system of liberal thought which gave expression and meaning to the mid-nineteenth century in Europe. But while his passion grew out of the events of his day, he gave his thoughts and values the imprint of the universal. That is why today they have a relevance as fresh as when they were newly minted.

"He has nae roots in his mind," said Carlyle once of his dearest enemy. To which Justice Holmes answered, when Harold Laski reported the anecdote to him, "I doubt if Carlyle gave the world as great a shove as Mill." There are many who will query whether the direction in which he shoved was the right one, but a shove it was.

WE learn from Mill's letters that his *Autobiography* was well under way by the time he reached the crisis in his writing plans brought on by his illness of 1853-4. He had been planning it even before his marriage with Harriet Taylor in 1851. After their marriage they moved to Blackheath Park, in the outskirts of London, and lived in retirement there while he wrote. What frightened and galvanized Mill into putting his literary house in order was serious illness and the fear of death. In January 1854 we find in his letters to his wife (who was at Hyères, on the French Riviera, recovering from a severe hemorrhage) repeated mention of the *Autobiography* project. "I too have thought very often lately about the life & am most anxious that we should complete it the soonest possible," he wrote on January 23, 1854. "What there is of it is in a perfectly publishable state. As far as the writing goes it could be printed tomorrow—& it contains a full writing out as far as anything can write out, what you are, as far as I am competent to describe you, & what I owe to you. . . ."

On February 12 he wrote again that he had "read through all that is written of the Life—I find it wants revision which I shall give to it but I do not well know what to do with some of the passages which we marked for alteration in the early part which we read together. They were mostly passages in which I had written, you thought, too much of the truth about my own defects. . . . Of course one does not, in writing a life, either one's own or another's, undertake to tell everything. . . . Still it va sans dire that it ought to be on the whole a fair representation. . . . I find there is a great deal of good matter written down in the Life which we have not written anywhere else, & which will make it as valuable in that respect (apart from its main object) as the best things we have published. But of what particularly concerns *our* life there is nothing yet written, except the descriptions of you, & of your effect on me. . . . We have to consider, which we can only do together, how much of our story it is advisable to tell, in order to make head against the representations of enemies when we shall not be alive to add anything to it. If it was not to be published for 100 years I should say, tell all, simply & without reserve. As it is there must be care taken not to put arms into the hands of the enemy."

To which Mrs. Mill answered from Hyères, in mid-February 1854: "I feel sure dear that the Life is not half written and that half that is written will not do. Should there not be a summary of our relationship from its commencement in 1830—I mean given in a dozen lines—so as to preclude other and different versions of our lives . . . —our summer excursions, etc. This ought to be done in its genuine truth and simplicity—strong affection, intimacy of friendship, and no impropriety. It seems to me an edifying picture for those poor wretches who cannot conceive friendship but in sex—nor believe that expediency and the consideration for feelings of others can conquer sensuality. . . ."

Mill's answer (February 20) lights up both his own personality and their relationship: "As to the Life—which I have been revising & correcting—the greater part, in bulk, of what is written consists in the history of my mind *up to* the time when your influence over it began—& I do not think there can be much objectionable in that part, even including as it does, sketches of the character of most of the people I was intimate with—if I could be said to be so with anyone. I quite agree in the sort of resumé of our relationship which you suggest—but if it is to be only as you say a dozen lines, or even three or four dozen, could you not my own love write it out your darling self & send it in one of your precious letters. . . ."

I have given these detailed passages from the letters (they are taken from F. A. Hayek, *John Stuart Mill and Harriet Taylor*, Chicago 1951) in order to describe the frame within which the *Autobiography* was written, and something of the emotional mood as well. There are, as I see it, three principal types of autobiography. There is the *confessional* type, as in

St. Augustine and Rousseau ("Here is my heart; see how it bled; see what I am now"). There is the *processional* type, as in Napoleon, Andrew Carnegie, Theodore Roosevelt ("I am a part of all that I have met; these are the men with whom I marched and fought"). There is, finally, the *intellectual* type, or the autobiography of the mind, as in Mill and Ruskin and Henry Adams ("This was my education, thus my mind was formed").

When I put Mill's *Autobiography* in the third category, I should add that it contains elements of the other two. The chapter on "A Crisis in My Mental History" belongs in the first category, and much of the last chapter, especially on his Parliamentary life, belongs in the second. Yet basically the book is, as Mill himself described it when he called it "the history of my mind," the story of the growth, unfolding, shaping of a mind. As such it is one of the half-dozen greatest books of its genre and will live (along with *On Liberty*) long after everything else of Mill's has become obsolescent.

As the story of a mind it has three great themes. The first is the Grand Design of education, of which Mill was at once guinea-pig, resplendent triumph, and victim. I have already spoken of this in my general Introduction, but I should like to add a few words here. James Mill regarded his son's mind as a *tabula rasa*—a clean blackboard on which he could inscribe the outlines of a great mind to his heart's desire. In a deep sense he failed. Certainly he failed in getting his son's love or gratitude. Quite understandably Mill resented being used as a guinea-pig.

There is another Victorian autobiography—*Father and Son*, by Edmund Gosse—which describes a wall of non-communication between the generations more typical of the era, the wall between the rigid religious orthodoxy of the older generation and the stirrings of doubt and desire in the younger. In the case of the Mills the cause of the discord was not the conception of God but of human nature. The elder Mill, in his simplified view of the human personality, made the mistake of many parents. In his eagerness to make something notable of his children, especially of his eldest, he pushed them beyond the margin of endurance.

In an early draft of the *Autobiography*, probably the one discussed in the Letters above, Mill had given a grim family portrait: "My father's older children neither loved him nor with any warmth of affection anyone else. That rarity in

England, a really warm-hearted mother would in the first place have made my father a totally different being and in the second have made the children grow up loving and loved. But my mother with the very best of intentions only knew how to pass her life in drudging for them. . . . I thus grew up in the absence of love and in the presence of fear; and many and indelible are the effects of this bringing-up in the stunting of my moral growth. . . . Another evil I shared with many of the sons of energetic fathers. To have been through childhood under the constant rule of a strong will certainly is not favorable to strength of will. . . . I acquired the habit of leaving my responsibility as a moral agent to rest on my father and my conscience never speaking to me except by his voice."

This passage was cut out of the final draft. In fact, Mill's mother is never even mentioned in that draft. What a dreary pitiful picture is presented here: a highly cultivated young man who resented his father and (as the boy grew away from him) was resented by him, and who despised and pitied his mother. And what a picture of self-pity is drawn! In this sense Mill is a writer attuned to the present "beat" generation, which is alienated from its elders, resentful, and somewhat self-pitying.

Yet it is an overstressed picture. The fact is that Mill became not only a great intellectual figure in his time, but (despite his lament about his moral dependence) a great moral figure as well. Mill was, I have said, not only the guinea-pig and victim of his father's educational method but its triumph as well. Despite his dependence on his father, and later on Mrs. Taylor he proved to be a self-starter and self-sustainer in all his projects.

His self-deprecatory language is not to be taken too seriously. He had, as he says, "a willingness and ability to learn from everybody." He *did* break away from his father's domination. He did learn, from Coleridge and Carlyle and the German thinkers, things which went contrary to his father's thinking. He did learn from the Saint-Simonians and Comte, and yet was able to break away from them when they threatened his intellectual integrity, just as he broke away from Carlyle and the Germans. He learned especially from Tocqueville, and found little there that needed breaking away from. The remarkable thing about Mill's education was that it did form his mind, and the remarkable thing about Mill's mind was that it did survive his education—and was deepened and strengthened by it.

The second great theme of the *Autobiography*, after the Grand Design, is the Great Love. Here again I can only add a few words to what I have written in the general Introduction. There is nothing quite like this story anywhere in world literature, not even in the relationship of George Sand with Benjamin Constant, although that comes perhaps closest. What Harriet Taylor offered John Mill was the fulfillment of all his hope of Heaven, a chance to find a replacement for his father as a lost love-object, a chance at the perfect love-work relationship, and an object for reverence which was the equivalent of religious feeling. What Mill offered Harriet was the love she wanted without the sex she scorned in her high-minded way, and a chance to give her ideas a permanence which she could not have achieved through her own abilities.

Every man woos and holds a woman in his own way. Mill's way of wooing was to convince Harriet of his intellectual dependence on her. There have been worse and more self-deluding ways. Despite his insistence that all his works are the product of a joint writing partnership, I am convinced that the bulk of the thinking and writing in them is Mill's own. But I am equally convinced that he was the kind of man who needs someone else, as catalyst, critic, and sanction, before he can feel intellectually fulfilled.

The *Autobiography* was written by Mill, but there is no question that Harriet went over every word of the earlier draft—though she did not live to go over everything in the final one. Mill identified it closely with her—more closely than any other book except *On Liberty*. The passages on her in the *Autobiography* have become famous. The superlatives about her in the preface to *On Liberty*, published soon after her death, stirred much comment at the time. But they were paled and dwarfed by the passages in the *Autobiography*, which was not published until 1873, shortly after Mill's own death. "I have often compared her, as she was at this time, to Shelley," he writes. "But in thought and intellect, Shelley . . . was but a child compared with what she ultimately became. Alike in the highest regions of speculation and in the smaller practical concerns of daily life, her mind was the same perfect instrument, piercing to the very heart and marrow of the matter." She might, Mill added, have been "a consummate artist," "a great orator," and (if such a career had been open to women) "among the rulers of mankind."

The question about these two people is not so much whether Mill's valuation was justified, but why and what her influence on him was. One should remember that throughout his *Autobiography*, and indeed throughout his life, Mill took a highly intellectual view of everything and everyone, including himself. After his early mental crisis, when he was desperately searching to find the springs of feeling, he found in Mrs. Taylor's intellectuality an intellectual reason for releasing the flood of his emotion. Once under the influence of this beautiful and fragile but also intelligent woman, he found in his feeling for her an emotional reason for being intellectual —for building and sustaining a highly intellectual life as a joint partnership. In both cases she served his life and mind well.

Add to this the fact that the seven and a half years of their married life were also the years when Mill felt sharply the impending danger of his own death and then of hers, so that love and anxiety, the sense of the shortness of the years that remained, the preciousness of every moment, the need to garner the intellectual harvest of the years, were all combined into a single feeling of reverence for Harriet as a kind of presiding goddess over it all. If I call her a fertility goddess I hope I shall not be misunderstood. Frigid in her sexual relations, she nevertheless (or perhaps *therefore*) played in Mill's life the role of the goddess of the fertility of their joint intellectual products.

I might add, as a curious footnote, the difference of view that two commentators on Mill, both at the London School of Economics, had of his relation to Mrs. Taylor. F. A. Hayek, the author of *The Road to Serfdom* as well as of the crucial study on Mill and Mrs. Taylor, is inclined to take Mill at his word about Mrs. Taylor's influence on his thought. Harold Laski, who did an edition of the *Autobiography*, and whose references to the Mills are plentifully scattered through his correspondence with Justice Holmes, made a mockery of Harriet and her influence. Is it possible that Hayek, a thoroughgoing anti-Socialist, preferred to believe that Mill's socialist phase was not really his own, and that Laski, a convinced Socialist, preferred to believe that Mill's Socialism was not just the product of the tyranny of a woman's mind?

If Laski was scornful of the relationship, this was not true of the other Fabian Socialists who followed Mill. The idea of a working intellectual partnership of the sexes, both outside marriage and within it, became a traditional Fabian idea. You find it best in the relation of Beatrice Potter and Sidney Webb, and it may be traced all the way from Beatrice Webb's *My Apprenticeship* to their joint (and naive) work on *Soviet Russia: a New Civilization.* You find it in H. G. Wells, especially in his relation to Rebecca West, and it will be found in fictional form in his *Ann Veronica* and *The New Machiavelli.* You may find it even, in attenuated and transmuted form, in the Platonic friendships of Bernard Shaw, immortalized in his letters to a succession of actresses.

There remains the third grand theme of the *Autobiography* —the life of thought and action in the cause of reform. Mill was primarily a thinker, but his constant question was the one that Robert S. Lynd later phrased as "Knowledge—for what?" He was also a fighting liberal and radical who felt that no great social reform could be accomplished unless grounded in an exacting and scrupulous intellectual analysis.

From Mill's activism in the area of social reform has come much of the liberal and labor movement, not only in England but in America—what has been described sometimes as the "Lib-Lab" mentality. But I fear that much of it, while deriving from Mill's fervor for reform, has lost sight of his fervor for fundamental thinking and re-thinking. "I pondered painfully on the subject," he writes at one point in the *Autobiography,* discussing "the doctrine of the formation of character by circumstances," "till gradually I saw light through it." The painful pondering on one subject after another, till the light comes through, is one of the best features of the *Autobiography,* and not the least of the habits of mind one may be able to acquire from it.

CONTENTS

AUTOBIOGRAPHY

I. CHILDHOOD AND EARLY EDUCATION.

IT seems proper that I should prefix to the following biographical sketch, some mention of the reasons which have made me think it desirable that I should leave behind me such a memorial of so uneventful a life as mine. I do not for a moment imagine that any part of what I have to relate can be interesting to the public as a narrative, or as being connected with myself. But I have thought that in an age in which education, and its improvement, are the subject of more, if not of profounder study than at any former period of English history, it may be useful that there should be some record of an education which was unusual and remarkable, and which, whatever else it may have done, has proved how much more than is commonly supposed may be taught, and well taught, in those early years which, in the common modes of what is called instruction, are little better than wasted. It has also seemed to me that in an age of transition in opinions, there may be somewhat both of interest and of benefit in noting the successive phases of any mind which was always pressing forward, equally ready to learn and to unlearn either from its own thoughts or from those of others. But a motive which weighs more with me than either of these, is a desire to make acknowledgment of the debts which my intellectual and moral development owes to other persons; some of them of recognized eminence, others less known than they deserve to be, and the one to whom most of all is due, one whom the world had no opportunity of knowing. The reader whom these things do not interest, has only himself to blame if he reads farther, and I do not desire any other indulgence from him than that of bearing in mind, that for him these pages were not written.

I was born in London, on the 20th of May, 1806, and was the eldest son of James Mill, the author of the History of British India. My father, the son of a petty tradesman and (I believe) small farmer, at Northwater Bridge, in the county of Angus, was, when a boy, recommended by his abilities to the notice of Sir John Stuart, of Fettercairn, one of the Barons of the Exchequer in Scotland, and was, in consequence, sent to the University of Edinburgh at the expense of a fund established by Lady Jane Stuart (the wife of Sir John Stuart) and some other ladies for educating young men for the Scottish Church. He there went through the usual course of study, and was licensed as a Preacher, but never followed the profession; having satisfied himself that he could not believe the doctrines of that or any other Church. For a few years he was a private tutor in various families in Scotland, among others that of the Marquis of Tweeddale; but ended by taking up his residence in London, and devoting himself to authorship. Nor had he any other means of support until 1819, when he obtained an appointment in the India House.

In this period of my father's life there are two things which it is impossible not to be struck with: one of them unfortunately a very common circumstance, the other a most uncommon one. The first is, that in his position, with no resource but the precarious one of writing in periodicals, he married and had a large family; conduct than which nothing could be more opposed, both as a matter of good sense and of duty, to the opinions which, at least at a later period of life, he strenuously upheld. The other circumstance is the extraordinary energy which was required to lead the life he led, with the disadvantages under which he laboured from the first, and with those which he brought upon himself by his marriage. It would have been no small thing, had he done no more than to support himself and his family during so many years by writing, without ever being in debt, or in any pecuniary difficulty; holding, as he did, opinions, both in politics and in religion, which were more odious to all persons of influence, and to the common run of prosperous Englishmen in that generation than either before or since; and being not only a man whom nothing would have induced to write against his convictions, but one who invariably threw into everything he wrote, as much of his convictions as he thought the circumstances would in any way permit: being, it must also be said, one who never did anything negligently; never undertook any task, literary or other, on which he did not conscientiously bestow all the labour necessary for performing it adequately. But he, with these burthens on him, planned, commenced, and completed, the History of India; and this in the course of about ten years, a shorter time than has been occupied (even by writers who had no other employment) in the production of almost any other historical work of equal bulk, and of anything approaching to the same amount of reading and research. And to this is to be added, that during the whole period, a considerable part of almost every day was employed in the instruction of his children: in the case of one of whom, myself, he exerted an amount of labour, care, and perseverance rarely, if ever, employed for a similar purpose, in endeavouring to give, according to his own conception, the highest order of intellectual education.

A man who, in his own practice, so vigorously acted up to the principle of losing no time, was likely to adhere to the same rule in the instruction of his pupil. I have no remembrance of the time when I began to learn Greek. I have been told that it was when I was three years old. My earliest recollection on the subject, is that of committing to memory what my father termed Vocables, being lists of common Greek words, with their signification in English, which he wrote out for me on cards. Of grammar, until some years later, I learnt no more than the inflexions of the nouns and verbs, but, after a course of vocables, proceeded at once to translation; and I faintly remember going through Æsop's Fables, the first Greek book which I read. The Anabasis, which I remember better, was the second. I learnt no Latin until my eighth year. At that time I had read, under my father's tuition, a number of Greek prose authors, among whom I remember the whole of Herodotus, and of Xenophon's Cyropædia and Memorials of Socrates; some of the lives of the philosophers by Diogenes Laertius; part of Lucian, and Isocrates' ad Demonicum and ad Nicoclem. I also read, in 1813, the first six dialogues (in the common arrangement) of Plato, from the Euthyphron to the Theætetus inclusive: which last dialogue, I venture to think, would have been better omitted, as it was totally impossible I should understand it. But my father, in all his teaching, demanded of me not only the utmost that I could do, but much that I could by no possibility have done. What he was himself willing to undergo for the sake of my instruction, may be judged from the fact, that I went through the whole process of preparing my Greek lessons in the same room and at the same table at which he was writing: and as in those days Greek and English lexicons were not, and I could make no more use of a Greek and Latin lexicon than could be made without having yet begun to learn Latin, I was forced to have recourse to him for the meaning of every word which I did not know. This incessant interruption, he, one of the most impatient of men, submitted to, and wrote under that interruption several volumes of his History and all else that he had to write during those years.

The only thing besides Greek, that I learnt as a lesson in this part of my childhood, was arithmetic: this also my father taught me: it was the task of the evenings, and I well remember its disagreeableness. But the lessons were only a part of the daily instruction I received. Much of it consisted in the books I read by myself, and my father's discourses to me, chiefly during our walks. From 1810 to the end of 1813 we were living in Newington Green, then an almost rustic neighbourhood. My father's health required considerable and constant exercise, and he walked habitually before breakfast, generally in the green lanes towards Hornsey. In these walks I always accompanied him, and with my earliest recollections of green fields and wild flowers, is mingled that of the account I gave him daily of what I had read the day before. To the best of my remembrance, this was a voluntary rather than a prescribed exercise. I made notes on slips of paper while reading, and from these, in the morning walks, I told the story to him; for the books were chiefly histories, of which I read in this manner a great number: Robertson's histories, Hume, Gibbon; but my greatest delight, then and for long afterwards, was Watson's Philip the Second and Third. The heroic defence of the Knights of Malta against the Turks, and of the revolted provinces of the Netherlands against Spain, excited in me an intense and lasting interest. Next to Watson, my favourite historical reading was Hooke's History of Rome. Of Greece I had seen at that time no regular history, except school abridgments and the last two or three volumes of a translation of Rollin's Ancient History, beginning with Philip of Macedon. But I read with great delight Langhorne's translation of Plutarch. In English history, beyond the time at which Hume leaves off, I remember reading Burnet's History

of his Own Time, though I cared little for anything in it except
the wars and battles; and the historical part of the Annual
Register, from the beginning to about 1788, when the volumes
my father borrowed for me from Mr. Bentham left off. I felt
a lively interest in Frederic of Prussia during his difficulties,
and in Paoli, the Corsican patriot; but when I came to the
American war, I took my part, like a child as I was (until set
right by my father) on the wrong side, because it was called
the English side. In these frequent talks about the books I
read, he used, as opportunity offered, to give me explanations
and ideas respecting civilization, government, morality, mental
cultivation, which he required me afterwards to restate to
him in my own words. He also made me read, and give him
a verbal account of, many books which would not have interested me sufficiently to induce me to read them of myself:
among others, Millar's Historical View of the English Government, a book of great merit for its time, and which he highly
valued; Mosheim's Ecclesiastical History, McCrie's Life of
John Knox, and even Sewel's and Rutty's Histories of the
Quakers. He was fond of putting into my hands books which
exhibited men of energy and resource in unusual circumstances, struggling against difficulties and overcoming them:
of such works I remember Beaver's African Memoranda, and
Collins's account of the first settlement of New South Wales.
Two books which I never wearied of reading were Anson's
Voyage, so delightful to most young persons, and a Collection
(Hawkesworth's, I believe) of Voyages round the World, in
four volumes, beginning with Drake and ending with Cook
and Bougainville. Of children's books, any more than of play-
things, I had scarcely any, except an occasional gift from a
relation or acquaintance: among those I had, Robinson Crusoe
was preeminent, and continued to delight me through all my
boyhood. It was no part however of my father's system to
exclude books of amusement, though he allowed them very
sparingly. Of such books he possessed at that time next to
none, but he borrowed several for me; those which I remember are the Arabian Nights, Cazotte's Arabian Tales, Don
Quixote, Miss Edgeworth's "Popular Tales," and a book of
some reputation in its day, Brooke's Fool of Quality.

In my eighth year I commenced learning Latin, in conjunction with a younger sister, to whom I taught it as I went on,
and who afterwards repeated the lessons to my father: and
from this time, other sisters and brothers being successively

added as pupils, a considerable part of my day's work consisted of this preparatory teaching. It was a part which I
greatly disliked; the more so, as I was held responsible for
the lessons of my pupils, in almost as full a sense as for my
own: I however derived from this discipline the great advantage of learning more thoroughly and retaining more lastingly
the things which I was set to teach: perhaps, too, the practice
it afforded in explaining difficulties to others, may even at
that age have been useful. In other respects, the experience
of my boyhood is not favourable to the plan of teaching children by means of one another. The teaching, I am sure, is
very inefficient as teaching, and I well knew that the relation
between teacher and taught is not a good moral discipline to
either. I went in this manner through the Latin grammar,
and a considerable part of Cornelius Nepos and Cæsar's Com-
mentaries, but afterwards added to the superintendence of
these lessons, much longer ones of my own.

In the same year in which I began Latin, I made my first
commencement in the Greek poets with the Iliad. After I had
made some progress in this, my father put Pope's translation
into my hands. It was the first English verse I had cared to
read, and it became one of the books in which for many years
I most delighted: I think I must have read it from twenty to
thirty times through. I should not have thought it worth while
to mention a taste apparently so natural to boyhood, if I had
not, as I think, observed that the keen enjoyment of this brilliant specimen of narrative and versification is not so universal
with boys, as I should have expected both *a priori* and from
my individual experience. Soon after this time I commenced
Euclid, and somewhat later, algebra, still under my father's
tuition.

From my eighth to my twelfth year the Latin books which
I remember reading were, the Bucolics of Virgil, and the first
six books of the Æneid; all Horace except the Epodes; the
Fables of Phædrus; the first five books of Livy (to which from
my love of the subject I voluntarily added, in my hours of
leisure, the remainder of the first decade); all Sallust; a considerable part of Ovid's Metamorphoses; some plays of Ter-
ence; two or three books of Lucretius; several of the Orations
of Cicero, and of his writings on oratory; also his letters to
Atticus, my father taking the trouble to translate to me from
the French the historical explanations in Mongault's notes. In
Greek I read the Iliad and Odyssey through; one or two plays

of Sophocles, Euripides, and Aristophanes, though by these I profited little; all Thucydides; the Hellenics of Xenophon; a great part of Demosthenes, Æschines, and Lysias; Theocritus; Anacreon; part of the Anthology; a little of Dionysius; several books of Polybius; and lastly Aristotle's Rhetoric, which, as the first expressly scientific treatise on any moral or psychological subject which I had read, and containing many of the best observations of the ancients on human nature and life, my father made me study with peculiar care, and throw the matter of it into synoptic tables. During the same years I learnt elementary geometry and algebra thoroughly, the differential calculus and other portions of the higher mathematics far from thoroughly: for my father, not having kept up this part of his early acquired knowledge, could not spare time to qualify himself for removing my difficulties, and left me to deal with them, with little other aid than that of books; while I was continually incurring his displeasure by my inability to solve difficult problems for which he did not see that I had not the necessary previous knowledge.

As to my private reading, I can only speak of what I remember. History continued to be my strongest predilection, and most of all ancient history. Mitford's Greece I read continually; my father had put me on my guard against the Tory prejudices of this writer, and his perversions of facts for the whitewashing of despots, and blackening of popular institutions. These points he discoursed on, exemplifying them from the Greek orators and historians, with such effect that in reading Mitford my sympathies were always on the contrary side to those of the author, and I could, to some extent, have argued the point against him: yet this did not diminish the ever new pleasure with which I read the book. Roman history, both in my old favourite, Hooke, and in Ferguson, continued to delight me. A book which, in spite of what is called the dryness of its style, I took great pleasure in, was the Ancient Universal History, through the incessant reading of which I had my head full of historical details concerning the obscurest ancient people, while about modern history, except detached passages, such as the Dutch war of independence, I knew and cared comparatively little. A voluntary exercise, to which throughout my boyhood I was much addicted, was what I called writing histories. I successively composed a Roman history, picked out of Hooke; an abridgment of the Ancient Universal History; a History of Holland, from my

favourite Watson and from an anonymous compilation; and
in my eleventh and twelfth year I occupied myself with writing what I flattered myself was something serious. This was
no less than a history of the Roman Government, compiled
(with the assistance of Hooke) from Livy and Dionysius: of
which I wrote as much as would have made an octavo volume,
extending to the epoch of the Licinian Laws. It was, in fact,
an account of the struggles between the patricians and plebeians, which now engrossed all the interest in my mind which
I had previously felt in the mere wars and conquests of the
Romans. I discussed all the constitutional points as they arose:
though quite ignorant of Niebuhr's researches, I, by such
lights as my father had given me, vindicated the Agrarian
Laws on the evidence of Livy, and upheld to the best of my
ability the Roman democratic party. A few years later, in my
contempt of my childish efforts, I destroyed all these papers,
not then anticipating that I could ever feel any curiosity about
my first attempts at writing and reasoning. My father encouraged me in this useful amusement, though, as I think judi-
ciously, he never asked to see what I wrote; so that I did not
feel that in writing it I was accountable to any one, nor had
the chilling sensation of being under a critical eye.

But though these exercises in history were never a compulsory lesson, there was another kind of composition which was
so, namely, writing verses, and it was one of the most disagreeable of my tasks. Greek and Latin verses I did not write,
nor learnt the prosody of those languages. My father, thinking
this not worth the time it required, contented himself with
making me read aloud to him, and correcting false quantities.
I never composed at all in Greek, even in prose, and but little
in Latin. Not that my father could be indifferent to the value
of this practice, in giving a thorough knowledge of those languages, but because there really was not time for it. The
verses I was required to write were English. When I first read
Pope's Homer, I ambitiously attempted to compose something
of the same kind, and achieved as much as one book of a
continuation of the Iliad. There, probably, the spontaneous
promptings of my poetical ambition would have stopped; but
the exercise, begun from choice, was continued by command.
Conformably to my father's usual practice of explaining to
me, as far as possible, the reasons for what he required me to
do, he gave me, for this, as I well remember, two reasons
highly characteristic of him: one was, that some things could

be expressed better and more forcibly in verse than in prose: this, he said, was a real advantage. The other was, that people in general attached more value to verse than it deserved, and the power of writing it, was, on this account, worth acquiring. He generally left me to choose my own subjects, which, as far as I remember, were mostly addresses to some mythological personage or allegorical abstractions; but he made me translate into English verse many of Horace's shorter poems: I also remember his giving me Thomson's "Winter" to read, and afterwards making me attempt (without book) to write something myself on the same subject. The verses I wrote were, of course, the merest rubbish, nor did I ever attain any facility of versification, but the practice may have been useful in making it easier for me, at a later period, to acquire readiness of expression.* I had read, up to this time, very little English poetry, Shakespeare my father had put into my hands, chiefly for the sake of the historical plays, from which, however, I went on to the others. My father never was a great admirer of Shakespeare, the English idolatry of whom he used to attack with some severity. He cared little for any English poetry except Milton (for whom he had the highest admiration), Goldsmith, Burns, and Gray's Bard, which he preferred to his Elegy: perhaps I may add Cowper and Beattie. He had some value for Spenser, and I remember his reading to me (unlike his usual practice of making me read to him), the first book of the Fairie Queene; but I took little pleasure in it. The poetry of the present century he saw scarcely any merit in, and I hardly became acquainted with any of it till I was grown up to manhood, except the metrical romances of Walter Scott, which I read at his recommendation and was intensely delighted with; as I always was with animated narrative. Dryden's Poems were among my father's books, and many of these he made me read, but I never cared for any of them except Alexander's Feast, which, as well as many of the songs in Walter Scott, I used to sing internally, to a music of my own: to some of the latter, indeed, I went so far as to compose airs, which I still remember. Cowper's short poems I read with some pleasure, but never got far into the longer ones; and nothing in the two volumes inter-

* In a subsequent stage of boyhood, when these exercises had ceased to be compulsory, like most youthful writers I wrote tragedies; under the inspiration not so much of Shakespeare as of Joanna Baillie, whose "Constantine Paleologus" in particular appeared to me one of the most glorious of human compositions. I still think it one of the best dramas of the last two centuries.

ested me like the prose account of his three hares. In my thirteenth year I met with Campbell's Poems, among which Lochiel, Hohenlinden, the Exile of Erin, and some others, gave me sensations I had never before experienced from poetry. Here, too, I made nothing of the longer poems, except the striking opening of Gertrude of Wyoming, which long kept its place in my feelings as the perfection of pathos.

During this part of my childhood, one of my greatest amusements was experimental science; in the theoretical, however, not the practical sense of the word; not trying experiments—a kind of discipline which I have often regretted not having had—nor even seeing, but merely reading about them. I never remember being so wrapt up in any book, as I was in Joyce's Scientific Dialogues; and I was rather recalcitrant to my father's criticisms of the bad reasoning respecting the first principles of physics, which abounds in the early part of that work. I devoured treatises on Chemistry, especially that of my father's early friend and schoolfellow, Dr. Thomson, for years before I attended a lecture or saw an experiment.

From about the age of twelve, I entered into another and more advanced stage in my course of instruction; in which the main object was no longer the aids and appliances of thought, but the thoughts themselves. This commenced with Logic, in which I began at once with the Organon, and read it to the Analytics inclusive, but profited little by the Posterior Analytics, which belongs to a branch of speculation I was not yet ripe for. Contemporaneously with the Organon, my father made me read the whole or parts of several of the Latin treatises on the scholastic logic; giving each day to him, in our walks, a minute account of what I had read, and answering his numerous and searching questions. After this, I went in a similar manner, through the "Computatio sive Logica" of Hobbes, a work of a much higher order of thought than the books of the school logicians, and which he estimated very highly; in my own opinion beyond its merits, great as these are. It was his invariable practice, whatever studies he exacted from me, to make me as far as possible understand and feel the utility of them: and this he deemed peculiarly fitting in the case of the syllogistic logic, the usefulness of which had been impugned by so many writers of authority. I well remember how, and in what particular walk, in the neighbourhood of Bagshot Heath (where we were on a visit to his old friend Mr. Wallace, then one of the Mathematical Professors at Sandhurst) he first attempted by questions to make me think on the subject, and frame some conception of what constituted the utility of the syllogistic logic, and when I had failed in this, to make me understand it by explanations. The explanations did not make the matter at all clear to me at the time; but they were not therefore useless; they remained as a nucleus for my observations and reflections to crystallize upon; the import of his general remarks being interpreted to me, by the particular instances which came under my notice afterwards. My own consciousness and experience ultimately led me to appreciate quite as highly as he did, the value of an early practical familiarity with the school logic. I know nothing, in my education, to which I think myself more indebted for whatever capacity of thinking I have attained. The first intellectual operation in which I arrived at any proficiency, was dissecting a bad argument, and finding in what part the fallacy lay: and though whatever capacity of this sort I attained was due to the fact that it was an intellectual exercise in which I was most perseveringly drilled by my father, yet it is also true that the school logic, and the mental habits acquired in studying it, were among the principal instruments of this drilling. I am persuaded that nothing, in modern education, tends so much, when properly used, to form exact thinkers, who attach a precise meaning to words and propositions, and are not imposed on by vague, loose, or ambiguous terms. The boasted influence of mathematical studies is nothing to it; for in mathematical processes, none of the real difficulties of correct ratiocination occur. It is also a study peculiarly adapted to an early stage in the education of philosophical students, since it does not presuppose the slow process of acquiring, by experience and reflection, valuable thoughts of their own. They may become capable of disentangling the intricacies of confused and self-contradictory thought, before their own thinking faculties are much advanced; a power which, for want of some such discipline, many otherwise able men altogether lack; and when they have to answer opponents, only endeavour, by such arguments as they can command, to support the opposite conclusion, scarcely even attempting to confute the reasonings of their antagonists; and, therefore, at the utmost, leaving the question, as far as it depends on argument, a balanced one.

During this time, the Latin and Greek books which I continued to read with my father were chiefly such as were worth studying, not for the language merely, but also for the thoughts. This included much of the orators, and especially Demosthenes, some of whose principal orations I read several times over, and wrote out, by way of exercise, a full analysis of them. My father's comments on these orations when I read them to him were very instructive to me. He not only drew my attention to the insight they afforded into Athenian institutions, and the principles of legislation and government which they often illustrated, but pointed out the skill and art of the orator—how everything important to his purpose was said at the exact moment when he had brought the minds of his audience into the state most fitted to receive it; how he made steal into their minds, gradually and by insinuation, thoughts which, if expressed in a more direct manner would have aroused their opposition. Most of these reflections were beyond my capacity of full comprehension at the time; but they left seed behind, which germinated in due season. At this time I also read the whole of Tacitus, Juvenal, and Quintilian. The latter, owing to his obscure style and to the scholastic details of which many parts of his treatise are made up, is little read, and seldom sufficiently appreciated. His book is a kind of encyclopædia of the thoughts of the ancients on the whole field of education and culture; and I have retained through life many valuable ideas which I can distinctly trace to my reading of him, even at that early age. It was at this period that I read, for the first time, some of the most important dialogues of Plato, in particular the Gorgias, the Protagoras, and the Republic. There is no author to whom my father thought himself more indebted for his own mental culture, than Plato, or whom he more frequently recommended to young students. I can bear similar testimony in regard to myself. The Socratic method, of which the Platonic dialogues are the chief example, is unsurpassed as a discipline for correcting the errors, and clearing up the confusions incident to the *intellectus sibi permissus*, the understanding which has made up all its bundles of associations under the guidance of popular phraseology. The close, searching *elenchus* by which the man of vague generalities is constrained either to express his meaning to himself in definite terms, or to confess that he does not know what he is talking about; the perpetual testing of all general statements by particular instances; the siege in form which is laid to the meaning of large abstract terms, by fixing upon some still larger class-name which includes that and more, and dividing down to the thing sought —marking out its limits and definition by a series of accurately drawn distinctions between it and each of the cognate objects which are successively parted off from it—all this, as an education for precise thinking, is inestimable, and all this, even at that age, took such hold of me that it became part of my own mind. I have felt ever since that the title of Platonist belongs by far better right to those who have been nourished in, and have endeavoured to practise Plato's mode of investigation, than to those who are distinguished only by the adoption of certain dogmatical conclusions, drawn mostly from the least intelligible of his works, and which the character of his mind and writings makes it uncertain whether he himself regarded as anything more than poetic fancies, or philosophic conjectures.

In going through Plato and Demosthenes, since I could now read these authors, as far as the language was concerned, with perfect ease, I was not required to construe them sentence by sentence, but to read them aloud to my father, answering questions when asked: but the particular attention which he paid to elocution (in which his own excellence was remarkable) made this reading aloud to him a most painful task. Of all things which he required me to do, there was none which I did so constantly ill, or in which he so perpetually lost his temper with me. He had thought much on the principles of the art of reading, especially the most neglected part of it, the inflections of the voice, or *modulation* as writers on elocution call it (in contrast with *articulation* on the one side, and *expression* on the other), and had reduced it to rules, grounded on the logical analysis of a sentence. These rules he strongly impressed upon me, and took me severely to task for every violation of them: but I even then remarked (though I did not venture to make the remark to him) that though he reproached me when I read a sentence ill, and *told* me how I ought to have read it, he never, by reading it himself, *showed* me how it ought to be read. A defect running through his otherwise admirable modes of instruction, as it did through all his modes of thought, was that of trusting too much to the intelligibleness of the abstract, when not embodied in the concrete. It was at a much later period of my youth, when practising elocution by myself, or with companions of my own age, that I for the first time understood the object of his rules, and saw the psychological grounds of them. At that time I and others followed out the subject into its ramifications and could have composed a very useful treatise, grounded on my father's principles. He himself left those principles and rules unwritten. I regret that when my mind was full of the subject, from systematic practice, I did not put them, and our improvements of them, into a formal shape.

A book which contributed largely to my education, in the best sense of the term, was my father's History of India. It was published in the beginning of 1818. During the year previous, while it was passing through the press, I used to read the proof sheets to him; or rather, I read the manuscript to him while he corrected the proofs. The number of new ideas which I received from this remarkable book, and the impulse and stimulus as well as guidance given to my thoughts by its criticisms and disquisitions on society and civilization in the Hindoo part, on institutions and the acts of governments in the English part, made my early familiarity with it eminently useful to my subsequent progress. And though I can perceive deficiencies in it now as compared with a perfect standard, I still think it, if not the most, one of the most instructive histories ever written, and one of the books from which most benefit may be derived by a mind in the course of making up its opinions.

The Preface, among the most characteristic of my father's writings, as well as the richest in materials of thought, gives a picture which may be entirely depended on, of the sentiments and expectations with which he wrote the History. Saturated as the book is with the opinions and modes of judgment of a democratic radicalism then regarded as extreme; and treating with a severity, at that time most unusual, the English Constitution, the English law, and all parties and classes who possessed any considerable influence in the country; he may have expected reputation, but certainly not advancement in life, from its publication; nor could he have supposed that it would raise up anything but enemies for him in powerful quarters: least of all could he have expected favour from the East India Company, to whose commercial privileges he was unqualifiedly hostile, and on the acts of whose government he had made so many severe comments: though, in various parts of his book, he bore a testimony in their favour, which he felt to be their just due, namely, that no government had on the whole given so much proof, to the extent of its lights, of good intention towards its subjects; and that if the acts of any other government had the light of publicity as completely let in upon them, they would, in all probability, still less bear scrutiny.

On learning, however, in the spring of 1819, about a year after the publication of the History, that the East India Directors desired to strengthen the part of their home establishment which was employed in carrying on the correspondence with India, my father declared himself a candidate for that employment, and, to the credit of the Directors, successfully. He was appointed one of the Assistants of the Examiner of India Correspondence; officers whose duty it was to prepare drafts of despatches to India, for consideration by the Directors, in the principal departments of administration. In this office, and in that of Examiner, which he subsequently attained, the influence which his talents, his reputation, and his decision of character gave him, with superiors who really desired the good government of India, enabled him to a great extent to throw into his drafts of despatches, and to carry through the ordeal of the Court of Directors and Board of Control, without having their force much weakened, his real opinions on Indian subjects. In his History he had set forth, for the first time, many of the true principles of Indian administration: and his despatches, following his History, did more than had ever been done before to promote the improvement of India, and teach Indian officials to understand their business. If a selection of them were published, they would, I am convinced, place his character as a practical statesman fully on a level with his eminence as a speculative writer.

This new employment of his time caused no relaxation in his attention to my education. It was in this same year, 1819, that he took me through a complete course of political economy. His loved and intimate friend, Ricardo, had shortly before published the book which formed so great an epoch in political economy; a book which never would have been published or written, but for the entreaty and strong encouragement of my father; for Ricardo, the most modest of men, though firmly convinced of the truth of his doctrines, deemed himself so little capable of doing them justice in exposition and expression, that he shrank from the idea of publicity. The same friendly encouragement induced Ricardo, a year or two later, to become a member of the House of Commons; where, during the few remaining years of his life, unhappily cut short in the full vigour of his intellect, he rendered so much service to his and my father's opinions both on political economy and on other subjects.

Though Ricardo's great work was already in print, no didactic treatise embodying its doctrines, in a manner fit for learners, had yet appeared. My father, therefore, commenced instructing me in the science by a sort of lectures, which he delivered to me in our walks. He expounded each day a portion of the subject, and I gave him next day a written account of it, which he made me rewrite over and over again until it was clear, precise, and tolerably complete. In this manner I went through the whole extent of the science; and the written outline of it which resulted from my daily *compte rendu*, served him afterwards as notes from which to write his Elements of Political Economy. After this I read Ricardo, giving an account daily of what I read, and discussing, in the best manner I could, the collateral points which offered themselves in our progress.

On Money, as the most intricate part of the subject, he made me read in the same manner Ricardo's admirable pamphlets, written during what was called the Bullion controversy; to these succeeded Adam Smith; and in this reading it was one of my father's main objects to make me apply to Smith's more superficial view of political economy, the superior lights of Ricardo, and detect what was fallacious in Smith's arguments, or erroneous in any of his conclusions. Such a mode of instruction was excellently calculated to form a thinker; but it required to be worked by a thinker, as close and vigorous as my father. The path was a thorny one, even to him, and I am sure it was so to me, notwithstanding the strong interest I took in the subject. He was often, and much beyond reason, provoked by my failures in cases where success could not have been expected; but in the main his method was right, and it succeeded. I do not believe that any scientific teaching ever was more thorough, or better fitted for training the faculties, than the mode in which logic and political economy were taught to me by my father. Striving, even in an exaggerated degree, to call forth the activity of my faculties, by making me find out everything for myself, he gave his explanations not before, but after, I had felt the full force of the difficulties; and not only gave me an accurate knowledge of these two great subjects, as far as they were then understood, but made me a thinker on both. I thought for myself almost from the first, and occasionally thought differently from him, though for a long time only on minor points, and making his opinion the ultimate standard. At a later period I even occasionally convinced him, and altered his opinion on some points of detail: which I state to his honour, not my own. It at once exemplifies his perfect candour, and the real worth of his method of teaching.

At this point concluded what can properly be called my lessons: when I was about fourteen I left England for more than a year; and after my return, though my studies went on under my father's general direction, he was no longer my schoolmaster. I shall therefore pause here, and turn back to matters of a more general nature connected with the part of my life and education included in the preceding reminiscences.

In the course of instruction which I have partially retraced, the point most superficially apparent is the great effort to give, during the years of childhood an amount of knowledge in what are considered the higher branches of education, which is seldom acquired (if acquired at all) until the age of manhood. The result of the experiment shows the ease with which this may be done, and places in a strong light the wretched waste of so many precious years as are spent in acquiring the modicum of Latin and Greek commonly taught to schoolboys; a waste, which has led so many educational reformers to entertain the ill-judged proposal of discarding these languages altogether from general education. If I had been by nature extremely quick of apprehension, or had possessed a very accurate and retentive memory, or were of a remarkably active and energetic character, the trial would not be conclusive; but in all these natural gifts I am rather below than above par; what I could do, could assuredly be done by any boy or girl of average capacity and healthy physical constitution: and if I have accomplished anything, I owe it, among other fortunate circumstances, to the fact that through the early training bestowed on me by my father, I started, I may fairly say, with an advantage of a quarter of a century over my contemporaries.

There was one cardinal point in this training, of which I have already given some indication, and which, more than anything else, was the cause of whatever good it effected. Most boys or youths who have had much knowledge drilled into them, have their mental capacities not strengthened, but overlaid by it. They are crammed with mere facts, and with the opinions or phrases of other people, and these are accepted as a substitute for the power to form opinions of their own: and thus the sons of eminent fathers, who have spared no pains in their education, so often grow up mere parroters of what they have learnt, incapable of using their minds except in the furrows traced for them. Mine, however, was not an education of cram. My father never permitted anything which I learnt to degenerate into a mere exercise of memory. He strove to make the understanding not only go along with every step of the teaching, but, if possible, precede it. Anything which could be found out by thinking I never was told, until I had exhausted my efforts to find it out for myself. As far as I can trust my remembrance, I acquitted myself very lamely in this department; my recollection of such matters is almost wholly of failures, hardly ever of success. It is true the failures were often in things in which success in so early a stage of my progress, was almost impossible. I remember at some time in my thirteenth year, on my happening to use the word idea, he asked me what an idea was; and expressed some displeasure at my ineffectual efforts to define the word: I recollect also his indignation at my using the common expression that something was true in theory but required correction in practice; and how, after making me vainly strive to define the word theory, he explained its meaning, and showed the fallacy of the vulgar form of speech which I had used; leaving me fully persuaded that in being unable to give a correct definition of Theory, and in speaking of it as something which might be at variance with practice, I had shown unparalleled ignorance. In this he seems, and perhaps was, very unreasonable; but I think, only in being angry at my failure. A pupil from whom nothing is ever demanded which he cannot do, never does all he can.

One of the evils most liable to attend on any sort of early proficiency, and which often fatally blights its promise, my father most anxiously guarded against. This was self-conceit. He kept me, with extreme vigilance, out of the way of hearing myself praised, or of being led to make self-flattering comparisons between myself and others. From his own intercourse with me I could derive none but a very humble opinion of myself; and the standard of comparison he always held up to me, was not what other people did, but what a man could and ought to do. He completely succeeded in preserving me from the sort of influences he so much dreaded. I was not at all aware that my attainments were anything unusual at my age. If I accidentally had my attention drawn to the fact that some other boy knew less than myself—which happened less often than might be imagined—I concluded, not that I knew much, but that he, for some reason or other, knew little, or that his knowledge was of a different kind from mine. My state of mind was not humility, but neither was it arrogance. I never thought of saying to myself, I am, or I can do, so and so. I neither estimated myself highly nor lowly: I did not estimate myself at all. If I thought anything about myself, it was that I was rather backward in my studies, since I always found myself so, in comparison with what my father expected from me. I assert this with confidence, though it was not the impression of various persons who saw me in my childhood. They, as I have since found, thought me greatly and disagreeably self-conceited; probably because I was disputatious, and did not scruple to give direct contradictions to things which I heard said. I suppose I acquired this bad habit from having been encouraged in an unusual degree to talk on matters beyond my age, and with grown persons, while I never had inculcated in me the usual respect for them. My father did not correct this ill-breeding and impertinence, probably from not being aware of it, for I was always too much in awe of him to be otherwise than extremely subdued and quiet in his presence. Yet with all this I had no notion of any superiority in myself; and well was it for me that I had not. I remember the very place in Hyde Park where, in my fourteenth year, on the eve of leaving my father's house for a long absence, he told me that I should find, as I got acquainted with new people, that I had been taught many things which youths of my age did not commonly know; and that many persons would be disposed to talk to me of this, and to compliment me upon it. What other things he said on this topic I remember very imperfectly; but he wound up by saying, that whatever I knew more than others, could not be ascribed to any merit in me, but to the very unusual advantage which had fallen to my lot, of having a father who was able to teach me, and willing to give the necessary trouble and time; that it was no matter of praise to me, if I knew more than those who had not had a similar advantage, but the deepest disgrace to me if I did not. I have a distinct remembrance, that the suggestion thus for the first time made to me, that I knew more than other youths who were considered well educated, was to me a piece of information, to which, as to all other things which my father told me, I gave implicit credence, but which did not at all impress me as a personal matter. I felt no disposition to glorify myself upon the circumstance that there were other persons who did not know what I knew; nor had I ever flattered myself that my acquirements, whatever they might be, were any merit of mine: but, now when my attention was called to the subject, I felt that what my father had said, respecting my peculiar advantages was exactly the truth and common sense of the matter, and it fixed my opinion and feeling from that time forward.

It is evident that this, among many other of the purposes of my father's scheme of education, could not have been accomplished if he had not carefully kept me from having any great amount of intercourse with other boys. He was earnestly bent upon my escaping not only the ordinary corrupting influence which boys exercise over boys, but the contagion of vulgar modes of thought and feeling; and for this he was willing that I should pay the price of inferiority in the accomplishments which schoolboys in all countries chiefly cultivate. The deficiencies in my education were principally in the things which boys learn from being turned out to shift for themselves, and from being brought together in large numbers. From temperance and much walking, I grew up healthy and hardy, though not muscular; but I could do no feats of skill or physical strength, and knew none of the ordinary bodily exercises. It was not that play, or time for it, was refused me. Though no holidays were allowed, lest the habit of work should be broken, and a taste for idleness acquired, I had ample leisure in every day to amuse myself; but as I had no boy companions, and the animal need of physical activity was satisfied by walking, my amusements, which were mostly solitary, were in general of a quiet, if not a bookish turn, and gave little stimulus to any other kind even of mental activity than that which was already called forth by my studies: I consequently remained long, and in a less degree have always remained, inexpert in anything requiring manual dexterity; my mind as well as my hands, did its work very lamely when it was applied, or ought to have been applied, to the practical details which, as they are the chief interest of life to the majority of men, are also the things in which whatever mental capacity they have, chiefly shows itself: I was constantly meriting reproof by inattention, inobservance, and general slackness of mind in matters of daily life. My father was the extreme opposite in these particulars: his senses and mental faculties were always on the alert; he carried decision and energy of character in his whole manner and into every action of life: and this, as much as his talents, contributed to the strong impression which he always made upon those with whom he came into personal contact. But the children of energetic parents, frequently grow up unenergetic, because they lean on their parents, and the parents are energetic for them. The education which my father gave me, was in itself much more fitted for training me to *know* than to *do*. Not that he was unaware of my deficiencies; both as a boy and as a youth I was incessantly smarting under his severe admonitions on the subject. There was anything but insensibility or tolerance on his part towards such shortcomings: but, while he saved me from the demoralizing effects of school life, he made no effort to provide me with any sufficient substitute for its practicalizing influences. Whatever qualities he himself, probably, had acquired without difficulty or special training, he seems to have supposed that I ought to acquire as easily. He had not, I think, bestowed the same amount of thought and attention on this, as on most other branches of education; and here, as well as in some other points of my tuition, he seems to have expected effects without causes.

II. MORAL INFLUENCES IN EARLY YOUTH. MY FATHER'S CHARACTER AND OPINIONS.

IN my education, as in that of everyone, the moral influences, which are so much more important than all others, are also the most complicated, and the most difficult to specify with any approach to completeness. Without attempting the hopeless task of detailing the circumstances by which, in this respect, my early character may have been shaped, I shall confine myself to a few leading points, which form an indispensable part of any true account of my education.

I was brought up from the first without any religious belief, in the ordinary acceptation of the term. My father, educated in the creed of Scotch presbyterianism, had by his own studies and reflections been early led to reject not only the belief in revelation, but the foundations of what is commonly called Natural Religion. I have heard him say, that the turning point of his mind on the subject was reading Butler's Analogy. That work, of which he always continued to speak with respect, kept him, as he said, for some considerable time, a believer in the divine authority of Christianity; by proving to him, that whatever are the difficulties in believing that the Old and New Testaments proceed from, or record the acts of, a perfectly wise and good being, the same and still greater difficulties stand in the way of the belief, that a being of such a character can have been the Maker of the universe. He considered Butler's argument as conclusive against the only opponents for whom it was intended. Those who admit an omnipotent as well as perfectly just and benevolent maker and ruler of such a world as this, can say little against Christianity but what can, with at least equal force, be retorted against themselves. Finding, therefore, no halting place in Deism, he remained in a state of perplexity, until, doubtless after many struggles, he yielded to the conviction, that, concerning the origin of things nothing whatever can be known. This is the only correct statement of his opinion; for dogmatic atheism he looked upon as absurd; as most of those, whom the world has considered Atheists, have always done. These particulars are important, because they show that my father's rejection of all that is called religious belief, was not, as many might suppose, primarily a matter of logic and evidence: the grounds of it were moral, still more than intellectual. He found it impossible to believe that a world so full of evil was the work of an Author combining infinite power with perfect goodness and righteousness. His intellect spurned the subtleties by which men attempt to blind themselves to this open contradiction. The Sabæan, or Manichæan theory of a Good and Evil Principle, struggling against each other for the government of the universe, he would not have equally condemned; and I have heard him express surprise, that no one revived it in our time. He would have regarded it as a mere hypothesis; but he would have ascribed to it no depraving influence. As it was, his aversion to religion, in the sense usually attached to the term, was of the same kind with that of Lucretius: he regarded it with the feelings due not to a mere mental delusion, but to a great moral evil. He looked upon it as the greatest enemy of morality: first, by setting up factitious excellencies, —belief in creeds, devotional feelings, and ceremonies, not connected with the good of human kind,—and causing these to be accepted as substitutes for genuine virtues: but above all,

by radically vitiating the standard of morals; making it consist in doing the will of a being, on whom it lavishes indeed
all the phrases of adulation, but whom in sober truth it de-
picts as eminently hateful. I have a hundred times heard him
say, that all ages and nations have represented their gods as
wicked, in a constantly increasing progression, that mankind
have gone on adding trait after trait till they reached the
most perfect conception of wickedness which the human mind
can devise, and have called this God, and prostrated themselves before it. This *ne plus ultra* of wickedness he considered
to be embodied in what is commonly presented to mankind as
the creed of Christianity. Think (he used to say) of a being
who would make a Hell—who would create the human race
with the infallible foreknowledge, and therefore with the intention, that the great majority of them were to be consigned
to horrible and everlasting torment. The time, I believe, is
drawing near when this dreadful conception of an object of
worship will be no longer identified with Christianity; and
when all persons, with any sense of moral good and evil, will
look upon it with the same indignation with which my father
regarded it. My father was as well aware as anyone that
Christians do not, in general, undergo the demoralizing consequences which seem inherent in such a creed, in the manner
or to the extent which might have been expected from it. The
same slovenliness of thought, and subjection of the reason to
fears, wishes, and affections, which enable them to accept a
theory involving a contradiction in terms, prevents them from
perceiving the logical consequences of the theory. Such is the
facility with which mankind believe at one and the same time
things inconsistent with one another, and so few are those who
draw from what they receive as truths, any consequences but
those recommended to them by their feelings, that multitudes
have held the undoubting belief in an Omnipotent Author of
Hell, and have nevertheless identified that being with the best
conception they were able to form of perfect goodness. Their
worship was not paid to the demon which such a being as
they imagined would really be, but to their own idea of excellence. The evil is, that such a belief keeps the ideal wretchedly low; and opposes the most obstinate resistance to all
thought which has a tendency to raise it higher. Believers
shrink from every train of ideas which would lead the mind
to a clear conception and an elevated standard of excellence,
because they feel (even when they do not distinctly see) that

such a standard would conflict with many of the dispensations of nature, and with much of what they are accustomed to consider as the Christian creed. And thus morality continues a matter of blind tradition, with no consistent principle, nor even any consistent feeling, to guide it.

It would have been wholly inconsistent with my father's ideas of duty, to allow me to acquire impressions contrary to his convictions and feelings respecting religion: and he impressed upon me from the first, that the manner in which the world came into existence was a subject on which nothing was known: that the question, "Who made me?" cannot be answered, because we have no experience or authentic information from which to answer it; and that any answer only throws the difficulty a step further back, since the question immediately presents itself, Who made God? He, at the same time, took care that I should be acquainted with what had been thought by mankind on these impenetrable problems. I have mentioned at how early an age he made me a reader of ecclesiastical history; and he taught me to take the strongest interest in the Reformation, as the great and decisive contest against priestly tyranny for liberty of thought.

I am thus one of the very few examples, in this country, of one who has, not thrown off religious belief, but never had it: I grew up in a negative state with regard to it. I looked upon the modern exactly as I did upon the ancient religion, as something which in no way concerned me. It did not seem to me more strange that English people should believe what I did not, than that the men I read of in Herodotus should have done so. History had made the variety of opinions among mankind a fact familiar to me, and this was but a prolongation of that fact. This point in my early education had, however, incidentally one bad consequence deserving notice. In giving me an opinion contrary to that of the world, my father thought it necessary to give it as one which could not prudently be avowed to the world. This lesson of keeping my thoughts to myself, at that early age, was attended with some moral disadvantages; though my limited intercourse with strangers, especially such as were likely to speak to me on religion, prevented me from being placed in the alternative of avowal or hypocrisy. I remember two occasions in my boyhood, on which I felt myself in this alternative, and in both cases I avowed my disbelief and defended it. My opponents were boys, considerably older than myself: one of them I certainly staggered at the time, but the subject was never renewed between us: the other who was surprised, and somewhat shocked, did his best to convince me for some time, without effect.

The great advance in liberty of discussion, which is one of the most important differences between the present time and that of my childhood, has greatly altered the moralities of this question; and I think that few men of my father's intellect and public spirit, holding with such intensity of moral conviction as he did, unpopular opinions on religion, or on any other of the great subjects of thought, would now either practise or inculcate the withholding of them from the world, unless in the cases, becoming fewer every day, in which frankness on these subjects would either risk the loss of means of subsistence, or would amount to exclusion from some sphere of usefulness peculiarly suitable to the capacities of the individual. On religion in particular the time appears to me to have come, when it is the duty of all who being qualified in point of knowledge, have on mature consideration satisfied themselves that the current opinions are not only false but hurtful, to make their dissent known; at least, if they are among those whose station or reputation, gives their opinion a chance of being attended to. Such an avowal would put an end, at once and for ever, to the vulgar prejudice, that what is called, very improperly, unbelief, is connected with any bad qualities either of mind or heart. The world would be astonished if it knew how great a proportion of its brightest ornaments—of those most distinguished even in popular estimation for wisdom and virtue—are complete sceptics in religion; many of them refraining from avowal, less from personal considerations, than from a conscientious, though now in my opinion a most mistaken apprehension, lest by speaking out what would tend to weaken existing beliefs, and by consequence (as they suppose) existing restraints, they should do harm instead of good.

Of unbelievers (so called) as well as of believers, there are many species, including almost every variety of moral type. But the best among them, as no one who has had opportunities of really knowing them will hesitate to affirm (believers rarely have that opportunity), are more genuinely religious, in the best sense of the word religion, than those who exclusively arrogate to themselves the title. The liberality of the age, or in other words the weakening of the obstinate prejudice which makes men unable to see what is before their eyes because it is contrary to their expectations, has caused it to be very commonly admitted that a Deist may be truly religious: but if religion stands for any graces of character and not for mere dogma, the assertion may equally be made of many whose belief is far short of Deism. Though they may think the proof incomplete that the universe is a work of design, and though they assuredly disbelieve that it can have an Author and Governor who is absolute in power as well as perfect in goodness, they have that which constitutes the principal worth of all religions whatever, an ideal conception of a Perfect Being, to which they habitually refer as the guide of their conscience; and this ideal of Good is usually far nearer to perfection than the objective Deity of those, who think themselves obliged to find absolute goodness in the author of a world so crowded with suffering and so deformed by injustice as ours.

My father's moral convictions, wholly dissevered from religion, were very much of the character of those of the Greek philosophers; and were delivered with the force and decision which characterized all that came from him. Even at the very early age at which I read with him the Memorabilia of Xenophon, I imbibed from that work and from his comments a deep respect for the character of Socrates; who stood in my mind as a model of ideal excellence: and I well remember how my father at that time impressed upon me the lesson of the "Choice of Hercules." At a somewhat later period the lofty moral standard exhibited in the writings of Plato operated upon me with great force. My father's moral inculcations were at all times mainly those of the "Socratici viri;" justice, temperance (to which he gave a very extended application), veracity, perseverance, readiness to encounter pain and especially labour; regard for the public good; estimation of persons according to their merits, and of things according to their intrinsic usefulness; a life of exertion in contradiction to one of self-indulgent sloth. These and other moralities he conveyed in brief sentences, uttered as occasion arose, of grave exhortation, or stern reprobation and contempt.

But though direct moral teaching does much, indirect does more; and the effect my father produced on my character, did not depend solely on what he said or did with that direct object, but also, and still more, on what manner of man he was.

In his views of life he partook of the character of the Stoic,
the Epicurean, and the Cynic, not in the modern but the ancient sense of the word. In his personal qualities the Stoic
predominated. His standard of morals was Epicurean, inasmuch as it was utilitarian, taking as the exclusive test of right
and wrong, the tendency of actions to produce pleasure or
pain. But he had (and this was the Cynic element) scarcely
any belief in pleasure; at least in his later years, of which
alone, on this point, I can speak confidently. He was not insensible to pleasures; but he deemed very few of them worth
the price which, at least in the present state of society, must
be paid for them. The greater number of miscarriages in life,
he considered to be attributable to the overvaluing of pleasures. Accordingly, temperance, in the large sense intended by
the Greek philosophers—stopping short at the point of mod-
eration in all indulgences—was with him, as with them, almost
the central point of educational precept. His inculcations of
this virtue fill a large place in my childish remembrances. He
thought human life a poor thing at best, after the freshness
of youth and of unsatisfied curiosity had gone by. This was a
topic on which he did not often speak, especially, it may be
supposed, in the presence of young persons: but when he did,
it was with an air of settled and profound conviction. He
would sometimes say, that if life were made what it might be,
by good government and good education, it would be worth
having: but he never spoke with anything like enthusiasm
even of that possibility. He never varied in rating intellectual
enjoyments above all others, even in value as pleasures, independently of their ulterior benefits. The pleasures of the benevolent affections he placed high in the scale; and used to
say, that he had never known a happy old man, except those
who were able to live over again in the pleasures of the young.
For passionate emotions of all sorts, and for everything which
has been said or written in exaltation of them, he professed
the greatest contempt. He regarded them as a form of madness. "The intense" was with him a bye-word of scornful disapprobation. He regarded as an aberration of the moral
standard of modern times, compared with that of the ancients,
the great stress laid upon feeling. Feelings, as such, he considered to be no proper subjects of praise or blame. Right and
wrong, good and bad, he regarded as qualities solely of conduct—of acts and omissions; there being no feeling which may
not lead, and does not frequently lead, either to good or to

bad actions: conscience itself, the very desire to act right, often leading people to act wrong. Consistently carrying out the doctrine, that the object of praise and blame should be the discouragement of wrong conduct and the encouragement of right, he refused to let his praise or blame be influenced by the motive of the agent. He blamed as severely what he thought a bad action, when the motive was a feeling of duty, as if the agents had been consciously evil doers. He would not have accepted as a plea in mitigation for inquisitors, that they sincerely believed burning heretics to be an obligation of conscience. But though he did not allow honesty of purpose to soften his disapprobation of actions, it had its full effect on his estimation of characters. No one prized conscientiousness and rectitude of intention more highly, or was more incapable of valuing any person in whom he did not feel assurance of it. But he disliked people quite as much for any other deficiency, provided he thought it equally likely to make them act ill. He disliked, for instance, a fanatic in any bad cause, as much or more than one who adopted the same cause from self-interest, because he thought him even more likely to be practically mischievous. And thus, his aversion to many intellectual errors, or what he regarded as such, partook, in a certain sense, of the character of a moral feeling. All this is merely saying that he, in a degree once common, but now very unusual, threw his feelings into his opinions; which truly it is difficult to understand how any one who possesses much of both, can fail to do. None but those who do not care about opinions, will confound it with intolerance. Those, who having opinions which they hold to be immensely important, and their contraries to be prodigiously hurtful, have any deep regard for the general good, will necessarily dislike, as a class and in the abstract, those who think wrong what they think right, and right what they think wrong: though they need not therefore be, nor was my father, insensible to good qualities in an opponent, nor governed in their estimation of individuals by one general presumption, instead of by the whole of their character. I grant that an earnest person, being no more infallible than other men, is liable to dislike people on account of opinions which do not merit dislike; but if he neither himself does them any ill office, nor connives at its being done by others, he is not intolerant: and the forbearance which flows from a conscientious sense of the importance to mankind of the equal freedom of all opinions, is the only tolerance which is commendable, or, to the highest moral order of minds, possible.

It will be admitted, that a man of the opinions, and the character, above described, was likely to leave a strong moral impression on any mind principally formed by him, and that his moral teaching was not likely to err on the side of laxity or indulgence. The element which was chiefly deficient in his moral relation to his children was that of tenderness. I do not believe that this deficiency lay in his own nature. I believe him to have had much more feeling than he habitually showed, and much greater capacities of feeling than were ever developed. He resembled most Englishmen in being ashamed of the signs of feeling, and by the absence of demonstration, starving the feelings themselves. If we consider further that he was in the trying position of sole teacher, and add to this that his temper was constitutionally irritable, it is impossible not to feel true pity for a father who did, and strove to do, so much for his children, who would have so valued their affection, yet who must have been constantly feeling that fear of him was drying it up at its source. This was no longer the case later in life, and with his younger children. They loved him tenderly: and if I cannot say so much of myself, I was always loyally devoted to him. As regards my own education, I hesitate to pronounce whether I was more a loser or gainer by his severity. It was not such as to prevent me from having a happy childhood. And I do not believe that boys can be induced to apply themselves with vigour, and what is so much more difficult, perseverance, to dry and irksome studies, by the sole force of persuasion and soft words. Much must be done, and much must be learnt, by children, for which rigid discipline, and known liability to punishment, are indispensable as means. It is, no doubt, a very laudable effort, in modern teaching, to render as much as possible of what the young are required to learn, easy and interesting to them. But when this principle is pushed to the length of not requiring them to learn anything *but* what has been made easy and interesting, one of the chief objects of education is sacrificed. I rejoice in the decline of the old brutal and tyrannical system of teaching, which, however, did succeed in enforcing habits of application; but the new, as it seems to me, is training up a race of men who will be incapable of doing anything which is disagreeable to them. I do not, then, believe that fear, as an element in education, can be dispensed with; but I am sure that it ought not to be

the main element; and when it predominates so much as to
preclude love and confidence on the part of the child to those
who should be the unreservedly trusted advisers of after years,
and perhaps to seal up the fountains of frank and spontaneous
communicativeness in the child's nature, it is an evil for which
a large abatement must be made from the benefits, moral and
intellectual, which may flow from any other part of the education.

During this first period of my life, the habitual frequenters
of my father's house were limited to a very few persons, most
of them little known to the world, but whom personal worth,
and more or less of congeniality with at least his political
opinions (not so frequently to be met with then as since) inclined him to cultivate; and his conversations with them I listened to with interest and instruction. My being an habitual
inmate of my father's study made me acquainted with the
dearest of his friends, David Ricardo, who by his benevolent
countenance, and kindliness of manner, was very attractive to
young persons, and who after I became a student of political
economy, invited me to his house and to walk with him in
order to converse on the subject. I was a more frequent visitor
(from about 1817 or 1818) to Mr. Hume, who, born in the
same part of Scotland as my father, and having been, I rather
think, a younger schoolfellow or college companion of his,
had on returning from India renewed their youthful acquaintance, and who coming like many others greatly under the influence of my father's intellect and energy of character, was
induced partly by that influence to go into Parliament, and
there adopt the line of conduct which has given him an honourable place in the history of his country. Of Mr. Bentham
I saw much more, owing to the close intimacy which existed
between him and my father. I do not know how soon after my
father's first arrival in England they became acquainted. But
my father was the earliest Englishman of any great mark, who
thoroughly understood, and in the main adopted, Bentham's
general views of ethics, government and law: and this was a
natural foundation for sympathy between them, and made
them familiar companions in a period of Bentham's life during which he admitted much fewer visitors than was the case
subsequently. At this time Mr. Bentham passed some part of
every year at Barrow Green House, in a beautiful part of the
Surrey hills, a few miles from Godstone, and there I each
summer accompanied my father in a long visit. In 1813, Mr.

Bentham, my father, and I made an excursion, which included Oxford, Bath and Bristol, Exeter, Plymouth, and Portsmouth. In this journey I saw many things which were instructive to me, and acquired my first taste for natural scenery, in the elementary form of fondness for a "view." In the succeeding winter we moved into a house very near Mr. Bentham's, which my father rented from him, in Queen Square, Westminster. From 1814 to 1817 Mr. Bentham lived during half of each year at Ford Abbey, in Somersetshire (or rather in a part of Devonshire surrounded by Somersetshire), which intervals I had the advantage of passing at that place. This sojourn was, I think, an important circumstance in my education. Nothing contributes more to nourish elevation of sentiments in a people, than the large and free character of their habitations. The middle-age architecture, the baronial hall, and the spacious and lofty rooms, of this fine old place, so unlike the mean and cramped externals of English middle class life, gave the sentiment of a large and freer existence, and were to me a sort of poetic cultivation, aided also by the character of the grounds in which the Abbey stood; which were riant and secluded, umbrageous, and full of the sound of falling waters.

I owed another of the fortunate circumstances in my education, a year's residence in France, to Mr. Bentham's brother, General Sir Samuel Bentham. I had seen Sir Samuel Bentham and his family at their house near Gosport in the course of the tour already mentioned (he being then Superintendent of the Dockyard at Portsmouth), and during a stay of a few days which they made at Ford Abbey shortly after the peace, before going to live on the Continent. In 1820 they invited me for a six months' visit to them in the South of France, which their kindness ultimately prolonged to nearly a twelvemonth. Sir Samuel Bentham, though of a character of mind different from that of his illustrous brother, was a man of very considerable attainments and general powers, with a decided genius for mechanical art. His wife, a daughter of the celebrated chemist, Dr. Fordyce, was a woman of strong will and decided character, much general knowledge, and great practical good sense of the Edgeworth kind: she was the ruling spirit of the household, as she deserved, and was well qualified, to be. Their family consisted of one son (the eminent botanist) and three daughters, the youngest about two years my senior. I am indebted to them for much and various instruction, and for an almost parental interest in my welfare. When I first joined them, in May 1820, they occupied the Château of Pompignan (still belonging to a descendant of Voltaire's enemy) on the heights overlooking the plain of the Garonne between Montauban and Toulouse. I accompanied them in an excursion to the Pyrenees, including a stay of some duration at Bagnères de Bigorre, a journey to Pau, Bayonne, and Bagnères de Luchon, and an ascent of the Pic du Midi de Bigorre.

This first introduction to the highest order of mountain scenery made the deepest impression on me, and gave a colour to my tastes through life. In October we proceeded by the beautiful mountain route of Castres and St. Pons, from Toulouse to Montpellier, in which last neighbourhood Sir Samuel had just bought the estate of Restinclière, near the foot of the singular mountain of St. Loup. During this residence in France I acquired a familiar knowledge of the French language, and acquaintance with the ordinary French literature; I took lessons in various bodily exercises, in none of which however I made any proficiency; and at Montpellier I attended the excellent winter courses of lectures at the Faculté des Sciences, those of M. Anglada on chemistry, of M. Provençal on zoology, and of a very accomplished representative of the eighteenth century metaphysics, M. Gergonne, on logic, under the name of Philosophy of the Sciences. I also went through a course of the higher mathematics under the private tuition of M. Lenthéric, a professor at the Lycée of Montpellier. But the greatest, perhaps, of the many advantages which I owed to this episode in my education, was that of having breathed for a whole year, the free and genial atmosphere of Continental life. This advantage was not the less real though I could not then estimate, nor even consciously feel it. Having so little experience of English life, and the few people I knew being mostly such as had public objects, of a large and personally disinterested kind, at heart, I was ignorant of the low moral tone of what, in England, is called society; the habit of, not indeed professing, but taking for granted in every mode of implication, that conduct is of course always directed towards low and petty objects; the absence of high feelings which manifests itself by sneering depreciation of all demonstrations of them, and by general abstinence (except among a few of the stricter religionists) from professing any high principles of action at all, except in those preordained cases in which such profession is put on as part of the costume and formalities of the occasion. I could not then know or estimate the difference between this manner of existence, and that of a people like the French, whose faults, if equally real, are at all events different; among whom sentiments, which by comparison at least may be called elevated, are the current coin of human intercourse, both in books and in private life; and though often evaporating in profession, are yet kept alive in the nation at large by constant exercise, and stimulated by sympathy, so as to form a living and active part of the existence of great numbers of persons, and to be recognized and understood by all. Neither could I then appreciate the general culture of the understanding, which results from the habitual exercise of the feelings, and is thus carried down into the most uneducated classes of several countries on the Continent, in a degree not equalled in England among the so-called educated, except where an unusual tenderness of conscience leads to a habitual exercise of the intellect on questions of right and wrong. I did not know the way in which, among the ordinary English, the absence of interest in things of an unselfish kind, except occasionally in a special thing here and there, and the habit of not speaking to others, nor much even to themselves, about the things in which they do feel interest, causes both their feelings and their intellectual faculties to remain undeveloped, or to develope themselves only in some single and very limited direction; reducing them, considered as spiritual beings, to a kind of negative existence. All these things I did not perceive till long afterwards; but I even then felt, though without stating it clearly to myself, the contrast between the frank sociability and amiability of French personal intercourse, and the English mode of existence in which everybody acts as if everybody else (with few, or no exceptions) was either an enemy or a bore. In France, it is true, the bad as well as the good points, both of individual and of national character, come more to the surface, and break out more fearlessly in ordinary intercourse, than in England: but the general habit of the people is to show, as well as to expect, friendly feeling in every one towards every other, wherever there is not some positive cause for the opposite. In England it is only of the best bred people, in the upper or upper middle ranks, that anything like this can be said.

In my way through Paris, both going and returning, I passed some time in the house of M. Say, the eminent political economist, who was a friend and correspondent of my father, having become acquainted with him on a visit to

England a year or two after the peace. He was a man of the later period of the French Revolution, a fine specimen of the best kind of French Republican, one of those who had never bent the knee to Bonaparte though courted by him to do so; a truly upright, brave, and enlightened man. He lived a quiet and studious life, made happy by warm affections, public and private. He was acquainted with many of the chiefs of the Liberal party, and I saw various noteworthy persons while staying at his house; among whom I have pleasure in the recollection of having once seen Saint-Simon, not yet the founder either of a philosophy or a religion, and considered only as a clever *original*. The chief fruit which I carried away from the society I saw, was a strong and permanent interest in Continental Liberalism, of which I ever afterwards kept myself *au courant*, as much as of English politics: a thing not at all usual in those days with Englishmen, and which had a very salutary influence on my development, keeping me free from the error always prevalent in England, and from which even my father with all his superiority to prejudice was not exempt, of judging universal questions by a merely English standard. After passing a few weeks at Caen with an old friend of my father's, I returned to England in July 1821; and my education resumed its ordinary course.

III. LAST STAGE OF EDUCATION AND FIRST OF SELF-EDUCATION.

For the first year or two after my visit to France, I continued my old studies, with the addition of some new ones. When I returned, my father was just finishing for the press his "Elements of Political Economy," and he made me perform an exercise on the manuscript, which Mr. Bentham practised on all his own writings, making what he called, "marginal contents"; a short abstract of every paragraph, to enable the writer more easily to judge of, and improve, the order of the ideas, and the general character of the exposition. Soon after, my father put into my hands Condillac's Traité des Sensations, and the logical and metaphysical volumes of his Cours d'Etudes; the first (notwithstanding the superficial resemblance between Condillac's psychological system and my father's) quite as much for a warning as for an example. I am not sure whether it was in this winter or the next that I first read a history of the French Revolution. I learnt with astonishment, that the principles of democracy, then apparently in so insignificant and hopeless a minority everywhere in Europe, had borne all before them in France thirty years earlier, and had been the creed of the nation. As may be supposed from this, I had previously a very vague idea of that great commotion. I knew only that the French had thrown off the absolute monarchy of Louis XIV. and XV., had put the King and Queen to death, guillotined many persons, one of whom was Lavoisier, and had ultimately fallen under the despotism of Bonaparte. From this time, as was natural, the subject took an immense hold of my feelings. It allied itself with all my juvenile aspirations to the character of a democratic champion. What had happened so lately, seemed as if it might easily happen again: and the most transcendant glory I was capable of conceiving, was that of figuring, successful or unsuccessful, as a Girondist in an English Convention.

During the winter of 1821–2, Mr. John Austin, with whom at the time of my visit to France my father had but lately become acquainted, kindly allowed me to read Roman law with him. My father, notwithstanding his abhorrence of the chaos of barbarism called English Law, had turned his thoughts towards the bar as on the whole less ineligible for me than any other profession: and these readings with Mr. Austin, who had made Bentham's best ideas his own, and added much to them from other sources and from his own mind, were not only a valuable introduction to legal studies, but an important portion of general education. With Mr. Austin I read Heineccius on the Institutes, his Roman Antiquities, and part of his exposition of the Pandects; to which was added a considerable portion of Blackstone. It was at the commencement of these studies that my father, as a needful accompaniment to them, put into my hands Bentham's principal speculations, as interpreted to the Continent, and indeed to all the world, by Dumont, in the Traité de Législation. The reading of this book was an epoch in my life; one of the turning points in my mental history.

My previous education had been, in a certain sense, already a course of Benthamism. The Benthamic standard of "the greatest happiness" was that which I had always been taught to apply; I was even familiar with an abstract discussion of it, forming an episode in an unpublished dialogue on Government, written by my father on the Platonic model. Yet in the first pages of Bentham it burst upon me with all the force of novelty. What thus impressed me was the chapter in which Bentham passed judgment on the common modes of reasoning in morals and legislation, deduced from phrases like "law of nature," "right reason," "the moral sense," "natural rectitude," and the like, and characterized them as dogmatism in disguise, imposing its sentiments upon others under cover of sounding expressions which convey no reason for the sentiment, but set up the sentiment as its own reason. It had not struck me before, that Bentham's principle put an end to all this. The feeling rushed upon me, that all previous moralists were superseded, and that here indeed was the commencement of a new era in thought. This impression was strengthened by the manner in which Bentham put into scientific form the application of the happiness principle to the morality of actions, by analysing the various classes and orders of their consequences. But what struck me at the time most of all, was the Classification of Offences, which is much more clear, compact and imposing in Dumont's *rédaction* than in the original work of Bentham from which it was taken. Logic and the dialectics of Plato, which had formed so large a part of my previous training, had given me a strong relish for accurate classification. This taste had been strengthened and enlightened by the study of botany, on the principles of what is called the Natural Method, which I had taken up with great zeal, though only as an amusement, during my stay in France; and when I found scientific classification applied to the great and complex subject of Punishable Acts, under the guidance of the ethical principle of Pleasurable and Painful Consequences, followed out in the method of detail introduced into these subjects by Bentham, I felt taken up to an eminence from which I could survey a vast mental domain, and see stretching out into the distance intellectual results beyond all computation. As I proceeded further, there seemed to be added to this intellectual clearness, the most inspiring prospects of practical improvements in human affairs. To Bentham's general view of the construction of a body of law I was not altogether a stranger, having read with attention that admirable compendium, my father's article "Jurisprudence": but I had read it with little profit and scarcely any interest, no doubt from its extremely general and abstract character, and also because it concerned the form more than the substance of the *corpus juris*, the logic rather than the ethics of law. But Bentham's subject was Legislation, of which Jurisprudence is only the formal part:

and at every page he seemed to open a clearer and broader conception of what human opinions and institutions ought to be, how they might be made what they ought to be, and how far removed from it they now are. When I laid down the last volume of the Traité, I had become a different being. The "principle of utility" understood as Bentham understood it, and applied in the manner in which he applied it through these three volumes, fell exactly into its place as the keystone which held together the detached and fragmentary component parts of my knowledge and beliefs. It gave unity to my conceptions of things. I now had opinions; a creed, a doctrine, a philosophy; in one among the best senses of the word, a religion; the inculcation and diffusion of which could be made the principal outward purpose of a life. And I had a grand conception laid before me of changes to be effected in the condition of mankind through that doctrine. The Traité de Législation wound up with what was to me a most impressive picture of human life as it would be made by such opinions and such laws as were recommended in the treatise. The anticipations of practicable improvement were studiously moderate, deprecating and discountenancing as reveries of vague enthusiasm many things which will one day seem so natural to human beings, that injustice will probably be done to those who once thought them chimerical. But, in my state of mind, this appearance of superiority to illusion added to the effect which Bentham's doctrines produced on me, by heightening the impression of mental power, and the vista of improvement which he did open was sufficiently large and brilliant to light up my life, as well as to give a definite shape to my aspirations.

After this I read, from time to time, the most important of the other works of Bentham which had then seen the light, either as written by himself or as edited by Dumont. This was my private reading: while, under my father's direction, my studies were carried into the higher branches of analytic psychology. I now read Locke's Essay, and wrote out an account of it, consisting of a complete abstract of every chapter, with such remarks as occurred to me: which was read by, or (I think) to, my father, and discussed throughout. I performed the same process with Helvetius de l'Esprit, which I read of my own choice. This preparation of abstracts, subject to my father's censorship, was of great service to me, by compelling precision in conceiving and expressing psychological doctrines,

whether accepted as truths or only regarded as the opinion of
others. After Helvetius, my father made me study what he
deemed the really master-production in the philosophy of
mind, Hartley's Observations on Man. This book, though it
did not, like the Traité de Législation, give a new colour to
my existence, made a very similar impression on me in regard
to its immediate subject. Hartley's explanation, incomplete as
in many points it is, of the more complex mental phenomena
by the law of association, commended itself to me at once as a
real analysis, and made me feel by contrast the insufficiency
of the merely verbal generalizations of Condillac, and even
of the instructive gropings and feelings about for psychological
explanations, of Locke. It was at this very time that my father
commenced writing his Analysis of the Mind, which carried
Hartley's mode of explaining the mental phenomena to so
much greater length and depth. He could only command the
concentration of thought necessary for this work, during the
complete leisure of his holiday of a month or six weeks annually: and he commenced it in the summer of 1822, in the
first holiday he passed at Dorking; in which neighbourhood,
from that time to the end of his life, with the exception of
two years, he lived, as far as his official duties permitted, for
six months of every year. He worked at the Analysis during
several successive vacations, up to the year 1829 when it was
published, and allowed me to read the manuscript, portion by
portion, as it advanced. The other principal English writers
on mental philosophy I read as I felt inclined, particularly
Berkeley, Hume's Essays, Reid, Dugald Stewart and Brown
on Cause and Effect. Brown's Lectures I did not read until
two or three years later, nor at that time had my father himself read them.

Among the works read in the course of this year, which
contributed materially to my development, I ought to mention
a book (written on the foundation of some of Bentham's manuscripts and published under the pseudonyme of Philip Beauchamp) entitled "Analysis of the Influence of Natural Religion
on the Temporal Happiness of Mankind." This was an examination not of the truth, but of the usefulness of religious
belief, in the most general sense, apart from the peculiarities
of any special Revelation; which, of all the parts of the discussion concerning religion, is the most important in this age,
in which real belief in any religious doctrine is feeble and
precarious, but the opinion of its necessity for moral and social

purposes almost universal; and when those who reject revelation, very generally take refuge in an optimistic Deism, a worship of the order of Nature, and the supposed course of Providence, at least as full of contradictions, and perverting to the moral sentiments, as any of the forms of Christianity, if only it is as completely realized. Yet, very little, with any claim to a philosophical character, has been written by sceptics against the usefulness of this form of belief. The volume bearing the name of Philip Beauchamp had this for its special object. Having been shown to my father in manuscript, it was put into my hands by him, and I made a marginal analysis of it as I had done of the Elements of Political Economy. Next to the Traité de Législation, it was one of the books which by the searching character of its analysis produced the greatest effect upon me. On reading it lately after an interval of many years, I find it to have some of the defects as well as the merits of the Benthamic modes of thought, and to contain, as I now think, many weak arguments, but with a great overbalance of sound ones, and much good material for a more completely philosophic and conclusive treatment of the subject.

I have now, I believe, mentioned all the books which had any considerable effect on my early mental development. From this point I began to carry on my intellectual cultivation by writing still more than by reading. In the summer of 1822 I wrote my first argumentative essay. I remember very little about it, except that it was an attack on what I regarded as the aristocratic prejudice, that the rich were, or were likely to be, superior in moral qualities to the poor. My performance was entirely argumentative, without any of the declamation which the subject would admit of, and might be expected to suggest to a young writer. In that department however I was, and remained, very inapt. Dry argument was the only thing I could manage, or willingly attempted; though passively I was very susceptible to the effect of all composition, whether in the form of poetry or oratory, which appealed to the feelings on any basis of reason. My father, who knew nothing of this essay until it was finished, was well satisfied, and as I learnt from others, even pleased with it; but, perhaps from a desire to promote the exercise of other mental faculties than the purely logical, he advised me to make my next exercise in composition one of the oratorical kind: on which suggestion, availing myself of my familiarity with Greek history and ideas and with the Athenian orators, I wrote two speeches, one an accusation, the other a defence of Pericles, on a supposed impeachment for not marching out to fight the Lacedæmonians on their invasion of Attica. After this I continued to write papers on subjects often very much beyond my capacity, but with great benefit both from the exercise itself, and from the discussions which it led to with my father.

I had now also begun to converse, on general subjects, with the instructed men with whom I came in contact: and the opportunities of such contact naturally became more numerous. The two friends of my father from whom I derived most, and with whom I most associated, were Mr. Grote and Mr. John Austin. The acquaintance of both with my father was recent, but had ripened rapidly into intimacy. Mr. Grote was introduced to my father by Mr. Ricardo, I think in 1819, (being then about twenty-five years old), and sought assiduously his society and conversation. Already a highly instructed man, he was yet, by the side of my father, a tyro on the great subjects of human opinion; but he rapidly seized on my father's best ideas; and in the department of political opinion he made himself known as early as 1820, by a pamphlet in defence of Radical Reform, in reply to a celebrated article by Sir James Mackintosh, then lately published in the Edinburgh Review. Mr. Grote's father, the banker, was, I believe, a thorough Tory, and his mother intensely Evangelical; so that for his liberal opinions he was in no way indebted to home influences. But, unlike most persons who have the prospect of being rich by inheritance, he had, though actively engaged in the business of banking, devoted a great portion of time to philosophic studies; and his intimacy with my father did much to decide the character of the next stage in his mental progress. Him I often visited, and my conversations with him on political, moral, and philosophical subjects gave me, in addition to much valuable instruction, all the pleasure and benefit of sympathetic communion with a man of the high intellectual and moral eminence which his life and writings have since manifested to the world.

Mr. Austin, who was four or five years older than Mr. Grote, was the eldest son of a retired miller in Suffolk, who had made money by contracts during the war, and who must have been a man of remarkable qualities, as I infer from the fact that all his sons were of more than common ability and all eminently gentlemen. The one with whom we are now concerned,

and whose writings on jurisprudence have made him celebrated, was for some time in the army, and served in Sicily
under Lord William Bentinck. After the peace he sold his
commission and studied for the bar, to which he had been
called for some time before my father knew him. He was not,
like Mr. Grote, to any extent a pupil of my father, but he had
attained, by reading and thought, a considerable number of
the same opinions, modified by his own very decided individuality of character. He was a man of great intellectual powers
which in conversation appeared at their very best; from the
vigour and richness of expression with which, under the excitement of discussion, he was accustomed to maintain some
view or other of most general subjects; and from an appearance of not only strong, but deliberate and collected will;
mixed with a certain bitterness, partly derived from temperament, and partly from the general cast of his feelings and
reflexions. The dissatisfaction with life and the world, felt
more or less in the present state of society and intellect by
every discerning and highly conscientious mind, gave in his
case a rather melancholy tinge to the character, very natural
to those whose passive moral susceptibilities are more than
proportioned to their active energies. For it must be said, that
the strength of will of which his manner seemed to give such
strong assurance, expended itself principally in manner. With
great zeal for human improvement, a strong sense of duty,
and capacities and acquirements the extent of which is proved
by the writings he has left, he hardly ever completed any
intellectual task of magnitude. He had so high a standard of
what ought to be done, so exaggerated a sense of deficiencies
in his own performances, and was so unable to content himself with the amount of elaboration sufficient for the occasion
and the purpose, that he not only spoilt much of his work for
ordinary use by overlabouring it, but spent so much time and
exertion in superfluous study and thought, that when his task
ought to have been completed, he had generally worked himself into an illness, without having half finished what he undertook. From this mental infirmity (of which he is not the sole
example among the accomplished and able men whom I have
known), combined with liability to frequent attacks of dis-
abling though not dangerous ill-health, he accomplished,
through life, little in comparison with what he seemed capable
of; but what he did produce is held in the very highest estimation by the most competent judges; and, like Coleridge, he

might plead as a set-off that he had been to many persons, through his conversation, a source not only of much instruction but of great elevation of character. On me his influence was most salutary. It was moral in the best sense. He took a sincere and kind interest in me, far beyond what could have been expected towards a mere youth from a man of his age, standing, and what seemed austerity of character. There was in his conversation and demeanour a tone of highmindedness which did not show itself so much, if the quality existed as much, in any of the other persons with whom at that time I associated. My intercourse with him was the more beneficial, owing to his being of a different mental type from all other intellectual men whom I frequented, and he from the first set himself decidedly against the prejudices and narrownesses which are almost sure to be found in a young man formed by a particular mode of thought or a particular social circle.

His younger brother, Charles Austin, of whom at this time and for the next year or two I saw much, had also a great effect on me, though of a very different description. He was but a few years older than myself, and had then just left the University, where he had shone with great éclat as a man of intellect and a brilliant orator and converser. The effect he produced on his Cambridge contemporaries deserves to be accounted an historical event; for to it may in part be traced the tendency towards Liberalism in general, and the Benthamic and politico-economic form of it in particular, which showed itself in a portion of the more active-minded young men of the higher classes from this time to 1830. The Union Debating Society, at that time at the height of its reputation, was an arena where what were then thought extreme opinions, in politics and philosophy, were weekly asserted, face to face with their opposites, before audiences consisting of the élite of the Cambridge youth: and though many persons afterwards of more or less note, (of whom Lord Macaulay is the most celebrated), gained their first oratorical laurels in those debates, the realy influential mind among these intellectual gladiators was Charles Austin. He continued, after leaving the University, to be, by his conversation and personal ascendancy, a leader among the same class of young men who had been his associates there; and he attached me among others to his car. Through him I became acquainted with Macaulay, Hyde and Charlies Villiers, Strutt (now Lord Belper), Romilly (now Lord Romilly and Master of the Rolls), and various

others who subsequently figured in literature or politics, and
among whom I heard discussions on many topics, as yet to a
certain degree new to me. The influence of Charles Austin
over me differed from that of the persons I have hitherto mentioned, in being not the influence of a man over a boy, but
that of an elder contemporary. It was through him that I first
felt myself, not a pupil under teachers, but a man among men.
He was the first person of intellect whom I met on a ground
of equality, though as yet much his inferior on that common
ground. He was a man who never failed to impress greatly
those with whom he came in contact, even when their opinions were the very reverse of his. The impression he gave was
that of boundless strength, together with talents which, combined with such apparent force of will and character, seemed
capable of dominating the world. Those who knew him,
whether friendly to him or not, always anticipated that he
would play a conspicuous part in public life. It is seldom that
men produce so great an immediate effect by speech, unless
they, in some degree, lay themselves out for it; and he did
this in no ordinary degree. He loved to strike, and even to
startle. He knew that decision is the greatest element of effect,
and he uttered his opinions with all the decision he could
throw into them, never so well pleased as when he astonished
any one by their audacity. Very unlike his brother, who made
war against the narrower interpretations and applications of
the principles they both professed, he, on the contrary, presented the Benthamic doctrines in the most startling form of
which they were susceptible, exaggerating everything in them
which tended to consequences offensive to any one's precon-
ceived feelings. All which, he defended with such verve and
vivacity, and carried off by a manner so agreeable as well as
forcible, that he always either came off victor, or divided the
honours of the field. It is my belief that much of the notion
popularly entertained of the tenets and sentiments of what
are called Benthamites or Utilitarians had its origin in paradoxes thrown out by Charles Austin. It must be said, however,
that his example was followed, *haud passibus æquis*, by
younger proselytes, and that to *outrer* whatever was by anybody considered offensive in the doctrines and maxims of
Benthanism, became at one time the badge of a small coterie
of youths. All of these who had anything in them, myself
among others, quickly outgrew this boyish vanity; and those
who had not, became tired of differing from other people, and

gave up both the good and the bad part of the heterodox opinions they had for some time professed.

It was in the winter of 1822–3 that I formed the plan of a little society, to be composed of young men agreeing in fundamental principles—acknowledging Utility as their standard in ethics and politics, and a certain number of the principal corollaries drawn from it in the philosophy I had accepted—and meeting once a fortnight to read essays and discuss questions conformably to the premises thus agreed on. The fact would hardly be worth mentioning, but for the circumstance, that the name I gave to the society I had planned was the Utilitarian Society. It was the first time that any one had taken the title of Utilitarian; and the term made its way into the language from this humble source. I did not invent the word, but found it in one of Galt's novels, the "Annals of the Parish," in which the Scotch clergyman, of whom the book is a supposed autobiography, is represented as warning his parishioners not to leave the Gospel and become utilitarians. With a boy's fondness for a name and a banner I seized on the word, and for some years called myself and others by it as a sectarian appellation; and it came to be occasionally used by some others holding the opinions which it was intended to designate. As those opinions attracted more notice, the term was repeated by strangers and opponents, and got into rather common use just about the time when those who had originally assumed it, laid down that along with other sectarian characteristics. The Society so called consisted at first of no more than three members, one of whom, being Mr. Bentham's amanuensis, obtained for us permission to hold our meetings in his house. The number never, I think, reached ten, and the society was broken up in 1826. It had thus an existence of about three years and a half. The chief effect of it as regards myself, over and above the benefit of practice in oral discussion, was that of bringing me in contact with several young men at that time less advanced than myself, among whom, as they professed the same opinions, I was for some time a sort of leader, and had considerable influence on their mental progress. Any young man of education who fell in my way, and whose opinions were not incompatible with those of the Society, I endeavoured to press into its service; and some others I probably should never have known, had they not joined it. Those of the members who became my intimate companions—no one of whom was in any sense of the word a disciple, but all of them independent thinkers on their own basis—were William Eyton Tooke, son of the eminent political economist, a young man of singular worth both moral and intellectual, lost to the world by an early death; his friend William Ellis, an original thinker in the field of political economy, now honourably known by his apostolic exertions for the improvement of education; George Graham, afterwards an official assignee of the Bankruptcy Court, a thinker of originality and power on almost all abstract subjects; and (from the time when he came first to England to study for the bar in 1824 or 1825) a man who has made considerably more noise in the world than any of these, John Arthur Roebuck.

In May, 1823, my professional occupation and status for the next thirty-five years of my life, were decided by my father's obtaining for me an appointment from the East India Company, in the office of the Examiner of India Correspondence, immediately under himself. I was appointed in the usual manner, at the bottom of the list of clerks, to rise, at least in the first instance, by seniority; but with the understanding that I should be employed from the beginning in preparing drafts of despatches, and be thus trained up as a successor to those who then filled the higher departments of the office. My drafts of course required, for some time, much revision from my immediate superiors, but I soon became well acquainted with the business, and by my father's instructions and the general growth of my own powers, I was in a few years qualified to be, and practically was, the chief conductor of the correspondence with India in one of the leading departments, that of the Native States. This continued to be my official duty until I was appointed Examiner, only two years before the time when the abolition of the East India Company as a political body determined my retirement. I do not know any one of the occupations by which a subsistence can now be gained, more suitable than such as this to any one who, not being in independent circumstances, desires to devote a part of the twenty-four hours to private intellectual pursuits. Writing for the press, cannot be recommended as a permanent resource to any one qualified to accomplish anything in the higher departments of literature or thought: not only on account of the uncertainty of this means of livelihood, especially if the writer has a conscience, and will not consent to serve any opinions except his own; but also because the writings by which one can live, are not the writings which themselves live, and are never those in which the writer does his best. Books destined to form future thinkers take too much time to write, and when written come, in general, too slowly into notice and repute, to be relied on for subsistence. Those who have to support themselves by their pen must depend on literary drudgery, or at best on writings addressed to the multitude; and can employ in the pursuits of their own choice, only such time as they can spare from those of necessity; which is generally less than the leisure allowed by office occupations, while the effect on the mind is far more enervating and fatiguing. For my own part I have, through life, found office duties an actual rest from the other mental occupations which I have carried on simultaneously with them. They were sufficiently intellectual not to be a distasteful drudgery, without being such as to cause any strain upon the mental powers of a person used to abstract thought, or to the labour of careful literary composition. The drawbacks, for every mode of life has its drawbacks, were not, however, unfelt by me. I cared little for the loss of the chances of riches and honours held out by some of the professions, particularly the bar, which had been, as I have already said, the profession thought of for me. But I was not indifferent to exclusion from Parliament, and public life: and I felt very sensibly the more immediate unpleasantness of confinement to London; the holiday allowed by India-house practice not exceeding a month in the year, while my taste was strong for a country life, and my sojourn in France had left behind it an ardent desire of travelling. But though these tastes could not be freely indulged, they were at no time entirely sacrificed. I passed most Sundays, throughout the year, in the country, taking long rural walks on that day even when residing in London. The month's holiday was, for a few years, passed at my father's house in the country: afterwards a part or the whole was spent in tours, chiefly pedestrian, with some one or more of the young men who were my chosen companions; and, at a later period, in longer journeys or excursions, alone or with other friends. France, Belgium, and Rhenish Germany were within easy reach of the annual holiday: and two longer absences, one of three, the other of six months, under medical advice, added Switzerland, the Tyrol, and Italy to my list. Fortunately, also, both these journeys occurred rather early, so as to give the benefit and charm of the remembrance to a large portion of life.

I am disposed to agree with what has been surmised by

others, that the opportunity which my official position gave me of learning by personal observation the necessary conditions of the practical conduct of public affairs, has been of considerable value to me as a theoretical reformer of the opinions and institutions of my time. Not, indeed, that public business transacted on paper, to take effect on the other side of the globe, was of itself calculated to give much practical knowledge of life. But the occupation accustomed me to see and hear the difficulties of every course, and the means of obviating them, stated and discussed deliberately with a view to execution; it gave me opportunities of perceiving when public measures, and other political facts, did not produce the effects which had been expected of them, and from what causes; above all, it was valuable to me by making me, in this portion of my activity, merely one wheel in a machine, the whole of which had to work together. As a speculative writer, I should have had no one to consult but myself, and should have encountered in my speculations none of the obstacles which would have started up whenever they came to be applied to practice. But as a Secretary conducting political correspondence, I could not issue an order or express an opinion, without satisfying various persons very unlike myself, that the thing was fit to be done. I was thus in a good position for finding out by practice the mode of putting a thought which gives it easiest admittance into minds not prepared for it by habit; while I became practically conversant with the difficulties of moving bodies of men, the necessities of compromise, the art of sacrificing the non-essential to preserve the essential. I learnt how to obtain the best I could, when I could not obtain everything; instead of being indignant or dispirited because I could not have entirely my own way, to be pleased and encouraged when I could have the smallest part of it; and when even that could not be, to bear with complete equanimity the being overruled altogether. I have found, through life, these acquisitions to be of the greatest possible importance for personal happiness, and they are also a very necessary condition for enabling any one, either as theorist or as practical man, to effect the greatest amount of good compatible with his opportunities.

IV. YOUTHFUL PROPAGANDISM. THE WESTMINSTER REVIEW.

THE occupation of so much of my time by office work did not
relax my attention to my own pursuits, which were never carried on more vigorously. It was about this time that I began
to write in newspapers. The first writings of mine which got
into print were two letters published towards the end of 1822,
in the Traveller evening newspaper. The Traveller (which
afterwards grew into the "Globe and Traveller," by the pur-
chase and incorporation of the Globe) was then the property
of the well-known political economist, Colonel Torrens, and
under the editorship of an able man, Mr. Walter Coulson
(who, after being an amanuensis of Mr. Bentham, became a
reporter, then an editor, next a barrister and conveyancer, and
died Counsel to the Home Office), it had become one of the
most important newspaper organs of liberal politics. Col. Torrens himself wrote much of the political economy of his paper;
and had at this time made an attack upon some opinion of
Ricardo and my father, to which, at my father's instigation, I
attempted an answer, and Coulson, out of consideration for
my father and goodwill to me, inserted it. There was a reply
by Torrens, to which I again rejoined. I soon after attempted
something considerably more ambitious. The prosecutions of
Richard Carlile and his wife and sister for publications hostile
to Christianity, were then exciting much attention, and nowhere more than among the people I frequented. Freedom of
discussion even in politics, much more in religion, was at that
time far from being, even in theory, the conceded point which
it at least seems to be now; and the holders of obnoxious opinions had to be always ready to argue and re-argue for the
liberty of expressing them. I wrote a series of five letters,
under the signature of Wickliffe, going over the whole length
and breadth of the question of free publication of all opinions
on religion, and offered them to the Morning Chronicle. Three
of them were published in January and February, 1823; the
other two, containing things too outspoken for that journal,
never appeared at all. But a paper which I wrote soon after
on the same subject, à propos of a debate in the House of
Commons, was inserted as a leading article; and during the
whole of this year, 1823, a considerable number of my contributions were printed in the Chronicle and Traveller: sometimes notices of books but oftener letters, commenting on some

nonsense talked in Parliament, or some defect of the law, or misdoings of the magistracy or the courts of justice. In this last department the Chronicle was now rendering signal service. After the death of Mr. Perry, the editorship and management of the paper had devolved on Mr. John Black, long a reporter on its establishment; a man of most extensive reading and information, great honesty and simplicity of mind; a particular friend of my father, imbued with many of his and Bentham's ideas, which he reproduced in his articles, among other valuable thoughts, with great facility and skill. From this time the Chronicle ceased to be the merely Whig organ it was before, and during the next ten years became to a considerable extent a vehicle of the opinions of the Utilitarian radicals. This was mainly by what Black himself wrote, with some assistance from Fonblanque, who first showed his eminent qualities as a writer by articles and *jeux d'esprit* in the Chronicle. The defects of the law, and of the administration of justice, were the subject on which that paper rendered most service to improvement. Up to that time hardly a word had been said, except by Bentham and my father, against that most peccant part of English institutions and of their administration. It was the almost universal creed of Englishmen, that the law of England, the judicature of England, the unpaid magistracy of England, were models of excellence. I do not go beyond the mark in saying, that after Bentham, who supplied the principal materials, the greatest share of the merit of breaking down this wretched superstition belongs to Black, as editor of the Morning Chronicle. He kept up an incessant fire against it, exposing the absurdities and vices of the law and the courts of justice, paid and unpaid, until he forced some sense of them into people's minds. On many other questions he became the organ of opinions much in advance of any which had ever before found regular advocacy in the newspaper press. Black was a frequent visitor of my father, and Mr. Grote used to say that he always knew by the Monday morning's article, whether Black had been with my father on the Sunday. Black was one of the most influential of the many channels through which my father's conversation and personal influence made his opinions tell on the world; co-operating with the effect of his writings in making him a power in the country, such as it has rarely been the lot of an individual in a private station to be, through the mere force of intellect and character: and a power which was often acting the most efficiently where it was least seen and suspected. I have already noticed how much of what was done by Ricardo, Hume, and Grote, was the result, in part, of his prompting and persuasion. He was the good genius by the side of Brougham in most of what he did for the public, either on education, law reform, or any other subject. And his influence flowed in minor streams too numerous to be specified. This influence was now about to receive a great extension by the foundation of the Westminster Review.

Contrary to what may have been supposed, my father was in no degree a party to setting up the Westminster Review. The need of a Radical organ to make head against the Edinburgh and Quarterly (then in the period of their greatest reputation and influence), had been a topic of conversation between him and Mr. Bentham many years earlier, and it had been a part of their *château en Espagne* that my father should be the editor; but the idea had never assumed any practical shape. In 1823, however, Mr. Bentham determined to establish the review at his own cost, and offered the editorship to my father, who declined it as incompatible with his India House appointment. It was then entrusted to Mr. (now Sir John) Bowring, at that time a merchant in the City. Mr. Bowring had been for two or three years previous an assiduous frequenter of Mr. Bentham, to whom he was recommended by many personal good qualities, by an ardent admiration for Bentham, a zealous adoption of many, though not all, of his opinions, and, not least, by an extensive acquaintanceship and correspondence with Liberals of all countries, which seemed to qualify him for being a powerful agent in spreading Bentham's fame and doctrines through all quarters of the world. My father had seen little of Bowring, but knew enough of him to have formed a strong opinion, that he was a man of an entirely different type from what my father considered suitable for conducting a political and philosophical review: and he augured so ill of the enterprise that he regretted it altogether, feeling persuaded not only that Mr. Bentham would lose his money, but that discredit would probably be brought upon radical principles. He could not, however, desert Mr. Bentham, and he consented to write an article for the first number. As it had been a favourite portion of the scheme formerly talked of, that part of the work should be devoted to reviewing the other Reviews, this article of my father's was to be a general criticism of the Edinburgh Review from its commencement. Before writing it he made me read through all the volumes of the Review, or as much of each as seemed of any importance (which was not so arduous a task in 1823 as it would be now), and make notes for him of the articles which I thought he would wish to examine, either on account of their good or their bad qualities. This paper of my father's was the chief cause of the sensation which the Westminster Review produced at its first appearance, and is, both in conception and in execution, one of the most striking of all his writings. He began by an analysis of the tendencies of periodical literature in general; pointing out, that it cannot, like books, wait for success, but must succeed immediately, or not at all, and is hence almost certain to profess and inculcate the opinions already held by the public to which it addresses itself, instead of attempting to rectify or improve those opinions. He next, to characterize the position of the Edinburgh Review as a political organ, entered into a complete analysis, from the Radical point of view, of the British Constitution. He held up to notice its thoroughly aristocratic character: the nomination of a majority of the House of Commons by a few hundred families; the entire identification of the more independent portion, the county members, with the great landholders; the different classes whom this narrow oligarchy was induced, for convenience, to admit to a share of power; and finally, what he called its two props, the Church, and the legal profession. He pointed out the natural tendency of an aristocratic body of this composition, to group itself into two parties, one of them in possession of the executive, the other endeavouring to supplant the former and become the predominant section by the aid of public opinion, without any essential sacrifice of the aristocratic predominance. He described the course likely to be pursued, and the political ground occupied, by an aristocratic party in opposition, coquetting with popular principles for the sake of popular support. He showed how this idea was realized in the conduct of the Whig party, and of the Edinburgh Review as its chief literary organ. He described, as their main characteristic, what he termed "seesaw;" writing alternately on both sides of every question which touched the power or interest of the governing classes; sometimes in different articles, sometimes in different parts of the same article: and illustrated his position by copious specimens. So formidable an attack on the Whig party and policy had never before been made; nor had so great a blow been ever struck, in this country, for radicalism; nor was there, I believe, any living person capable of writing that article, except my father.*

In the meantime the nascent review had formed a junction with another project, of a purely literary periodical, to be edited by Mr. Henry Southern, afterwards a diplomatist, then a literary man by profession. The two editors agreed to unite their corps, and divide the editorship, Bowring taking the political, Southern the literary department. Southern's review was to have been published by Longman, and that firm, though part proprietors of the Edinburgh, were willing to be the publishers of the new journal. But when all the arrangements had been made, and the prospectuses sent out, the Longmans saw my father's attack on the Edinburgh, and drew back. My father was now appealed to for his interest with his own publisher, Baldwin, which was exerted with a successful result. And so, in April, 1824, amidst anything but hope on my father's part, and that of most of those who afterwards aided in carrying on the review, the first number made its appearance.

That number was an agreeable surprise to most of us. The average of the articles was of much better quality than had been expected. The literary and artistic department had rested chiefly on Mr. Bingham, a barrister (subsequently a Police Magistrate), who had been for some years a frequenter of Bentham, was a friend of both the Austins, and had adopted with great ardour Mr. Bentham's philosophical opinions. Partly from accident, there were in the first number as many as five articles by Bingham; and we were extremely pleased with them. I well remember the mixed feeling I myself had about the Review; the joy at finding, what we did not at all expect, that it was sufficiently good to be capable of being made a creditable organ of those who held the opinions it professed; and extreme vexation, since it was so good on the whole, at what we thought the blemishes of it. When, however, in addition to our generally favourable opinion of it, we learned that it had an extraordinarily large sale for a first number, and found that the appearance of a Radical review, with pretensions equal to those of the established organs of parties, had excited much attention, there could be no room for hesi-

---

* The continuation of this article in the second number of the review was written by me under my father's eye, and (except as practice in composition, in which respect it was, to me, more useful than anything else I ever wrote) was of little or no value.

tation, and we all became eager in doing everything we could to strengthen and improve it.

My father continued to write occasional articles. The Quarterly Review received its exposure, as a sequel to that of the Edinburgh. Of his other contributions, the most important were an attack on Southey's Book of the Church, in the fifth number, and a political article in the twelfth. Mr. Austin only contributed one paper, but one of great merit, an argument against primogeniture, in reply to an article then lately published in the Edinburgh Review by McCulloch. Grote also was a contributor only once; all the time he could spare being already taken up with his History of Greece. The article he wrote was on his own subject, and was a very complete exposure and castigation of Mitford. Bingham and Charles Austin continued to write for some time; Fonblanque was a frequent contributor from the third number. Of my particular associates, Ellis was a regular writer up to the ninth number; and about the time when he left off, others of the set began; Eyton Tooke, Graham, and Roebuck. I was myself the most frequent writer of all, having contributed, from the second number to the eighteenth, thirteen articles; reviews of books on history and political economy, or discussions on special political topics, as corn laws, game laws, laws of libel. Occasional articles of merit came in from other acquaintances of my father's, and, in time, of mine; and some of Mr. Bowring's writers turned out well. On the whole, however, the conduct of the Review was never satisfactory to any of the persons strongly interested in its principles, with whom I came in contact. Hardly ever did a number come out without containing several things extremely offensive to us, either in point of opinion, of taste, or by mere want of ability. The unfavourable judgments passed by my father, Grote, the two Austins, and others, were re-echoed with exaggeration by us younger people; and as our youthful zeal rendered us by no means backward in making complaints, we led the two editors a sad life. From my knowledge of what I then was, I have no doubt that we were at least as often wrong as right; and I am very certain that if the Review had been carried on according to our notions (I mean those of the juniors), it would have been no better, perhaps not even so good as it was. But it is worth noting as a fact in the history of Benthanism, that the periodical organ, by which it was best known, was from the first

extremely unsatisfactory to those whose opinions on all subjects it was supposed specially to represent.

Meanwhile, however, the Review made considerable noise
in the world, and gave a recognised *status*, in the arena of
opinion and discussion, to the Benthamic type of radicalism,
out of all proportion to the number of its adherents, and to
the personal merits and abilities, at that time, of most of
those who could be reckoned among them. It was a time, as
is known, of rapidly rising Liberalism. When the fears and
animosities accompanying the war with France had been
brought to an end, and people had once more a place in their
thoughts for home politics, the tide began to set towards reform. The renewed oppression of the Continent by the old
reigning families, the countenance apparently given by the
English Government to the conspiracy against liberty called
the Holy Alliance, and the enormous weight of the national
debt and taxation occasioned by so long and costly a war,
rendered the government and parliament very unpopular.
Radicalism, under the leadership of the Burdetts and Cobbetts,
had assumed a character and importance which seriously
alarmed the Administration: and their alarm had scarcely been
temporarily assuaged by the celebrated Six Acts, when the
trial of Queen Caroline roused a still wider and deeper feeling
of hatred. Though the outward signs of this hatred passed
away with its exciting cause, there arose on all sides a spirit
which had never shown itself before, of opposition to abuses
in detail. Mr. Hume's persevering scrutiny of the public expenditure, forcing the House of Commons to a division on
every objectionable item in the estimates, had begun to tell
with great force on public opinion, and had extorted many
minor retrenchments from an unwilling administration. Political economy had asserted itself with great vigour in public
affairs, by the Petition of the Merchants of London for Free
Trade, drawn up in 1820 by Mr. Tooke and presented by Mr.
Alexander Baring; and by the noble exertions of Ricardo during the few years of his parliamentary life. His writings,
following up the impulse given by the Bullion controversy,
and followed up in their turn by the expositions and comments of my father and McCulloch (whose writings in the
Edinburgh Review during those years were most valuable),
had drawn general attention to the subject, making at least
partial converts in the Cabinet itself; and Huskisson, supported by Canning, had commenced that gradual demolition

of the protective system, which one of their colleagues virtually completed in 1846, though the last vestiges were only
swept away by Mr. Gladstone in 1860. Mr. Peel, then Home
Secretary, was entering cautiously into the untrodden and
peculiarly Benthamic path of Law Reform. At this period,
when Liberalism seemed to be becoming the tone of the time,
when improvement of institutions was preached from the
highest places, and a complete change of the constitution of
Parliament was loudly demanded in the lowest, it is not
strange that attention should have been roused by the regular
appearance in controversy of what seemed a new school of
writers, claiming to be the legislators and theorists of this new
tendency. The air of strong conviction with which they wrote,
when scarcely any one else seemed to have an equally strong
faith in as definite a creed; the boldness with which they
tilted against the very front of both the existing political parties; their uncompromising profession of opposition to many
of the generally received opinions, and the suspicion they lay
under of holding others still more heterodox than they professed; the talent and verve of at least my father's articles,
and the appearance of a corps behind him sufficient to carry
on a review; and finally, the fact that the review was bought
and read, made the so-called Bentham school in philosophy
and politics fill a greater place in the public mind than it had
held before, or has ever again held since other equally earnest
schools of thought have arisen in England. As I was in the
headquarters of it, knew of what it was composed, and as one
of the most active of its very small number, might say without undue assumption, *quorum pars magna fui*, it belongs to
me more than to most others, to give some account of it.

This supposed school, then, had no other existence than
what was constituted by the fact, that my father's writings
and conversation drew round him a certain number of young
men who had already imbibed, or who imbibed from him, a
greater or smaller portion of his very decided political and
philosophical opinions. The notion that Bentham was surrounded by a band of disciples who received their opinions
from his lips, is a fable to which my father did justice in his
"Fragment on Mackintosh," and which, to all who knew Mr.
Bentham's habits of life and manner of conversation, is simply
ridiculous. The influence which Bentham exercised was by
his writings. Through them he has produced, and is producing, effects on the condition of mankind, wider and deeper,

no doubt, than any which can be attributed to my father. He is a much greater name in history. But my father exercised a far greater personal ascendancy. He *was* sought for the vigour and instructiveness of his conversation, and did use it largely as an instrument for the diffusion of his opinions. I have never known any man who could do such ample justice to his best thoughts in colloquial discussion. His perfect command over his great mental resources, the terseness and expressiveness of his language and the moral earnestness as well as intellectual force of his delivery, made him one of the most striking of all argumentative conversers: and he was full of anecdote, a hearty laugher, and, when with people whom he liked, a most lively and amusing companion. It was not solely, or even chiefly, in diffusing his merely intellectual convictions that his power showed itself: it was still more through the influence of a quality, of which I have only since learnt to appreciate the extreme rarity: that exalted public spirit, and regard above all things to the good of the whole, which warmed into life and activity every germ of similar virtue that existed in the minds he came in contact with: the desire he made them feel for his approbation, the shame at his disapproval; the moral support which his conversation and his very existence gave to those who were aiming to the same objects, and the encouragement he afforded to the fainthearted or desponding among them, by the firm confidence which (though the reverse of sanguine as to the results to be expected in any one particular case) he always felt in the power of reason, the general progress of improvement, and the good which individuals could do by judicious effort.

It was my father's opinions which gave the distinguishing character to the Benthamic or utilitarian propagandism of that time. They fell singly, scattered from him in many directions, but they flowed from him in a continued stream principally in three channels. One was through me, the only mind directly formed by his instructions, and through whom considerable influence was exercised over various young men, who became, in their turn, propagandists. A second was through some of the Cambridge contemporaries of Charles Austin, who, either initiated by him or under the general mental impulse which he gave, had adopted many opinions allied to those of my father, and some of the more considerable of whom afterwards sought my father's acquaintance and frequented his house. Among these may be mentioned Strutt, afterwards Lord Belper, and the present Lord Romilly, with whose eminent father, Sir Samuel, my father had of old been on terms of friendship. The third channel was that of a younger generation of Cambridge undergraduates, contemporary, not with Austin, but with Eyton Tooke, who were drawn to that estimable person by affinity of opinions, and introduced by him to my father: the most notable of these was Charles Buller. Various other persons individually received and transmitted a considerable amount of my father's influence: for example, Black (as before mentioned) and Fonblanque: most of these, however, we accounted only partial allies; Fonblanque, for instance, was always divergent from us on many important points. But indeed there was by no means complete unanimity among any portion of us, nor had any of us adopted implicitly all my father's opinions. For example, although his Essay on Government was regarded probably by all of us as a masterpiece of political wisdom, our adhesion by no means extended to the paragraph of it, in which he maintains that women may consistently with good government, be excluded from the suffrage, because their interest is the same with that of men. From this doctrine, I, and all those who formed my chosen associates, most positively dissented. It is due to my father to say that he denied having intended to affirm that women *should* be excluded, any more than men under the age of forty, concerning whom he maintained, in the very next paragraph, an exactly similar thesis. He was, as he truly said, not discussing whether the suffrage had better be restricted, but only (assuming that it is to be restricted) what is the utmost limit of restriction, which does not necessarily involve a sacrifice of the securities for good government. But I thought then, as I have always thought since, that the opinion which he acknowledged, no less than that which he disclaimed, is as great an error as any of those against which the Essay was directed; that the interest of women is included in that of men exactly as much and no more, as the interest of subjects is included in that of kings; and that every reason which exists for giving the suffrage to anybody, demands that it should not be withheld from women. This was also the general opinion of the younger proselytes; and it is pleasant to be able to say that Mr. Bentham, on this important point, was wholly on our side.

But though none of us, probably, agreed in every respect with my father, his opinions, as I said before, were the princi-

pal element which gave its colour and character to the little
group of young men who were the first propagators of what
was afterwards called "philosophic radicalism." Their mode
of thinking was not characterized by Benthamism in any sense
which has relation to Bentham as a chief or guide, but rather
by a combination of Bentham's point of view with that of the
modern political economy, and with the Hartleian metaphysics. Malthus's population principle was quite as much a banner, and point of union among us, as any opinion specially
belonging to Bentham. This great doctrine, originally brought
forward as an argument against the indefinite improvability
of human affairs, we took up with ardent zeal in the contrary
sense, as indicating the sole means of realizing that improvability by securing full employment at high wages to the whole
labouring population through a voluntary restriction of the
increase of their numbers. The other leading characteristics
of the creed, which we held in common with my father, may
be stated as follows:

In politics, an almost unbounded confidence in the efficacy
of two things: representative government, and complete freedom of discussion. So complete was my father's reliance on
the influence of reason over the minds of mankind, whenever
it is allowed to reach them, that he felt as if all would be
gained if the whole population were taught to read, if all sorts
of opinions were allowed to be addressed to them by word
and in writing, and if by means of the suffrage they could
nominate a legislature to give effect to the opinions they
adopted. He thought that when the legislature no longer
represented a class interest, it would aim at the general interest, honestly and with adequate wisdom; since the people
would be sufficiently under the guidance of educated intelligence, to make in general a good choice of persons to represent them, and having done so, to leave to those whom they
had chosen a liberal discretion. Accordingly aristocratic rule,
the government of the Few in any of its shapes, being in his
eyes the only thing which stood between mankind and an
administration of their affairs by the best wisdom to be found
among them, was the object of his sternest disapprobation,
and a democratic suffrage the principal article of his political
creed, not on the ground of liberty, Rights of Man, or any of
the phrases, more or less significant, by which, up to that
time, democracy had usually been defended, but as the most
essential of "securities for good government." In this, too, he

held fast only to what he deemed essentials; he was comparatively indifferent to monarchical or republican forms—far more so than Bentham, to whom a king, in the character of "corrupter-general," appeared necessarily very noxious. Next to aristocracy, an established church, or corporation of priests, as being by position the great depravers of religion, and interested in opposing the progress of the human mind, was the object of his greatest detestation; though he disliked no clergyman personally who did not deserve it, and was on terms of sincere friendship with several. In ethics, his moral feelings were energetic and rigid on all points which he deemed important to human well being, while he was supremely indifferent in opinion (though his indifference did not show itself in personal conduct) to all those doctrines of the common morality, which he thought had no foundation but in asceticism and priestcraft. He looked forward, for example, to a considerable increase of freedom in the relations between the sexes, though without pretending to define exactly what would be, or ought to be, the precise conditions of that freedom. This opinion was connected in him with no sensuality either of a theoretical or of a practical kind. He anticipated, on the contrary, as one of the beneficial effects of increased freedom, that the imagination would no longer dwell upon the physical relation and its adjuncts, and swell this into one of the principal objects of life; a perversion of the imagination and feelings, which he regarded as one of the deepest seated and most pervading evils in the human mind. In psychology, his fundamental doctrine was the formation of all human character by circumstances, through the universal Principle of Association, and the consequent unlimited possibility of improving the moral and intellectual condition of mankind by education. Of all his doctrines none was more important than this, or needs more to be insisted on: unfortunately there is none which is more contradictory to the prevailing tendencies of speculation, both in his time and since.

These various opinions were seized on with youthful fanaticism by the little knot of young men of whom I was one: and we put into them a sectarian spirit, from which, in intention at least, my father was wholly free. What we (or rather a phantom substituted in the place of us) were sometimes, by a ridiculous exaggeration, called by others, namely a "school," some of us for a time really hoped and aspired to be. The French *philosophes* of the eighteenth century were the example we sought to imitate, and we hoped to accomplish no less results. No one of the set went to so great excesses in this boyish ambition as I did; which might be shown by many particulars, were it not an useless waste of space and time.

All this, however, is properly only the outside of our existence; or, at least, the intellectual part alone, and no more than one side of that. In attempting to penetrate inward, and give any indication of what we were as human beings, I must be understood as speaking only of myself, of whom alone I can speak from sufficient knowledge; and I do not believe that the picture would suit any of my companions without many and great modifications.

I conceive that the description so often given of a Benthamite, as a mere reasoning machine, though extremely inapplicable to most of those who have been designated by that title, was during two or three years of my life not altogether untrue of me. It was perhaps as applicable to me as it can well be to any one just entering into life, to whom the common objects of desire must in general have at least the attraction of novelty. There is nothing very extraordinary in this fact: no youth of the age I then was, can be expected to be more than one thing, and this was the thing I happened to be. Ambition and desire of distinction, I had in abundance; and zeal for what I thought the good of mankind was my strongest sentiment, mixing with and colouring all others. But my zeal was as yet little else, at that period of my life, than zeal for speculative opinions. It had not its root in genuine benevolence, or sympathy with mankind; though these qualities held their due place in my ethical standard. Nor was it connected with any high enthusiasm for ideal nobleness. Yet of this feeling I was imaginatively very susceptible; but there was at that time an intermission of its natural ailment, poetical culture, while there was a superabundance of the discipline antagonistic to it, that of mere logic and analysis. Add to this that, as already mentioned, my father's teachings tended to the undervaluing of feeling. It was not that he was himself cold-hearted or insensible; I believe it was rather from the contrary quality; he thought that feeling could take care of itself; that there was sure to be enough of it if actions were properly cared about. Offended by the frequency with which, in ethical and philosophical controversy, feeling is made the ultimate reason and justification of conduct, instead of being itself called on for a justification, while, in practice, actions, the effect of which on human happiness is mischievous, are defended as being required by feeling, and the character of a person of feeling obtains a credit for desert, which he thought only due to actions, he had a real impatience of attributing praise to feeling, or of any but the most sparing reference to it, either in the estimation of persons or in the discussion of things. In addition to the influence which this characteristic in him had on me and others, we found all the opinions to which we attached most importance, constantly attacked on the ground of feeling. Utility was denounced as cold calculation; political economy as hard-hearted; anti-population doctrines as repulsive to the natural feelings of mankind. We retorted by the word "sentimentality," which, along with "declamation" and "vague generalities," served us as common terms of opprobrium. Although we were generally in the right, as against those who were opposed to us, the effect was that the cultivation of feeling (except the feelings of public and private duty), was not in much esteem among us, and had very little place in the thoughts of most of us, myself in particular. What we principally thought of, was to alter people's opinions; to make them believe according to evidence, and know what was their real interest, which when they once knew, they would, we thought, by the instrument of opinion, enforce a regard to it upon one another. While fully recognizing the superior excellence of unselfish benevolence and love of justice, we did not expect the regeneration of mankind from any direct action on those sentiments, but from the effect of educated intellect, enlightening the selfish feelings. Although this last is prodigiously important as a means of improvement in the hands of those who are themselves impelled by nobler principles of action, I do not believe that any one of the survivors of the Benthamites or Utilitarians of that day, now relies mainly upon it for the general amendment of human conduct.

From this neglect both in theory and in practice of the cultivation of feeling, naturally resulted, among other things, an undervaluing of poetry, and of Imagination generally, as an element of human nature. It is, or was, part of the popular notion of Benthamites, that they are enemies of poetry: this was partly true of Bentham himself; he used to say that "all poetry is misrepresentation:" but in the sense in which he said it, the same might have been said of all impressive speech; of all representation or inculcation more oratorical in its character than a sum in arithmetic. An article of Bingham's in the first number of the Westminster Review, in which he offered as an explanation of something which he disliked in Moore, that "Mr. Moore *is* a poet, and therefore is *not* a reasoner," did a good deal to attach the notion of hating poetry to the writers in the Review. But the truth was that many of us were great readers of poetry; Bingham himself had been a writer of it, while as regards me (and the same thing might be said of my father), the correct statement would be, not that I disliked poetry, but that I was theoretically indifferent to it. I disliked any sentiments in poetry which I should have disliked in prose; and that included a great deal. And I was wholly blind to its place in human culture, as a means of educating the feelings. But I was always personally very susceptible to some kinds of it. In the most sectarian period of my Benthamism, I happened to look into Pope's Essay on Man, and though every opinion in it was contrary to mine, I well remember how powerfully it acted on my imagination. Perhaps at that time poetical composition of any higher type than eloquent discussion in verse, might not have produced a similar effect on me: at all events I seldom gave it an opportunity. This, however, was a mere passive state. Long before I had enlarged in any considerable degree, the basis of my intellectual creed, I had obtained in the natural course of my mental progress, poetic culture of the most valuable kind, by means of reverential admiration for the lives and characters of heroic persons; especially the heroes of philosophy. The same inspiring effect which so many of the benefactors of mankind have left on record that they had experienced from Plutarch's Lives, was produced on me by Plato's pictures of Socrates, and by some modern biographies, above all by Condorcet's Life of Turgot; a book well calculated to rouse the best sort of enthusiasm, since it contains one of the wisest and noblest of lives, delineated by one of the wisest and noblest of men. The heroic virtue of these glorious representatives of the opinions with which I sympathized, deeply affected me, and I perpetually recurred to them as others do to a favourite poet, when needing to be carried up into the more elevated regions of feeling and thought. I may observe by the way that this book cured me of my sectarian follies. The two or three pages beginning "Il regardait toute secte comme nuisible," and explaining why Turgot always kept himself perfectly distinct from the Encyclopedists, sank deeply into my mind. I left off designating myself and others as Utilitarians, and by the pronoun "we" or any other collective designation, I ceased to *afficher* sectarianism. My real inward sectarianism I did not get rid of till later, and much more gradually.

About the end of 1824, or beginning of 1825, Mr. Bentham, having lately got back his papers on Evidence from M. Dumont (whose Traité des Preuves Judiciaires, grounded on them, was then first completed and published) resolved to have them printed in the original, and bethought himself of me as capable of preparing them for the press; in the same manner as his Book of Fallacies had been recently edited by Bingham. I gladly undertook this task, and it occupied nearly all my leisure for about a year, exclusive of the time afterwards spent in seeing the five large volumes through the press. Mr. Bentham had begun this treatise three times, at considerable intervals, each time in a different manner, and each time without reference to the preceding: two of the three times he had gone over nearly the whole subject. These three masses of manuscript it was my business to condense into a single treatise; adopting the one last written as the groundwork, and incorporating with it as much of the two others as it had not completely superseded. I had also to unroll such of Bentham's involved and parenthetical sentences, as seemed to overpass by their complexity the measure of what readers were likely to take the pains to understand. It was further Mr. Bentham's particular desire that I should, from myself, endeavour to supply any *lacunæ* which he had left; and at his instance I read, for this purpose, the most authoritative treatises on the English Law of Evidence, and commented on a few of the objectionable points of the English rules, which had escaped Bentham's notice. I also replied to the objections which had been made to some of his doctrines by reviewers of Dumont's book, and added a few supplementary remarks on some of the more abstract parts of the subject, such as the theory of improbability and impossibility. The controversial part of these editorial additions was written in a more assuming tone than became one so young and inexperienced as I was: but indeed I had never contemplated coming forward in my own person; and as an anonymous editor of Bentham, I fell into the tone of my author, not thinking it unsuitable to him or to the subject, however it might be so to me. My name as editor was put to the book after it was printed, at Mr.

Bentham's positive desire, which I in vain attempted to persuade him to forego.

The time occupied in this editorial work was extremely well employed in respect to my own improvement. The "Rationale of Judicial Evidence" is one of the richest in matter of all Bentham's productions. The theory of evidence being in itself one of the most important of his subjects, and ramifying into most of the others, the book contains, very fully developed, a great proportion of all his best thoughts: while, among more special things, it comprises the most elaborate exposure of the vices and defects of English law, as it then was, which is to be found in his works; not confined to the law of evidence, but including, by way of illustrative episode, the entire procedure or practice of Westminster Hall. The direct knowledge, therefore, which I obtained from the book, and which was imprinted upon me much more thoroughly than it could have been by mere reading, was itself no small acquisition. But this occupation did for me what might seem less to be expected; it gave a great start to my powers of composition. Everything which I wrote subsequently to this editorial employment, was markedly superior to anything that I had written before it. Bentham's later style, as the world knows, was heavy and cumbersome, from the excess of a good quality, the love of precision, which made him introduce clause within clause into the heart of every sentence, that the reader might receive into his mind all the modifications and qualifications simultaneously with the main proposition: and the habit grew on him until his sentences became, to those not accustomed to them, most laborious reading. But his earlier style, that of the Fragment on Government, Plan of a Judicial Establishment, &c., is a model of liveliness and ease combined with fulness of matter, scarcely ever surpassed: and of this earlier style there were many striking specimens in the manuscripts on Evidence, all of which I endeavoured to preserve. So long a course of this admirable writing had a considerable effect upon my own; and I added to it by the assiduous reading of other writers, both French and English, who combined, in a remarkable degree, ease with force, such as Goldsmith, Fielding, Pascal, Voltaire, and Courier. Through these influences my writing lost the jejuneness of my early compositions; the bones and cartilages began to clothe themselves with flesh, and the style became, at times, lively and almost light.

This improvement was first exhibited in a new field. Mr.

Marshall, of Leeds, father of the present generation of Marshalls, the same who was brought into Parliament for Yorkshire, when the representation forfeited by Grampound was transferred to it, an earnest parliamentary reformer, and a man of large fortune, of which he made a liberal use, had been much struck with Bentham's Book of Fallacies: and the thought had occurred to him that it would be useful to publish annually the Parliamentary Debates, not in the chronological order of Hansard, but classified according to subjects, and accompanied by a commentary pointing out the fallacies of the speakers. With this intention, he very naturally addressed himself to the editor of the Book of Fallacies; and Bingham, with the assistance of Charles Austin, undertook the editorship. The work was called "Parliamentary History and Review." Its sale was not sufficient to keep it in existence, and it only lasted three years. It excited, however, some attention among parliamentary and political people. The best strength of the party was put forth in it; and its execution did them much more credit than that of the Westminster Review had ever done. Bingham and Charles Austin wrote much in it; as did Strutt, Romilly, and several other liberal lawyers. My father wrote one article in his best style; the elder Austin another. Coulson wrote one of great merit. It fell to my lot to lead off the first number by an article on the principal topic of the session (that of 1825), the Catholic Association and the Catholic disabilities. In the second number I wrote an elaborate Essay on the commercial crisis of 1825 and the Currency Debates. In the third I had two articles, one on a minor subject, the other on the Reciprocity principle in commerce, à propos of a celebrated diplomatic correspondence between Canning and Gallatin. These writings were no longer mere reproductions and applications of the doctrines I had been taught; they were original thinking, as far as that name can be applied to old ideas in new forms and connexions: and I do not exceed the truth in saying that there was a maturity, and a well-digested character about them, which there had not been in any of my previous performances. In execution, therefore, they were not at all juvenile; but their subjects have either gone by, or have been so much better treated since, that they are entirely superseded, and should remain buried in the same oblivion with my contributions to the first dynasty of the Westminster Review.

While thus engaged in writing for the public, I did not

neglect other modes of self-cultivation. It was at this time
that I learnt German; beginning it on the Hamiltonian method,
for which purpose I and several of my companions formed
a class. For several years from this period, our social studies
assumed a shape which contributed very much to my mental
progress. The idea occurred to us of carrying on, by reading
and conversation, a joint study of several of the branches of
science which we wished to be masters of. We assembled to
the number of a dozen or more. Mr. Grote lent a room of his
house in Threadneedle Street for the purpose, and his partner,
Prescott, one of the three original members of the Utilitarian
Society, made one among us. We met two mornings in every
week, from half-past eight till ten, at which hour most of
us were called off to our daily occupations. Our first subject
was Political Economy. We chose some systematic treatise as
our text-book; my father's "Elements" being our first choice.
One of us read aloud a chapter, or some smaller portion of
the book. The discussion was then opened, and any one who
had an objection, or other remark to make, made it. Our rule
was to discuss thoroughly every point raised, whether great
or small, prolonging the discussion until all who took part
were satisfied with the conclusion they had individually
arrived at; and to follow up every topic of collateral speculation which the chapter or the conversation suggested, never
leaving it until we had untied every knot which we found.
We repeatedly kept up the discussion of some one point for
several weeks, thinking intently on it during the intervals of
our meetings, and contriving solutions of the new difficulties
which had risen up in the last morning's discussion. When we
had finished in this way my father's Elements, we went in
the same manner through Ricardo's Principles of Political
Economy, and Bailey's Dissertation on Value. These close
and vigorous discussions were not only improving in a high
degree to those who took part in them, but brought out new
views of some topics of abstract Political Economy. The
theory of International Values which I afterwards published,
emanated from these conversations, as did also the modified
form of Ricardo's theory of Profits, laid down in my Essay on
Profits and Interest. Those among us with whom new speculations chiefly originated, were Ellis, Graham, and I; though
others gave valuable aid to the discussions, especially Prescott and Roebuck, the one by his knowledge, the other by his
dialectical acuteness. The theories of International Values and

of Profits were excogitated and worked out in about equal proportions by myself and Graham: and if our original project had been executed, my "Essays on some Unsettled Questions of Political Economy" would have been brought out along with some papers of his, under our joint names. But when my exposition came to be written, I found that I had so much over-estimated my agreement with him, and he dissented so much from the most original of the two Essays, that on International Values, that I was obliged to consider the theory as now exclusively mine, and it came out as such when published many years later. I may mention that among the alterations which my father made in revising his Elements for the third edition, several were founded on criticisms elicited by these conversations; and in particular he modified his opinions (though not to the extent of our new speculations) on both the points to which I have adverted.

When we had enough of political economy, we took up the syllogistic logic in the same manner, Grote now joining us. Our first text-book was Aldrich, but being disgusted with its superficiality, we reprinted one of the most finished among the many manuals of the school logic, which my father, a great collector of such books, possessed, the Manuductio ad Logicam of the Jesuit Du Trieu. After finishing this, we took up Whately's Logic, then first republished from the Encyclopædia Metropolitana, and finally the "Computatio sive Logica" of Hobbes. These books, dealt with in our manner, afforded a wide range for original metaphysical speculation: and most of what has been done in the First Book of my System of Logic, to rationalize and correct the principles and distinctions of the school logicians, and to improve the theory of the Import of Propositions, had its origin in these discussions; Graham and I originating most of the novelties, while Grote and others furnished an excellent tribunal or test. From this time I formed the project of writing a book on Logic, though on a much humbler scale than the one I ultimately executed.

Having done with Logic, we launched into analytic psychology, and having chosen Hartley for our text-book, we raised Priestley's edition to an extravagant price by searching through London to furnish each of us with a copy. When we had finished Hartley, we suspended our meetings; but my father's Analysis of the Mind being published soon after, we reassembled for the purpose of reading it. With this our exercises ended. I have always dated from these conversations my own real inauguration as an original and independent thinker. It was also through them that I acquired, or very much strengthened, a mental habit to which I attribute all that I have ever done, or ever shall do, in speculation; that of never accepting half-solutions of difficulties as complete; never abandoning a puzzle, but again and again returning to it until it was cleared up; never allowing obscure corners of a subject to remain unexplored, because they did not appear important; never thinking that I perfectly understood any part of a subject until I understood the whole.

Our doings from 1825 to 1830 in the way of public speaking, filled a considerable place in my life during those years, and as they had important effects on my development, something ought to be said of them.

There was for some time in existence a society of Owenites, called the Co-operative Society, which met for weekly public discussions in Chancery Lane. In the early part of 1825, accident brought Roebuck in contact with several of its members, and led to his attending one or two of the meetings and taking part in the debate in opposition to Owenism. Some of us started the notion of going there in a body and having a general battle: and Charles Austin and some of his friends who did not usually take part in our joint exercises, entered into the project. It was carried out by concert with the principal members of the Society, themselves nothing loth, as they naturally preferred a controversy with opponents to a tame discussion among their own body. The question of population was proposed as the subject of debate: Charles Austin led the case on our side with a brilliant speech, and the fight was kept up by adjournment through five or six weekly meetings before crowded auditories, including along with the members of the Society and their friends, many hearers and some speakers from the Inns of Court. When this debate was ended, another was commenced on the general merits of Owen's system: and the contest altogether lasted about three months. It was a *lutte corps-à-corps* between Owenites and political economists, whom the Owenites regarded as their most inveterate opponents: but it was a perfectly friendly dispute. We who represented political economy, had the same objects in view as they had, and took pains to show it; and the principal champion on their side was a very estimable man, with whom I was well acquainted, Mr. William Thompson, of Cork, author of a book on the Distribution of Wealth, and of an

"Appeal" in behalf of women against the passage relating to them in my father's Essay on Government. Ellis, Roebuck, and I took an active part in the debate, and among those from the Inns of Court who joined in it, I remember Charles Villiers. The other side obtained also, on the population question, very efficient support from without. The well-known Gale Jones, then an elderly man, made one of his florid speeches; but the speaker with whom I was most struck, though I dissented from nearly every word he said, was Thirlwall, the historian, since Bishop of St. David's, then a Chancery barrister, unknown except by a high reputation for eloquence acquired at the Cambridge Union before the era of Austin and Macaulay. His speech was in answer to one of mine. Before he had uttered ten sentences, I set him down as the best speaker I had ever heard, and I have never since heard any one whom I placed above him.

The great interest of these debates predisposed some of those who took part in them, to catch at a suggestion thrown out by McCulloch, the political economist, that a society was wanted in London similar to the Speculative Society at Edinburgh, in which Brougham, Horner, and others first cultivated public speaking. Our experience at the Co-operative Society seemed to give cause for being sanguine as to the sort of men who might be brought together in London for such a purpose. McCulloch mentioned the matter to several young men of influence, to whom he was then giving private lessons in political economy. Some of these entered warmly into the project, particularly George Villiers, afterwards Earl of Clarendon. He and his brothers, Hyde and Charles, Romilly, Charles Austin and I, with some others, met and agreed on a plan. We determined to meet once a fortnight from November to June, at the Freemasons' Tavern, and we had soon a splendid list of members, containing, along with several members of parliament, nearly all the most noted speakers of the Cambridge Union and of the Oxford United Debating Society. It is curiously illustrative of the tendencies of the time, that our principal difficulty in recruiting for the Society was to find a sufficient number of Tory speakers. Almost all whom we could press into the service were Liberals, of different orders and degrees. Besides those already named, we had Macaulay, Thirlwall, Praed, Lord Howick, Samuel Wilberforce (afterwards Bishop of Oxford), Charles Poulett Thomson (afterwards Lord Sydenham), Edward and Henry Lytton Bulwer,

Fonblanque, and many others whom I cannot now recollect, but who made themselves afterwards more or less conspicuous in public or literary life. Nothing could seem more promising. But when the time for action drew near, and it was necessary to fix on a President, and find somebody to open the first debate, none of our celebrities would consent to perform either office. Of the many who were pressed on the subject, the only one who could be prevailed on was a man of whom I knew very little, but who had taken high honours at Oxford and was said to have acquired a great oratorical reputation there; who some time afterwards became a Tory member of parliament. He accordingly was fixed on, both for filling the President's chair and for making the first speech. The important day arrived; the benches were crowded; all our great speakers were present, to judge of, but not to help our efforts. The Oxford orator's speech was a complete failure. This threw a damp on the whole concern: the speakers who followed were few, and none of them did their best: the affair was a complete *fiasco*; and the oratorical celebrities we had counted on went away never to return, giving to me at least a lesson in knowledge of the world. This unexpected breakdown altered my whole relation to the project. I had not anticipated taking a prominent part, or speaking much or often, particularly at first, but I now saw that the success of the scheme depended on the new men, and I put my shoulder to the wheel. I opened the second question, and from that time spoke in nearly every debate. It was very uphill work for some time. The three Villiers' and Romilly stuck to us for some time longer, but the patience of all the founders of the Society was at last exhausted, except me and Roebuck. In the season following, 1826-7, things began to mend. We had acquired two excellent Tory speakers, Hayward and Shee (afterwards Sergeant Shee): the radical side was reinforced by Charles Buller, Cockburn, and others of the second generation of Cambridge Benthamites; and with their and other occasional aid, and the two Tories as well as Roebuck and me for regular speakers, almost every debate was a *bataille rangée* between the "philosophic radicals" and the Tory lawyers; until our conflicts were talked about, and several persons of note and consideration came to hear us. This happened still more in the subsequent seasons, 1828 and 1829, when the Coleridgians, in the persons of Maurice and Sterling, made their appearance in the Society as a second Liberal and even Radical party, on totally different grounds from Benthamism and vehemently opposed to it; bringing into these discussions the general doctrines and modes of thought of the European reaction against the philosophy of the eighteenth century; and adding a third and very important belligerent party to our contests, which were now no bad exponent of the movement of opinion among the most cultivated part of the new generation. Our debates were very different from those of common debating societies, for they habitually consisted of the strongest arguments and most philosophic principles which either side was able to produce, thrown often into close and *serré* confutations of one another. The practice was necessarily very useful to us, and eminently so to me. I never, indeed, acquired real fluency, and had always a bad and ungraceful delivery; but I could make myself listened to: and as I always wrote my speeches when, from the feelings involved, or the nature of the ideas to be developed, expression seemed important, I greatly increased my power of effective writing; acquiring not only an ear for smoothness and rhythm, but a practical sense for *telling* sentences, and an immediate criterion of their telling property, by their effect on a mixed audience.

The Society, and the preparation for it, together with the preparation for the morning conversations which were going on simultaneously, occupied the greater part of my leisure; and made me feel it a relief when, in the spring of 1828, I ceased to write for the Westminster. The Review had fallen into difficulties. Though the sale of the first number had been very encouraging, the permanent sale had never, I believe, been sufficient to pay the expenses, on the scale on which the review was carried on. Those expenses had been considerably, but not sufficiently, reduced. One of the editors, Southern, had resigned; and several of the writers, including my father and me, who had been paid like other contributors for our earlier articles, had latterly written without payment. Nevertheless, the original funds were nearly or quite exhausted, and if the Review was to be continued some new arrangement of its affairs had become indispensable. My father and I had several conferences with Bowring on the subject. We were willing to do our utmost for maintaining the Review as an organ of our opinions, but not under Bowring's editorship: while the impossibility of its any longer supporting a paid editor, afforded a ground on which, without affront to him, we could propose to dispense with his services. We and some

of our friends were prepared to carry on the Review as unpaid writers, either finding among ourselves an unpaid editor,
or sharing the editorship among us. But while this negotiation
was proceeding with Bowring's apparent acquiescence, he
was carrying on another in a different quarter (with Colonel
Perronet Thompson), of which we received the first intimation
in a letter from Bowring as editor, informing us merely that
an arrangement had been made, and proposing to us to write
for the next number, with promise of payment. We did not
dispute Bowring's right to bring about, if he could, an arrangement more favourable to himself than the one we had proposed; but we thought the concealment which he had practised towards us, while seemingly entering into our own
project, an affront: and even had we not thought so, we were
indisposed to expend any more of our time and trouble in attempting to write up the Review under his management.
Accordingly my father excused himself from writing; though
two or three years later, on great pressure, he did write one
more political article. As for me, I positively refused. And
thus ended my connexion with the original Westminster. The
last article which I wrote in it had cost me more labour than
any previous; but it was a labour of love, being a defence
of the early French Revolutionists against the Tory misrepre-
sentations of Sir Walter Scott, in the introduction to his Life
of Napoleon. The number of books which I read for this purpose, making notes and extracts—even the number I had to
buy (for in those days there was no public or subscription
library from which books of reference could be taken home),
far exceeded the worth of the immediate object; but I had at
that time a half-formed intention of writing a History of the
French Revolution; and though I never executed it, my col-
lections afterwards were very useful to Carlyle for a similar
purpose.

V. A CRISIS IN MY MENTAL HISTORY. ONE STAGE ONWARD.

FOR some years after this I wrote very little, and nothing
regularly, for publication: and great were the advantages
which I derived from the intermission. It was of no common
importance to me, at this period, to be able to digest and
mature my thoughts for my own mind only, without any immediate call for giving them out in print. Had I gone on
writing, it would have much disturbed the important trans-

formation in my opinions and character, which took place during those years. The origin of this transformation, or at least the process by which I was prepared for it, can only be explained by turning some distance back.

From the winter of 1821, when I first read Bentham, and especially from the commencement of the Westminster Review, I had what might truly be called an object in life; to be a reformer of the world. My conception of my own happiness was entirely identified with this object. The personal sympathies I wished for were those of fellow labourers in this enterprise. I endeavoured to pick up as many flowers as I could by the way; but as a serious and permanent personal satisfaction to rest upon, my whole reliance was placed on this; and I was accustomed to felicitate myself on the certainty of a happy life which I enjoyed, through placing my happiness in something durable and distant, in which some progress might be always making, while it could never be exhausted by complete attainment. This did very well for several years, during which the general improvement going on in the world and the idea of myself as engaged with others in struggling to promote it, seemed enough to fill up an interesting and animated existence. But the time came when I awakened from this as from a dream. It was in the autumn of 1826. I was in a dull state of nerves, such as everybody is occasionally liable to; unsusceptible to enjoyment or pleasurable excitement; one of those moods when what is pleasure at other times, becomes insipid or indifferent; the state, I should think, in which converts to Methodism usually are, when smitten by their first "conviction of sin." In this frame of mind it occurred to me to put the question directly to myself: "Suppose that all your objects in life were realized; that all the changes in institutions and opinions which you are looking forward to, could be completely effected at this very instant: would this be a great joy and happiness to you?" And an irrepressible self-consciousness distinctly answered, "No!" At this my heart sank within me: the whole foundation on which my life was constructed fell down. All my happiness was to have been found in the continual pursuit of this end. The end had ceased to charm, and how could there ever again be any interest in the means? I seemed to have nothing left to live for.

At first I hoped that the cloud would pass away of itself; but it did not. A night's sleep, the sovereign remedy for the smaller vexations of life, had no effect on it. I awoke to a renewed consciousness of the woful fact. I carried it with me into all companies, into all occupations. Hardly anything had power to cause me even a few minutes oblivion of it. For some months the cloud seemed to grow thicker and thicker. The lines in Coleridge's "Dejection"—I was not then acquainted with them—exactly describe my case:

> "A grief without a pang, void, dark and drear,
> A drowsy, stifled, unimpassioned grief,
> Which finds no natural outlet or relief
> In word, or sigh, or tear."

In vain I sought relief from my favourite books; those memorials of past nobleness and greatness from which I had always hitherto drawn strength and animation. I read them now without feeling, or with the accustomed feeling *minus* all its charm; and I became persuaded, that my love of mankind, and of excellence for its own sake, had worn itself out. I sought no comfort by speaking to others of what I felt. If I had loved any one sufficiently to make confiding my griefs a necessity, I should not have been in the condition I was. I felt, too, that mine was not an interesting, or in any way respectable distress. There was nothing in it to attract sympathy. Advice, if I had known where to seek it, would have been most precious. The words of Macbeth to the physician often occurred to my thoughts. But there was no one on whom I could build the faintest hope of such assistance. My father, to whom it would have been natural to me to have recourse in any practical difficulties, was the last person to whom, in such a case as this, I looked for help. Everything convinced me that he had no knowledge of any such mental state as I was suffering from, and that even if he could be made to understand it, he was not the physician who could heal it. My education, which was wholly his work, had been conducted without any regard to the possibility of its ending in this result; and I saw no use in giving him the pain of thinking that his plans had failed, when the failure was probably irremediable, and, at all events, beyond the power of *his* remedies. Of other friends, I had at that time none to whom I had any hope of making my condition intelligible. It was however abundantly intelligible to myself; and the more I dwelt upon it, the more hopeless it appeared.

My course of study had led me to believe, that all mental and moral feelings and qualities, whether of a good or of a bad kind, were the results of association; that we love one thing, and hate another, take pleasure in one sort of action or contemplation, and pain in another sort, through the clinging of pleasurable or painful ideas to those things, from the effect of education or of experience. As a corollary from this, I had always heard it maintained by my father, and was myself convinced, that the object of education should be to form the strongest possible associations of the salutary class; associations of pleasure with all things beneficial to the great whole, and of pain with all things hurtful to it. This doctrine appeared inexpugnable; but it now seemed to me, on retrospect, that my teachers had occupied themselves but superficially with the means of forming and keeping up these salutary associations. They seemed to have trusted altogether to the old familiar instruments, praise and blame, reward and punishment. Now, I did not doubt that by these means, begun early, and applied unremittingly, intense associations of pain and pleasure, especially of pain, might be created, and might produce desires and aversions capable of lasting undiminished to the end of life. But there must always be something artificial and casual in associations thus produced. The pains and pleasures thus forcibly associated with things, are not connected with them by any natural tie; and it is therefore, I thought, essential to the durability of these associations, that they should have become so intense and inveterate as to be practically indissoluble, before the habitual exercise of the power of analysis had commenced. For I now saw, or thought I saw, what I had always before received with incredulity—that the habit of analysis has a tendency to wear away the feelings: as indeed it has, when no other mental habit is cultivated, and the analysing spirit remains without its natural complements and correctives. The very excellence of analysis (I argued) is that it tends to weaken and undermine whatever is the result of prejudice; that it enables us mentally to separate ideas which have only casually clung together: and no associations whatever could ultimately resist this dissolving force, were it not that we owe to analysis our clearest knowledge of the permanent sequences in nature; the real connexions between Things, not dependent on our will and feelings; natural laws, by virtue of which, in many cases, one thing is inseparable from another in fact; which laws, in proportion as they are clearly perceived and imaginatively realized, cause our ideas of things which are always joined together in Nature, to cohere more and more closely in our thoughts. Analytic habits may thus even strengthen the associations between causes and effects, means and ends, but tend altogether to weaken those which are, to speak familiarly, a *mere* matter of feeling. They are therefore (I thought) favourable to prudence and clear-sightedness, but a perpetual worm at the root both of the passions and of the virtues; and, above all, fearfully undermine all desires, and all pleasures, which are the effects of association, that is, according to the theory I held, all except the purely physical and organic; of the entire insufficiency of which to make life desirable, no one had a stronger conviction than I had. These were the laws of human nature, by which, as it seemed to me, I had been brought to my present state. All those to whom I looked up, were of opinion that the pleasure of sympathy with human beings, and the feelings which made the good of others, and especially of mankind on a large scale, the object of existence, were the greatest and surest sources of happiness. Of the truth of this I was convinced, but to know that a feeling would make me happy if I had it, did not give me the feeling. My education, I thought, had failed to create these feelings in sufficient strength to resist the dissolving influence of analysis, while the whole course of my intellectual cultivation had made precocious and premature analysis the inveterate habit of my mind. I was thus, as I said to myself, left stranded at the commencement of my voyage, with a well-equipped ship and a rudder, but no sail; without any real desire for the ends which I had been so carefully fitted out to work for: no delight in virtue, or the general good, but also just as little in anything else. The fountains of vanity and ambition seemed to have dried up within me, as completely as those of benevolence. I had had (as I reflected) some gratification of vanity at too early an age: I had obtained some distinction, and felt myself of some importance, before the desire of distinction and of importance had grown into a passion: and little as it was which I had attained, yet having been attained too early, like all pleasures enjoyed too soon, it had made me *blasé* and indifferent to the pursuit. Thus neither selfish nor unselfish pleasures were pleasures to me. And there seemed no power in nature sufficient to begin the formation of my character anew, and create in a mind now irretrievably analytic, fresh associations of pleasure with any of the objects of human desire.

These were the thoughts which mingled with the dry heavy dejection of the melancholy winter of 1826–7. During this time I was not incapable of my usual occupations. I went on with them mechanically, by the mere force of habit. I had been so drilled in a certain sort of mental exercise, that I could still carry it on when all the spirit had gone out of it. I even composed and spoke several speeches at the debating society, how, or with what degree of success, I know not. Of four years continual speaking at that society, this is the only year of which I remember next to nothing. Two lines of Coleridge, in whom alone of all writers I have found a true description of what I felt, were often in my thoughts, not at this time (for I had never read them), but in a later period of the same mental malady:

"Work without hope draws nectar in a sieve,
    And hope without an object cannot live."

In all probability my case was by no means so peculiar as I fancied it, and I doubt not that many others have passed through a similar state; but the idiosyncrasies of my education had given to the general phenomenon a special character, which made it seem the natural effect of causes that it was hardly possible for time to remove. I frequently asked myself, if I could, or if I was bound to go on living, when life must be passed in this manner. I generally answered to myself, that I did not think I could possibly bear it beyond a year. When, however, not more than half that duration of time had elapsed, a small ray of light broke in upon my gloom. I was reading, accidentally, Marmontel's "Mémoires," and came to the passage which relates his father's death, the distressed position of the family, and the sudden inspiration by which he, then a mere boy, felt and made them feel that he would be everything to them—would supply the place of all that they had lost. A vivid conception of the scene and its feelings came over me, and I was moved to tears. From this moment my burthen grew lighter. The oppression of the thought that all feeling was dead within me, was gone. I was no longer hopeless: I was not a stock or a stone. I had still, it seemed, some of the material out of which all worth of character, and all capacity for happiness, are made. Relieved from my ever present sense of irremediable wretchedness, I gradually found that the ordinary incidents of life could again give me some pleasure; that I could again find enjoyment, not intense, but sufficient for cheerfulness, in sunshine and sky, in books, in conversation, in public affairs; and that there was, once more, excitement, though of a moderate kind, in exerting myself for my opinions, and for the public good. Thus the cloud gradually drew off, and I again enjoyed life: and though I had several relapses, some of which lasted many months, I never again was as miserable as I had been.

The experiences of this period had two very marked effects on my opinions and character. In the first place, they led me to adopt a theory of life, very unlike that on which I had before acted, and having much in common with what at that time I certainly had never heard of, the anti-self-consciousness theory of Carlyle. I never, indeed, wavered in the conviction that happiness is the test of all rules of conduct, and the end of life. But I now thought that this end was only to be attained by not making it the direct end. Those only are happy (I thought) who have their minds fixed on some object other than their own happiness; on the happiness of others, on the improvement of mankind, even on some art or pursuit, followed not as a means, but as itself an ideal end. Aiming thus at something else, they find happiness by the way. The enjoyments of life (such was now my theory) are sufficient to make it a pleasant thing, when they are taken *en passant*, without being made a principal object. Once make them so, and they are immediately felt to be insufficient. They will not bear a scrutinizing examination. Ask yourself whether you are happy, and you cease to be so. The only chance is to treat, not happiness, but some end external to it, as the purpose of life. Let your self-consciousness, your scrutiny, your self-interrogation, exhaust themselves on that; and if otherwise fortunately circumstanced you will inhale happiness with the air you breathe, without dwelling on it or thinking about it, without either forestalling it in imagination, or putting it to flight by fatal questioning. This theory now became the basis of my philosophy of life. And I still hold to it as the best theory for all those who have but a moderate degree of sensibility and of capacity for enjoyment, that is, for the great majority of mankind.

The other important change which my opinions at this time underwent, was that I, for the first time, gave its proper place, among the prime necessities of human well-being, to the internal culture of the individual. I ceased to attach almost exclusive importance to the ordering of outward circumstances, and the training of the human being for speculation and for action.

I had now learnt by experience that the passive susceptibilities needed to be cultivated as well as the active capacities, and required to be nourished and enriched as well as guided. I did not, for an instant, lose sight of, or undervalue, that part of the truth which I had seen before; I never turned recreant to intellectual culture, or ceased to consider the power and practice of analysis as an essential condition both of individual and of social improvement. But I thought that it had consequences which required to be corrected, by joining other kinds of cultivation with it. The maintenance of a due balance among the faculties, now seemed to me of primary importance. The cultivation of the feelings became one of the cardinal points in my ethical and philosophical creed. And my thoughts and inclinations turned in an increasing degree towards whatever seemed capable of being instrumental to that object.

I now began to find meaning in the things which I had read or heard about the importance of poetry and art as instruments of human culture. But it was some time longer before I began to know this by personal experience. The only one of the imaginative arts in which I had from childhood taken great pleasure, was music; the best effect of which (and in this it surpasses perhaps every other art) consists in exciting enthusiasm; in winding up to a high pitch those feelings of an elevated kind which are already in the character, but to which this excitement gives a glow and a fervour, which, though transitory at its utmost height, is precious for sustaining them at other times. This effect of music I had often experienced; but like all my pleasurable susceptibilities it was suspended during the gloomy period. I had sought relief again and again from this quarter, but found none. After the tide had turned, and I was in process of recovery, I had been helped forward by music, but in a much less elevated manner. I at this time first became acquainted with Weber's Oberon, and the extreme pleasure which I drew from its delicious melodies did me good, by showing me a source of pleasure to which I was as susceptible as ever. The good, however, was much impaired by the thought, that the pleasure of music (as is quite true of such pleasure as this was, that of mere tune) fades with familiarity, and requires either to be revived by intermittence, or fed by continual novelty. And it is very characteristic both of my then state, and of the general tone of my mind at this period of my life, that I was seriously tormented by the thought of the exhaustibility of musical combinations. The octave consists only of five tones and two semi-tones, which can be put together in only a limited number of ways, of which but a small proportion are beautiful: most of these, it seemed to me, must have been already discovered, and there could not be room for a long succession of Mozarts and Webers, to strike out, as these had done, entirely new and surpassingly rich veins of musical beauty. This source of anxiety may, perhaps, be thought to resemble that of the philosophers of Laputa, who feared lest the sun should be burnt out. It was, however, connected with the best feature in my character, and the only good point to be found in my very unromantic and in no way honourable distress. For though my dejection, honestly looked at, could not be called other than egotistical, produced by the ruin, as I thought, of my fabric of happiness, yet the destiny of mankind in general was ever in my thoughts, and could not be separated from my own. I felt that the flaw in my life, must be a flaw in life itself; that the question was, whether, if the reformers of society and government could succeed in their objects, and every person in the community were free and in a state of physical comfort, the pleasures of life, being no longer kept up by struggle and privation, would cease to be pleasures. And I felt that unless I could see my way to some better hope than this for human happiness in general, my dejection must continue; but that if I could see such an outlet, I should then look on the world with pleasure; content as far as I was myself concerned, with any fair share of the general lot.

This state of my thoughts and feelings made the fact of my reading Wordsworth for the first time (in the autumn of 1828), an important event in my life. I took up the collection of his poems from curiosity, with no expectation of mental relief from it, though I had before resorted to poetry with that hope. In the worst period of my depression, I had read through the whole of Byron (then new to me), to try whether a poet, whose peculiar department was supposed to be that of the intenser feelings, could rouse any feeling in me. As might be expected, I got no good from this reading, but the reverse. The poet's state of mind was too like my own. His was the lament of a man who had worn out all pleasures, and who seemed to think that life, to all who possess the good things of it, must necessarily be the vapid, uninteresting thing which I found it. His Harold and Manfred had the same burthen on them which I had; and I was not in a frame of mind to derive any comfort from the vehement sensual passion of his Giaours,

or the sullenness of his Laras. But while Byron was exactly
what did not suit my condition, Wordsworth was exactly what
did. I had looked into the Excursion two or three years before,
and found little in it; and I should probably have found as
little, had I read it at this time. But the miscellaneous poems,
in the two-volume edition of 1815 (to which little of value
was added in the latter part of the author's life), proved to be
the precise thing for my mental wants at that particular juncture.

In the first place, these poems addressed themselves powerfully to one of the strongest of my pleasurable susceptibilities,
the love of rural objects and natural scenery; to which I had
been indebted not only for much of the pleasure of my life,
but quite recently for relief from one of my longest relapses
into depression. In this power of rural beauty over me, there
was a foundation laid for taking pleasure in Wordsworth's
poetry; the more so, as his scenery lies mostly among moun-
tains, which, owing to my early Pyrenean excursion, were my
ideal of natural beauty. But Wordsworth would never have
had any great effect on me, if he had merely placed before
me beautiful pictures of natural scenery. Scott does this still
better than Wordsworth, and a very second-rate landscape
does it more effectually than any poet. What made Wordsworth's poems a medicine for my state of mind, was that they
expressed, not mere outward beauty, but states of feeling,
and of thought coloured by feeling, under the excitement of
beauty. They seemed to be the very culture of the feelings,
which I was in quest of. In them I seemed to draw from a
source of inward joy, of sympathetic and imaginative pleasure,
which could be shared in by all human beings; which had no
connexion with struggle or imperfection, but would be made
richer by every improvement in the physical or social condition of mankind. From them I seemed to learn what would
be the perennial sources of happiness, when all the greater
evils of life shall have been removed. And I felt myself at
once better and happier as I came under their influence.
There have certainly been, even in our own age, greater poets
than Wordsworth; but poetry of deeper and loftier feeling
could not have done for me at that time what his did. I
needed to be made to feel that there was real, permanent
happiness in tranquil contemplation. Wordsworth taught me
this, not only without turning away from, but with a greatly
increased interest in the common feelings and common destiny

of human beings. And the delight which these poems gave me, proved that with culture of this sort, there was nothing to dread from the most confirmed habit of analysis. At the conclusion of the Poems came the famous Ode, falsely called Platonic, "Intimations of Immortality:" in which, along with more than his usual sweetness of melody and rhythm, and along with the two passages of grand imagery but bad philosophy so often quoted, I found that he too had had similar experience to mine; that he also had felt that the first freshness of youthful enjoyment of life was not lasting; but that he had sought for compensation, and found it, in the way in which he was now teaching me to find it. The result was that I gradually, but completely, emerged from my habitual depression, and was never again subject to it. I long continued to value Wordsworth less according to his intrinsic merits, than by the measure of what he had done for me. Compared with the greatest poets, he may be said to be the poet of unpoetical natures, possessed of quiet and contemplative tastes. But unpoetical natures are precisely those which require poetic cultivation. This cultivation Wordsworth is much more fitted to give, than poets who are intrinsically far more poets than he.

It so fell out that the merits of Wordsworth were the occasion of my first public declaration of my new way of thinking, and separation from those of my habitual companions who had not undergone a similar change. The person with whom at that time I was most in the habit of comparing notes on such subjects was Roebuck, and I induced him to read Wordsworth, in whom he also at first seemed to find much to admire: but I, like most Wordsworthians, threw myself into strong antagonism to Byron, both as a poet and as to his influence on the character. Roebuck, all whose instincts were those of action and struggle, had, on the contrary, a strong relish and great admiration of Byron, whose writings he regarded as the poetry of human life, while Wordsworth's, according to him, was that of flowers and butterflies. We agreed to have the fight out at our Debating Society, where we accordingly discussed for two evenings the comparative merits of Byron and Wordsworth, propounding and illustrating by long recitations our respective theories of poetry: Sterling also, in a brilliant speech, putting forward his particular theory. This was the first debate on any weighty subject in which Roebuck and I had been on opposite sides. The schism between us widened from this time more and more, though we continued for some years longer to be companions. In the beginning, our chief divergence related to the cultivation of the feelings. Roebuck was in many respects very different from the vulgar notion of a Benthamite or Utilitarian. He was a lover of poetry and of most of the fine arts. He took great pleasure in music, in dramatic performances, especially in painting, and himself drew and designed landscapes with great facility and beauty. But he never could be made to see that these things have any value as aids in the formation of character. Personally, instead of being, as Benthamites are supposed to be, void of feeling, he had very quick and strong sensibilities. But, like most Englishmen who have feelings, he found his feelings stand very much in his way. He was much more susceptible to the painful sympathies than to the pleasurable, and looking for his happiness elsewhere, he wished that his feelings should be deadened rather than quickened. And, in truth, the English character, and English social circumstances, make it so seldom possible to derive happiness from the exercise of the sympathies, that it is not wonderful if they count for little in an Englishman's scheme of life. In most other countries the paramount importance of the sympathies as a constituent of individual happiness is an axiom, taken for granted rather than needing any formal statement; but most English thinkers almost seem to regard them as necessary evils, required for keeping men's actions benevolent and compassionate. Roebuck was, or appeared to be, this kind of Englishman. He saw little good in any cultivation of the feelings, and none at all in cultivating them through the imagination, which he thought was only cultivating illusions. It was in vain I urged on him that the imaginative emotion which an idea, when vividly conceived, excites in us, is not an illusion but a fact, as real as any of the other qualities of objects; and far from implying anything erroneous and delusive in our mental apprehension of the object, is quite consistent with the most accurate knowledge and most perfect practical recognition of all its physical and intellectual laws and relations. The intensest feeling of the beauty of a cloud lighted by the setting sun, is no hindrance to my knowing that the cloud is vapour of water, subject to all the laws of vapours in a state of suspension; and I am just as likely to allow for, and act on, these physical laws whenever there is occasion to do so, as if I had been incapable of perceiving any distinction between beauty and ugliness.

While my intimacy with Roebuck diminished, I fell more and more into friendly intercourse with our Coleridgian adversaries in the Society, Frederick Maurice and John Sterling, both subsequently so well known, the former by his writings, the latter through the biographies by Hare and Carlyle. Of these two friends, Maurice was the thinker, Sterling the orator, and impassioned expositor of thoughts which, at this period, were almost entirely formed for him by Maurice. With Maurice I had for some time been acquainted through Eyton Tooke, who had known him at Cambridge, and though my discussions with him were almost always disputes, I had carried away from them much that helped to build up my new fabric of thought, in the same way as I was deriving much from Coleridge, and from the writings of Goethe and other German authors which I read during those years. I have so deep a respect for Maurice's character and purposes, as well as for his great mental gifts, that it is with some unwillingness I say anything which may seem to place him on a less high eminence than I would gladly be able to accord to him. But I have always thought that there was more intellectual power wasted in Maurice than in any other of my contemporaries. Few of them certainly have had so much to waste. Great powers of generalization, rare ingenuity and subtlety, and a wide perception of important and unobvious truths, served him not for putting something better into the place of the worthless heap of received opinions on the great subjects of thought, but for proving to his own mind that the Church of England had known everything from the first, and that all the truths on the ground of which the Church and orthodoxy have been attacked (many of which he saw as clearly as any one) are not only consistent with the Thirty-nine articles, but are better understood and expressed in those articles than by any one who rejects them. I have never been able to find any other explanation of this, than by attributing it to that timidity of conscience, combined with original sensitiveness of temperament, which has so often driven highly gifted men into Romanism from the need of a firmer support than they can find in the independent conclusions of their own judgment. Any more vulgar kind of timidity no one who knew Maurice would ever think of imputing to him, even if he had not given public proof of his freedom from it, by his ultimate collision with some of the opinions commonly regarded as orthodox, and by his noble origination of the Christian Socialist movement. The nearest parallel to him, in a moral point of view, is Coleridge, to whom, in merely intellectual power, apart from poetical genius, I think him decidedly superior. At this time, however, he might be described as a disciple of Coleridge, and Sterling as a disciple of Coleridge and of him. The modifications which were taking place in my old opinions gave me some points of contact with them; and both Maurice and Sterling were of considerable use to my development. With Sterling I soon became very intimate, and was more attached to him than I have ever been to any other man. He was indeed one of the most lovable of men. His frank, cordial, affectionate, and expansive character; a love of truth alike conspicuous in the highest things and the humblest; a generous and ardent nature which threw itself with impetuosity into the opinions it adopted, but was as eager to do justice to the doctrines and the men it was opposed to, as to make war on what it thought their errors; and an equal devotion to the two cardinal points of Liberty and Duty, formed a combination of qualities as attractive to me, as to all others who knew him as well as I did. With his open mind and heart, he found no difficulty in joining hands with me across the gulf which as yet divided our opinions. He told me how he and others had looked upon me (from hearsay information), as a "made" or manufactured man, having had a certain impress of opinion stamped on me which I could only reproduce; and what a change took place in his feelings when he found, in the discussion on Wordsworth and Byron, that Wordsworth, and all which that names implies, "belonged" to me as much as to him and his friends. The failure of his health soon scattered all his plans of life, and compelled him to live at a distance from London; so that after the first year or two of our acquaintance, we only saw each other at distant intervals. But (as he said himself in one of his letters to Carlyle) when we did meet it was like brothers. Though he was never, in the full sense of the word, a profound thinker, his openness of mind, and the moral courage in which he greatly surpassed Maurice, made him outgrow the dominion which Maurice and Coleridge had once exercised over his intellect; though he retained to the last a great but discriminating admiration of both, and towards Maurice a warm affection. Except in that short and transitory phasis of his life, during which he made the mistake of becoming a clergyman, his mind was ever progressive: and the advance he always seemed to have made when I saw him after an interval, made me apply to him what Goethe said of Schiller, "Er hatte eine fürchterliche Fortschreitung." He and I started from intellectual points almost as wide apart as the poles, but the distance between us was always diminishing: if I made steps towards some of his opinions, he, during his short life, was constantly approximating more and more to several of mine: and if he had lived, and had health and vigour to prosecute his ever assiduous self-culture, there is no knowing how much further this spontaneous assimilation might have proceeded.

After 1829 I withdrew from attendance on the Debating Society. I had had enough of speech-making, and was glad to carry on my private studies and meditations without any immediate call for outward assertion of their results. I found the fabric of my old and taught opinions giving way in many fresh places, and I never allowed it to fall to pieces, but was incessantly occupied in weaving it anew. I never, in the course of my transition, was content to remain, for ever so short a time, confused and unsettled. When I had taken in any new idea, I could not rest till I had adjusted its relation to my old opinions, and ascertained exactly how far its effect ought to extend in modifying or superseding them.

The conflicts which I had so often had to sustain in defending the theory of government laid down in Bentham's and my father's writings, and the acquaintance I had obtained with other schools of political thinking, made me aware of many things which that doctrine, professing to be a theory of government in general, ought to have made room for, and did not. But these things, as yet, remained with me rather as corrections to be made in applying the theory to practice, than as defects in the theory. I felt that politics could not be a science of specific experience; and that the accusations against the Benthamic theory of *being* a theory, of proceeding *à priori* by way of general reasoning, instead of Baconian experiment, showed complete ignorance of Bacon's principles, and of the necessary conditions of experimental investigation. At this juncture appeared in the Edinburgh Review, Macaulay's famous attack on my father's Essay on Government. This gave me much to think about. I saw that Macaulay's conception of the logic of politics was erroneous; that he stood up for the empirical mode of treating political phenomena, against the philosophical; that even in physical science his notion of philosophizing might have recognized Kepler, but would have excluded Newton and Laplace. But I could not help feeling, that though the tone was unbecoming (an error for which the writer, at a later period, made the most ample and honourable amends), there was truth in several of his strictures on my father's treatment of the subject; that my father's premises were really too narrow, and included but a small number of the general truths, on which, in politics, the important consequences depend. Identity of interest between the governing body and the community at large, is not, in any practical sense which can be attached to it, the only thing on which good government depends; neither can this identity of interest be secured by the mere conditions of election. I was not at all satisfied with the mode in which my father met the criticisms of Macaulay. He did not, as I thought he ought to have done, justify himself by saying, "I was not writing a scientific treatise on politics, I was writing an argument for parliamentary reform." He treated Macaulay's argument as simply irrational; an attack upon the reasoning faculty; an example of the saying of Hobbes, that when reason is against a man, a man will be against reason. This made me think that there was really something more fundamentally erroneous in my father's conception of philosophical method, as applicable to politics, than I had hitherto supposed there was. But I did not at first see clearly what the error might be. At last it flashed upon me all at once in the course of other studies. In the early part of 1830 I had begun to put on paper the ideas on Logic (chiefly on the distinctions among Terms, and the import of Propositions) which had been suggested and in part worked out in the morning conversations already spoken of. Having secured these thoughts from being lost, I pushed on into the other parts of the subject, to try whether I could do anything further towards clearing up the theory of Logic generally. I grappled at once with the problem of Induction, postponing that of Reasoning, on the ground that it is necessary to obtain premises before we can reason from them. Now, Induction is mainly a process for finding the causes of effects: and in attempting to fathom the mode of tracing causes and effects in physical science, I soon saw that in the more perfect of the sciences, we ascend, by generalization from particulars, to the tendencies of causes considered singly, and then reason downward from those separate tendencies, to the effect of the same causes when combined. I then asked myself, what is the ultimate analysis of this deductive process; the common theory of the syllogism evidently throwing no light upon it. My practice (learnt from Hobbes and my father) being to study abstract principles by means of the best concrete instances I could find, the Composition of Forces, in dynamics, occurred to me as the most complete example of the logical process I was investigating. On examining, accordingly, what the mind does when it applies the principle of the Composition of Forces, I found that it performs a simple act of addition. It adds the separate effect of the one force to the separate effect of the other, and puts down the sum of these separate effects as the joint effect. But is this a legitimate process? In dynamics, and in all the mathematical branches of physics, it is; but in some other cases, as in chemistry, it is not; and I then recollected that something not unlike this was pointed out as one of the distinctions between chemical and mechanical phenomena, in the introduction to that favourite of my boyhood, Thomson's System of Chemistry. This distinction at once made my mind clear as to what was perplexing me in respect to the philosophy of politics. I now saw, that a science is either deductive or experimental, according as, in the province it deals with, the effects of causes when conjoined, are or are not the sums of the effects which the same causes produce when separate. It followed that politics must be a deductive science. It thus appeared, that both Macaulay and my father were wrong; the one in assimilating the method of philosophizing in politics to the purely experimental method of chemistry; while the other, though right in adopting a deductive method, had made a wrong selection of one, having taken as the type of deduction, not the appropriate process, that of the deductive branches of natural philosophy, but the inappropriate one of pure geometry, which, not being a science of causation at all, does not require or admit of any summing-up of effects. A foundation was thus laid in my thoughts for the principal chapters of what I aferwards published on the Logic of the Moral Sciences; and my new position in respect to my old political creed, now became perfectly definite.

If I am asked, what system of political philosophy I substituted for that which, as a philosophy, I had abandoned, I answer, no system: only a conviction that the true system was something much more complex and many-sided than I had previously had any idea of, and that its office was to supply, not a set of model institutions, but principles from which the institutions suitable to any given circumstances might be deduced. The influences of European, that is to say, Continental, thought, and especially those of the reaction of the nineteenth century against the eighteenth, were now streaming in upon me. They came from various quarters: from the writings of Coleridge, which I had begun to read with interest even before the change in my opinions; from the Coleridgians with whom I was in personal intercourse; from what I had read of Goethe; from Carlyle's early articles in the Edinburgh and Foreign Reviews, though for a long time I saw nothing in these (as my father saw nothing in them to the last) but insane rhapsody. From these sources, and from the acquaintance I kept up with the French literature of the time, I derived, among other ideas which the general turning upside down of the opinions of European thinkers had brought uppermost, these in particular: That the human mind has a certain order of possible progress, in which some things must precede others, an order which governments and public instructors can modify to some, but not to an unlimited extent: That all questions of political institutions are relative, not absolute, and that different stages of human progress not only *will* have, but *ought* to have, different institutions: That government is always either in the hands, or passing into the hands, of whatever is the strongest power in society, and that what this power is, does not depend on institutions, but institutions on it: That any general theory or philosophy of politics supposes a previous theory of human progress, and that this is the same thing with a philosophy of history. These opinions, true in the main, were held in an exaggerated and violent manner by the thinkers with whom I was now most accustomed to compare notes, and who, as usual with a reaction, ignored that half of the truth which the thinkers of the eighteenth century saw. But though, at one period of my progress, I for some time undervalued that great century, I never joined in the reaction against it, but kept as firm hold of one side of the truth as I took of the other. The fight between the nineteenth century and the eighteenth always reminded me of the battle about the shield, one side of which was white and the other black. I marvelled at the blind rage with which the combatants rushed against one another. I applied to them, and to Coleridge himself, many of Coleridge's sayings about half truths; and Goethe's device, "many-sidedness," was one which I would most willingly, at this period, have taken for mine.

The writers by whom, more than by any others, a new

mode of political thinking was brought home to me, were
those of the St. Simonian school in France. In 1829 and 1830
I became acquainted with some of their writings. They were
then only in the earlier stages of their speculations. They had
not yet dressed out their philosophy as a religion, nor had
they organized their scheme of Socialism. They were just beginning to question the principle of hereditary property. I
was by no means prepared to go with them even this length;
but I was greatly struck with the connected view which they
for the first time presented to me, of the natural order of
human progress; and especially with their division of all history into organic periods and critical periods. During the
organic periods (they said) mankind accept with firm conviction some positive creed, claiming jurisdiction over all their
actions, and containing more or less of truth and adaptation
to the needs of humanity. Under its influence they make all
the progress compatible with the creed, and finally outgrow
it; when a period follows of criticism and negation, in which
mankind lose their old convictions without acquiring any new
ones, of a general or authoritative character, except the conviction that the old are false. The period of Greek and Roman
polytheism, so long as really believed in by instructed Greeks
and Romans, was an organic period, succeeded by the critical
or sceptical period of the Greek philosophers. Another organic
period came in with Christianity. The corresponding critical
period began with the Reformation, has lasted ever since, still
lasts, and cannot altogether cease until a new organic period
has been inaugurated by the triumph of a yet more advanced
creed. These ideas, I knew, were not peculiar to the St.
Simonians; on the contrary, they were the general property
of Europe, or at least of Germany and France, but they had
never, to my knowledge, been so completely systematized as
by these writers, nor the distinguishing characteristics of a
critical period so powerfully set forth; for I was not then
acquainted with Fichte's Lectures on "the Characteristics of
the Present Age." In Carlyle, indeed, I found bitter denunciations of an "age of unbelief," and of the present as such,
which I, like most people at that time, supposed to be passionate protests in favour of the old modes of belief. But all that
was true in these denunciations, I thought that I found more
calmly and philosophically stated by the St. Simonians. Among
their publications, too, there was one which seemed to me far
superior to the rest; in which the general idea was matured

into something much more definite and instructive. This was an early work of Auguste Comte, who then called himself, and even announced himself in the title-page as, a pupil of Saint-Simon. In this tract M. Comte first put forth the doctrine, which he afterwards so copiously illustrated, of the natural succession of three stages in every department of human knowledge: first, the theological, next the metaphysical, and lastly, the positive stage; and contended, that social science must be subject to the same law; that the feudal and Catholic system was the concluding phasis of the theological state of the social science, Protestantism the commencement, and the doctrines of the French Revolution the consummation of the metaphysical; and that its positive state was yet to come. This doctrine harmonized well with my existing notions, to which it seemed to give a scientific shape. I already regarded the methods of physical science as the proper models for political. But the chief benefit which I derived at this time from the trains of thought suggested by the St. Simonians and by Comte, was, that I obtained a clear conception than ever before of the peculiarities of an era of transition in opinion, and ceased to mistake the moral and intellectual characteristics of such an era, for the normal attributes of humanity. I looked forward, through the present age of loud disputes but generally weak convictions, to a future which shall unite the best qualities of the critical with the best qualities of the organic periods; unchecked liberty of thought, unbounded freedom of individual action in all modes not hurtful to others; but also, convictions as to what is right and wrong, useful and pernicious, deeply engraven on the feelings by early education and general unanimity of sentiment, and so firmly grounded in reason and in the true exigencies of life, that they shall not, like all former and present creeds, religious, ethical, and political, require to be periodically thrown off and replaced by others.

M. Comte soon left the St. Simonians, and I lost sight of him and his writings for a number of years. But the St. Simonians I continued to cultivate. I was kept *au courant* of their progress by one of their most enthusiastic disciples, M. Gustave d'Eichthal, who about that time passed a considerable interval in England. I was introduced to their chiefs, Bazard and Enfantin, in 1830; and as long as their public teachings and proselytism continued, I read nearly everything they wrote. Their criticisms on the common doctrines of

Liberalism seemed to me full of important truth; and it was partly by their writings that my eyes were opened to the very limited and temporary value of the old political economy, which assumes private property and inheritance as indefeasible facts, and freedom of production and exchange as the *dernier mot* of social improvement. The scheme gradually unfolded by the St. Simonians, under which the labour and capital of society would be managed for the general account of the community, every individual being required to take a share of labour, either as thinker, teacher, artist, or producer, all being classed according to their capacity, and remunerated according to their works, appeared to me a far superior description of Socialism to Owen's. Their aim seemed to me desirable and rational, however their means might be inefficacious; and though I neither believed in the practicability, nor in the beneficial operation of their social machinery, I felt that the proclamation of such an ideal of human society could not but tend to give a beneficial direction to the efforts of others to bring society, as at present constituted, nearer to some ideal standard. I honoured them most of all for what they have been most cried down for—the boldness and freedom from prejudice with which they treated the subject of family, the most important of any, and needing more fundamental alterations than remain to be made in any other great social institution, but on which scarcely any reformer has the courage to touch. In proclaiming the perfect equality of men and women, and an entirely new order of things in regard to their relations with one another, the St. Simonians, in common with Owen and Fourier, have entitled themselves to the grateful remembrance of future generations.

In giving an account of this period of my life, I have only specified such of my new impressions as appeared to me, both at the time and since, to be a kind of turning points, marking a definite progress in my mode of thought. But these few selected points give a very insufficient idea of the quantity of thinking which I carried on respecting a host of subjects during these years of transition. Much of this, it is true, consisted in rediscovering things known to all the world, which I had previously disbelieved, or disregarded. But the rediscovery was to me a discovery, giving me plenary possession of the truths, not as traditional platitudes, but fresh from their source: and it seldom failed to place them in some new light, by which they were reconciled with, and seemed to confirm while they modified, the truths less generally known which lay in my early opinions, and in no essential part of which I at any time wavered. All my new thinking only laid the foundation of these more deeply and strongly, while it often removed misapprehension and confusion of ideas which had perverted their effect. For example, during the later returns of my dejection, the doctrine of what is called Philosophical Necessity weighed on my existence like an incubus. I felt as if I was scientifically proved to be the helpless slave of antecedent circumstances; as if my character and that of all others had been formed for us by agencies beyond our control, and was wholly out of our own power. I often said to myself, what a relief it would be if I could disbelieve the doctrine of the formation of character by circumstances; and remembering the wish of Fox respecting the doctrine of resistance to governments, that it might never be forgotten by kings, nor remembered by subjects, I said that it would be a blessing if the doctrine of necessity could be believed by all *quoad* the characters of others, and disbelieved in regard to their own. I pondered painfully on the subject, till gradually I saw light through it. I perceived, that the word Necessity, as a name for the doctrine of Cause and Effect applied to human action, carried with it a misleading association; and that this association was the operative force in the depressing and paralysing influence whcih I had experienced: I saw that though our character is formed by circumstances, our own desires can do much to shape those circumstances; and that what is really inspiriting and ennobling in the doctrine of free-will, is the conviction that we have real power over the formation of our own character; that our will, by influencing some of our circumstances, can modify our future habits or capabilities of willing. All this was entirely consistent with the doctrine of circumstances, or rather, was that doctrine itself, properly understood. From that time I drew in my own mind, a clear distinction between the doctrine of circumstances, and Fatalism; discarding altogether the misleading word Necessity. The theory, which I now for the first time rightly apprehended, ceased altogether to be discouraging, and besides the relief to my spirits, I no longer suffered under the burthen, so heavy to one who aims at being a reformer in opinions, of thinking one doctrine true, and the contrary doctrine morally beneficial. The train of thought which had extricated me from this dilemma, seemed to me, in after years, fitted to render a similar service to others; and it now forms the chapter on Liberty and Necessity in the concluding Book of my "System of Logic."

Again, in politics, though I no longer accepted the doctrine of the Essay on Government as a scientific theory; though I ceased to consider representative democracy as an absolute principle, and regarded it as a question of time, place, and circumstance; though I now looked upon the choice of political institutions as a moral and educational question more than one of material interests, thinking that it ought to be decided mainly by the consideration, what great improvement in life and culture stands next in order for the people concerned, as the condition of their further progress, and what institutions are most likely to promote that; nevertheless, this change in the premises of my political philosophy did not alter my practical political creed as to the requirements of my own time and country. I was as much as ever a radical and democrat for Europe, and especially for England. I thought the predominance of the aristocratic classes, the noble and the rich, in the English Constitution, an evil worth any struggle to get rid of; not on account of taxes, or any such comparatively small inconvenience, but as the great demoralizing agency in the country. Demoralizing, first, because it made the conduct of the government an example of gross public immorality, through the predominance of private over public interests in the State, and the abuse of the powers of legislation for the advantage of classes. Secondly, and in a still greater degree, because the respect of the multitude always attaching itself principally to that which, in the existing state of society, is the chief passport to power; and under English institutions, riches, hereditary or acquired, being the almost exclusive source of political importance; riches, and the signs of riches, were almost the only things really respected, and the life of the people was mainly devoted to the pursuit of them. I thought, that while the higher and richer classes held the power of government, the instruction and improvement of the mass of the people were contrary to the self-interest of those classes, because tending to render the people more powerful for throwing off the yoke: but if the democracy obtained a large, and perhaps the principal, share in the governing power, it would become the interest of the opulent classes to promote their education, in order to ward off really mischievous errors, and especially those which would lead to unjust violations of property. On these grounds I was not only as ardent as ever for democratic institutions, but earnestly hoped that Owenite, St. Simonian, and all other anti-property doctrines might spread widely among the poorer classes; not that I thought those doctrines true, or desired that they should be acted on, but in order that the higher classes might be made to see that they had more to fear from the poor when uneducated, than when educated.

In this frame of mind the French Revolution of July found me. It aroused my utmost enthusiasm, and gave me, as it were, a new existence. I went at once to Paris, was introduced to Lafayette, and laid the groundwork of the intercourse I afterwards kept up with several of the active chiefs of the extreme popular party. After my return I entered warmly, as a writer, into the political discussions of the time; which soon became still more exciting, by the coming in of Lord Grey's ministry, and the proposing of the Reform Bill. For the next few years I wrote copiously in newspapers. It was about this time that Fonblanque, who had for some time written the political articles in the Examiner, became the proprietor and editor of the paper. It is not forgotten with what verve and talent, as well as fine wit, he carried it on, during the whole period of Lord Grey's ministry, and what importance it assumed as the principal representative, in the newspaper press, of radical opinions. The distinguishing character of the paper was given to it entirely by his own articles, which formed at least three-fourths of all the original writing contained in it: but of the remaining fourth I contributed during those years a much larger share than any one else. I wrote nearly all the articles on French subjects, including a weekly summary of French politics, often extending to considerable length; together with many leading articles on general politics, commercial and financial legislation, and any miscellaneous subjects in which I felt interested, and which were suitable to the paper, including occasional reviews of books. Mere newspaper articles on the occurrences or questions of the moment, gave no opportunity for the development of any general mode of thought; but I attempted, in the beginning of 1831, to embody in a series of articles, headed "The Spirit of the Age," some of my new opinions, and especially to point out in the character of the present age, the anomalies and evils characteristic of the transition from a system of opinions which had worn out, to another only in process of being formed. These articles were, I fancy, lumbering in style, and not lively or

striking enough to be at any time, acceptable to newspaper
readers; but had they been far more attractive, still, at that
particular moment, when great political changes were impending, and engrossing all minds, these discussions were ill-timed,
and missed fire altogether. The only effect which I know to
have been produced by them, was that Carlyle, then living in
a secluded part of Scotland, read them in his solitude, and
saying to himself (as he afterwards told me) "here is a new
Mystic," inquired on coming to London that autumn respecting their authorship; an inquiry which was the immediate
cause of our becoming personally acquainted.

I have already mentioned Carlyle's earlier writings as one
of the channels through which I received the influences which
enlarged my early narrow creed; but I do not think that those
writings, by themselves, would ever have had any effect on
my opinions. What truths they contained, though of the very
kind which I was already receiving from other quarters, were
presented in a form and vesture less suited than any other to
give them access to a mind trained as mine had been. They
seemed a haze of poetry and German metaphysics, in which
almost the only clear thing was a strong animosity to most of
the opinions which were the basis of my mode of thought;
religious scepticism, utilitarianism, the doctrine of circumstances, and the attaching any importance to democracy, logic,
or political economy. Instead of my having been taught anything, in the first instance, by Carlyle, it was only in proportion as I came to see the same truths through media more
suited to my mental constitution, that I recognized them in
his writings. Then, indeed, the wonderful power with which
he put them forth made a deep impression upon me, and I
was during a long period one of his most fervent admirers;
but the good his writings did me, was not as philosophy to
instruct, but as poetry to animate. Even at the time when our
acquaintance commenced, I was not sufficiently advanced in
my new modes of thought, to appreciate him fully; a proof
of which is, that on his showing me the manuscript of Sartor
Resartus, his best and greatest work, which he had just then
finished, I made little of it; though when it came out about
two years afterwards in Fraser's Magazine I read it with enthusiastic admiration and the keenest delight. I did not seek
and cultivate Carlyle less on account of the fundamental differences in our philosophy. He soon found out that I was not
"another mystic," and when for the sake of my own integrity

I wrote to him a distinct profession of all those of my opinions which I knew he most disliked, he replied that the chief difference between us was that I "was as yet consciously nothing of a mystic." I do not know at what period he gave up the expectation that I was destined to become one; but though both his and my opinions underwent in subsequent years considerable changes, we never approached much nearer to each other's modes of thought than we were in the first years of our acquaintance. I did not, however, deem myself a competent judge of Carlyle. I felt that he was a poet, and that I was not; that he was a man of intuition, which I was not; and that as such, he not only saw many things long before me, which I could only when they were pointed out to me, hobble after and prove, but that it was highly probable he could see many things which were not visible to me even after they were pointed out. I knew that I could not see round him, and could never be certain that I saw over him; and I never presumed to judge him with any definiteness, until he was interpreted to me by one greatly the superior of us both—who was more a poet than he, and more a thinker than I—whose own mind and nature included his, and infinitely more.

Among the persons of intellect whom I had known of old, the one with whom I had now most points of agreement was the elder Austin. I have mentioned that he always set himself in opposition to our early sectarianism; and latterly he had, like myself, come under new influences. Having been appointed Professor of Jurisprudence in the London University (now University College), he had lived for some time at Bonn to study for his Lectures; and the influences of German literature and of the German character and state of society had made a very perceptible change in his views of life. His personal disposition was much softened; he was less militant and polemic; his tastes had begun to turn themselves towards the poetic and contemplative. He attached much less importance than formerly to outward changes; unless accompanied by a better cultivation of the inward nature. He had a strong distaste for the general meanness of English life, the absence of enlarged thoughts and unselfish desires, the low objects on which the faculties of all classes of the English are intent. Even the kind of public interests which Englishmen care for, he held in very little esteem. He thought that there was more practical good government, and (which is true enough) infinitely more care for the education and mental improvement of all ranks of the people, under the Prussian monarchy, than under the English representative government: and he held, with the French Economistes, that the real security for good government is "un peuple éclairé," which is not always the fruit of popular institutions, and which if it could be had without them, would do their work better than they. Though he approved of the Reform Bill, he predicted, what in fact occurred, that it would not produce the great immediate improvements in government, which many expected from it. The men, he said, who could do these great things, did not exist in the country. There were many points of sympathy between him and me, both in the new opinions he had adopted and in the old ones which he retained. Like me, he never ceased to be an utilitarian, and with all his love of the Germans, and enjoyment of their literature, never became in the smallest degree reconciled to the innate-principle metaphysics. He cultivated more and more a kind of German religion, a religion of poetry and feeling with little, if anything, of positive dogma; while, in politics (and here it was that I most differed with him) he acquired an indifference, bordering on contempt, for the progress of popular institutions: though he rejoiced in that of Socialism, as the most effectual means of compelling the powerful classes to educate the people, and to impress on them the only real means of permanently improving their material condition, a limitation of their numbers. Neither was he, at this time, fundamentally opposed to Socialism in itself as an ultimate result of improvement. He professed great disrespect for what he called "the universal principles of human nature of the political economists," and insisted on the evidence which history and daily experience afford of the "extraordinary pliability of human nature" (a phrase which I have somewhere borrowed from him), nor did he think it possible to set any positive bounds to the moral capabilities which might unfold themselves in mankind, under an enlightened direction of social and educational influences. Whether he retained all these opinions to the end of life I know not. Certainly the modes of thinking of his later years, and especially of his last publication, were much more Tory in their general character than those which he held at this time.

My father's tone of thought and feeling, I now felt myself at a great distance from: greater, indeed, than a full and calm explanation and reconsideration on both sides, might have shown to exist in reality. But my father was not one with whom calm and full explanations on fundamental points of doctrine could be expected, at least with one whom he might consider as, in some sort, a deserter from his standard. Fortunately we were almost always in strong agreement on the political questions of the day which engrossed a large part of his interest and of his conversation. On those matters of opinion on which we differed, we talked little. He knew that the habit of thinking for myself, which his mode of education had fostered, sometimes led me to opinions different from his, and he perceived from time to time that I did not always tell him *how* different. I expected no good, but only pain to both of us, from discussing our differences: and I never expressed them but when he gave utterance to some opinion of feeling repugnant to mine, in a manner which would have made it disingenuousness on my part to remain silent.

It remains to speak of what I wrote during these years, which, independently of my contributions to newspapers, was considerable. In 1830 and 1831 I wrote the five Essays since published under the title of "Essays on some Unsettled Questions of Political Economy," almost as they now stand, except that in 1833 I partially rewrote the fifth Essay. They were written with no immediate purpose of publication; and when, some years later, I offered them to a publisher, he declined them. They were only printed in 1844, after the success of the "System of Logic." I also resumed my speculations on this last subject, and puzzled myself, like others before me, with the great paradox of the discovery of new truths by general reasoning. As to the fact, there could be no doubt. As little could it be doubted, that all reasoning is resolvable into syllogisms, and that in every syllogism the conclusion is actually contained and implied in the premises. How, being so contained and implied, it could be new truth, and how the theorems of geometry, so different in appearance from the definitions and axioms, could be all contained in these, was a difficulty which no one, I thought, had sufficiently felt, and which, at all events, no one had succeeded in clearing up. The explanations offered by Whately and others, though they might give a temporary satisfaction, always, in my mind, left a mist still hanging over the subject. At last, when reading a second or third time the chapters on Reasoning in the second volume of Dugald Stewart, interrogating myself on every point, and following out, as far as I knew how, every topic of thought which the book suggested, I came upon an idea of his respecting the use of axioms in ratiocination, which I did not remember to have before noticed, but which now, in meditating on it, seemed to me not only true of axioms, but of all general propositions whatever, and to be the key of the whole perplexity. From this germ grew the theory of the Syllogism propounded in the Second Book of the Logic; which I immediately fixed by writing it out. And now, with greatly increased hope of being able to produce a work on Logic, of some originality and value, I proceeded to write the First Book, from the rough and imperfect draft I had already made. What I now wrote became the basis of that part of the subsequent Treatise; except that it did not contain the Theory of Kinds, which was a later addition, suggested by otherwise inextricable difficulties which met me in my first attempt to work out the subject of some of the concluding chapters of the Third Book. At the point which I had now reached I made a halt, which lasted five years. I had come to the end of my tether; I could make nothing satisfactory of Induction, at this time. I continued to read any book which seemed to promise light on the subject, and appropriated, as well as I could, the results; but for a long time I found nothing which seemed to open to me any very important vein of meditation.

In 1832 I wrote several papers for the first series of Tait's Magazine, and one for a quarterly periodical called the Jurist, which had been founded, and for a short time carried on, by a set of friends, all lawyers and law reformers, with several of whom I was acquainted. The paper in question is the one on the rights and duties of the State respecting Corporation and Church Property, now standing first among the collected "Dissertations and Discussions;" where one of my articles in Tait, "The Currency Juggle," also appears. In the whole mass of what I wrote previous to these, there is nothing of sufficient permanent value to justify reprinting. The paper in the Jurist, which I still think a very complete discussion of the rights of the State over Foundations, showed both sides of my opinions, asserting as firmly as I should have done at any time, the doctrine that all endowments are national property, which the government may and ought to control; but not, as I should once have done, condemning endowments in themselves, and proposing that they should be taken to pay off the national debt. On the contrary, I urged strenuously the importance of having a provision for education, not dependent on the mere demand of the market, that is, on the knowledge and discernment of average parents, but calculated to establish and keep up a higher standard of instruction than is likely to be spontaneously demanded by the buyers of the article. All these opinions have been confirmed and strengthened by the whole course of my subsequent reflections.

VI. COMMENCEMENT OF THE MOST VALUABLE FRIENDSHIP OF MY LIFE. MY FATHER'S DEATH. WRITINGS AND OTHER PROCEEDINGS UP TO 1840.

IT was the period of my mental progress which I have now reached that I formed the friendship which has been the honour and chief blessing of my existence, as well as the source of a great part of all that I have attempted to do, or hope to effect hereafter, for human improvement. My first introduction to the lady who, after a friendship of twenty years, consented to become my wife, was in 1830, when I was in my twenty-fifth and she in her twenty-third year. With her husband's family it was the renewal of an old acquaintanceship. His grandfather lived in the next house to my father's in Newington Green, and I had sometimes when a boy been invited to play in the old gentleman's garden. He was a fine specimen of the old Scotch puritan; stern, severe, and powerful, but very kind to children, on whom such men make a lasting impression. Although it was years after my introduction to Mrs. Taylor before my acquaintance with her became at all intimate or confidential, I very soon felt her to be the most admirable person I had ever known. It is not to be supposed that she was, or that any one, at the age at which I first saw her, could be, all that she afterwards became. Least of all could this be true of her, with whom self-improvement, progress in the highest and in all senses, was a law of her nature; a necessity equally from the ardour with which she sought it, and from the spontaneous tendency of faculties which could not receive an impression or an experience without making it the source or the occasion of an accession of wisdom. Up to the time when I first saw her, her rich and powerful nature had chiefly unfolded itself according to the received type of feminine genius. To her outer circle she was a beauty and a wit, with an air of natural distinction, felt by all who approached her: to the inner, a woman of deep and strong feeling, of penetrating and intuitive intelligence, and

of an eminently meditative and poetic nature. Married at a
very early age, to a most upright, brave, and honourable man,
of liberal opinions and good education, but without the intellectual or* artistic tastes which would have made him a
companion for her, though a steady and affectionate friend,
for whom she had true esteem and the strongest affection
through life, and whom she most deeply lamented when dead;
shut out by the social disabilities of women from any adequate
exercise of her highest faculties in action on the world without; her life was one of inward meditation, varied by familiar
intercourse with a small circle of friends, of whom† one only
(long since deceased) was a person of genius, or of capacities
of feeling or intellect kindred with her own, but all had more
or less of alliance with her in sentiments and opinions. Into
this circle I had the good fortune to be admitted, and I soon
perceived that she possessed in combination, the qualities
which in all other persons whom I had known I had been
only too happy to find singly. In her, complete emancipation
from every kind of superstition (including that which attributes a pretended perfection to the order of nature and the
universe), and an earnest protest against many things which
are still part of the established constitution of society, resulted
not from the hard intellect, but from strength of noble and
elevated feeling, and co-existed with a highly reverential
nature. In general spiritual characteristics, as well as in temperament and organisation, I have often compared her, as
she was at this time, to Shelley: but in thought and intellect,
Shelley, so far as his powers were developed in his short life,
was but a child compared with what she ultimately became.
Alike in the highest regions of speculation and in the smaller
practical concerns of daily life, her mind was the same perfect
instrument, piercing to the very heart and marrow of the
matter; always seizing the essential idea or principle. The
same exactness and rapidity of operation, pervading as it did
her sensitive as well as her mental faculties, would, with her
gifts of feeling and imagination, have fitted her to be a consummate artist, as her fiery and tender soul and her vigorous
eloquence would certainly have made her a great orator, and
her profound knowledge of human nature and discernment
and sagacity in practical life, would, in the times when such
a *carrière* was open to women, have made her eminent among

* Pencil note by H. T. on MS. "not true."
† Pencil note on MS. "Miss Flower, H. T."

the rulers of mankind. Her intellectual gifts did but minister to a moral character at once the noblest and the best balanced which I have ever met with in life. Her unselfishness was not that of a taught system of duties, but of a heart which thoroughly identified itself with the feelings of others, and often went to excess in consideration for them by imaginatively investing their feelings with the intensity of its own. The passion of justice might have been thought to be her strongest feeling, but for her boundless generosity, and a lovingness ever ready to pour itself forth upon any or all human beings who were capable of giving the smallest feeling in return. The rest of her moral characteristics were such as naturally accompany these qualities of mind and heart: the most genuine modesty combined with the loftiest pride; a simplicity and sincerity which were absolute, towards all who were fit to receive them; the utmost scorn of whatever was mean and cowardly, and a burning indignation at everything brutal or tyrannical, faithless or dishonourable in conduct and character, while making the broadest distinction between *mala in se* and mere *mala prohibita*—between acts giving evidence of intrinsic badness in feeling and character, and those which are only violations of conventions either good or bad, violations which whether in themselves right or wrong, are capable of being committed by persons in every other respect lovable or admirable.

To be admitted into any degree of mental intercourse with a being of these qualities, could not but have a most beneficial influence on my development; though the effect was only gradual, and many years elapsed before her mental progress and mine went forward in the complete companionship they at last attained. The benefit I received was far greater than any which I could hope to give; though to her, who had at first reached her opinions by the moral intuition of a character of strong feeling, there was doubtless help as well as encouragement to be derived from one who had arrived at many of the same results by study and reasoning: and in the rapidity of her intellectual growth, her mental activity, which converted everything into knowledge, doubtless drew from me, as it did from other sources, many of its materials. What I owe, even intellectually, to her, is in its detail, almost infinite; of its general character a few words will give some, though a very imperfect, idea. With those who, like all the best and wisest of mankind, are dissatisfied with human life as it is, and whose feelings are wholly identified with its radical amendment, there are two main regions of thought. One is the region of ultimate aims; the constituent elements of the highest realizable ideal of human life. The other is that of the immediately useful and practically attainable. In both these departments, I have acquired more from her teaching, than from all other sources taken together. And, to say truth, it is in these two extremes principally, that real certainty lies. My own strength lay wholly in the uncertain and slippery intermediate region, that of theory, or moral and political science: respecting the conclusions of which, in any of the forms in which I have received or originated them, whether as political economy, analytic psychology, logic, philosophy of history, or anything else, it is not the least of my intellectual obligations to her that I have derived from her a wise scepticism, which, while it has not hindered me from following out the honest exercise of my thinking faculties to whatever conclusions might result from it, has put me on my guard against holding or announcing these conclusions with a degree of confidence which the nature of such speculations does not warrant, and has kept my mind not only open to admit, but prompt to welcome and eager to seek, even on the questions on which I have most meditated, any prospect of clearer perceptions and better evidence. I have often received praise, which in my own right I only partially deserve, for the greater practicality which is supposed to be found in my writings, compared with those of most thinkers who have been equally addicted to large generalizations. The writings in which this quality has been observed, were not the work of one mind, but of the fusion of two, one of them as pre-eminently practical in its judgments and perceptions of things present, as it was high and bold in its anticipations for a remote futurity.

At the present period, however, this influence was only one among many which were helping to shape the character of my future development: and even after it became, I may truly say, the presiding principle of my mental progress, it did not alter the path, but only made me move forward more boldly, and, at the same time, more cautiously, in the same course. The only actual revolution which has ever taken place in my modes of thinking, was already complete. My new tendencies had to be confirmed in some respects, moderated in others: but the only substantial changes of opinion that were yet to come, related to politics, and consisted, on one hand, in a greater approximation, so far as regards the ultimate prospects of humanity, to a qualified Socialism, and on the other, a shifting of my political ideal from pure democracy, as commonly understood by its partizans, to the modified form of it, which is set forth in my "Considerations on Representative Government."

This last change, which took place very gradually, dates its commencement from my reading, or rather study, of M. de Tocqueville's "Democracy in America," which fell into my hands immediately after its first appearance. In that remarkable work, the excellences of Democracy were pointed out in a more conclusive, because a more specific manner than I had ever known them to be, even by the most enthusiastic democrats; while the specific dangers which beset Democracy, considered as the government of the numerical majority, were brought into equally strong light, and subjected to a masterly analysis, not as reasons for resisting what the author considered as an inevitable result of human progress, but as indications of the weak points of popular government, the defences by which it needs to be guarded, and the correctives which must be added to it in order that while full play is given to its beneficial tendencies, those which are of a different nature may be neutralized or mitigated. I was now well prepared for speculations of this character, and from this time onward my own thoughts moved more and more in the same channel, though the consequent modifications in my practical political creed were spread over many years, as would be shown by comparing my first review of "Democracy in America," written and published in 1835, with the one in 1840 (reprinted in the "Dissertations"), and this last, with the "Considerations on Representative Government."

A collateral subject on which also I derived great benefit from the study of Tocqueville, was the fundamental question of Centralization. The powerful philosophic analysis which he applied to American and to French experience, led him to attach the utmost importance to the performance of as much of the collective business of society, as can safely be so performed, by the people themselves, without any intervention of the executive government, either to supersede their agency, or to dictate the manner of its exercise. He viewed this practical political activity of the individual citizen, not only as one of the most effectual means of training the social feelings and practical intelligence of the people, so important in themselves and so indispensable to good government, but also as the specific counteractive to some of the characteristic infirmities of Democracy, and a necessary protection against its degenerating into the only despotism of which, in the modern world, there is real danger—the absolute rule of the head of the executive over a congregation of isolated individuals, all equals but all slaves. There was, indeed, no immediate peril from this source on the British side of the channel, where nine-tenths of the internal business which elsewhere devolves on the government, was transacted by agencies independent of it; where Centralization was, and is, the subject not only of rational disapprobation, but of unreasoning prejudice; where jealousy of Government interference was a blind feeling preventing or resisting even the most beneficial exertion of legislative authority to correct the abuses of what pretends to be local self-government, but is, too often, selfish mismanagement of local interests, by a jobbing and borné local oligarchy. But the more certain the public were to go wrong on the side opposed to Centralization, the greater danger was there lest philosophic reformers should fall into the contrary error, and overlook the mischiefs of which they had been spared the painful experience. I was myself, at this very time, actively engaged in defending important measures, such as the great Poor Law Reform of 1834, against an irrational clamour grounded on the Anti-Centralization prejudice: and had it not been for the lessons of Tocqueville, I do not know that I might not, like many reformers before me, have been hurried into the excess opposite to that, which, being the one prevalent in my own country, it was generally my business to combat. As it is, I have steered carefully between the two errors, and whether I have or have not drawn the line between them exactly in the right place, I have at least insisted with equal emphasis upon the evils on both sides, and have made the means of reconciling the advantages of both, a subject of serious study.

In the meanwhile had taken place the election of the first Reformed Parliament, which included several of the most notable of my Radical friends and acquaintances—Grote, Roebuck, Buller, Sir William Molesworth, John and Edward Romilly, and several more; besides Warburton, Strutt, and others, who were in parliament already. Those who thought themselves, and were called by their friends, the philosophic radicals, had now, it seemed, a fair opportunity, in a more advantageous position than they had ever before occupied, for showing what was in them; and I, as well as my father, founded great hopes on them. These hopes were destined to be disappointed. The men were honest, and faithful to their opinions, as far as votes were concerned; often in spite of much discouragement. When measures were proposed, flagrantly at variance with their principles, such as the Irish Coercion Bill, or the Canada coercion in 1837, they came forward manfully, and braved any amount of hostility and prejudice rather than desert the right. But on the whole they did very little to promote any opinions; they had little enterprise, little activity: they left the lead of the radical portion of the House to the old hands, to Hume and O'Connell. A partial exception must be made in favour of one or two of the younger men; and in the case of Roebuck, it is his title to permanent remembrance, that in the very first year during which he sat in Parliament, he originated (or re-originated after the unsuccessful attempt of Mr. Brougham) the parliamentary movement for National Education; and that he was the first to commence, and for years carried on almost alone, the contest for the self-government of the Colonies. Nothing, on the whole equal to these two things, was done by any other individual, even of those from whom most was expected. And now, on a calm retrospect, I can perceive that the men were less in fault than we supposed, and that we had expected too much from them. They were in unfavourable circumstances. Their lot was cast in the ten years of inevitable reaction, when, the Reform excitement being over, and the few legislative improvements which the public really called for having been rapidly effected, power gravitated back in its natural direction, to those who were for keeping things as they were; when the public mind desired rest, and was less disposed than at any other period since the peace, to let itself be moved by attempts to work up the reform feeling into fresh activity in favour of new things. It would have required a great political leader, which no one is to be blamed for not being, to have effected really great things by parliamentary discussion when the nation was in this mood. My father and I had hoped that some competent leader might arise; some man of philosophic attainments and popular talents, who could have put heart into the many younger or less distinguished men that would have been ready to join him—could have made them available, to the extent of their talents, in bringing advanced ideas before the public— could have used the House of Commons as a rostra or a

teacher's chair for instructing and impelling the public mind;
and would either have forced the Whigs to receive their measures from him, or have taken the lead of the Reform party out
of their hands. Such a leader there would have been, if my
father had been in Parliament. For want of such a man, the
instructed Radicals sank into a mere *côté gauche* of the Whig
party. With a keen, and as I now think, an exaggerated sense
of the possibilities which were open to the Radicals if they
made even ordinary exertion for their opinions, I laboured
from this time till 1839, both by personal influence with some
of them, and by writings, to put ideas into their heads, and
purpose into their hearts. I did some good with Charles Buller,
and some with Sir William Molesworth; both of whom did
valuable service, but were unhappily cut off almost in the beginning of their usefulness. On the whole, however, my attempt was vain. To have had a chance of succeeding in it,
required a different position from mine. It was a task only for
one who, being himself in Parliament, could have mixed with
the radical members in daily consultation, could himself have
taken the initiative, and instead of urging others to lead, could
have summoned them to follow.

What I could do by writing, I did. During the year 1833 I
continued working in the Examiner with Fonblanque who at
that time was zealous in keeping up the fight for radicalism
against the Whig ministry. During the session of 1834 I wrote
comments on passing events, of the nature of newspaper articles (under the title "Notes on the Newspapers"), in the
Monthly Repository, a magazine conducted by Mr. Fox, well
known as a preacher and political orator, and subsequently
as member of parliament for Oldham; with whom I had lately
become acquainted, and for whose sake chiefly I wrote in his
Magazine. I contributed several other articles to this periodical, the most considerable of which (on the theory of poetry),
is reprinted in the "Dissertations." Altogether, the writings
(independently of those in newspapers) which I published
from 1832 to 1834, amount to a large volume. This, however,
includes abstracts of several of Plato's Dialogues, with intro-
ductory remarks, which, though not published until 1834, had
been written several years earlier; and which I afterwards, on
various occasions, found to have been read, and their authorship known, by more people than were aware of anything else
which I had written, up to that time. To complete the tale of
my writings at this period, I may add that in 1833, at the re-

quest of Bulwer, who was just then completing his "England and the English" (a work, at that time, greatly in advance of the public mind), I wrote for him a critical account of Bentham's philosophy, a small part of which he incorporated in his text, and printed the rest (with an honourable acknowledgment), as an appendix. In this, along with the favourable, a part also of the unfavourable side of my estimation of Bentham's doctrines, considered as a complete philosophy, was for the first time put into print.

But an opportunity soon offered, by which, as it seemed, I might have it in my power to give more effectual aid, and at the same time, stimulus, to the "philosophic radical" party, than I had done hitherto. One of the projects occasionally talked of between my father and me, and some of the parliamentary and other Radicals who frequented his house, was the foundation of a periodical organ of philosophic radicalism, to take the place which the Westminster Review had been intended to fill: and the scheme had gone so far as to bring under discussion the pecuniary contributions which could be looked for, and the choice of an editor. Nothing, however, came of it for some time: but in the summer of 1834 Sir William Molesworth, himself a laborious student, and a precise and metaphysical thinker, capable of aiding the cause by his pen as well as by his purse, spontaneously proposed to establish a Review, provided I would consent to be the real, if I could not be the ostensible, editor. Such a proposal was not to be refused; and the review was founded, at first under the title of the London Review, and afterwards under that of the London and Westminster, Molesworth having bought the Westminster from its proprietor, General Thompson, and merged the two into one. In the years between 1834 and 1840 the conduct of this review occupied the greater part of my spare time. In the beginning, it did not, as a whole, by any means represent my opinions. I was under the necessity of conceding much to my inevitable associates. The Review was established to be the representative of the "philosophic radicals," with most of whom I was now at issue on many essential points, and among whom I could not even claim to be the most important individual. My father's co-operation as a writer we all deemed indispensable, and he wrote largely in it until prevented by his last illness. The subjects of his articles, and the strength and decision with which his opinions were expressed in them, made the Review at first derive its tone and colouring from him much more than from any of the other writers. I could not exercise editorial control over his articles, and I was sometimes obliged to sacrifice to him portions of my own. The old Westminster Review doctrines, but little modified, thus formed the staple of the review; but I hoped by the side of these, to introduce other ideas and another tone, and to obtain for my own shade of opinion a fair representation, along with those of other members of the party. With this end chiefly in view, I made it one of the peculiarities of the work that every article should bear an initial, or some other signature, and be held to express the opinions solely of the individual writer; the editor being only responsible for its being worth publishing and not in conflict with the objects for which the Review was set on foot. I had an opportunity of putting in practice my scheme of conciliation betwen the old and the new "philosophic radicalism," by the choice of a subject for my own first contribution. Professor Sedgwick, a man of eminence in a particular walk of natural science, but who should not have trespassed into philosophy, had lately published his Discourse on the Studies of Cambridge, which had as its most prominent feature an intemperate assault on analytic psychology and utilitarian ethics, in the form of an attack on Locke and Paley. This had excited great indignation in my father and others, which I thought it fully deserved. And here, I imagined, was an opportunity of at the same time repelling an unjust attack, and inserting into my defence of Hartleianism and Utilitarianism a number of the opinions which constituted my view of those subjects, as distinguished from that of my old associates. In this I partially succeeded, though my relation to my father would have made it painful to me in any case, and impossible in a review for which he wrote, to speak out my whole mind on the subject at this time.

I am, however, inclined to think that my father was not so much opposed as he seemed, to the modes of thought in which I believed myself to differ from him; that he did injustice to his own opinions by the unconscious exaggerations of an intellect emphatically polemical; and that when thinking without an adversary in view, he was willing to make room for a great portion of the truths he seemed to deny. I have frequently observed that he made large allowance in practice for considerations which seemed to have no place in his theory. His "Fragment on Mackintosh," which he wrote and published about this time, although I greatly admired some parts of it, I read as a whole with more pain than pleasure; yet on reading it again, long after, I found little in the opinions it contains, but what I think in the main just; and I can even sympathize in his disgust at the *verbiage* of Mackintosh, though his asperity towards it went not only beyond what was judicious, but beyond what was even fair. One thing, which I thought, at the time, of good augury, was the very favourable reception he gave to Tocqueville's "Democracy in America." It is true, he said and thought much more about what Tocqueville said in favour of Democracy, than about what he said of its disadvantages. Still, his high appreciation of a book which was at any rate an example of a mode of treating the question of government almost the reverse of his—wholly inductive and analytical, instead of purely ratiocinative—gave me great encouragement. He also approved of an article which I published in the first number following the junction of the two reviews, the essay reprinted in the Dissertations, under the title "Civilization;" into which I threw many of my new opinions, and criticised rather emphatically the mental and moral tendencies of the time, on grounds and in a manner which I certainly had not learnt from him.

All speculation, however, on the possible future developments of my father's opinions, and on the probabilities of permanent co-operation between him and me in the promulgation of our thoughts, was doomed to be cut short. During the whole of 1835 his health had been declining: his symptoms became unequivocally those of pulmonary consumption, and after lingering to the last stage of debility, he died on the 23rd of June, 1836. Until the last few days of his life there was no apparent abatement of intellectual vigour; his interest in all things and persons that had interested him through life was undiminished, nor did the approach of death cause the smallest wavering (as in so strong and firm a mind it was impossible that it should) in his convictions on the subject of religion. His principal satisfaction, after he knew that his end was near, seemed to be the thought of what he had done to make the world better than he found it; and his chief regret in not living longer, that he had not had time to do more.

His place is an eminent one in the literary, and even in the political history of his country; and it is far from honourable to the generation which has benefited by his worth, that he is so seldom mentioned, and, compared with men far his inferiors, so little remembered. This is probably to be ascribed mainly to two causes. In the first place, the thought of him merges too much in the deservedly superior fame of Bentham. Yet he was anything but Bentham's mere follower or disciple. Precisely because he was himself one of the most original thinkers of his time, he was one of the earliest to appreciate and adopt the most important mass of original thought which had been produced by the generation preceding him. His mind and Bentham's were essentially of different construction. He had not all Bentham's high qualities, but neither had Bentham all his. It would, indeed, be ridiculous to claim for him the praise of having accomplished for mankind such splendid services as Bentham's. He did not revolutionize, or rather create, one of the great departments of human thought. But, leaving out of the reckoning all that portion of his labours in which he benefited by what Bentham had done, and counting only what he achieved in a province in which Bentham had done nothing, that of analytic psychology, he will be known to posterity as one of the greatest names in that most important branch of speculation, on which all the moral and political sciences ultimately rest, and will mark one of the essential stages in its progress. The other reason which has made his fame less than he deserved, is that notwithstanding the great number of his opinions which, partly through his own efforts, have now been generally adopted, there was, on the whole, a marked opposition between his spirit and that of the present time. As Brutus was called the last of the Romans, so was he the last of the eighteenth century: he continued its tone of thought and sentiment into the nineteenth (though not unmodified nor unimproved), partaking neither in the good nor in the bad influences of the reaction against the eighteenth century, which was the great characteristic of the first half of the nineteenth. The eighteenth century was a great age, an age of strong and brave men, and he was a fit companion for its strongest and bravest. By his writings and his personal influence he was a great centre of light to his generation. During his later years he was quite as much the head and leader of the intellectual radicals in England, as Voltaire was of the *philosophes* of France. It is only one of his minor merits, that he was the originator of all sound statesmanship in regard to the subject of his largest work, India. He wrote on no subject which he did not enrich with valuable thought, and excepting the "Elements of Political Economy," a very useful book when

first written, but which has now for some time finished its
work, it will be long before any of his books will be wholly
superseded, or will cease to be instructive reading to students
of their subjects. In the power of influencing by mere force of
mind and character, the convictions and purposes of others,
and in the strenuous exertion of that power to promote freedom and progress, he left, as far as my knowledge extends,
no equal among men and but one among women.

Though acutely sensible of my own inferiority in the qualities by which he acquired his personal ascendancy, I had now
to try what it might be possible for me to accomplish without
him: and the Review was the instrument on which I built my
chief hopes of establishing a useful influence over the liberal
and democratic section of the public mind. Deprived of my
father's aid, I was also exempted from the restraints and
reticences by which that aid had been purchased. I did not
feel that there was any other radical writer or politician to
whom I was bound to defer, further than consisted with my
own opinions: and having the complete confidence of Molesworth, I resolved henceforth to give full scope to my own
opinions and modes of thought, and to open the Review
widely to all writers who were in sympathy with Progress as
I understood it, even though I should lose by it the support
of my former associates. Carlyle, consequently, became from
this time a frequent writer in the Review; Sterling, soon after,
an occasional one; and though each individual article continued to be the expression of the private sentiments of its
writer, the general tone conformed in some tolerable degree
to my opinions. For the conduct of the Review, under, and
in conjunction with me, I associated with myself a young
Scotchman of the name of Robertson, who had some ability
and information, much industry, and an active scheming head,
full of devices for making the Review more saleable, and on
whose capacities in that direction I founded a good deal of
hope: insomuch, that when Molesworth, in the beginning of
1837, became tired of carrying on the Review at a loss, and
desirous of getting rid of it (he had done *his* part honourably,
and at no small pecuniary cost,) I, very imprudently for my
own pecuniary interest, and very much from reliance on
Robertson's devices, determined to continue it at my own risk,
until his plans should have had a fair trial. The devices were
good, and I never had any reason to change my opinion of
them. But I do not believe that any devices would have made

a radical and democratic review defray its expenses, including a paid editor or sub-editor, and a liberal payment to writers. I myself and several frequent contributors gave our labour gratuitously, as we had done for Molesworth; but the paid contributors continued to be remunerated on the usual scale of the Edinburgh and Quarterly Reviews; and this could not be done from the proceeds of the sale.

In the same year, 1837, and in the midst of these occupations, I resumed the Logic. I had not touched my pen on the subject for five years, having been stopped and brought to a halt on the threshold of Induction. I had gradually discovered that what was mainly wanting, to overcome the difficulties of that branch of the subject, was a comprehensive, and, at the same time, accurate view of the whole circle of physical science, which I feared it would take me a long course of study to acquire; since I knew not of any book, or other guide, that would spread out before me the generalities and processes of the sciences, and I apprehended that I should have no choice but to extract them for myself, as I best could, from the details. Happily for me, Dr. Whewell, early in this year, published his History of the Inductive Sciences. I read it with eagerness, and found in it a considerable approximation to what I wanted. Much, if not most, of the philosophy of the work appeared open to objection; but the materials were there, for my own thoughts to work upon: and the author had given to those materials that first degree of elaboration, which so greatly facilitates and abridges the subsequent labour. I had now obtained what I had been waiting for. Under the impulse given me by the thoughts excited by Dr. Whewell, I read again Sir J. Herschel's Discourse on the Study of Natural Philosophy: and I was able to measure the progress my mind had made, by the great help I now found in this work—though I had read and even reviewed it several years before with little profit. I now set myself vigorously to work out the subject in thought and in writing. The time I bestowed on this had to be stolen from occupations more urgent. I had just two months to spare, at this period, in the intervals of writing for the Review. In these two months I completed the first draft of about a third, the most difficult third, of the book. What I had before written, I estimate at another third, so that only one-third remained. What I wrote at this time consisted of the remainder of the doctrine of Reasoning (the theory of Trains of Reasoning, and Demonstrative Science), and the greater part of the Book on Induction. When this was done, I had, as it seemed to me, untied all the really hard knots, and the completion of the book had become only a question of time. Having got thus far, I had to leave off in order to write two articles for the next number of the Review. When these were written, I returned to the subject, and now for the first time fell in with Comte's Cours de Philosophie Positive, or rather with the two volumes of it which were all that had at that time been published.

My theory of Induction was substantially completed before I knew of Comte's book; and it is perhaps well that I came to it by a different road from his, since the consequence has been that my treatise contains, what his certainly does not, a reduction of the inductive process to strict rules and to a scientific test, such as the Syllogism is for ratiocination. Comte is always precise and profound on the methods of investigation, but he does not even attempt any exact definition of the conditions of proof: and his writings show that he never attained a just conception of them. This, however, was specifically the problem, which, in treating of Induction, I had proposed to myself. Nevertheless, I gained much from Comte, with which to enrich my chapters in the subsequent rewriting: and his book was essential service to me in some of the parts which still remained to be thought out. As his subsequent volumes successively made their appearance, I read them with avidity, but, when he reached the subject of Social Science, with varying feelings. The fourth volume disappointed me: it contained those of his opinions on social subjects with which I most disagree. But the fifth, containing the connected view of history, rekindled all my enthusiasm; which the sixth (or concluding) volume did not materially abate. In a merely logical point of view, the only leading conception for which I am indebted to him is that of the Inverse Deductive Method, as the one chiefly applicable to the complicated subjects of History and Statistics: a process differing from the more common form of the Deductive Method in this—that instead of arriving at its conclusions by general reasoning, and verifying them by specific experience (as is the natural order in the deductive branches of physical science), it obtains its generalizations by a collation of specific experience, and verifies them by ascertaining whether they are such as would follow from known general principles. This was an idea entirely new to me when I found it in Comte: and but for him I might not soon (if ever) have arrived at it.

I had been long an ardent admirer of Comte's writings before I had any communication with himself; nor did I ever, to the last, see him in the body. But for some years we were frequent correspondents, until our correspondence became controversial, and our zeal cooled. I was the first to slacken correspondence; he was the first to drop it. I found, and he probably found likewise, that I could do no good to his mind, and that all the good he could do to mine, he did by his books. This would never have led to discontinuance of intercourse, if the differences between us had been on matters of simple doctrine. But they were chiefly on those points of opinion which blended in both of us with our strongest feelings, and determined the entire direction of our aspirations. I had fully agreed with him when he maintained that the mass of mankind, including even their rulers in all the practical departments of life, must, from the necessity of the case, accept most of their opinions on political and social matters, as they do on physical, from the authority of those who have bestowed more study on those subjects than they generally have it in their power to do. This lesson had been strongly impressed on me by the early work of Comte, to which I have adverted. And there was nothing in his great Treatise which I admired more than his remarkable exposition of the benefits which the nations of modern Europe have historically derived from the separation, during the middle ages, of temporal and spiritual power, and the distinct organization of the latter. I agreed with him that the moral and intellectual ascendancy, once exercised by priests, must in time pass into the hands of philosophers, and will naturally do so when they become sufficiently unanimous, and in other respects worthy to possess it. But when he exaggerated this line of thought into a practical system, in which philosophers were to be organized into a kind of corporate hierarchy, invested with almost the same spiritual supremacy (though without any secular power) once possessed by the Catholic church; when I found him relying on this spiritual authority as the only security for good government, the sole bulwark against practical oppression, and expecting that by it a system of despotism in the state and despotism in the family would be rendered innocuous and beneficial; it is not surprising, that while as logicians we were nearly at one, as sociologists we could travel together no further. M. Comte lived to carry out these doctrines to their extremest consequences, by planning, in his last work, the "Système de Politique Positive," the completest system of spiritual and temporal despotism which ever yet emanated from a human brain, unless possibly that of Ignatius Loyola: a system by which the yoke of general opinion, wielded by an organized body of spiritual teachers and rulers, would be made supreme over every action, and as far as is in human possibility, every thought, of every member of the community, as well in the things which regard only himself, as in those which concern the interests of others. It is but just to say that this work is a considerable improvement, in many points of feeling, over Comte's previous writings on the same subjects: but as an accession to social philosophy, the only value it seems to me to possess, consists in putting an end to the notion that no effectual moral authority can be maintained over society without the aid of religious belief; for Comte's work recognises no religion except that of Humanity, yet it leaves an irresistible conviction that any moral beliefs concurred in by the community generally, may be brought to bear upon the whole conduct and lives of its individual members, with an energy and potency truly alarming to think of. The book stands a monumental warning to thinkers on society and politics, of what happens when once men lose sight in their speculations, of the value of Liberty and of Individuality.

To return to myself. The Review engrossed, for some time longer, nearly all the time I could devote to authorship, or to thinking with authorship in view. The articles from the London and Westminster Review which are reprinted in the "Dissertations," are scarcely a fourth part of those I wrote. In the conduct of the Review I had two principal objects. One was to free philosophic radicalism from the reproach of sectarian Benthamism. I desired, while retaining the precision of expression, the definiteness of meaning, the contempt of declamatory phrases and vague generalities, which were so honourably characteristic both of Bentham and of my father, to give a wider basis and a more free and genial character to Radical speculations; to show that there was a Radical philosophy, better and more complete than Bentham's, while recognizing and incorporating all of Bentham's which is permanently valuable. In this first object I, to a certain extent, succeeded. The other thing I attempted, was to stir up the educated

Radicals, in and out of Parliament, to exertion, and induce them to make themselves, what I thought by using the proper means they might become—a powerful party capable of taking the government of the country, or at least of dictating the terms on which they should share it with the Whigs. This attempt was from the first chimerical: partly because the time was unpropitious, the Reform fervour being in its period of ebb, and the Tory influences powerfully rallying; but still more, because, as Austin so truly said, "the country did not contain the men." Among the Radicals in Parliament there were several qualified to be useful members of an enlightened Radical party, but none capable of forming and leading such a party. The exhortations I addressed to them found no response. One occasion did present itself when there seemed to be room for a bold and successful stroke for Radicalism. Lord Durham had left the ministry, by reason, as was thought, of their not being sufficiently liberal; he afterwards accepted from them the task of ascertaining and removing the causes of the Canadian rebellion; he had shown a disposition to surround himself at the outset with Radical advisers; one of his earliest measures, a good measure both in intention and in effect, having been disapproved and reversed by the Government at home, he had resigned his post, and placed himself openly in a position of quarrel with the ministers. Here was a possible chief for a Radical party in the person of a man of importance, who was hated by the Tories and had just been injured by the Whigs. Any one who had the most elementary notions of party tactics, must have attempted to make something of such an opportunity. Lord Durham was bitterly attacked from all sides, inveighed against by enemies, given up by timid friends; while those who would willingly have defended him did not know what to say. He appeared to be returning a defeated and discredited man. I had followed the Canadian events from the beginning; I had been one of the prompters of his prompters; his policy was almost exactly what mine would have been, and I was in a position to defend it. I wrote and published a manifesto in the Review, in which I took the very highest ground in his behalf, claiming for him not mere acquittal, but praise and honour. Instantly a number of other writers took up the tone: I believe there was a portion of truth in what Lord Durham, soon after, with polite exaggeration, said to me—that to this article might be ascribed the almost triumphal reception which he met with on his arrival in England. I believe it to have been the word in season, which, at a critical moment, does much to decide the result; the touch which determines whether a stone, set in motion at the top of an eminence, shall roll down on one side or on the other. All hopes connected with Lord Durham as a politician soon vanished; but with regard to Canadian, and generally to colonial policy, the cause was gained: Lord Durham's report, written by Charles Buller, partly under the inspiration of Wakefield, began a new era; its recommendations, extending to complete internal self-government, were in full operation in Canada within two or three years, and have been since extended to nearly all the other colonies, of European race, which have any claim to the character of important communities. And I may say that in successfully upholding the reputation of Lord Durham and his advisers at the most important moment, I contributed materially to this result.

One other case occurred during my conduct of the Review, which similarly illustrated the effect of taking a prompt initiative. I believe that the early success and reputation of Carlyle's French Revolution, were considerably accelerated by what I wrote about it in the Review. Immediately on its publication, and before the commonplace critics, all whose rules and modes of judgment it set at defiance, had time to preoccupy the public with their disapproval of it, I wrote and published a review of the book, hailing it as one of those productions of genius which are above all rules, and are a law to themselves. Neither in this case nor in that of Lord Durham do I ascribe the impression, which I think was produced by what I wrote, to any particular merit of execution: indeed, in at least one of the cases (the article on Carlyle) I do not think the execution was good. And in both instances, I am persuaded that anybody, in a position to be read, who had expressed the same opinion at the same precise time, and had made any tolerable statement of the just grounds for it, would have produced the same effects. But, after the complete failure of my hopes of putting a new life into radical politics by means of the Review, I am glad to look back on these two instances of success in an honest attempt to do immediate service to things and persons that deserved it.

After the last hope of the formation of a Radical party had disappeared, it was time for me to stop the heavy expenditure of time and money which the Review cost me. It had to some extent answered my personal purpose as a vehicle for my opinions. It had enabled me to express in print much of my altered mode of thought, and to separate myself in a marked manner from the narrower Benthamism of my early writings. This was done by the general tone of all I wrote, including various purely literary articles, but especially by the two papers (reprinted in the Dissertations) which attempted a philosophical estimate of Bentham and of Coleridge. In the first of these, while doing full justice to the merits of Bentham, I pointed out what I thought the errors and deficiencies of his philosophy. The substance of this criticism I still think perfectly just; but I have sometimes doubted whether it was right to publish it at that time. I have often felt that Bentham's philosophy, as an instrument of progress, has been to some extent discredited before it had done its work, and that to lend a hand towards lowering its reputation was doing more harm than service to improvement. Now, however, when a counter-reaction appears to be setting in towards what is good in Benthamism, I can look with more satisfaction on this criticism of its defects, especially as I have myself balanced it by vindications of the fundamental principles of Bentham's philosophy, which are reprinted along with it in the same collection. In the essay on Coleridge I attempted to characterize the European reaction against the negative philosophy of the eighteenth century: and here, if the effect only of this one paper were to be considered, I might be thought to have erred by giving undue prominence to the favourable side, as I had done in the case of Bentham to the unfavourable. In both cases, the impetus with which I had detached myself from what was untenable in the doctrines of Bentham and of the eighteenth century, may have carried me, though in appearance rather than in reality, too far on the contrary side. But as far as relates to the article on Coleridge, my defence is, that I was writing for Radicals and Liberals, and it was my business to dwell most on that in writers of a different school, from the knowledge of which they might derive most improvement.

The number of the Review which contained the paper on Coleridge, was the last which was published during my proprietorship. In the spring of 1840 I made over the Review to Mr. Hickson, who had been a frequent and very useful unpaid contributor under my management: only stipulating that the change should be marked by a resumption of the old name, that of Westminster Review. Under that name Mr. Hickson conducted it for ten years, on the plan of dividing among contributors only the net proceeds of the Review, giving his own labour as writer and editor gratuitously. Under the difficulty in obtaining writers, which arose from this low scale of payment, it is highly creditable to him that he was able to maintain, in some tolerable degree, the character of the Review as an organ of radicalism and progress. I did not cease altogether to write for the Review, but continued to send it occasional contributions, not, however, exclusively; for the greater circulation of the Edinburgh Review induced me from this time to offer articles to it also when I had anything to say for which it appeared to be a suitable vehicle. And the concluding volumes of "Democracy in America," having just then come out, I inaugurated myself as a contributor to the Edinburgh, by the article on that work, which heads the second volume of the "Dissertations."

VII. GENERAL VIEW OF THE REMAINDER OF MY LIFE.

FROM this time, what is worth relating of my life will come into a very small compass; for I have no further mental changes to tell of, but only, as I hope, a continued mental progress; which does not admit of a consecutive history, and the results of which, if real, will be best found in my writings. I shall, therefore, greatly abridge the chronicle of my subsequent years.

The first use I made of the leisure which I gained by disconnecting myself from the Review, was to finish the Logic. In July and August, 1838, I had found an interval in which to execute what was still undone of the original draft of the Third Book. In working out the logical theory of those laws of nature which are not laws of Causation, nor corollaries from such laws, I was led to recognize kinds as realities in nature, and not mere distinctions for convenience; a light which I had not obtained when the First Book was written, and which made it necessary for me to modify and enlarge several chapters of that Book. The Book on Language and Classification, and the chapter on the Classification of Fallacies, were drafted in the autumn of the same year; the remainder of the work, in the summer and autumn of 1840. From April following to the end of 1841, my spare time was devoted to a complete rewriting of the book from its commencement. It is in this way that all my books have been composed. They were always written at least twice over; a first draft of the entire work was completed to the very end of the subject, then the whole begun again *de novo;* but incorporating, in the second writing, all sentences and parts of sentences of the old draft, which appeared as suitable to my purpose as anything which I could write in lieu of them. I have found great advantages in this system of double redaction. It combines, better than any other mode of composition, the freshness and vigour of the first conception, with the superior precision and completeness resulting from prolonged thought. In my own case, moreover, I have found that the patience necessary for a careful elaboration of the details of composition and expression, costs much less effort after the entire subject has been once gone through, and the substance of all that I find to say has in some manner, however imperfect, been got upon paper. The only thing which I am careful, in the first draft, to make as perfect as I am able, is the arrangement. If that is bad, the whole thread on which the ideas string themselves becomes · twisted; thoughts placed in a wrong connexion are not expounded in a manner that suits the right, and a first draft with this original vice is next to useless as a foundation for the final treatment.

During the re-writing of the Logic, Dr. Whewell's Philosophy of the Inductive Sciences made its appearance; a circumstance fortunate for me, as it gave me what I greatly desired, a full treatment of the subject by an antagonist, and enabled me to present my ideas with greater clearness and emphasis as well as fuller and more varied development, in defending them against definite objections, or confronting them distinctly with an opposite theory. The controversies with Dr. Whewell, as well as much matter derived from Comte, were first introduced into the book in the course of the re-writing.

At the end of 1841, the book being ready for the press, I offered it to Murray, who kept it until too late for publication that season, and then refused it, for reasons which could just as well have been given at first. But I have had no cause to regret a rejection which led to my offering it to Mr. Parker, by whom it was published in the spring of 1843. My original expectations of success were extremely limited. Archbishop Whately had, indeed, rehabilitated the name of Logic, and the study of the forms, rules, and fallacies of Ratiocination; and Dr. Whewell's writings had begun to excite an interest in the other part of my subject, the theory of Induction. A treatise, however, on a matter so abstract, could not be expected to be popular; it could only be a book for students, and students on such subjects were not only (at least in England) few, but addicted chiefly to the opposite school of metaphysics, the ontological and "innate principles" school. I therefore did not expect that the book would have many readers, or approvers; and looked for little practical effect from it, save that of keeping the tradition unbroken of what I thought a better philosophy. What hopes I had of exciting any immediate attention, were mainly grounded on the polemical propensities of Dr. Whewell; who, I thought, from observation of his conduct in other cases, would probably do something to bring the book into notice, by replying, and that promptly, to the attack on his opinions. He did reply, but not till 1850, just in time for me to answer him in the third edition. How the book came to have, for a work of the kind, so much success, and what sort of persons compose the bulk of those who have bought, I will not venture to say read, it, I have never thoroughly understood. But taken in conjunction with the many proofs which have since been given of a revival of speculation, speculation too of a free kind, in many quarters, and above all (where at one time I should have least expected it) in the Universities, the fact becomes partially intelligible. I have never indulged the illusion that the book had made any considerable impression on philosophical opinion. The German, or à priori view of human knowledge, and of the knowing faculties, is likely for some time longer (though it may be hoped in a diminishing degree) to predominate among those who occupy themselves with such inquiries, both here and on the Continent. But the "System of Logic" supplies what was much wanted, a text-book of the opposite doctrine—that which derives all knowledge from experience, and all moral and intellectual qualities principally from the direction given to the associations. I make as humble an estimate as anybody of what either an analysis of logical processes, or any possible canons of evidence, can do by themselves, towards guiding or rectifying the operations of the understanding. Combined with other requisites, I certainly do think them of great use; but whatever may be the practical value of a true philosophy of these matters, it is hardly possible to exaggerate the mischiefs of a false one. The notion that truths external to the mind may be known by intuition or consciousness, independently of observation and experience, is, I am persuaded, in these times, the great intellectual support of false doctrines and bad institutions. By the aid of this theory, every inveterate belief and every intense feeling, of which the origin is not remembered, is enabled to dispense with the obligation of justifying itself by reason, and is erected into its own all-sufficient voucher and justification. There never was such an instrument devised for consecrating all deep-seated prejudices. And the chief strength of this false philosophy in morals, politics, and religion, lies in the appeal which it is accustomed to make to the evidence of mathematics and of the cognate branches of physical science. To expel it from these, is to drive it from its stronghold: and because this had never been effectually done, the intuitive school, even after what my father had written in his Analysis of the Mind, had in appearance, and as far as published writings were concerned, on the whole the best of the argument. In attempting to clear up the real nature of the evidence of mathematical and physical truths, the "System of Logic" met the intuitive philosophers on ground on which they had previously been deemed unassailable; and gave its own explanation, from experience and association, of that peculiar character of what are called necessary truths, which is adduced as proof that their evidence must come from a deeper source than experience. Whether this has been done effectually, is still *sub judice;* and even then, to deprive a mode of thought so strongly rooted in human prejudices and partialities, of its mere speculative support, goes but a very little way towards overcoming it; but though only a step, it is a quite indispensable one; for since, after all, prejudice can only be successfully combated by philosophy, no way can really be made against it permanently until it has been shown not to have philosophy on its side.

Being now released from any active concern in temporary politics, and from any literary occupation involving personal communication with contributors and others, I was enabled to indulge the inclination, natural to thinking persons when the age of boyish vanity is once past, for limiting my own society to a very few persons. General society, as now carried on in England, is so insipid an affair, even to the persons who make it what it is, that it is kept up for any reason rather than the pleasure it affords. All serious discussion on matters on which opinions differ, being considered ill-bred, and the national deficiency in liveliness and sociability having prevented the cultivation of the art of talking agreeably on trifles, in

which the French of the last century so much excelled, the
sole attraction of what is called society to those who are not at
the top of the tree, is the hope of being aided to climb a little
higher in it; while to those who are already at the top, it is
chiefly a compliance with custom, and with the supposed requirements of their station. To a person of any but a very
common order in thought or feeling, such society, unless he
has personal objects to serve by it, must be supremely unat-
tractive: and most people, in the present day, of any really
high class of intellect, make their contact with it so slight,
and at such long intervals, as to be almost considered as re-
tiring from it altogether. Those persons of any mental superiority who do otherwise, are, almost without exception,
greatly deteriorated by it. Not to mention loss of time, the
tone of their feelings is lowered: they become less in earnest
about those of their opinions respecting which they must remain silent in the society they frequent: they come to look
upon their most elevated objects as unpractical, or, at least,
too remote from realization to be more than a vision, or a
theory; and if, more fortunate than most, they retain their
higher principles unimpaired, yet with respect to the persons
and affairs of their own day they insensibly adopt the modes
of feeling and judgment in which they can hope for sympathy
from the company they keep. A person of high intellect
should never go into unintellectual society unless he can enter
it as an apostle; yet he is the only person with high objects
who can safely enter it at all. Persons even of intellectual
aspirations had much better, if they can, make their habitual
associates of at least their equals, and, as far as possible, their
superiors, in knowledge, intellect, and elevation of sentiment.
Moreover, if the character is formed, and the mind made up,
on the few cardinal points of human opinion, agreement of
conviction and feeling on these, has been felt in all times to
be an essential requisite of anything worthy the name of
friendship, in a really earnest mind. All these circumstances
united, made the number very small of those whose society,
and still more whose intimacy, I now voluntarily sought.

Among these, by far the principal was the incomparable
friend of whom I have already spoken. At this period she lived
mostly with one young daughter, in a quiet part of the country, and only occasionally in town, with her first husband, Mr.
Taylor. I visited her equally in both places; and was greatly
indebted to the strength of character which enabled her to

disregard the false interpretations liable to be put on the frequency of my visits to her while living generally apart from Mr. Taylor, and on our occasionally travelling together, though in all other respects our conduct during those years gave not the slightest ground for any other supposition than the true one, that our relation to each other at that time was one of strong affection and confidential intimacy only. For though we did not consider the ordinances of society binding on a subject so entirely personal, we did feel bound that our conduct should be such as in no degree to bring discredit on her husband, nor therefore on herself.

In this third period (as it may be termed) of my mental progress, which now went hand in hand with hers, my opinions gained equally in breadth and depth, I understood more things, and those which I had understood before, I now understood more thoroughly. I had now completely turned back from what there had been of excess in my reaction against Benthamism. I had, at the height of that reaction, certainly become much more indulgent to the common opinions of society and the world, and more willing to be content with seconding the superficial improvement which had begun to take place in those common opinions, than became one whose convictions on so many points, differed fundamentally from them. I was much more inclined, than I can now approve, to put in abeyance the more decidedly heretical part of my opinions, which I now look upon as almost the only ones, the assertion of which tends in any way to regenerate society. But in addition to this, our opinions were far *more* heretical than mine had been in the days of my most extreme Benthamism. In those days I had seen little further than the old school of political economists into the possibilities of fundamental improvement in social arrangements. Private property, as now understood, and inheritance, appeared to me, as to them, the *dernier mot* of legislation: and I looked no further than to mitigating the inequalities consequent on these institutions, by getting rid of primogeniture and entails. The notion that it was possible to go further than this in removing the injustice—for injustice it is, whether admitting of a complete remedy or not—involved in the fact that some are born to riches and the vast majority to poverty, I then reckoned chimerical, and only hoped that by universal education, leading to voluntary restraint on population, the portion of the poor might be made more tolerable. In short, I was a democrat, but not the least of a Socialist. We were now much less democrats than I had been, because so long as education continues to be so wretchedly imperfect, we dreaded the ignorance and especially the selfishness and brutality of the mass: but our ideal of ultimate improvement went far beyond Democracy, and would class us decidedly under the general designation of Socialists. While we repudiated with the greatest energy that tyranny of society over the individual which most Socialistic systems are supposed to involve, we yet looked forward to a time when society will no longer be divided into the idle and the industrious; when the rule that they who do not work shall not eat, will be applied not to paupers only, but impartially to all; when the division of the produce of labour, instead of depending, as in so great a degree it now does, on the accident of birth, will be made by concert on an acknowledged principle of justice; and when it will no longer either be, or be thought to be, impossible for human beings to exert themselves strenuously in procuring benefits which are not to be exclusively their own, but to be shared with the society they belong to. The social problem of the future we considered to be, how to unite the greatest individual liberty of action, with a common ownership in the raw material of the globe, and an equal participation of all in the benefits of combined labour. We had not the presumption to suppose that we could already foresee, by what precise form of institutions these objects could most effectually be attained, or at how near or how distant a period they would become practicable. We saw clearly that to render any such social transformation either possible or desirable, an equivalent change of character must take place both in the uncultivated herd who now compose the labouring masses, and in the immense majority of their employers. Both these classes must learn by practice to labour and combine for generous, or at all events for public and social purposes, and not, as hitherto, solely for narrowly interested ones. But the capacity to do this has always existed in mankind, and is not, nor is ever likely to be, extinct. Education, habit, and the cultivation of the sentiments, will make a common man dig or weave for his country, as readily as fight for his country. True enough, it is only by slow degrees, and a system of culture prolonged through successive generations, that men in general can be brought up to this point. But the hindrance is not in the essential constitution of human nature. Interest in the common good is at present so weak a motive in the generality, not because it can never be otherwise, but because the mind is not accustomed to dwell on it as it dwells from morning till night on things which tend only to personal advantage. When called into activity, as only self-interest now is, by the daily course of life, and spurred from behind by the love of distinction and the fear of shame, it is capable of producing, even in common men, the most strenuous exertions as well as the most heroic sacrifices. The deep-rooted selfishness which forms the general character of the existing state of society, is *so* deeply rooted, only because the whole course of existing institutions tends to foster it; modern institutions in some respects more than ancient, since the occasions on which the individual is called on to do anything for the public without receiving its pay, are far less frequent in modern life, than the smaller commonwealths of antiquity. These considerations did not make us overlook the folly of premature attempts to dispense with the inducements of private interest in social affairs, while no substitute for them has been or can be provided: but we regarded all existing institutions and social arrangements as being (in a phrase I once heard from Austin) "merely provisional," and we welcomed with the greatest pleasure and interest all socialistic experiments by select individuals (such as the Co-operative Societies), which, whether they succeeded or failed, could not but operate as a most useful education of those who took part in them, by cultivating their capacity of acting upon motives pointing directly to the general good, or making them aware of the defects which render them and others incapable of doing so.

In the "Principles of Political Economy," these opinions were promulgated, less clearly and fully in the first edition, rather more so in the second, and quite unequivocally in the third. The difference arose partly from the change of times, the first edition having been written and sent to press before the French Revolution of 1848, after which the public mind became more open to the reception of novelties in opinion, and doctrines appeared moderate which would have been thought very startling a short time before. In the first edition the difficulties of Socialism were stated so strongly, that the tone was on the whole that of opposition to it. In the year or two which followed, much time was given to the study of the best Socialistic writers on the Continent, and to meditation and discussion on the whole range of topics involved in the controversy: and the result was that most of what had been written on the subject in the first edition was cancelled, and replaced by arguments and reflections which represent a more advanced opinion.

The Political Economy was far more rapidly executed than the Logic, or indeed than anything of importance which I had previously written. It was commenced in the autumn of 1845, and was ready for the press before the end of 1847. In this period of little more than two years there was an interval of six months during which the work was laid aside, while I was writing articles in the Morning Chronicle (which unexpectedly entered warmly into my purpose) urging the formation of peasant properties on the waste lands of Ireland. This was during the period of the Famine, the winter of 1846–47, when the stern necessities of the time seemed to afford a chance of gaining attention for what appeared to me the only mode of combining relief to immediate destitution with permanent improvement of the social and economical condition of the Irish people. But the idea was new and strange; there was no English precedent for such a proceeding: and the profound ignorance of English politicians and the English public concerning all social phenomena not generally met with in England (however common elsewhere), made my endeavours an entire failure. Instead of a great operation on the waste lands, and the conversion of cottiers into proprietors, Parliament passed a Poor Law for maintaining them as paupers: and if the nation has not since found itself in inextricable difficulties from the joint operation of the old evils and the quack remedy, it is indebted for its deliverance to that most unexpected and surprising fact, the depopulation of Ireland, commenced by famine, and continued by emigration.

The rapid success of the Political Economy showed that the public wanted, and were prepared for such a book. Published early in 1848, an edition of a thousand copies was sold in less than a year. Another similar edition was published in the spring of 1849; and a third, of 1250 copies, early in 1852. It was, from the first, continually cited and referred to as an authority, because it was not a book merely of abstract science, but also of application, and treated Political Economy not as a thing by itself, but as a fragment of a greater whole; a branch of Social Philosophy, so interlinked with all the other branches, that its conclusions, even in its own peculiar province, are only true conditionally, subject to interference and counteraction from causes not directly within its scope:

while to the character of a practical guide it has no pretension, apart from other classes of considerations. Political Economy, in truth, has never pretended to give advice to mankind with no lights but its own; though people who knew nothing but political economy (and therefore knew that ill) have taken upon themselves to advise, and could only do so by such lights as they had. But the numerous sentimental enemies of political economy, and its still more numerous interested enemies in sentimental guise, have been very successful in gaining belief for this among other unmerited imputations against it, and the "Principles" having, in spite of the freedom of many of its opinions, become for the present the most popular treatise on the subject, has helped to disarm the enemies of so important a study. The amount of its worth as an exposition of the science, and the value of the different applications which it suggests, others of course must judge.

For a considerable time after this, I published no work of magnitude; though I still occasionally wrote in periodicals, and my correspondence (much of it with persons quite unknown to me), on subjects of public interest, swelled to a considerable bulk. During these years I wrote or commenced various Essays, for eventual publication, on some of the fundamental questions of human and social life, with regard to several of which I have already much exceeded the severity of the Horatian precept. I continued to watch with keen interest the progress of public events. But it was not, on the whole, very encouraging to me. The European reaction after 1848, and the success of an unprincipled usurper in December, 1851, put an end, as it seemed, to all present hope for freedom or social improvement in France and the Continent. In England, I had seen and continued to see many of the opinions of my youth obtain general recognition, and many of the reforms in institutions, for which I had through life contended, either effected or in course of being so. But these changes had been attended with much less benefit to human well-being than I should formerly have anticipated, because they had produced very little improvement in that which all real amelioration in the lot of mankind depends on, their intellectual and moral state: and it might even be questioned if the various causes of deterioration which had been at work in the meanwhile, had not more than counterbalanced the tendencies to improvement. I had learnt from experience that many false opinions may be exchanged for true ones, without in the least altering the habits of mind of which false opinions are the result. The English public, for example, are quite as raw and undiscerning on subjects of political economy since the nation has been converted to free-trade, as they were before; and are still further from having acquired better habits of thought and feeling, or being in any way better fortified against error, on subjects of a more elevated character. For, though they have thrown off certain errors, the general discipline of their minds, intellectually and morally, is not altered. I am now convinced, that no great improvements in the lot of mankind are possible, until a great change takes place in the fundamental constitution of their modes of thought. The old opinions in religion, morals, and politics, are so much discredited in the more intellectual minds as to have lost the greater part of their efficacy for good, while they have still life enough in them to be a powerful obstacle to the growing up of any better opinions on those subjects. When the philosophic minds of the world can no longer believe its religion, or can only believe it with modifications amounting to an essential change of its character, a transitional period commences, of weak convictions, paralysed intellects, and growing laxity of principle, which cannot terminate until a renovation has been effected in the basis of their belief leading to the elevation of some faith, whether religious or merely human, which they can really believe: and when things are in this state, all thinking or writing which does not tend to promote such a renovation, is of very little value beyond the moment. Since there was little in the apparent condition of the public mind, indicative of any tendency in this direction, my view of the immediate prospects of human improvement was not sanguine. More recently a spirit of free speculation has sprung up, giving a more encouraging prospect of the gradual mental emancipation of England; and concurring with the renewal under better auspices, of the movement for political freedom in the rest of Europe, has given to the present condition of human affairs a more hopeful aspect.

Between the time of which I have now spoken, and the present, took place the most important events of my private life. The first of these was my marriage, in April, 1851, to the lady whose incomparable worth had made her friendship the greatest source to me both of happiness and of improvement, during many years in which we never expected to be in any closer relation to one another. Ardently as I should have aspired to this complete union of our lives at any time in the course of my existence at which it had been practicable, I, as much as my wife, would far rather have foregone that privilege for ever, than have owed it to the premature death of one for whom I had the sincerest respect, and she the strongest affection. That event, however, having taken place in July, 1849, it was granted to me to derive from that evil my own greatest good, by adding to the partnership of thought, feeling, and writing which had long existed, a partnership of our entire existence. For seven and a half years that blessing was mine; for seven and a half only! I can say nothing which could describe, even in the faintest manner, what that loss was and is. But because I know that she would have wished it, I endeavour to make the best of what life I have left, and to work on for her purposes with such diminished strength as can be derived from thoughts of her, and communion with her memory.

During the years which intervened between the commencement of my married life and the catastrophe which closed it, the principal occurrences of my outward existence (unless I count as such a first attack of the family disease, and a consequent journey of more than six months for the recovery of health, in Italy, Sicily, and Greece) had reference to my position in the India House. In 1856 I was promoted to the rank of chief of the office in which I had served for upwards of thirty-three years. The appointment, that of Examiner of India Correspondence, was the highest, next to that of Secretary, in the East India Company's home service, involving the general superintendence of all the correspondence with the Indian Governments, except the military, naval, and financial. I held this office as long as it continued to exist, being a little more than two years; after which it pleased Parliament, in other words Lord Palmerston, to put an end to the East India Company as a branch of the government of India under the Crown, and convert the administration of that country into a thing to be scrambled for by the second and third class of English parliamentary politicians. I was the chief manager of the resistance which the Company made to their own political extinction. To the letters and petitions I wrote for them, and the concluding chapter of my treatise on Representative Government, I must refer for my opinions on the folly and mischief of this ill-considered change. Personally I considered myself a gainer by it, as I had given enough of my life to

India, and was not unwilling to retire on the liberal compensation granted. After the change was consummated, Lord Stanley, the first Secretary of State for India, made me the honourable offer of a seat in the Council, and the proposal was subsequently renewed by the Council itself, on the first occasion of its having to supply a vacancy in its own body. But the conditions of Indian government under the new system made me anticipate nothing but useless vexation and waste of effort from any participation in it: and nothing that has since happened has had any tendency to make me regret my refusal.

During the two years which immediately preceded the cessation of my official life, my wife and I were working together at the "Liberty." I had first planned and written it as a short essay in 1854. It was in mounting the steps of the Capitol, in January, 1855, that the thought first arose of converting it into a volume. None of my writings have been either so carefully composed, or so sedulously corrected as this. After it had been written as usual twice over, we kept it by us, bringing it out from time to time, and going through it *de novo*, reading, weighing, and criticizing every sentence. Its final revision was to have been a work of the winter of 1858–9, the first after my retirement, which we had arranged to pass in the South of Europe. That hope and every other were frustrated by the most unexpected and bitter calamity of her death—at Avignon, on our way to Montpellier, from a sudden attack of pulmonary congestion.

Since then I have sought for such alleviation as my state admitted of, by the mode of life which most enabled me to feel her still near me. I bought a cottage as close as possible to the place where she is buried, and there her daughter (my fellow-sufferer and now my chief comfort) and I, live constantly during a great portion of the year. My objects in life are solely those which were hers; my pursuits and occupations those in which she shared, or sympathized, and which are indissolubly associated with her. Her memory is to me a religion, and her approbation the standard by which, summing up as it does all worthiness, I endeavour to regulate my life.

In resuming my pen some years after closing the preceding narrative, I am influenced by a desire not to leave incomplete the record, for the sake of which chiefly this biographical sketch was undertaken, of the obligations I owe to those who have either contributed essentially to my own mental development or had a direct share in my writings and in whatever else of a public nature I have done. In the preceding pages, this record, so far as it relates to my wife, is not so detailed and precise as it ought to be; and since I lost her, I have had other help, not less deserving and requiring acknowledgment.

When two persons have their thoughts and speculations completely in common; when all subjects of intellectual or moral interest are discussed between them in daily life, and probed to much greater depths than are usually or conveniently sounded in writings intended for general readers; when they set out from the same principles, and arrive at their conclusions by processes pursued jointly, it is of little consequence in respect to the question of originality, which of them holds the pen; the one who contributes least to the composition may contribute most to the thought; the writings which result are the joint product of both, and it must often be impossible to disentangle their respective parts, and affirm that this belongs to one and that to the other. In this wide sense, not only during the years of our married life, but during many of the years of confidential friendship which preceded it, all my published writings were as much my wife's work as mine; her share in them constantly increasing as years advanced. But in certain cases, what belongs to her can be distinguished, and specially identified. Over and above the general influence which her mind had over mine, the most valuable ideas and features in these joint productions—those which have been most fruitful of important results, and have contributed most to the success and reputation of the works themselves—originated with her, were emanations from her mind, my part in them being no greater than in any of the thoughts which I found in previous writers, and made my own only by incorporating them with my own system of thought. During the greater part of my literary life I have performed the office in relation to her, which from a rather early period I had considered as the most useful part that I was qualified to take in the domain of thought, that of an interpreter of original thinkers, and mediator between them and the public; for I had always a humble opinion of my own powers as an original thinker, except in abstract science (logic, metaphysics, and the theoretic principles of political economy and politics), but thought myself much superior to most of my contemporaries in willingness and ability to learn from everybody; as I found

hardly any one who made such a point of examining what was
said in defence of all opinions, however new or however old,
in the conviction that even if they were errors there might be
a substratum of truth underneath them, and that in any case
the discovery of what it was that made them plausible, would
be a benefit to truth. I had, in consequence, marked out this
as a sphere of usefulness in which I was under a special obligation to make myself active: the more so, as the acquaintance I had formed with the ideas of the Coleridgians, of the
German thinkers, and of Carlyle, all of them fiercely opposed
to the mode of thought in which I had been brought up, had
convinced me that along with much error they possessed
much truth, which was veiled from minds otherwise capable
of receiving it by the transcendental and mystical phraseology
in which they were accustomed to shut it up, and from which
they neither cared, nor knew how, to disengage it; and I did
not despair of separating the truth from the error, and expressing it in terms which would be intelligible and not repulsive to those on my own side in philosophy. Thus prepared,
it will easily be believed that when I came into close intellectual communion with a person of the most eminent faculties, whose genius, as it grew and unfolded itself in thought,
continually struck out truths far in advance of me, but in
which I could not, as I had done in those others, detect any
mixture of error, the greatest part of my mental growth consisted in the assimilation of those truths, and the most valuable
part of my intellectual work was in building the bridges and
clearing the paths which connected them with my general
system of thought.*

* The steps in my mental growth for which I was indebted to her were far
from being those which a person wholly uninformed on the subject would
probably suspect. It might be supposed, for instance, that my strong convictions on the complete equality in all legal, political, social and domestic relations, which ought to exist between men and women, may have been adopted
or learnt from her. This was so far from being the fact, that those convictions
were among the earliest results of the application of my mind to political
subjects, and the strength with which I held them was, as I believe, more
than anything else, the originating cause of the interest she felt in me. What
is true is, that until I knew her, the opinion was in my mind, little more than
an abstract principle. I saw no more reason why women should be held in
legal subjection to other people, than why men should. I was certain that
their interests required fully as much protection as those of men, and were
quite as little likely to obtain it without an equal voice in making the laws
by which they are to be bound. But that perception of the vast practical
bearings of women's disabilities which found expression in the book on the
"Subjection of Women" was acquired mainly through her teaching. But for
her rare knowledge of human nature and comprehension of moral and social
influences, though I should doubtless have held my present opinions, I should
have had a very insufficient perception of the mode in which the consequences

The first of my books in which her share was conspicuous was the "Principles of Political Economy." The "System of Logic" owed little to her except in the minuter matters of composition, in which respect my writings, both great and small, have largely benefited by her accurate and clear-sighted criticism.* The chapter of the Political Economy which has had a greater influence on opinion than all the rest, that on "the Probable Future of the Labouring Classes," is entirely due to her: in the first draft of the book, that chapter did not exist. She pointed out the need of such a chapter, and the extreme imperfection of the book without it: she was the cause of my writing it; and the more general part of the chapter, the statement and discussion of the two opposite theories respecting the proper condition of the labouring classes, was wholly an exposition of her thoughts, often in words taken from her own lips. The purely scientific part of the Political Economy I did not learn from her; but it was chiefly her influence that gave to the book that general tone by which it is distinguished from all previous expositions of Political Economy that had any pretension to being scientific, and which has made it so useful in conciliating minds which those previous expositions had repelled. This tone consisted chiefly in making the proper distinction between the laws of the Production of Wealth, which are real laws of nature, dependent on the properties of objects, and the modes of its Distribution,

---

of the inferior position of women intertwine themselves with all the evils of existing society and with all the difficulties of human improvement. I am indeed painfully conscious how much of her best thoughts on the subject I have failed to reproduce, and how greatly that little treatise falls short of what would have been if she had put on paper her entire mind on this question, or had lived to revise and improve, as she certainly would have done, my imperfect statement of the case.

* The only person from whom I received any direct assistance in the preparation of the "System of Logic" was Mr. Bain, since so justly celebrated for his philosophical writings. He went carefully through the manuscript before it was sent to press, and enriched it with a great number of additional examples and illustrations from science; many of which, as well as some detached remarks of his own in confirmation of my logical views, I inserted nearly in his own words.

My obligations to Comte were only to his writings—to the part which had then been published of his "Système de Philosophie Positive:" and, as has been seen from what I have said in the Narrative, the amount of these obligations is far less than has sometimes been asserted. The first volume, which contains all the fundamental doctrines of the book, was substantially complete before I had seen Comte's treatise. I derived from him many valuable thoughts, conspicuously in the chapter on Hypotheses and in the view taken of the logic of algebra: but it is only in the concluding Book, on the Logic of the Moral Sciences, that I owe to him any radical improvement in my conception of the application of logical methods. This improvement I have stated and characterized in a former part of the present Memoir.

which, subject to certain conditions, depend on human will. The common run of political economists confuse these together, under the designation of economic laws, which they deem incapable of being defeated or modified by human effort; ascribing the same necessity to things dependent on the unchangeable conditions of our earthly existence, and to those which, being but the necessary consequences of particular social arrangements, are merely co-extensive with these: given certain institutions and customs, wages, profits, and rent will be determined by certain causes; but this class of political economists drop the indispensable presupposition, and argue that these causes must, by an inherent necessity, against which no human means can avail, determine the shares which fall, in the division of the produce, to labourers, capitalists, and landlords. The "Principles of Political Economy" yielded to none of its predecessors in aiming at the scientific appreciation of the action of these causes, under the conditions which they presuppose; but it set the example of not treating those conditions as final. The economic generalizations which depend, not on necessities of nature but on those combined with the existing arrangements of society, it deals with only as provisional, and as liable to be much altered by the progress of social improvement. I had indeed partially learnt this view of things from the thoughts awakened in me by the speculations of the St. Simonians; but it was made a living principle pervading and animating the book by my wife's promptings. This example illustrates well the general character of what she contributed to my writings. What was abstract and purely scientific was generally mine; the properly human element came from her: in all that concerned the application of philosophy to the exigencies of human society and progress, I was her pupil, alike in boldness of speculation and cautiousness of practical judgment. For, on the one hand, she was much more courageous and far-sighted than without her I should have been, in anticipations of an order of things to come, in which many of the limited generalizations now so often confounded with universal principles will cease to be applicable. Those parts of my writings, and especially of the Political Economy, which contemplate possibilities in the future such as, when affirmed by Socialists, have in general been fiercely denied by political economists, would, but for her, either have been absent, or the suggestions would have been made much more timidly and in a more qualified form. But while she thus rendered me bolder in speculation on human affairs, her practical turn of mind, and her almost unerring estimate of practical obstacles, repressed in me all tendencies that were really visionary. Her mind invested all ideas in a concrete shape, and formed to itself a conception of how they would actually work: and her knowledge of the existing feelings and conduct of mankind was so seldom at fault, that the weak point in any unworkable suggestion seldom escaped her.

The "Liberty" was more directly and literally our joint production than anything else which bears my name, for there was not a sentence of it that was not several times gone through by us together, turned over in many ways, and carefully weeded of any faults, either in thought or expression, that we detected in it. It is in consequence of this that, although it never underwent her final revision, it far surpasses, as a mere specimen of composition, anything which has proceeded from me either before or since. With regard to the thoughts, it is difficult to identify any particular part or element as being more hers than all the rest. The whole mode of thinking of which the book was the expression, was emphatically hers. But I also was so thoroughly imbued with it, that the same thoughts naturally occurred to us both. That I was thus penetrated with it, however, I owe in a great degree to her. There was a moment in my mental progress when I might easily have fallen into a tendency towards over-government, both social and political; as there was also a moment when, by reaction from a contrary excess, I might have become a less thorough radical and democrat than I am. In both these points, as in many others, she benefited me as much by keeping me right where I was right, as by leading me to new truths, and ridding me of errors. My great readiness and eagerness to learn from everybody, and to make room in my opinions for every new acquisition by adjusting the old and the new to one another, might, but for her steadying influence, have seduced me into modifying my early opinions too much. She was in nothing more valuable to my mental development than by her just measure of the relative importance of different considerations, which often protected me from allowing to truths I had only recently learnt to see, a more important place in my thoughts than was properly their due.

The "Liberty" is likely to survive longer than anything else

* A few dedicatory lines acknowledging what the book owed to her, were prefixed to some of the presentation copies of the Political Economy on its first publication. Her dislike of publicity alone prevented their insertion in the other copies of the work.

that I have written (with the possible exception of the
"Logic"), because the conjunction of her mind with mine has
rendered it a kind of philosophic text-book of a single truth,
which the changes progressively taking place in modern society tend to bring out into ever stronger relief: the importance,
to man and society, of a large variety in types of character,
and of giving full freedom to human nature to expand itself
in innumerable and conflicting directions. Nothing can better
show how deep are the foundations of this truth, than the
great impression made by the exposition of it at a time which,
to superficial observation, did not seem to stand much in need
of such a lesson. The fears we expressed, lest the inevitable
growth of social equality and of the government of public
opinion, should impose on mankind an oppressive yoke of uniformity in opinion and practice, might easily have appeared
chimerical to those who looked more at present facts than at
tendencies; for the gradual revolution that is taking place in
society and institutions has, thus far, been decidedly favourable to the development of new opinions, and has procured
for them a much more unprejudiced hearing than they previously met with. But this is a feature belonging to periods of
transition, when old notions and feelings have been unsettled,
and no new doctrines have yet succeeded to their ascendancy.
At such times people of any mental activity, having given up
many of their old beliefs, and not feeling quite sure that those
they still retain can stand unmodified, listen eagerly to new
opinions. But this state of things is necessarily transitory: some
particular body of doctrine in time rallies the majority round
it, organizes social institutions and modes of action conformably to itself, education impresses this new creed upon the new
generations without the mental processes that have led to it,
and by degrees it acquires the very same power of compression, so long exercised by the creeds of which it had taken
the place. Whether this noxious power will be exercised, depends on whether mankind have by that time become aware
that it cannot be exercised without stunting and dwarfing
human nature. It is then that the teachings of the "Liberty"
will have their greatest value. And it is to be feared that they
will retain that value a long time.

As regards originality, it has of course no other than that
which every thoughtful mind gives to its own mode of conceiving and expressing truths which are common property.
The leading thought of the book is one which though in many
ages confined to insulated thinkers, mankind have probably

at no time since the beginning of civilization been entirely
without. To speak only of the last few generations, it is distinctly contained in the vein of important thought respecting
education and culture, spread through the European mind by
the labours and genius of Pestalozzi. The unqualified cham-
pionship of it by Wilhelm von Humboldt is referred to in the
book; but he by no means stood alone in his own country.
During the early part of the present century the doctrine of
the rights of individuality, and the claim of the moral nature
to develop itself in its own way, was pushed by a whole
school of German authors even to exaggeration; and the writings of Goethe, the most celebrated of all German authors,
though not belonging to that or to any other school, are penetrated throughout by views of morals and of conduct in life,
often in my opinion not defensible, but which are incessantly
seeking whatever defence they admit of in the theory of the
right and duty of self-development. In our own country, before the book "On Liberty" was written, the doctrine of Individuality had been enthusiastically asserted, in a style of
vigorous declamation sometimes reminding one of Fichte, by
Mr. William Maccall, in a series of writings of which the most
elaborate is entitled "Elements of Individualism:" and a remarkable American, Mr. Warren, had framed a System of
Society, on the foundation of "the Sovereignty of the Individual," had obtained a number of followers, and had actually
commenced the formation of a Village Community (whether
it now exists I know not), which, though bearing a superficial
resemblance to some of the projects of Socialists, is diametri-
cally opposite to them in principle, since it recognizes no
authority whatever in Society over the individual, except to
enforce equal freedom of development for all individualities.
As the book which bears my name claimed no originality for
any of its doctrines, and was not intended to write their history, the only author who had preceded me in their assertion,
of whom I thought it appropriate to say anything, was Humboldt, who furnished the motto to the work; although in one
passage I borrowed from the Warrenites their phrase, the
sovereignty of the individual. It is hardly necessary here to
remark that there are abundant differences in detail, between
the conception of the doctrine by any of the predecessors I
have mentioned, and that set forth in the book.

After my irreparable loss, one of my earliest cares was to
print and publish the treatise, so much of which was the work
of her whom I had lost, and consecrate it to her memory. I

have made no alteration or addition to it, nor shall I ever. Though it wants the last touch of her hand, no substitute for that touch shall ever be attempted by mine.

The political circumstances of the time induced me, shortly after, to complete and publish a pamphlet ("Thoughts on Parliamentary Reform"), part of which had been written some years previously, on the occasion of one of the abortive Reform Bills, and had at the time been approved and revised by her. Its principal features were, hostility to the Ballot (a change of opinion in both of us, in which she rather preceded me), and a claim of representation for minorities; not, however, at that time going beyond the cumulative vote proposed by Mr. Garth Marshall. In finishing the pamphlet for publication, with a view to the discussions on the Reform Bill of Lord Derby's and Mr. Disraeli's Government in 1859, I added a third feature, a plurality of votes, to be given, not to property, but to proved superiority of education. This recommended itself to me as a means of reconciling the irresistible claim of every man or woman to be consulted, and to be allowed a voice, in the regulation of affairs which vitally concern them, with the superiority of weight justly due to opinions grounded on superiority of knowledge. The suggestion, however, was one which I had never discussed with my almost infallible counsellor, and I have no evidence that she would have concurred in it. As far as I have been able to observe, it has found favour with nobody; all who desire any sort of inequality in the electoral vote, desiring it in favour of property and not of intelligence or knowledge. If it ever overcomes the strong feeling which exists against it, this will only be after the establishment of a systematic National Education by which the various grades of politically valuable acquirement may be accurately defined and authenticated. Without this it will always remain liable to strong, possibly conclusive, objections; and with this, it would perhaps not be needed.

It was soon after the publication of "Thoughts on Parliamentary Reform," that I became acquainted with Mr. Hare's admirable system of Personal Representation, which, in its present shape, was then for the first time published. I saw in this great practical and philosophical idea, the greatest improvement of which the system of representative government is susceptible; an improvement which, in the most felicitous manner, exactly meets and cures the grand, and what before seemed the inherent, defect of the representative system; that of giving to a numerical majority all power, instead of only a power proportional to its numbers, and enabling the strongest party to exclude all weaker parties from making their opinions heard in the assembly of the nation, except through such opportunity as may be given to them by the accidentally unequal distribution of opinions in different localities. To these great evils nothing more than very imperfect palliatives had seemed possible; but Mr. Hare's system affords a radical cure. This great discovery, for it is no less, in the political art, inspired me, as I believe it has inspired all thoughtful persons who have adopted it, with new and more sanguine hopes respecting the prospects of human society; by freeing the form of political institutions towards which the whole civilized world is manifestly and irresistibly tending, from the chief part of what seemed to qualify, or render doubtful, its ultimate benefits. Minorities, so long as they remain minorities, are, and ought to be, outvoted; but under arrangements which enable any assemblage of voters, amounting to a certain number, to place in the legislature a representative of its own choice, minorities cannot be suppressed. Independent opinions will force their way into the council of the nation and make themselves heard there, a thing which often cannot happen in the existing forms of representative democracy; and the legislature, instead of being weeded of individual peculiarities and entirely made up of men who simply represent the creed of great political or religious parties, will comprise a large proportion of the most eminent individual minds in the country, placed there, without reference to party, by voters who appreciate their individual eminence. I can understand that persons, otherwise intelligent, should, for want of sufficient examination, be repelled from Mr. Hare's plan by what they think the complex nature of its machinery. But any one who does not feel the want which the scheme is intended to supply; any one who throws it over as a mere theoretical subtlety or crotchet, tending to no valuable purpose, and unworthy of the attention of practical men, may be pronounced an incompetent statesman, unequal to the politics of the future. I mean, unless he is a minister or aspires to become one: for we are quite accustomed to a minister continuing to profess unqualified hostility to an improvement almost to the very day when his conscience or his interest induces him to take it up as a public measure, and carry it.

Had I met with Mr. Hare's system before the publication of my pamphlet, I should have given an account of it there. Not having done so, I wrote an article in Fraser's Magazine (reprinted in my miscellaneous writings) principally for that purpose, though I included in it, along with Mr. Hare's book, a review of two other productions on the question of the day; one of them a pamphlet by my early friend, Mr. John Austin, who had in his old age become an enemy to all further Parliamentary reform; the other an able and ingenious, though partially erroneous, work by Mr. Lorimer.

In the course of the same summer I fulfilled a duty particularly incumbent upon me, that of helping (by an article in the Edinburgh Review) to make known Mr. Bain's profound treatise on the Mind, just then completed by the publication of its second volume. And I carried through the press a selection of my minor writings, forming the first two volumes of "Dissertations and Discussions." The selection had been made during my wife's lifetime, but the revision, in concert with her, with a view to republication, had been barely commenced; and when I had no longer the guidance of her judgment I despaired of pursuing it further, and republished the papers as they were, with the exception of striking out such passages as were no longer in accordance with my opinions. My literary work of the year was terminated with an essay in Fraser's magazine (afterwards republished in the third volume of "Dissertations and Discussions,") entitled "A Few Words on Non-Intervention." I was prompted to write this paper by a desire, while vindicating England from the imputations commonly brought against her on the Continent, of a peculiar selfishness in matters of foreign policy, to warn Englishmen of the colour given to this imputation by the low tone in which English statesmen are accustomed to speak of English policy as concerned only with English interests, and by the conduct of Lord Palmerston at that particular time in opposing the Suez Canal: and I took the opportunity of expressing ideas which had long been in my mind (some of them generated by my Indian experience, and others by the international questions which then greatly occupied the European public), respecting the true principles of international morality, and the legitimate modifications made in it by difference of times and circumstances; a subject I had already, to some extent, discussed in the vindication of the French Provisional Government of 1848 against the attacks of Lord Brougham and others, which I published at the time in the Westminster Review, and which is reprinted in the "Dissertations."

I had now settled, as I believed, for the remainder of my existence into a purely literary life; if that can be called liter-

ary which continued to be occupied in a pre-eminent degree
with politics, and not merely with theoretical, but practical
politics, although a great part of the year was spent at a dis-
stance of many hundred miles from the chief seat of the
politics of my own country, to which, and primarily for which,
I wrote. But, in truth, the modern facilities of communication
have not only removed all the disadvantages, to a political
writer in tolerably easy circumstances, of distance from the
scene of political action, but have converted them into advantages. The immediate and regular receipt of newspapers and
periodicals keeps him *au courant* of even the most temporary
politics, and gives him a much more correct view of the state
and progress of opinion than he could acquire by personal
contact with individuals: for every one's social intercourse is
more or less limited to particular sets or classes, whose impressions and no others reach him through that channel; and
experience has taught me that those who give their time to
the absorbing claims of what is called society, not having
leisure to keep up a large acquaintance with the organs of
opinion, remain much more ignorant of the general state either
of the public mind, or of the active and instructed part of it,
than a recluse who reads the newspapers need be. There are,
no doubt, disadvantages in too long a separation from one's
country—in not occasionally renewing one's impressions of the
light in which men and things appear when seen from a position in the midst of them; but the deliberate judgment formed
at a distance, and undisturbed by inequalities of perspective,
is the most to be depended on, even for application to practice.
Alternating between the two positions, I combined the advantages of both. And, though the inspirer of my best thoughts was
no longer with me, I was not alone: she had left a daughter,
my stepdaughter, Miss Helen Taylor, the inheritor of much
of her wisdom, and of all her nobleness of character, whose
ever growing and ripening talents from that day to this have
been devoted to the same great purposes, and have already
made her name better and more widely known than was that
of her mother, though far less so than I predict, that if she
lives it is destined to become. Of the value of her direct co-
operation with me, something will be said hereafter, of what
I owe in the way of instruction to her great powers of original
thought and soundness of practical judgment, it would be a
vain attempt to give an adequate idea. Surely no one ever
before was so fortunate, as, after such a loss as mine, to draw
another prize in the lottery of life—another companion, stimu-

lator, adviser, and instructor of the rarest quality. Whoever, either now or hereafter, may think of me and of the work I have done, must never forget that it is the product not of one intellect and conscience, but of three, the least considerable of whom, and above all the least original, is the one whose name is attached to it.

The work of the years 1860 and 1861 consisted chiefly of two treatises, only one of which was intended for immediate publication. This was the "Considerations on Representative Government"; a connected exposition of what, by the thoughts of many years, I had come to regard as the best form of a popular constitution. Along with as much of the general theory of government as is necessary to support this particular portion of its practice, the volume contains many matured views of the principal questions which occupy the present age, within the province of purely organic institutions, and raises, by anticipation, some other questions to which growing necessities will sooner or later compel the attention both of theoretical and of practical politicians. The chief of these last, is the distinction between the function of making laws, for which a numerous popular assembly is radically unfit, and that of getting good laws made, which is its proper duty and cannot be satisfactorily fulfilled by any other authority: and the consequent need of a Legislative Commission, as a permanent part of the constitution of a free country; consisting of a small number of highly trained political minds, on whom, when Parliament has determined that a law shall be made, the task of making it should be devolved: Parliament retaining the power of passing or rejecting the bill when drawn up, but not of altering it otherwise than by sending proposed amendments to be dealt with by the Commission. The question here raised respecting the most important of all public functions, that of legislation, is a particular case of the great problem of modern political organization, stated, I believe, for the first time in its full extent by Bentham, though in my opinion not always satisfactorily resolved by him; the combination of complete popular control over public affairs, with the greatest attainable perfection of skilled agency.

The other treatise written at this time is the one which was published some years later under the title of "The Subjection of Women." It was written at my daughter's suggestion that there might, in any event, be in existence a written exposition of my opinions on that great question, as full and conclusive as I could make it. The intention was to keep this among other unpublished papers, improving it from time to time if I was able, and to publish it at the time when it should seem likely to be most useful. As ultimately published it was enriched with some important ideas of my daughter's, and passages of her writing. But in what was of my own composition, all that is most striking and profound belongs to my wife; coming from the fund of thought which had been made common to us both, by our innumerable conversations and discussions on a topic which filled so large a place in our minds.

Soon after this time I took from their repository a portion of the unpublished papers which I had written during the last years of our married life, and shaped them, with some additional matter, into the little work entitled "Utilitarianism"; which was first published, in three parts, in successive numbers of Fraser's Magazine, and afterwards reprinted in a volume.

Before this, however, the state of public affairs had become extremely critical, by the commencement of the American civil war. My strongest feelings were engaged in this struggle, which, I felt from the beginning, was destined to be a turning point, for good or evil, of the course of human affairs for an indefinite duration. Having been a deeply interested observer of the Slavery quarrel in America, during the many years that preceded the open breach, I knew that it was in all its stages an aggressive enterprise of the slave-owners to extend the territory of slavery; under the combined influences of pecuniary interest, domineering temper, and the fanaticism of a class for its class privileges, influences so fully and powerfully depicted in the admirable work of my friend Professor Cairnes, "The Slave Power." Their success, if they succeeded, would be a victory of the powers of evil which would give courage to the enemies of progress and damp the spirits of its friends all over the civilized world, while it would create a formidable military power, grounded on the worst and most anti-social form of the tyranny of men over men, and, by destroying for a long time the prestige of the great democratic republic, would give to all the privileged classes of Europe a false confidence, probably only to be extinguished in blood. On the other hand, if the spirit of the North was sufficiently roused to carry the war to a successful termination, and if that termination did not come too soon and too easily, I foresaw, from the laws of human nature, and the experience of revolutions, that when it did come it would in all probability be thorough: that the bulk of the Northern population, whose conscience had as yet been awakened only to the point of resisting the further extension of slavery, but whose fidelity to the Constitution of the United States made them disapprove of any attempt by the Federal Government to interfere with slavery in the States where it already existed, would acquire feelings of another kind when the Constitution had been shaken off by armed rebellion, would determine to have done for ever with the accursed thing, and would join their banner with that of the noble body of Abolitionists, of whom Garrison was the courageous and single-minded apostle, Wendell Phillips the eloquent orator, and John Brown the voluntary martyr.* Then, too, the whole mind of the United States would be let loose from its bonds, no longer corrupted by the supposed necessity of apologizing to foreigners for the most flagrant of all possible violations of the free principles of their Constitution; while the tendency of a fixed state of society to stereotype a set of national opinions would be at least temporarily checked, and the national mind would become more open to the recognition of whatever was bad in either the institutions or the customs of the people. These hopes, so far as related to Slavery, have been completely, and in other respects are in course of being progressively realized. Foreseeing from the first this double set of consequences from the success or failure of the rebellion, it may be imagined with what feelings I contemplated the rush of nearly the whole upper and middle classes of my own country, even those who passed for Liberals, into a furious pro-Southern partisanship: the working classes, and some of the literary and scientific men, being almost the sole exceptions to the general frenzy. I never before felt so keenly how little permanent improvement had reached the minds of our influential classes, and of what small value were the liberal opinions they had got into the habit of professing. None of the Continental Liberals committed the same frightful mistake. But the generation which had extorted negro emancipation from our West India planters had passed away; another had succeeded which had not learnt by many years of discussion and exposure to feel strongly the enormities of slavery; and the inattention habitual with Englishmen to whatever is going on in the world outside their own island, made them profoundly ignorant of all the antecedents of the struggle, insomuch that it was not generally believed in England, for the

---

* The saying of this true hero, after his capture, that he was worth more for hanging than for any other purpose, reminds one, by its combination of wit, wisdom, and self-devotion, of Sir Thomas More.

first year or two of the war, that the quarrel was one of slavery. There were men of high principle and unquestionable liberality of opinion, who thought it a dispute about tariffs, or assimilated it to the cases in which they were accustomed to sympathize, of a people struggling for independence.

It was my obvious duty to be one of the small minority who protested against this perverted state of public opinion. I was not the first to protest. It ought to be remembered to the honour of Mr. Hughes and of Mr. Ludlow, that they, by writings published at the very beginning of the struggle, began the protestation. Mr. Bright followed in one of the most powerful of his speeches, followed by others not less striking. I was on the point of adding my words to theirs, when there occurred, towards the end of 1861, the seizure of the Southern envoys on board a British vessel, by an officer of the United States. Even English forgetfulness has not yet had time to lose all remembrance of the explosion of feeling in England which then burst forth, the expectation, prevailing for some weeks, of war with the United States, and the warlike preparations actually commenced on this side. While this state of things lasted, there was no chance of a hearing for anything favourable to the American cause; and, moreover, I agreed with those who thought the act unjustifiable, and such as to require that England should demand its disavowal. When the disavowal came, and the alarm of war was over, I wrote, in January, 1862, the paper, in Fraser's Magazine, entitled "The Contest in America." And I shall always feel grateful to my daughter that her urgency prevailed on me to write it when I did, for we were then on the point of setting out for a journey of some months in Greece and Turkey, and but for her, I should have deferred writing till our return. Written and published when it was, this paper helped to encourage those Liberals who had felt overborne by the tide of illiberal opinion, and to form in favour of the good cause a nucleus of opinion which increased gradually, and, after the success of the North began to seem probable, rapidly. When we returned from our journey I wrote a second article, a review of Professor Cairnes' book, published in the Westminster Review. England is paying the penalty, in many uncomfortable ways, of the durable resentment which her ruling classes stirred up in the United States by their ostentatious wishes for the ruin of America as a nation: they have reason to be thankful that a few, if only a few, known writers and speakers, standing firmly by the Americans in the time of their greatest difficulty, effected a partial diversion of these bitter feelings, and made Great Britain not altogether odious to the Americans.

This duty having been performed, my principal occupation for the next two years was on subjects not political. The publication of Mr. Austin's Lectures on Jurisprudence after his decease, gave me an opportunity of paying a deserved tribute to his memory, and at the same time expressing some thoughts on a subject on which, in my old days of Benthamism, I had bestowed much study. But the chief product of those years was the Examination of Sir William Hamilton's Philosophy. His Lectures, published in 1860 and 1861, I had read towards the end of the latter year, with a half-formed intention of giving an account of them in a Review, but I soon found that this would be idle, and that justice could not be done to the subject in less than a volume. I had then to consider whether it would be advisable that I myself should attempt such a performance. On consideration, there seemed to be strong reasons for doing so. I was greatly disappointed with the Lectures. I read them, certainly, with no prejudice against Sir W. Hamilton. I had up to that time deferred the study of his Notes to Reid on account of their unfinished state, but I had not neglected his "Discussions in Philosophy;" and though I knew that his general mode of treating the facts of mental philosophy differed from that of which I most approved, yet his vigorous polemic against the later Transcendentalists, and his strenuous assertion of some important principles, especially the Relativity of human knowledge, gave me many points of sympathy with his opinions, and made me think that genuine psychology had considerably more to gain than to lose by his authority and reputation. His Lectures and the Dissertations on Reid dispelled this illusion: and even the Discussions, read by the light which these throw on them, lost much of their value. I found that the points of apparent agreement between his opinions and mine were more verbal than real; that the important philosophical principles which I had thought he recognised, were so explained away by him as to mean little or nothing, or were continually lost sight of, and doctrines entirely inconsistent with them were taught in nearly every part of his philosophical writings. My estimation of him was therefore so far altered, that instead of regarding him as occupying a kind of intermediate position between the two rival philosophies, holding some of the principles of both, and supplying to both powerful weapons of attack and defence, I now looked upon him as one of the pillars, and in this country from his high philosophical reputation the chief pillar, of that one of the two which seemed to me to be erroneous.

Now, the difference between these two schools of philosophy, that of Intuition, and that of Experience and Association, is not a mere matter of abstract speculation; it is full of practical consequences, and lies at the foundation of all the greatest differences of practical opinion in an age of progress. The practical reformer has continually to demand that changes be made in things which are supported by powerful and widely-spread feelings, or to question the apparent necessity and indefeasibleness of established facts; and it is often an indispensable part of his argument to show, how those powerful feelings had their origin, and how those facts came to seem necessary and indefeasible. There is therefore a natural hostility between him and a philosophy which discourages the explanation of feelings and moral facts by circumstances and association, and prefers to treat them as ultimate elements of human nature; a philosophy which is addicted to holding up favourite doctrines as intuitive truths, and deems intuition to be the voice of Nature and of God, speaking with an authority higher than that of our reason. In particular, I have long felt that the prevailing tendency to regard all the marked distinctions of human character as innate, and in the main indelible, and to ignore the irresistible proofs that by far the greater part of those differences, whether between individuals, races, or sexes, are such as not only might but naturally would be produced by differences in circumstances, is one of the chief hindrances to the rational treatment of great social questions, and one of the greatest stumbling blocks to human improvement. This tendency has its source in the intuitional metaphysics which characterized the reaction of the nineteenth century against the eighteenth, and it is a tendency so agreeable to human indolence, as well as to conservative interests generally, that unless attacked at the very root, it is sure to be carried to even a greater length than is really justified by the more moderate forms of the intuitional philosophy. That philosophy, not always in its moderate forms, had ruled the thought of Europe for the greater part of a century. My father's Analysis of the Mind, my own Logic, and Professor Bain's great treatise, had attempted to re-introduce a better mode of philosophizing, latterly with quite as much success as could be expected; but I had for some time felt that the mere contrast of the two philosophies was not enough, that there ought to be a hand-to-hand fight between them, that controversial as well as expository writings were needed, and that the time was come when such controversy would be useful. Considering then the writings and fame of Sir W. Hamilton as the great fortress of the intuitional philosophy in this country, a fortress the more formidable from the imposing character, and the in many respects great personal merits and mental endowments, of the man, I thought it might be a real service to philosophy to attempt a thorough examination of all his most important doctrines, and an estimate of his general claims to eminence as a philosopher, and I was confirmed in this resolution by observing that in the writings of at least one, and him one of the ablest, of Sir W. Hamilton's followers, his peculiar doctrines were made the justification of a view of religion which I hold to be profoundly immoral—that it is our duty to bow down in worship before a Being whose moral attributes are affirmed to be unknowable by us, and to be perhaps extremely different from those which, when we are speaking of our fellow creatures, we call by the same names.

As I advanced in my task, the damage to Sir W. Hamilton's reputation became greater than I at first expected, through the almost incredible multitude of inconsistencies which showed themselves on comparing different passages with one another. It was my business, however, to show things exactly as they were, and I did not flinch from it. I endeavoured always to treat the philosopher whom I criticized with the most scrupulous fairness; and I knew that he had abundance of disciples and admirers to correct me if I ever unintentionally did him injustice. Many of them accordingly have answered me, more or less elaborately; and they have pointed out oversights and misunderstandings, though few in number, and mostly very unimportant in substance. Such of those as had (to my knowledge) been pointed out before the publication of the latest edition (at present the third) have been corrected there, and the remainder of the criticisms have been, as far as seemed necessary, replied to. On the whole, the book has done its work: it has shown the weak side of Sir W. Hamilton, and has reduced his too great philosophical reputation within more moderate bounds; and by some of its discussions, as well as by two expository chapters, on the notions of Matter and of Mind, it has perhaps thrown additional light on some of the disputed questions in the domain of psychology and metaphysics.

After the completion of the book on Hamilton, I applied myself to a task which a variety of reasons seemed to render

specially incumbent upon me; that of giving an account, and
forming an estimate, of the doctrines of Auguste Comte. I
had contributed more than any one else to make his speculations known in England. In consequence chiefly of what I had
said of him in my Logic, he had readers and admirers among
thoughtful men on this side of the Channel at a time when
his name had not yet in France emerged from obscurity. So
unknown and unappreciated was he at the time when my
Logic was written and published, that to criticize his weak
points might well appear superfluous, while it was a duty to
give as much publicity as one could to the important contributions he had made to philosophic thought. At the time,
however, at which I have now arrived, this state of affairs
had entirely changed. His name, at least, was known almost
universally, and the general character of his doctrines very
widely. He had taken his place in the estimation both of
friends and opponents, as one of the conspicuous figures in
the thought of the age. The better parts of his speculations
had made great progress in working their way into those
minds, which, by their previous culture and tendencies, were
fitted to receive them: under cover of those better parts those
of a worse character, greatly developed and added to in his
later writings, had also made some way, having obtained
active and enthusiastic adherents, some of them of no incon-
siderable personal merit, in England, France, and other countries. These causes not only made it desirable that some one
should undertake the task of sifting what is good from what
is bad in M. Comte's speculations, but seemed to impose on
myself in particular a special obligation to make the attempt.
This I accordingly did in two Essays, published in successive
numbers of the Westminster Review, and reprinted in a small
volume under the title "Auguste Comte and Positivism."

The writings which I have now mentioned, together with
a small number of papers in periodicals which I have not
deemed worth preserving, were the whole of the products of
my activity as a writer during the years from 1859 to 1865.
In the early part of the last-mentioned year, in compliance
with a wish frequently expressed to me by working men, I
published cheap People's Editions of those of my writings
which seemed the most likely to find readers among the working classes; viz, Principles of Political Economy, Liberty, and
Representative Government. This was a considerable sacrifice
of my pecuniary interest, especially as I resigned all idea of
deriving profit from the cheap editions, and after ascertaining

from my publishers the lowest price which they thought would remunerate them on the usual terms of an equal division of profits, I gave up my half share to enable the price to be fixed still lower. To the credit of Messrs. Longman they fixed, unasked, a certain number of years after which the copyright and stereotype plates were to revert to me, and a certain number of copies after the sale of which I should receive half of any further profit. This number of copies (which in the case of the Political Economy was 10,000) has for some time been exceeded, and the People's Editions have begun to yield me a small but unexpected pecuniary return, though very far from an equivalent for the diminution of profit from the Library Editions.

In this summary of my outward life I have now arrived at the period at which my tranquil and retired existence as a writer of books was to be exchanged for the less congenial occupation of a member of the House of Commons. The proposal made to me, early in 1865, by some electors of Westminster, did not present the idea to me for the first time. It was not even the first offer I had received, for, more than ten years previous, in consequence of my opinions on the Irish Land question, Mr. Lucas and Mr. Duffy, in the name of the popular party in Ireland, offered to bring me into Parliament for an Irish County, which they could easily have done: but the incompatibility of a seat in Parliament with the office I then held in the India House, precluded even consideration of the proposal. After I had quitted the India House, several of my friends would gladly have seen me a member of Parliament; but there seemed no probability that the idea would ever take any practical shape. I was convinced that no numerous or influential portion of any electoral body, really wished to be represented by a person of my opinions; and that one who possessed no local connexion or popularity, and who did not choose to stand as the mere organ of a party, had small chance of being elected anywhere unless through the expenditure of money. Now it was, and is, my fixed conviction, that a candidate ought not to incur one farthing of expense for undertaking a public duty. Such of the lawful expenses of an election as have no special reference to any particular candidate, ought to be borne as a public charge, either by the State or by the locality. What has to be done by the supporters of each candidate in order to bring his claims properly before the constituency, should be done by unpaid agency, or by voluntary subscription. If members of the electoral body, or others, are willing to subscribe money of their own for the purpose of bringing, by lawful means, into Parliament some one who they think would be useful there, no one is entitled to object: but that the expense, or any part of it, should fall on the candidate, is fundamentally wrong; because it amounts in reality to buying his seat. Even on the most favourable supposition as to the mode in which the money is expended, there is a legitimate suspicion that any one who gives money for leave to undertake a public trust, has other than public ends to promote by it; and (a consideration of the greatest importance) the cost of elections, when borne by the candidates, deprives the nation of the services, as members of Parliament, of all who cannot or will not afford to incur a heavy expense. I do not say that, so long as there is scarcely a chance for an independent candidate to come into Parliament without complying with this vicious practice, it must always be morally wrong in him to spend money, provided that no part of it is either directly or indirectly employed in corruption. But, to justify it, he ought to be very certain that he can be of more use to his country as a member of Parliament than in any other mode which is open to him; and this assurance, in my own case, I did not feel. It was by no means clear to me that I could do more to advance the public objects which had a claim on my exertions, from the benches of the House of Commons, than from the simple position of a writer. I felt, therefore, that I ought not to seek election to Parliament, much less to expend any money in procuring it.

But the conditions of the question were considerably altered when a body of electors sought me out, and spontaneously offered to bring me forward as their candidate. If it should appear, on explanation, that they persisted in this wish, knowing my opinions, and accepting the only conditions on which I could conscientiously serve, it was questionable whether this was not one of those calls upon a member of the community by his fellow-citizens, which he was scarcely justified in rejecting. I therefore put their disposition to the proof by one of the frankest explanations ever tendered, I should think, to an electoral body by a candidate. I wrote, in reply to the offer, a letter for publication, saying that I had no personal wish to be a member of parliament, that I thought a candidate ought neither to canvass nor to incur any expense, and that I could not consent to do either. I said further, that if elected, I could not undertake to give any of my time and labour to their local interests. With respect to general politics, I told them without reserve, what I thought on a number of important subjects on which they had asked my opinion; and one of these being the suffrage, I made known to them, among other things, my conviction (as I was bound to do, since I intended, if elected, to act on it), that women were entitled to representation in Parliament on the same terms with men. It was the first time, doubtless, that such a doctrine had ever been mentioned to English electors; and the fact that I was elected after proposing it, gave the start to the movement which has since become so vigorous, in favour of women's suffrage. Nothing, at the time, appeared more unlikely than that a candidate (if candidate I could be called) whose professions and conduct set so completely at defiance all ordinary notions of electioneering, should nevertheless be elected. A well-known literary man, who was also a man of society, was heard to say that the Almighty himself would have no chance of being elected on such a programme. I strictly adhered to it, neither spending money nor canvassing, nor did I take any personal part in the election, until about a week preceding the day of nomination, when I attended a few public meetings to state my principles and give to any questions which the electors might exercise their just right of putting to me for their own guidance, answers as plain and unreserved as my Address. On one subject only, my religious opinions, I announced from the beginning that I would answer no questions; a determination which appeared to be completely approved by those who attended the meetings. My frankness on all other subjects on which I was interrogated, evidently did me far more good than my answers, whatever they might be, did harm. Among the proofs I received of this, one is too remarkable not to be recorded. In the pamphlet, "Thoughts on Parliamentary Reform," I had said, rather bluntly, that the working classes, though differing from those of some other countries, in being ashamed of lying, are yet generally liars. This passage some opponent got printed in a placard, which was handed to me at a meeting, chiefly composed of the working classes, and I was asked whether I had written and published it. I at once answered "I did." Scarcely were these two words out of my mouth, when vehement applause resounded through the whole meeting. It was evident that the working people were so accustomed to expect equivocation and evasion from those who sought their suffrages, that when they found, instead of that, a direct avowal of what was likely to be disagreeable to them, instead of being offended, they concluded at once that this was a person whom they could trust. A more striking instance never came under my notice of what, I believe, is the experience of those who best know the working classes, that the most essential of all recommendations to their favour is that of complete straightforwardness; its presence outweighs in their minds very strong objections, while no amount of other qualities will make amends for its apparent absence. The first working man who spoke after the incident I have mentioned (it was Mr. Odger) said, that the working classes had no desire not to be told of their faults; they wanted friends, not flatterers, and felt under obligation to any one who told them anything in themselves which he sincerely believed to require amendment. And to this the meeting heartily responded.

Had I been defeated in the election, I should still have had no reason to regret the contact it had brought me into with large bodies of my countrymen; which not only gave me much new experience, but enabled me to scatter my political opinions rather widely, and, by making me known in many quarters where I had never before been heard of, increased the number of my readers, and the presumable influence of my writings. These latter effects were of course produced in a still greater degree, when, as much to my surprise as to that of any one, I was returned to Parliament by a majority of some hundreds over my Conservative competitor.

I was a member of the House during the three sessions of the Parliament which passed the Reform Bill; during which time Parliament was necessarily my main occupation, except during the recess. I was a tolerably frequent speaker, sometimes of prepared speeches, sometimes extemporaneously. But my choice of occasions was not such as I should have made if my leading object had been parliamentary influence. When I had gained the ear of the House, which I did by a successful speech on Mr. Gladstone's Reform Bill, the idea I proceeded on was that when anything was likely to be as well done, or sufficiently well done, by other people, there was no necessity for me to meddle with it. As I, therefore, in general reserved myself for work which no others were likely to do, a great proportion of my appearances were on points on which the bulk of the Liberal party, even the advanced portion of it, either were of a different opinion from mine, or were comparatively indifferent. Several of my speeches, especially one against the motion for the abolition of capital punishment, and another in favour of resuming the right of seizing enemies' goods in neutral vessels, were opposed to what then was, and probably still is, regarded as the advanced liberal opinion. My advocacy of women's suffrage and of Personal Representation, were at the time looked upon by many as whims of my own; but the great progress since made by those opinions, and especially the zealous response made from almost all parts of the kingdom to the demand for women's suffrage, fully justified the timeliness of those movements, and have made what was undertaken as a moral and social duty, a personal success. Another duty which was particularly incumbent on me as one of the Metropolitan Members, was the attempt to obtain a Municipal Government for the Metropolis: but on that subject the indifference of the House of Commons was such that I found hardly any help or support within its walls. On this subject, however, I was the organ of an active and intelligent body of persons outside, with whom, and not with me, the scheme originated, and who carried on all the agitation on the subject and drew up the Bills. My part was to bring in Bills already prepared, and to sustain the discussion of them during the short time they were allowed to remain before the House; after having taken an active part in the work of a Committee presided over by Mr. Ayrton, which sat through the greater part of the Session of 1866, to take evidence on the subject. The very different position in which the question now stands (1870) may justly be attributed to the preparation which went on during those years, and which produced but little visible effect at the time; but all questions on which there are strong private interests on one side, and only the public good on the other, have a similar period of incubation to go through.

The same idea, that the use of my being in Parliament was to do work which others were not able or not willing to do, made me think it my duty to come to the front in defence of advanced Liberalism on occasions when the obloquy to be encountered was such as most of the advanced Liberals in the House, preferred not to incur. My first vote in the House was in support of an amendment in favour of Ireland, moved by an Irish member, and for which only five English and Scotch votes were given, including my own: the other four were Mr. Bright, Mr. McLaren, Mr. T. B. Potter, and Mr. Hadfield.

And the second speech I delivered* was on the bill to prolong
the suspension of the Habeas Corpus in Ireland. In denouncing, on this occasion, the English mode of governing Ireland,
I did no more than the general opinion of England now admits
to have been just; but the anger against Fenianism was then
in all its freshness; any attack on what Fenians attacked was
looked upon as an apology for them; and I was so unfavour-
ably received by the House, that more than one of my friends
advised me (and my own judgment agreed with the advice)
to wait, before speaking again, for the favourable opportunity
that would be given by the first great debate on the Reform
Bill. During this silence, many flattered themselves that I had
turned out a failure, and that they should not be troubled
with me any more. Perhaps their uncomplimentary comments
may, by the force of reaction, have helped to make my speech
on the Reform Bill the success it was. My position in the
House was further improved by a speech in which I insisted
on the duty of paying off the National Debt before our coal
supplies are exhausted, and by an ironical reply to some of
the Tory leaders who had quoted against me certain passages
of my writings, and called me to account for others, especially
for one in my "Considerations on Representative Government," which said that the Conservative party was, by the law
of its composition, the stupidest party. They gained nothing
by drawing attention to the passage, which up to that time had
not excited any notice, but the *sobriquet* of "the stupid party"
stuck to them for a considerable time afterwards. Having now
no longer any apprehension of not being listened to, I confined
myself, as I have since thought too much, to occasions on
which my services seemed specially needed, and abstained
more than enough from speaking on the great party questions.
With the exception of Irish questions, and those which concerned the working classes, a single speech on Mr. Disraeli's
Reform Bill was nearly all that I contributed to the great
decisive debates of the last two of my three sessions.

I have, however, much satisfaction in looking back to the
part I took on the two classes of subjects just mentioned. With
regard to the working classes, the chief topic of my speech
on Mr. Gladstone's Reform Bill was the assertion of their
claims to the suffrage. A little later, after the resignation

* The first was in answer to Mr. Lowe's reply to Mr. Bright on the Cattle
Plague Bill, and was thought at the time to have helped to get rid of a provision in the Government measure which would have given to landholders a
second indemnity, after they had already been once indemnified for the loss
of some of their cattle by the increased selling price of the remainder.

of Lord Russell's ministry and the succession of a Tory Government, came the attempt of the working classes to hold a meeting in Hyde Park, their exclusion by the police, and the breaking down of the park railing by the crowd. Though Mr. Beales and the leaders of the working men had retired under protest before this took place, a scuffle ensued in which many innocent persons were maltreated by the police, and the exasperation of the working men was extreme. They showed a determination to make another attempt at a meeting in the Park, to which many of them would probably have come armed; the Government made military preparations to resist the attempt, and something very serious seemed impending. At this crisis I really believe that I was the means of preventing much mischief. I had in my place in Parliament taken the side of the working men, and strongly censured the conduct of the Government. I was invited, with several other Radical members, to a conference with the leading members of the Council of the Reform League; and the task fell chiefly upon myself, of persuading them to give up the Hyde Park project, and hold their meeting elsewhere. It was not Mr. Beales and Colonel Dickson who needed persuading; on the contrary, it was evident that these gentlemen had already exerted their influence in the same direction, thus far without success. It was the working men who held out, and so bent were they on their original scheme, that I was obliged to have recourse to *les grands moyens*. I told them that a proceeding which would certainly produce a collision with the military, could only be justifiable on two conditions: if the position of affairs had become such that a revolution was desirable, and if they thought themselves able to accomplish one. To this argument, after considerable discussion, they at last yielded: and I was able to inform Mr. Walpole that their intention was given up. I shall never forget the depth of his relief or the warmth of his expressions of gratitude. After the working men had conceded so much to me, I felt bound to comply with their request that I would attend and speak at their meeting at the Agricultural Hall; the only meeting called by the Reform League which I ever attended. I had always declined being a member of the League, on the avowed ground that I did not agree in its programme of manhood suffrage and the ballot: from the ballot I dissented entirely; and I could not consent to hoist the flag of manhood suffrage, even on the assurance that the exclusion of women was not intended to be implied; since if one goes beyond what can be immediately carried, and professes to take one's stand on a principle, one should go the whole length of the principle. I have entered thus particularly into this matter because my conduct on this occasion gave great displeasure to the Tory and Tory-Liberal press, who have charged me ever since with having shown myself, in the trials of public life, intemperate and passionate. I do not know what they expected from me; but they had reason to be thankful to me if they knew from what I had, in all probability, preserved them. And I do not believe it could have been done, at that particular juncture, by any one else. No other person, I believe, had at that moment the necessary influence for restraining the working classes, except Mr. Gladstone and Mr. Bright, neither of whom was available: Mr. Gladstone, for obvious reasons; Mr. Bright because he was out of town.

When, some time later, the Tory Government brought in a bill to prevent public meetings in the Parks, I not only spoke strongly in opposition to it, but formed one of a number of advanced Liberals, who, aided by the very late period of the Session, succeeded in defeating the Bill by what is called talking it out. It has not since been renewed.

On Irish affairs also I felt bound to take a decided part. I was one of the foremost in the deputation of Members of Parliament who prevailed on Lord Derby to spare the life of the condemned Fenian insurgent, General Burke. The Church question was so vigorously handled by the leaders of the party, in the session of 1868, as to require no more from me than an emphatic adhesion: but the land question was by no means in so advanced a position; the superstitions of landlordism had up to that time been little challenged, especially in Parliament, and the backward state of the question, so far as concerned the Parliamentary mind, was evidenced by the extremely mild measure brought in by Lord Russell's Government in 1866, which nevertheless could not be carried. On that bill I delivered one of my most careful speeches, in which I attempted to lay down some of the principles of the subject, in a manner calculated less to stimulate friends, than to conciliate and convince opponents. The engrossing subject of Parliamentary Reform prevented either this bill, or one of a similar character brought in by Lord Derby's Government, from being carried through. They never got beyond the second reading. Meanwhile the signs of Irish disaffection had become much more decided; the demand for complete separation between the two countries had assumed a menacing aspect, and there were few who did not feel that if there was still any chance of reconciling Ireland to the British connexion, it could only be by the adoption of much more thorough reforms in the territorial and social relations of the country, than had yet been contemplated. The time seemed to me to have come when it would be useful to speak out my whole mind; and the result was my pamphlet "England and Ireland," which was written in the winter of 1867, and published shortly before the commencement of the session of 1868. The leading features of the pamphlet were, on the one hand, an argument to show the undesirableness, for Ireland as well as England, of separation between the countries, and on the other, a proposal for settling the land question by giving to the existing tenants a permanent tenure, at a fixed rent, to be assessed after due inquiry by the State.

The pamphlet was not popular, except in Ireland, as I did not expect it to be. But, if no measure short of that which I proposed would do full justice to Ireland, or afford a prospect of conciliating the mass of the Irish people, the duty of proposing it was imperative; while if, on the other hand, there was any intermediate course which had a claim to a trial, I well knew that to propose something which would be called extreme, was the true way not to impede but to facilitate a more moderate experiment. It is most improbable that a measure conceding so much to the tenantry as Mr. Gladstone's Irish Land Bill, would have been proposed by a Government, or could have been carried through Parliament, unless the British public had been led to perceive that a case might be made, and perhaps a party formed, for a measure considerably stronger. It is the character of the British people, or at least of the higher and middle classes who pass muster for the British people, that to induce them to approve of any change, it is necessary that they should look upon it as a middle course: they think every proposal extreme and violent unless they hear of some other proposal going still farther, upon which their antipathy to extreme views may discharge itself. So it proved in the present instance; my proposal was condemned, but any scheme of Irish Land reform, short of mine, came to be thought moderate by comparison. I may observe that the attacks made on my plan usually gave a very incorrect idea of its nature. It was usually discussed as a proposal that the State should buy up the land and become the universal landlord; though in fact it only offered to each individual landlord this as an alternative, if he liked better to sell his estate than to retain it on the new conditions; and I fully anticipated that most landlords would continue to prefer the position of landowners to that of Government annuitants, and would retain their existing relation to their tenants, often on more indulgent terms than the full rents on which the compensation to be given them by Government would have been based. This and many other explanations I gave in a speech on Ireland, in the debate on Mr. Maguire's Resolution, early in the session of 1868. A corrected report of this speech, together with my speech on Mr. Fortescue's Bill, has been published (not by me, but with my permission) in Ireland.

Another public duty, of a most serious kind, it was my lot to have to perform, both in and out of Parliament, during these years. A disturbance in Jamaica, provoked in the first instance by injustice, and exaggerated by rage and panic into a premeditated rebellion, had been the motive or excuse for taking hundreds of innocent lives by military violence, or by sentence of what were called courts-martial, continuing for weeks after the brief disturbance had been put down; with many added atrocities of destruction of property, flogging women as well as men, and a general display of the brutal recklessness which usually prevails when fire and sword are let loose. The perpetrators of those deeds were defended and applauded in England by the same kind of people who had so long upheld negro slavery: and it seemed at first as if the British nation was about to incur the disgrace of letting pass without even a protest, excesses of authority as revolting as any of those for which, when perpetrated by the instruments of other governments, Englishmen can hardly find terms sufficient to express their abhorrence. After a short time, however, an indignant feeling was roused: a voluntary Association formed itself under the name of the Jamaica Committee, to take such deliberation and action as the case might admit of, and adhesions poured in from all parts of the country. I was abroad at the time, but I sent in my name to the Committee as soon as I heard of it, and took an active part in the proceedings from the time of my return. There was much more at stake than only justice to the Negroes, imperative as was that consideration. The question was, whether the British dependencies, and eventually, perhaps, Great Britain itself, were to be under the government of law, or of military licence; whether the lives and persons of British subjects are at the mercy of any two or three officers however raw and inexperienced or reckless and brutal, whom a panic-stricken Governor, or other functionary, may assume the right to constitute into a so-called Court-martial. This question could only be decided by an appeal to the tribunals; and such an appeal the Committee determined to make. Their determination led to a change in the Chairmanship of the Committee, as the Chairman, Mr. Charles Buxton, thought it not unjust indeed, but inexpedient, to prosecute Governor Eyre and his principal subordinates in a criminal court: but a numerously attended general meeting of the Association having decided this point against him, Mr. Buxton withdrew from the Committee, though continuing to work in the cause, and I was, quite unexpectedly on my own part, proposed and elected Chairman. It became, in consequence, my duty to represent the Committee in the House, sometimes by putting questions to the Government, sometimes as the recipient of questions, more or less provocative, addressed by individual members to myself; but especially as speaker in the important debate originated in the session of 1866, by Mr. Buxton: and the speech I then delivered is that which I should probably select as the best of my speeches in Parliament.* For more than two years we carried on the combat, trying every avenue legally open to us, to the courts of criminal justice. A bench of magistrates in one of the most Tory counties in England dismissed our case: we were more successful before the magistrates at Bow Street; which gave an opportunity to the Lord Chief Justice of the Queen's Bench, Sir Alexander Cockburn, for delivering his celebrated charge, which settled the law of the question in favour of liberty, as far as it is in the power of a judge's charge to settle it. There, however, our success ended, for the Old Bailey Grand Jury by throwing out our bill prevented the case from coming to trial. It was clear that to bring English functionaries to the bar of a criminal court for abuses of power committed against negroes and mulattoes was not a popular proceeding with the English middle classes. We had, however, redeemed, so far as lay in us, the character of our country, by showing that there was at any rate a body of persons determined to use all the means which the law afforded to obtain justice for the injured. We had elicited from the highest criminal judge in the nation an authoritative declaration that the law was what we maintained it to be; and we

---

* Among the most active members of the Committee were Mr. P. A. Taylor, M.P., always faithful and energetic in every assertion of the principles of liberty; Mr. Goldwin Smith, Mr. Frederic Harrison, Mr. Slack, Mr. Chamerovzow, Mr. Shaen, and Mr. Chesson, the Honorary Secretary of the Association.

had given an emphatic warning to those who might be tempted to similar guilt hereafter, that, though they might escape the actual sentence of a criminal tribunal, they were not safe against being put to some trouble and expense in order to avoid it. Colonial governors and other persons in authority, will have a considerable motive to stop short of such extremities in future.

As a matter of curiosity I kept some specimens of the abusive letters, almost all of them anonymous, which I received while these proceedings were going on. They are evidence of the sympathy felt with the brutalities in Jamaica by the brutal part of the population at home. They graduated from coarse jokes, verbal and pictorial, up to threats of* assassination.

Among other matters of importance in which I took an active part, but which excited little interest in the public, two deserve particular mention. I joined with several other independent Liberals in defeating an Extradition Bill introduced at the very end of the session of 1866, and by which, though surrender avowedly for political offences was not authorized, political refugees, if charged by a foreign government with acts which are necessarily incident to all attempts at insurrection, would have been surrendered to be dealt with by the criminal courts of the government against which they had rebelled: thus making the British Government an accomplice in the vengeance of foreign despotisms. The defeat of this proposal led to the appointment of a Select Committee (in which I was included), to examine and report on the whole subject of Extradition Treaties; and the result was, that in the Extradition Act which passed through Parliament after I had ceased to be a member, opportunity is given to any one whose extradition is demanded, of being heard before an English Court of justice to prove that the offence with which he is charged, is really political. The cause of European freedom has thus been saved from a serious misfortune, and our own country from a great iniquity. The other subject to be mentioned is the fight kept up by a body of advanced Liberals

---

* At one time I reckoned that threats of assassination were received at least once a week; and I remarked that threatening letters were always especially numerous by Tuesday morning's post. I inferred that they were meditated during the Sunday's leisure and posted on the Mondays. It might be worth while to collect evidence as to the proportions of crime committed on the different days of the week. It may be observed however that in England Sunday is generally used for all kinds of letter-writing, innocent as well as guilty. Helen Taylor.

in the session of 1868, on the Bribery Bill of Mr. Disraeli's Government, in which I took a very active part. I had taken counsel with several of those who had applied their minds most carefully to the details of the subject—Mr. W. D. Christie, Serjeant Pulling, Mr. Chadwick—as well as bestowed much thought of my own, for the purpose of framing such amendments and additional clauses as might make the Bill really effective against the numerous modes of corruption, direct and indirect, which might otherwise, as there was much reason to fear, be increased instead of diminished by the Reform Act. We also aimed at engrafting on the Bill, measures for diminishing the mischievous burthen of what are called the legitimate expenses of elections. Among our many amendments, was that of Mr. Fawcett for making the returning officer's expenses a charge on the rates, instead of on the candidates; another was the prohibition of paid canvassers, and the limitation of paid agents to one for each candidate; a third was the extension of the precautions and penalties against bribery, to municipal elections, which are well known to be not only a preparatory school for bribery at parliamentary elections, but an habitual cover for it. The Conservative Government, however, when once they had carried the leading provision of their Bill (for which I voted and spoke), the transfer of the jurisdiction in elections from the House of Commons to the Judges, made a determined resistance to all other improvements; and after one of our most important proposals, that of Mr. Fawcett, had actually obtained a majority, they summoned the strength of their party and threw out the clause in a subsequent stage. The Liberal party in the House was greatly dishonoured by the conduct of many of its members in giving no help whatever to this attempt to secure the necessary conditions of an honest representation of the people. With their large majority in the House they could have carried all the amendments, or better ones if they had better to propose. But it was late in the Session; members were eager to set about their preparations for the impending General Election: and while some (such as Sir Robert Anstruther) honourably remained at their post, though rival candidates were already canvassing their constituency, a much greater number placed their electioneering interests before their public duty. Many Liberals also looked with indifference on legislation against bribery, thinking that it merely diverted public interest from the Ballot, which they considered, very mistakenly as I expect it will turn out, to be a sufficient, and the only, remedy. From these causes our fight, though kept up with great vigour for several nights, was wholly unsuccessful, and the practices which we sought to render more difficult, prevailed more widely than ever in the first General Election held under the new electoral law.

In the general debates on Mr. Disraeli's Reform Bill, my participation was limited to the one speech already mentioned; but I made the Bill an occasion for bringing the two great improvements which remain to be made in representative government, formally before the House and the nation. One of them was Personal, or, as it is called with equal propriety, Proportional Representation. I brought this under the consideration of the House, by an expository and argumentative speech on Mr. Hare's plan; and subsequently I was active in support of the very imperfect substitute for that plan, which, in a small number of constituencies, Parliament was induced to adopt. This poor makeshift had scarcely any recommendation, except that it was a partial recognition of the evil which it did so little to remedy. As such, however, it was attacked by the same fallacies, and required to be defended on the same principles, as a really good measure; and its adoption in a few parliamentary elections, as well as the subsequent introduction of what is called the Cumulative Vote in the elections for the London School Board, have had the good effect of converting the equal claim of all electors to a proportional share in the representation, from a subject of merely speculative discussion, into a question of practical politics, much sooner than would otherwise have been the case.

This assertion of my opinions on Personal Representation cannot be credited with any considerable or visible amount of practical result. It was otherwise with the other motion which I made in the form of an amendment to the Reform Bill, and which was by far the most important, perhaps the only really important, public service I performed in the capacity of a Member of Parliament: a motion to strike out the words which were understood to limit the electoral franchise to males, and thereby admitting to the suffrage all women who, as householders or otherwise, possessed the qualification required of male electors. For women not to make their claim to the suffrage, at the time when the elective franchise was being largely extended, would have been to abjure the claim altogether; and a movement on the subject was begun in 1866, when I presented a petition for the suffrage, signed by a considerable number of distinguished women. But it was as yet uncertain whether the proposal would obtain more than a few stray votes in the House: and when, after a debate in which the speakers on the contrary side were conspicuous by their feebleness, the votes recorded in favour of the motion amounted to 73—made up by pairs and tellers to above 80— the surprise was general, and the encouragement great: the greater, too, because one of those who voted for the motion was Mr. Bright, a fact which could only be attributed to the impression made on him by the debate, as he had previously made no secret of his nonconcurrence in the proposal. The time appeared to my daughter, Miss Helen Taylor, to have come for forming a Society for the extension of the suffrage to women. The existence of the Society is due to my daughter's initiative; its constitution was planned entirely by her, and she was the soul of the movement during its first years, though delicate health and superabundant occupation made her decline to be a member of the Executive Committee. Many distinguished members of parliament, professors, and others, and some of the most eminent women of whom the country can boast, became members of the Society, a large proportion either directly or indirectly through my daughter's influence, she having written the greater number, and all the best, of the letters by which adhesions was obtained, even when those letters bore my signature. In two remarkable instances, those of Miss Nightingale and Miss Mary Carpenter, the reluctance those ladies had at first felt to come forward, (for it was not on their past difference of opinion) was overcome by appeals written by my daughter though signed by me. Associations for the same object were formed in various local centres, Manchester, Edinburgh, Birmingham, Bristol, and Glasgow; and others which have done much valuable work for the cause. All the Societies take the title of branches of the National Society for Women's Suffrage; but each has its own governing body, and acts in complete independence of the others.

I believe I have mentioned all that is worth remembering of my proceedings in the House. But their enumeration, even if complete, would give but an inadequate idea of my occupations during that period, and especially of the time taken up by correspondence. For many years before my election to Parliament, I had been continually receiving letters from strangers, mostly addressed to me as a writer on philosophy, and either propounding difficulties or communicating thoughts on subjects connected with logic or political economy. In common, I suppose, with all who are known as political economists, I was a recipient of all the shallow theories and absurd proposals by which people are perpetually endeavouring to show the way to universal wealth and happiness by some artful reorganization of the currency. When there were signs of sufficient intelligence in the writers to make it worth while attempting to put them right, I took the trouble to point out their errors, until the growth of my correspondence made it necessary to dismiss such persons with very brief answers. Many, however, of the communications I received were more worthy of attention than these, and in some, oversights of detail were pointed out in my writings, which I was thus enabled to correct. Correspondence of this sort naturally multiplied with the multiplication of the subjects on which I wrote, especially those of a metaphysical character. But when I became a member of parliament, I began to receive letters on private grievances and on every imaginable subject that related to any kind of public affairs, however remote from my knowledge or pursuits. It was not my constituents in Westminster who laid this burthen on me: they kept with remarkable fidelity the understanding on which I had consented to serve. I received, indeed, now and then an application from some ingenuous youth to procure for him a small government appointment; but these were few, and how simple and ignorant the writers were, was shown by the fact that the applications came in about equally whichever party was in power. My invariable answer was, that it was contrary to the principles on which I was elected to ask favours of any Government. But, on the whole, hardly any part of the country gave me less trouble than my own constituents. The general mass of correspondence, however, swelled into an oppressive burthen.

At this time, and thenceforth, a great proportion of all my letters (including many which found their way into the newspapers*) were not written by me but by my daughter; at first merely from her willingness to help in disposing of a mass of letters greater than I could get through without assistance, but afterwards because I thought the letters she wrote superior to mine, and more so in proportion to the difficulty and im-

---

* One which deserves particular mention is a letter respecting the Habitual Criminals Act and the functions of a police generally, written in answer to a private application for my opinion, but which got into the newspapers and excited some notice. This letter which was full of original and valuable thoughts was entirely my daughter's; the fertility and aptness which distinguishes her practical conceptions of the adaptation of means to ends is such as I can never hope to rival.

portance of the occasion. Even those which I wrote myself were generally much improved by her, as is also the case with all the more recent of my prepared speeches, of which, and of some of my published writings, not a few passages, and those the most successful, were hers.

While I remained in Parliament my work as an author was unavoidably limited to the recess. During that time I wrote (besides the pamphlet on Ireland, already mentioned), the Essay on Plato, published in the Edinburgh Review, and reprinted in the third volume of "Dissertations and Discussions;" and the Address which, conformably to custom, I delivered to the University of St. Andrew's, whose students had done me the honour of electing me to the office of Rector. In this Discourse I gave expression to many thoughts and opinions which had been accumulating in me through life, respecting the various studies which belong to a liberal education, their uses and influences, and the mode in which they should be pursued to render their influences most beneficial. The position I took up, vindicating the high educational value alike of the old classic and the new scientific studies, on even stronger grounds than are urged by most of their advocates, and insisting that it is only the stupid inefficiency of the usual teaching which makes those studies be regarded as competitors instead of allies, was, I think, calculated, not only to aid and stimulate the improvement which has happily commenced in the national institutions for higher education, but to diffuse juster ideas than we often find, even in highly educated men, on the conditions of the highest mental cultivation.

During this period also I commenced (and completed soon after I had left Parliament) the performance of a duty to philosophy and to the memory of my father, by preparing and publishing an edition of the "Analysis of the Phenomena of the Human Mind," with notes bringing up the doctrines of that admirable book to the latest improvements in science and in speculation. This was a joint undertaking: the psychological notes being furnished in about equal proportions by Mr. Bain and myself, while Mr. Grote supplied some valuable contributions on points in the history of philosophy incidentally raised, and Dr. Andrew Findlater supplied the deficiencies in the book which had been occasioned by the imperfect philological knowledge of the time when it was written. Having been originally published at a time when the current of metaphysical speculation ran in a quite opposite direction to the psychology of Experience and Association, the "Analysis" had not obtained the amount of immediate success which it deserved, though it had made a deep impression on many individual minds, and had largely contributed, through those minds, to create that more favourable atmosphere for the Association Psychology of which we now have the benefit. Admirably adapted for a class-book of the Experience Metaphysics, it only required to be enriched, and in some cases corrected, by the results of more recent labours in the same school of thought, to stand, as it now does, in company with Mr. Bain's treatises, at the head of the systematic works on Analytic psychology.

In the autumn of 1868 the Parliament which passed the Reform Act was dissolved, and at the new election for Westminster I was thrown out; not to my surprise, nor, I believe, to that of my principal supporters, though in the few days preceding the election they had become more sanguine than before. That I should not have been elected at all would not have required any explanation; what excites curiosity is that I should have been elected the first time, or, having been elected then, should have been defeated afterwards. But the efforts made to defeat me were far greater on the second occasion than on the first. For one thing, the Tory Government was now struggling for existence, and success in any contest was of more importance to them. Then, too, all persons of Tory feelings were far more embittered against me individually than on the previous occasion; many who had at first been either favourable or indifferent, were vehemently opposed to my re-election. As I had shown in my political writings that I was aware of the weak points in democratic opinions, some Conservatives, it seems, had not been without hopes of finding me an opponent of democracy: as I was able to see the Conservative side of the question, they presumed that, like them, I could not see any other side. Yet if they had really read my writings, they would have known that after giving full weight to all that appeared to me well grounded in the arguments against democracy, I unhesitatingly decided in its favour, while recommending that it should be accompanied by such institutions as were consistent with its principle and calculated to ward off its inconveniences: one of the chief of these remedies being Proportional Representation, on which scarcely any of the Conservatives gave me any support. Some Tory expectations appear to have been founded on the approbation I had expressed of plural voting, under certain conditions: and it has been surmised that the suggestion of this sort made in

one of the Resolutions which Mr. Disraeli introduced into the
House preparatory to his Reform Bill (a suggestion which
meeting with no favour he did not press), may have been
occasioned by what I had written on the point: but if so, it
was forgotten that I had made it an express condition that
the privilege of a plurality of votes should be annexed to
education, not to property, and even so, had approved of it
only on the supposition of universal suffrage. How utterly in-
admissible such plural voting would be under the suffrage
given by the present Reform Act, is proved, to any who could
otherwise doubt it, by the very small weight which the working classes are found to possess in elections, even under the
law which gives no more votes to any one elector than to any
other.

While I thus was far more obnoxious to the Tory interest,
and to many Conservative Liberals than I had formerly been,
the course I pursued in Parliament had by no means been such
as to make Liberals generally at all enthusiastic in my support.
It has already been mentioned, how large a proportion of my
prominent appearances had been on questions on which I
differed from most of the Liberal party, or about which they
cared little, and how few occasions there had been on which
the line I took was such as could lead them to attach any great
value to me as an organ of their opinions. I had moreover done
things which had excited, in many minds, a personal prejudice
against me. Many were offended by what they called the
persecution of Mr. Eyre: and still greater offence was taken at
my sending a subscription to the election expenses of Mr.
Bradlaugh. Having refused to be at any expense for my own
election, and having had all its expenses defrayed by others,
I felt under a peculiar obligation to subscribe in my turn
where funds were deficient for candidates whose election was
desirable. I accordingly sent subscriptions to nearly all the
working class candidates, and among others to Mr. Bradlaugh.
He had the support of the working classes; having heard him
speak, I knew him to be a man of ability, and he had proved
that he was the reverse of a demagogue, by placing himself in
strong opposition to the prevailing opinion of the democratic
party on two such important subjects as Malthusianism and
Personal Representation. Men of this sort, who, while sharing
the democratic feelings of the working classes, judged political questions for themselves, and had courage to assert
their individual convictions against popular opposition, were
needed, as it seemed to me, in Parliament, and I did not think

that Mr. Bradlaugh's anti-religious opinions (even though he had been intemperate in the expression of them) ought to exclude him. In subscribing, however, to his election, I did what would have been highly imprudent if I had been at liberty to consider only the interests of my own re-election; and, as might be expected, the utmost possible use, both fair and unfair, was made of this act of mine to stir up the electors of Westminster against me. To these various causes, combined with an unscrupulous use of the usual pecuniary and other influences on the side of my Tory competitor, while none were used on my side, it is to be ascribed that I failed at my second election after having succeeded at the first. No sooner was the result of the election known than I received three or four invitations to become a candidate for other constituencies, chiefly counties; but even if success could have been expected, and this without expense, I was not disposed to deny myself the relief of returning to private life. I had no cause to feel humiliated at my rejection by the electors; and if I had, the feeling would have been far outweighed by the numerous expressions of regret which I received from all sorts of persons and places, and in a most marked degree from those members of the liberal party in Parliament, with whom I had been accustomed to act.

Since that time little has occurred which there is need to commemorate in this place. I returned to my old pursuits and to the enjoyment of a country life in the South of Europe, alternating twice a year with a residence of some weeks or months in the neighbourhood of London. I have written various articles in periodicals (chiefly in my friend Mr. Morley's Fortnightly Review), have made a small number of speeches on public occasions, especially at the meetings of the Women's Suffrage Society, have published the "Subjection of Women," written some years before, with some additions by my daughter and myself, and have commenced the preparation of matter for future books, of which it will be time to speak more particularly if I live to finish them. Here, therefore, for the present, this Memoir may close.

ONE of the subjects which Mill, during the crisis year of 1854, planned to include in his two volumes of basic essays was "Foundation of Morals." The progress of his illness forced him to leave for a six-week walking trip through Brittany, in an effort to build up his strength. Crossing from Jersey to St. Malo he worked out the plan for an essay on Justice, and when he was held up the next day by rain at St. Malo he started writing it. A letter to his wife in London, at the end of June, still from Brittany, reports: "I do not find the essay on Justice goes on well. I wrote a good long piece of it at Quimper, but it is too metaphysical, & not what is most wanted— but I must finish it now in that vein & then strike into another." It is fair to assume that this theme and related ones were being turned over in his mind during his long walks in Brittany, and that they were continued on his return home.

There is evidence that much of the material of what later became *Utilitarianism* was written that year, although not under that title. After his wife's death Mill (as he reports it in his *Autobiography*) "took from their repository a portion of the unpublished papers which I had written during the last years of our married life, and shaped them, with some additional matter, into the little work entitled *Utilitarianism*." It first appeared in three issues of *Fraser's Magazine*, and then (in 1863) as a book.

The title came, of course, from the name of a discussion group Mill had formed when he was only sixteen—a group which started with three members and never reached more than ten. The youngster had found, in a novel by Galt called

Annals of the Parish, a sentence in which a Scotch clergyman warned his parishioners not to leave the Gospel and become "utilitarians." "With a boy's fondness for a name and a banner I seized on the word." The Utilitarian Society became famous, and the young philosophical radicals of the day grouped themselves around the name and banner.

Mill himself tired of the label. He was begining to develop some differences from the Benthamites, and something he read about Turgot's independence from the French Encyclopedists made him resolve to end sectarianism. "I left off designating myself and others as Utilitarians," he writes. And yet, writing later about John Austin, the great English legal philosopher, he says, "Like me, he never ceased to be a utilitarian." The point was, of course, that Mill tired of the label but clung to the substance of doctrine. Almost forty years after he had dissolved the Utilitarian Society, seeking a title for his papers on Justice, and on what he had once called "Foundation of Morals," he went back to the direct unadorned word *Utilitarianism*.

It was, I think, a gesture of affirmation and of the continuity of his thinking through his whole career. And it was a gage of battle flung equally at several groups whom he regarded as dangerous—at the school of "innate ideas," which followed mysticism and revealed religion and social orthodoxy, instead of reforming social institutions by the test of utility; at the vulgar critics of utilitarianism, who saw in it only the morals of the pigsty; and at the Utilitarian enthusiasts of the old Benthamite school, who followed Bentham's table of pleasures and pains too mechanically, and did not allow poetry and emotion as elements in the shaping of character and personality, and as valid constituents of the good society.

In this book then the "Saint of Rationalism," almost sixty when it was published, was coming back full circle to the days of his early manhood, and was coming to terms with his father, with Bentham, with his own early days, and squaring accounts with all the enemies of the life of reason. If I were allowed, by anachronism, to use the titles of three later books by other authors to indicate what the term "Utilitarianism" must have meant in Mill's day to him and his readers, I should cite one title by Santayana—the "Life of Reason," and two by Lippmann—the "Good Society" and "A Preface to Morals." Mill deals in this book with all three of these central themes— the foundations of morals, the nature of a good society, and the quality and temper of the life of reason. Thrown in for good measure are discussions of politics, of law, and of education in the sense of the lifting of the levels and standards of social intelligence.

Thus, although slight in bulk and deceptively lucid in manner, this is not a lightweight book. No one had ever before rounded out the full implications of the principle of social utility—what man can do for man, not by rigid conventions and taboos or by religion, but by applying the standard of human welfare to laws, decisions, and institutions. If today we read the term "welfare" for Mill's terms "happiness" and "utility," we shall come closer to the spirit of Mill's book.

But if you talk either of welfare, or (as Mill did) of happiness and utility, you come up against knotty questions. How can you decide of what happiness and utility consist, and *who* decides? Mill insisted that the tests were not only material, as the Benthamites had thought. He includes the emotional life of man as well—the whole range of music, poetry, the arts. The man who played the piano every day at Blackheath, who had wandered through France and Italy and Greece, was not a man to exclude from the tests of social welfare the receptivity of as many people as possible to the best creations of the human mind and spirit. Mill deplored the English fear and repression of the emotions, and attacked the insensitivity of so many of the English middle-class to the life of the intellect and the sensibilities.

Yet if he managed to crowd the non-rational into the house of utility, he never quite answered the question of who was to decide what was good for the good society and what was not. And even when he brought in the emotional and aesthetic life, he did it not by their own standards and for their own sake, but by making them pass the scrutiny of reason. Nor did he ever get away from his faulty and almost rudimentary psychology of association, and reach deep into the tangled and tragic nature of life. Thus with all its courage and nobility, this little book (I fear) leaves a trace of dust in the mouth.

CONTENTS

UTILITARIANISM

I. GENERAL REMARKS

THERE are few circumstances among those which make up the present condition of human knowledge more unlike what might have been expected, or more significant of the backward state in which speculation on the most important subjects still lingers, than the little progress which has been made in the decision of the controversy respecting the criterion of right and wrong. From the dawn of philosophy the question concerning the *summum bonum*, or, what is the same thing, concerning the foundation of morality, has been accounted the main problem in speculative thought, has occupied the most gifted intellects, and divided them into sects and schools, carrying on a vigorous warfare against one another. And after more than two thousand years the same discussions continue, philosophers are still ranged under the same contending banners, and neither thinkers nor mankind at large seem nearer to being unanimous on the subject than when the youth Socrates listened to the old Protagoras, and asserted (if Plato's dialogue be grounded on a real conversation) the theory of utilitarianism against the popular morality of the so-called Sophist.

It is true that similar confusion and uncertainty, and in some cases similar discordance, exist respecting the first principles of all the sciences, not excepting that which is deemed the most certain of them, mathematics; without much impairing, generally indeed without impairing at all, the trustworthiness of the conclusions of those sciences. An apparent anomaly, the explanation of which is that the detailed doctrines of a science are not usually deduced from, or depend for their evidence upon, what are called its first principles. Were it not so, there would be no science more precarious, or whose conclusions were more insufficiently made out, than algebra; which derives none of its certainty from what are commonly taught to learners as its elements, since these, as laid down by some of its most eminent teachers, are as full of fictions as English law, and of mysteries as theology.

The truths which are ultimately accepted as the first principles of a science, are really the last results of metaphysical analysis, practised on the elementary notions with which the science is conversant; and their relation to the science is not that of foundations to an edifice, but of roots to a tree, which may perform their office equally well though they be never dug down to and exposed to light. But though in science the particular truths precede the general theory, the contrary might be expected to be the case with a practical art, such as morals or legislation. All action is for the sake of some end, and rules of action, it seems natural to suppose, must take their whole character and colour from the end to which they are subservient. When we engage in a pursuit, a clear and precise conception of what we are pursuing would seem to be the first thing we need, instead of the last we are to look forward to. A test of right and wrong must be the means, one would think, of ascertaining what is right or wrong, and not a consequence of having already ascertained it.

The difficulty is not avoided by having recourse to the popular theory of a natural faculty, a sense or instinct, informing us of right and wrong. For—besides that the existence of such a moral instinct is itself one of the matters in dispute—those believers in it who have any pretensions to philosophy, have been obliged to abandon the idea that it discerns what is right or wrong in the particular case in hand, as our other senses discern the sight or sound actually present. Our moral faculty, according to all those of its interpreters who are entitled to the name of thinkers, supplies us only with the general principles of moral judgments; it is a branch of our reason, not of our sensitive faculty; and must be looked to for the abstract doctrines of morality, not for perception of it in the concrete. The intuitive, no less than what may be termed the inductive, school of ethics, insists on the necessity of general laws. They both agree that the morality of an individual action is not a question of direct perception, but the application of a law to an individual case. They recognise also, to a great extent, the same moral laws; but differ as to their evidence, and the source from which they derive their authority. According to the one opinion, the principles of morals are evident à priori, requiring nothing to command assent except that the meaning of the terms be understood. According to the other doctrine, right and wrong, as well as truth and falsehood, are questions of observation and experience. But both hold equally that morality must be deduced from principles; and the intuitive school affirm as strongly as the inductive that there is a science of morals. Yet they seldom attempt to make out a list of the *à priori* principles which are to serve as the premises of the science; still more rarely do they make any effort to reduce those various principles to one first principle, or common ground of obligation. They either assume the ordinary precepts of morals as of *à priori* authority, or they lay down as the common groundwork of those maxims some generality which is much less obviously authoritative than the maxims themselves, and which has never succeeded in gaining popular acceptance. Yet to support their pretensions there ought either to be some one fundamental principle or law at the root of all morality, or, if there be several, there should be a determinate order of precedence among them; and the one principle, or the rule for deciding between the various principles when they conflict, ought to be self-evident.

To inquire how far the bad effects of this deficiency have been mitigated in practice, or to what extent the moral beliefs of mankind have been vitiated or made uncertain by the absence of any distinct recognition of an ultimate standard, would imply a complete survey and criticism of past and present ethical doctrine. It would, however, be easy to show that whatever steadiness or consistency these moral beliefs have attained has been mainly due to the tacit influence of a standard not recognized. Although the non-existence of an acknowledged first principle has made ethics not so much a guide as a consecration of men's actual sentiments, still, as men's sentiments, both of favour and aversion, are greatly influenced by what they suppose to be the effects of things upon their happiness, the principle of utility, or as Bentham latterly called it, the greatest happiness principle, has had a large share in forming the moral doctrines even of those who most scornfully reject its authority. Nor is there any school of thought which refuses to admit that the influence of actions on happiness is a most material and even predominant consideration in many of the details of morals, however unwilling to acknowledge it as the fundamental principle of morality, and the source of moral obligation. I might go much further, and say that to all those *à priori* moralists who deem it necessary to argue at all utilitarian arguments are indispensable. It is not my present purpose to criticize these thinkers; but I cannot help referring, for illustration, to a systematic treatise by one of the most illustrious of them, *The Metaphysics of Ethics*, by Kant.

This remarkable man, whose system of thought will long remain one of the landmarks in the history of philosophical speculation, does, in the treatise in question, lay down a universal first principle as the origin and ground of moral obligation; it is this: 'So act that the rule on which thou actest would admit of being adopted as a law by all rational beings.' But when he begins to deduce from this precept any of the actual duties of morality, he fails, almost grotesquely, to show that there would be any contradiction, any logical (not to say physical) impossibility, in the adoption by all rational beings of the most outrageously immoral rules of conduct. All he shows is that the *consequences* of their universal adoption would be such as no one would choose to incur.

On the present occasion, I shall, without further discussion of the other theories, attempt to contribute something towards the understanding and appreciation of the Utilitarian or Happiness theory, and towards such proof as it is susceptible of. It is evident that this cannot be proof in the ordinary and popular meaning of the term. Questions of ultimate ends are not amenable to direct proof. Whatever can be proved to be good must be so by being shown to be a means to something admitted to be good without proof. The medical art is proved to be good, by its conducing to health; but how is it possible to prove that health is good? The art of music is good, for the reason, among others, that it produces pleasure; but what proof is it possible to give that pleasure is good? If, then, it is asserted that there is a comprehensive formula, including all things which are in themselves good, and that whatever else is good is not so as an end but as a mean, the formula may be accepted or rejected, but is not a subject of what is commonly understood by proof. We are not, however, to infer that its acceptance or rejection must depend on blind impulse or arbitrary choice. There is a larger meaning of the word proof, in which this question is as amenable to it as any other of the disputed questions of philosophy. The subject is within the cognizance of the rational faculty; and neither does that faculty deal with it solely in the way of intuition. Considerations may be presented capable of determining the intellect either to give or withhold its assent to the doctrine; and this is equivalent to proof.

We shall examine presently of what nature are these considerations; in what manner they apply to the case, and what rational grounds, therefore, can be given for accepting or rejecting the utilitarian formula. But it is a preliminary condition of rational acceptance or rejection that the formula should be correctly understood. I believe that the very imperfect notion ordinarily formed of its meaning is the chief obstacle which impedes its reception; and that could it be cleared, even from only the grosser misconceptions, the question would be greatly simplified, and a large proportion of its difficulties removed. Before, therefore, I attempt to enter into the philosophical grounds which can be given for assenting to the utilitarian standard I shall offer some illustrations of the doctrine itself, with the view of showing more clearly what it is, distinguishing it from what it is not, and disposing of such of the practical objections to it as either originate in, or are closely connected with, mistaken interpretations of its meaning. Having thus prepared the ground, I shall afterwards endeavour to throw such light as I can upon the question, considered as one of philosophical theory.

II. WHAT UTILITARIANISM IS

A PASSING remark is all that needs be given to the ignorant blunder of supposing that those who stand up for utility as the test of right and wrong use the term in that restricted and merely colloquial sense in which utility is opposed to pleasure. An apology is due to the philosophical opponents of utilitarianism, for even the momentary appearance of confounding them with any one capable of so absurd a misconception, which is the more extraordinary, inasmuch as the contrary accusation, of referring everything to pleasure, and that too in its grossest form, is another of the common charges against utilitarianism: and, as has been pointedly remarked by an able writer, the same sort of persons, and often the very same persons, denounce the theory 'as impracticably dry when the word utility precedes the word pleasure, and as too practicably voluptuous when the word pleasure precedes the word utility.'

Those who know anything about the matter are aware that every writer from Epicurus to Bentham who maintained the theory of utility meant by it, not something to be contradistinguished from pleasure, but pleasure itself, together with exemption from pain; and, instead of opposing the useful to the agreeable or the ornamental, have always declared that the useful means these, among other things.

Yet the common herd, including the herd of writers not only in newspapers and periodicals but in books of weight and pretension, are perpetually falling into this shallow mistake. Having caught up the word utilitarian, while knowing nothing whatever about it but its sound, they habitually express by it the rejection, or the neglect, of pleasure in some of its forms: of beauty, of ornament, or of amusement. Nor is the term thus ignorantly misapplied solely in disparagement, but occasionally in compliment; as though it implied superiority to frivolity and the mere pleasures of the moment. And this perverted use is the only one in which the word is popularly known, and the one from which the new generation are acquiring their sole notion of its meaning. Those who introduced the word, but who had for many years discontinued it as a distinctive appellation, may well feel themselves called upon to resume it, if by doing so they can hope to contribute anything towards rescuing it from this utter degradation.*

The creed which accepts as the foundation of morals, Utility, or the Greatest Happiness Principle, holds that actions are right in proportion as they tend to promote happiness, wrong as they tend to produce the reverse of happiness. By happiness is intended pleasure and the absence of pain; by unhappiness, pain and the privation of pleasure. To give a clear view of the moral standard set up by the theory much more requires to be said; in particular, what things it includes in the ideas of pain and pleasure; and to what extent this is left an open question. But these supplementary explanations do not affect the theory of life on which this theory of morality is grounded—namely, that pleasure and freedom from pain are the only things desirable as ends; and that all desirable things (which are as numerous in the utilitarian as in any other scheme) are desirable either for the pleasure inherent in themselves, or as means to the promotion of pleasure and the prevention of pain.

Now, such a theory of life excites in many minds, and

* The author of this essay has reason for believing himself to be the first person who brought the word utilitarian into use. He did not invent it, but adopted it from a passing expression in Mr. Galt's *Annals of the Parish.* After using it as a designation for several years, he and others abandoned it from a growing dislike to anything resembling a badge or watchword of sectarian distinction. But as a name for one single opinion, not a set of opinions —to denote the recognition of utility as a standard, not any particular way of applying it—the term supplies a want in the language, and offers, in many cases, a convenient mode of avoiding tiresome circumlocution.

among them in some of the most estimable in feeling and purpose, inveterate dislike. To suppose that life has (as they express it) no higher end than pleasure—no better and nobler object of desire and pursuit—they designate as utterly mean and grovelling; as a doctrine worthy only of swine, to whom the followers of Epicurus were, at a very early period, contemptuously likened; and modern holders of the doctrine are occasionally made the subject of equally polite comparisons by its German, French, and English assailants.

When thus attacked, the Epicureans have always answered that it is not they, but their accusers, who represent human nature in a degrading light; since the accusation supposes human beings to be capable of no pleasures except those of which swine are capable. If this supposition were true, the charge could not be gainsaid, but would then be no longer an imputation; for if the sources of pleasure were precisely the same to human beings and to swine, the rule of life which is good enough for the one would be good enough for the other. The comparison of the Epicurean life to that of beasts is felt as degrading, precisely because a beast's pleasures do not satisfy a human being's conceptions of happiness. Human beings have faculties more elevated than the animal appetites, and, when once made conscious of them, do not regard anything as happiness which does not include their gratification. I do not, indeed, consider the Epicureans to have been by any means faultless in drawing out their scheme of consequences from the utilitarian principle. To do this is any sufficient manner, many Stoic, as well as Christian, elements require to be included. But there is no known Epicurean theory of life which does not assign to the pleasures of the intellect, of the feelings and imagination, and of the moral sentiments, a much higher value as pleasures than to those of mere sensation.

It must be admitted, however, that utilitarian writers in general have placed the superiority of mental over bodily pleasures chiefly in the greater permanency, safety, uncostliness, etc., of the former—that is, in their circumstantial advantages rather than in their intrinsic nature. And on all these points utilitarians have fully proved their case; but they might have taken the other, and, as it may be called, higher ground, with entire consistency. It is quite compatible with the principle of utility to recognize the fact that some *kinds* of pleasure are more desirable and more valuable than others. It would be absurd that while, in estimating all other things, quality is considered as well as quantity, the estimation of pleasures should be supposed to depend on quantity alone.

If I am asked what I mean by difference of quality in pleasures, or what makes one pleasure more valuable than another, merely as a pleasure, except its being greater in amount, there is but one possible answer. Of two pleasures, if there be one to which all or almost all who have experience of both give a decided preference, irrespective of any feeling of moral obligation to prefer it, that is the more desirable pleasure. If one of the two is, by those who are competently acquainted with both, placed so far above the other that they prefer it, even though knowing it to be attended with a greater amount of discontent, and would not resign it for any quantity of the other pleasure of which their nature is capable, we are justified in ascribing to the preferred enjoyment a superiority in quality so far outweighing quantity as to render it, in comparison, of small account.

Now, it is an unquestionable fact that those who are equally acquainted with, and equally capable of appreciating and enjoying, both do give a most marked preference to the manner of existence which employs their higher faculties. Few human creatures would consent to be changed into any of the lower animals for a promise of the fullest allowance of a beast's pleasures; no intelligent human being would consent to be a fool, no instructed person would be an ignoramus, no person of feeling and conscience would be selfish and base, even though they should be persuaded that the fool, the dunce, or the rascal is better satisfied with his lot than they are with theirs. They would not resign what they possess more than he for the most complete satisfaction of all the desires which they have in common with him. If they ever fancy they would, it is only in cases of unhappiness so extreme that to escape from it they would exchange their lot for almost any other, however undesirable in their own eyes. A being of higher faculties requires more to make him happy, is capable probably of more acute suffering, and certainly accessible to it at more points, than one of an inferior type; but in spite of these liabilities, he can never really wish to sink into what he feels to be a lower grade of existence.

We may give what explanation we please of this unwillingness; we may attribute it to pride, a name which is given indiscriminately to some of the most and to some of the least estimable feelings of which mankind are capable; we may refer it to the love of liberty and personal independence, an appeal to which was with the Stoics one of the most effective

means for the inculcation of it, to the love of power, or to the
love of excitement, both of which do really enter into and
contribute to it: but its most appropriate appellation is a sense
of dignity, which all human beings possess in one form or another, and in some, though by no means in exact, proportion
to their higher faculties, and which is so essential a part of
the happiness of those in whom it is strong that nothing which
conflicts with it could be, otherwise than momentarily, an
object of desire to them. Whoever supposes that this preference takes place at a sacrifice of happiness—that the superior
being, in anything like equal circumstances, is not happier
than the inferior—confounds the two very different ideas, of
happiness, and content. It is indisputable that the being whose
capacities of enjoyment are low, has the greatest chance of
having them fully satisfied; and a highly endowed being will
always feel that any happiness which he can look for, as the
world is constituted, is imperfect. But he can learn to bear its
imperfections, if they are at all bearable; and they will not
make him envy the being who is indeed unconscious of the
imperfections, but only because he feels not at all the good
which those imperfections qualify. It is better to be a human
being dissatisfied than a pig satisfied; better to be Socrates
dissatisfied than a fool satisfied. And if the fool, or the pig,
are of a different opinion, it is because they only know their
own side of the question. The other party to the comparison
knows both sides.

It may be objected that many who are capable of the
higher pleasures, occasionally, under the influence of temptation, postpone them to the lower. But this is quite compatible
with a full appreciation of the intrinsic superiority of the
higher. Men often, from infirmity of character, make their
election for the nearer good, though they know it to be the
less valuable; and this no less when the choice is between
two bodily pleasures than when it is between bodily and
mental. They pursue sensual indulgences to the injury of
health, though perfectly aware that health is the greater good.

It may be further objected that many who begin with
youthful enthusiasm for everything noble, as they advance in
years sink into indolence and selfishness. But I do not believe
that those who undergo this very common change voluntarily
choose the lower description of pleasures in preference to the
higher. I believe that before they devote themselves exclusively to the one, they have already become incapable of the
other. Capacity for the nobler feelings is in most natures a

very tender plant, easily killed not only by hostile influences but by mere want of sustenance; and in the majority of young persons it speedily dies away if the occupations to which their position in life has devoted them, and the society into which it has thrown them, are not favourable to keeping that higher capacity in exercise. Men lose their high aspirations as they lose their intellectual tastes, because they have not time or opportunity for indulging them; and they addict themselves to inferior pleasures not because they deliberately prefer them, but because they are either the only ones to which they have access, or the only ones which they are any longer capable of enjoying. It may be questioned whether any one who has remained equally susceptible to both classes of pleasures ever knowingly and calmly preferred the lower; though many, in all ages, have broken down in an ineffectual attempt to combine both.

From this verdict of the only competent judges I apprehend there can be no appeal. On a question which is the best worth having of two pleasures, or which of two modes of existence is the most grateful to the feelings, apart from its moral attributes and from its consequences, the judgment of those who are qualified by knowledge of both, or, if they differ, that of the majority among them, must be admitted as final. And there needs be the less hesitation to accept this judgment respecting the quality of pleasures, since there is no other tribunal to be referred to even on the question of quantity. What means are there of determining which is the acuter of two pains, or the intenser of two pleasurable sensations, except the general suffrage of those who are familiar with both? Neither pains nor pleasures are homogeneous, and pain is always heterogeneous with pleasure. What is there to decide whether a particular pleasure is worth purchasing at the cost of a particular pain, except the feelings and judgment of the experienced? When, therefore, those feelings and judgment declare the pleasures derived from the higher faculties to be preferable *in kind*, apart from the question of intensity, to those of which the animal nature, disjoined from the higher faculties is susceptible, they are entitled on this subject to the same regard.

I have dwelt on this point, as being a necessary part of a perfectly just conception of Utility or Happiness, considered as the directive rule of human conduct. But it is by no means an indispensable condition to the acceptance of the utilitarian standard; for that standard is not the agent's own greatest happiness, but the greatest amount of happiness altogether; and, if it may possibly be doubted whether a noble character is always the happier for its nobleness, there can be no doubt that it makes other people happier, and that the world in general is immensely a gainer by it. Utilitarianism, therefore, could only attain its end by the general cultivation of nobleness of character, even if each individual were only benefited by the nobleness of others, and his own, so far as happiness is concerned, were a sheer deduction from the benefit. But the bare enunciation of such an absurdity as this last renders refutation superfluous.

According to the Greatest Happiness Principle, as above explained, the ultimate end, with reference to and for the sake of which all other things are desirable (whether we are considering our own good or that of other people), is an existence exempt as far as possible from pain, and as rich as possible in enjoyments, both in point of quantity and quality; the test of quality, and the rule for measuring it against quantity, being the preference felt by those who in their opportunities of experience, to which must be added their habits of self-consciousness and self-observation, are best furnished with the means of comparison. This, being, according to the utilitarian opinion, the end of human action, is necessarily also the standard of morality, which may accordingly be defined, the rules and precepts for human conduct, by the observance of which an existence such as has been described might be, to the greatest extent possible, secured to all mankind; and not to them only, but, so far as the nature of things admits, to the whole sentient creation.

Against this doctrine, however, arises another class of objectors, who say that happiness, in any form, cannot be the rational purpose of human life and action; because in the first place, it is unattainable: and they contemptuously ask What right hast thou to be happy?, a question which Mr. Carlyle clenches by the addition, What right, a short time ago, hadst thou even *to be?* Next, they say that men can do *without* happiness; that all noble human beings have felt this, and could not have become noble but by learning the lesson of *Entsagen,* or renunciation; which lesson, thoroughly learnt and submitted to, they affirm to be the beginning and necessary condition of all virtue.

The first of these objections would go to the root of the matter were it well founded; for, if no happiness is to be had at all by human beings, the attainment of it cannot be the end

of morality, or of any rational conduct. Though, even in tha
case, something might still be said for the utilitarian theory
since utility includes not solely the pursuit of happiness, bu
the prevention or mitigation of unhappiness; and, if the forme
aim be chimerical, there will be all the greater scope and mor
imperative need for the latter, so long at least as mankin
think fit to live, and do not take refuge in the simultaneou
act of suicide recommended under certain conditions b
Novalis.

When, however, it is thus positively asserted to be impossi
ble that human life should be happy, the assertion, if no
something like a verbal quibble, is at least an exaggeration. I
by happiness be meant a continuity of highly pleasurable ex
citement, it is evident enough that this is impossible. A state o
exalted pleasure lasts only moments, or in some cases, an
with some intermissions, hours or days, and is the occasiona
brilliant flash of enjoyment, not its permanent and stead
flame. Of this the philosophers who have taught that happi
ness is the end of life were as fully aware as those who taun
them. The happiness which they meant was not a life of rap
ture, but moments of such, in an existence made up of fev
and transitory pains, many and various pleasures, with a de
cided predominance of the active over the passive, and havin
as the foundation of the whole not to expect more from lif
than it is capable of bestowing. A life thus composed, to thos
who have been fortunate enough to obtain it, has always ap
peared worthy of the name of happiness. And such an ex
istence is even now the lot of many, during some considerabl
portion of their lives. The present wretched education an
wretched social arrangements are the only real hindrance t
its being attainable by almost all.

The objectors perhaps may doubt whether human beings
if taught to consider happiness as the end of life, would b
satisfied with such a moderate share of it. But great number
of mankind have been satisfied with much less. The main con
stituents of a satisfied life appear to be two, either of whic
by itself is often found sufficient for the purpose: tranquillit
and excitement. With much tranquillity, many find that the
can be content with very little pleasure: with much excite
ment, many can reconcile themselves to a considerable quan
tity of pain.

There is assuredly no inherent impossibility in enablin
even the mass of mankind to unite both; since the two are s
far from being incompatible that they are in natural alliance

the prolongation of either being a preparation for, and exciting a wish for, the other. It is only those in whom indolence amounts to a vice that do not desire excitement after an interval of repose: it is only those in whom the need of excitement is a disease that feel the tranquillity which follows excitement dull and insipid, instead of pleasurable in direct proportion to the excitement which preceded it. When people who are tolerably fortunate in their outward lot do not find in life sufficient enjoyment to make it valuable to them, the cause generally is caring for nobody but themselves. To those who have neither public nor private affections, the excitements of life are much curtailed, and in any case dwindle in value as the time approaches when all selfish interests must be terminated by death; while those who leave after them objects of personal affection, and especially those who have also cultivated a fellow-feeling with the collective interests of mankind, retain as lively an interest in life on the eve of death as in the vigour of youth and health.

Next to selfishness, the principal cause which makes life unsatisfactory is want of mental cultivation. A cultivated mind —I do not mean that of a philosopher, but any mind to which the fountains of knowledge have been opened, and which has been taught, in any tolerable degree, to exercise its faculties— finds sources of inexhaustible interest in all that surrounds it: in the objects of nature, the achievements of art, the imaginations of poetry, the incidents of history, the ways of mankind, past and present, and their prospects in the future. It is possible, indeed, to become indifferent to all this, and that too without having exhausted a thousandth part of it; but only when one has had from the beginning no moral or human interest in these things, and has sought in them only the gratification of curiosity.

Now, there is absolutely no reason in the nature of things why an amount of mental culture sufficient to give an intelligent interest in these objects of contemplation should not be the inheritance of every one born in a civilized country. As little is there an inherent necessity that any human being should be a selfish egoist, devoid of every feeling or care but those which centre in his own miserable individuality. Something far superior to this is sufficiently common even now, to give ample earnest of what the human species may be made. Genuine private affections, and a sincere interest in the public good, are possible, though in unequal degrees, to every rightly brought up human being. In a world in which there is so

much to interest, so much to enjoy, and so much also to correct and improve, every one who has this moderate amount
of moral and intellectual requisites is capable of an existence
which may be called enviable; and, unless such a person,
through bad laws, or subjection to the will of others, is denied
the liberty to use the sources of happiness within his reach, he
will not fail to find this enviable existence, if he escape the
positive evils of life, the great sources of physical and mental
suffering—such as indigence, disease, and the unkindness,
worthlessness, or premature loss of objects of affection.

The main stress of the problem lies, therefore, in the contest
with these calamities, from which it is a rare good fortune
entirely to escape; which, as things now are, cannot be obvi-
ated, and often cannot be in any material degree mitigated.
Yet no one whose opinion deserves a moment's consideration
can doubt that most of the great positive evils of the world
are in themselves removable, and will, if human affairs continue to improve, be in the end reduced within narrow limits.
Poverty, in any sense implying suffering, may be completely
extinguished by the wisdom of society, combined with the
good sense and providence of individuals. Even that most intractable of enemies, disease, may be indefinitely reduced in
dimensions by good physical and moral education, and proper
control of noxious influences; while the progress of science
holds out a promise for the future of still more direct conquests over this detestable foe. And every advance in that
direction relieves us from some, not only of the chances which
cut short our own lives, but, what concerns us still more,
which deprive us of those in whom our happiness is wrapt up.
As for vicissitudes of fortune and other disappointments connected with worldly circumstances, these are principally the
effect either of gross imprudence, of ill-regulated desires, or
of bad or imperfect social institutions. All the grand sources,
in short, of human suffering are in a great degree, many of
them almost entirely, conquerable by human care and effort;
and though their removal is grievously slow—though a long
succession of generations will perish in the breach before the
conquest is completed, and this world becomes all that, if
will and knowledge were not wanting, it might easily be made
—yet every mind sufficiently intelligent and generous to bear
a part, however small and unconspicuous, in the endeavour
will draw a noble enjoyment from the contest itself, which he
would not for any bribe in the form of selfish indulgence consent to be without.

And this leads to the true estimation of what is said by the objectors concerning the possibility, and the obligation, of learning to do without happiness. Unquestionably it is possible to do without happiness; it is done involuntarily by nineteen-twentieths of mankind, even in those parts of our present world which are least deep in barbarism; and it often has to be done voluntarily by the hero or the martyr, for the sake of something which he prizes more than his individual happiness. But this something, what is it, unless the happiness of others, or some of the requisites of happiness? It is noble to be capable of resigning entirely one's own portion of happiness, or chances of it; but, after all, this self-sacrifice must be for some end: it is not its own end; and if we are told that its end is not happiness but virtue, which is better than happiness, I ask would the sacrifice be made if the hero or martyr did not believe that it would earn for others immunity from similar sacrifices? Would it be made if he thought that his renunciation of happiness for himself would produce no fruit for any of his fellow creatures but to make their lot like his, and place them also in the condition of persons who have renounced happiness? All honour to those who can abnegate for themselves the personal enjoyment of life, when by such renunciation they contribute worthily to increase the amount of happiness in the world; but he who does it, or professes to do it, for any other purpose, is no more deserving of admiration than the ascetic mounted on his pillar. He may be an inspiriting proof of what men *can* do, but assuredly not an example of what they *should*.

Though it is only in a very imperfect state of the world's arrangements that any one can best serve the happiness of others by the absolute sacrifice of his own, yet, so long as the world is in that imperfect state, I fully acknowledge that the readiness to make such a sacrifice is the highest virtue which can be found in man. I will add that in this condition of the world, paradoxical as the assertion may be, the conscious ability to do without happiness gives the best prospect of realizing such happiness as is attainable. For nothing except that consciousness can raise a person above the chances of life, by making him feel that, let fate and fortune do their worst, they have not power to subdue him: which, once felt, frees him from excess of anxiety concerning the evils of life, and enables him, like many a Stoic in the worst times of the Roman Empire, to cultivate in tranquillity the sources of satisfaction accessible to him, without concerning himself about the uncertainty of their duration, any more than about their inevitable end.

Meanwhile, let utilitarians never cease to claim the morality of self-devotion as a possession which belongs by as good a right to them as either to the Stoic or to the Transcendentalist. The utilitarian morality does recognize in human beings the power of sacrificing their own greatest good for the good of others. It refuses only to admit that the sacrifice is itself a good. A sacrifice which does not increase, nor tend to increase, the sum total of happiness it considers as wasted. The only self-renunciation which it applauds is devotion to the happiness, or to some of the means of happiness, of others; either of mankind collectively, or of individuals within the limits imposed by the collective interests of mankind.

I must again repeat, what the assailants of utilitarianism seldom have the justice to acknowledge, that the happiness which forms the utilitarian standard of what is right in conduct is not the agent's own happiness, but that of all concerned. As between his own happiness and that of others, utilitarianism requires him to be as strictly impartial as a disinterested and benevolent spectator. In the golden rule of Jesus of Nazareth we read the complete spirit of the ethics of utility. To do as you would be done by, and to love your neighbour as yourself, constitute the ideal perfection of utilitarian morality. As the means of making the nearest approach to this ideal, utility would enjoin first, that laws and social arrangements should place the happiness, or (as speaking practically it may be called) the interest, of every individual, as nearly as possible in harmony with the interest of the whole; and secondly, that education and opinion, which have so vast a power over human character, should so use that power as to establish in the mind of every individual an indissoluble association between his own happiness and the good of the whole; especially between his own happiness and the practice of such modes of conduct, negative and positive, as regard for the universal happiness prescribes; so that not only he may be unable to conceive the possibility of happiness to himself, consistently with conduct opposed to the general good, but also that a direct impulse to promote the general good may be in every individual one of the habitual motives of action, and the sentiments connected therewith may fill a large and prominent place in every human being's sentient existence. If the impugners of the utilitarian morality represented it to their own minds in this its true character, I know not what recommendation possessed by any other morality they could possibly affirm to be wanting to it; what more beautiful or more exalted developments of human nature any other ethical system can be supposed to foster, or what springs of action, not accessible to the utilitarian, such systems rely on for giving effect to their mandates.

The objectors to utilitarianism cannot always be charged with representing it in a discreditable light. On the contrary, those among them who entertain anything like a just idea of its disinterested character, sometimes find fault with its standard as being too high for humanity. They say it is exacting too much to require that people shall always act from the inducement of promoting the general interests of society. But this is to mistake the very meaning of a standard of morals, and confound the rule of action with the motive of it. It is the business of ethics to tell us what are our duties, or by what test we may know them; but no system of ethics requires that the sole motive of all we do shall be a feeling of duty: on the contrary, ninety-nine hundredths of all our actions are done from other motives, and rightly so done, if the rule of duty does not condemn them. It is the more unjust to utilitarianism that this particular misapprehension should be made a ground of objection to it, inasmuch as utilitarian moralists have gone beyond almost all others in affirming that the motive has nothing to do with the morality of the action, though much with the worth of the agent. He who saves a fellow creature from drowning does what is morally right, whether his motive be duty, or the hope of being paid for his trouble; he who betrays the friend that trusts him, is guilty of a crime, even if his object be to serve another friend to whom he is under greater obligations. But to speak only of actions done from the motive of duty, and in direct obedience to principle: it is a misapprehension of the utilitarian mode of thought to conceive it as implying that people should fix their minds upon so wide a generality as the world, or society at large. The great majority of good actions are intended not for the benefit of the world, but for that of individuals, of which the good of the world is made up; and the thoughts of the most virtuous man need not on these occasions travel beyond the particular persons concerned, except so far as is necessary to assure himself that in benefiting them he is not violating the rights, that is the legitimate and authorized expectations, of any one else. The multiplication of happiness is, according to the utilitarian ethics, the object of virtue: the occasions on which any person (except one in a thousand) has it in his power to do this on an extended scale, in other words to be a public benefactor, are but exceptional; and on these occasions alone is he called on to consider public utility; in every other case, private utility, the interest or happiness of some few persons, is all he has to attend to. Those alone the influence of whose actions extends to society in general need concern themselves habitually about so large an object. In the case of abstinences indeed —of things which people forbear to do from moral considerations, though the consequences in the particular case might be beneficial—it would be unworthy of an intelligent agent not to be consciously aware that the action is of a class which, if practised generally, would be generally injurious, and that this is the ground of the obligation to abstain from it. The amount of regard for the public interest implied in this recognition, is no greater than is demanded by every system of morals, for they all enjoin to abstain from whatever is manifestly pernicious to society.

The same considerations dispose of another reproach against the doctrine of utility, founded on a still grosser misconception of the purpose of a standard of morality, and of the very meaning of the words right and wrong. It is often affirmed that utilitarianism renders men cold and unsympathizing; that it chills their moral feelings towards individuals; that it makes them regard only the dry and hard consideration of the consequences of actions, not taking into their moral estimate the qualities from which those actions emanate. If the assertion means that they do not allow their judgment respecting the rightness or wrongness of an action to be influenced by their opinion of the qualities of the person who does it, this is a complaint not against utilitarianism, but against having any standard of morality at all; for certainly no known ethical standard decides an action to be good or bad because it is done by a good or a bad man, still less because done by an amiable, a brave, or a benevolent man, or the contrary. These considerations are relevant, not to the estimation of actions, but of persons; and there is nothing in the utilitarian theory inconsistent with the fact that there are other things which interest us in persons besides the rightness and wrongness of their actions.

The Stoics, indeed, with the paradoxical misuse of language which was part of their system, and by which they strove to raise themselves above all concern about anything but virtue, were fond of saying that he who has that has everything; that he, and only he, is rich, is beautiful, is a king. But no claim of this description is made for the virtuous man by the utilitarian doctrine. Utilitarians are quite aware that there are other desirable possessions and qualities besides virtue, and are perfectly willing to allow to all of them their full worth. They are also aware that a right action does not necessarily indicate a virtuous character, and that actions which are blameable, often proceed from qualities entitled to praise. When this is apparent in any particular case, it modifies their estimation, not certainly of the act, but of the agent. I grant that they are, notwithstanding, of opinion that in the long run the best proof of a good character is good actions; and resolutely refuse to consider any mental disposition as good, of which the predominant tendency is to produce bad conduct. This makes them unpopular with many people; but it is an unpopularity which they must share with every one who regards the distinction between right and wrong in a serious light; and the reproach is not one which a conscientious utilitarian need be anxious to repel.

If no more be meant by the objection than that many utilitarians look on the morality of actions, as measured by the utilitarian standard, with too exclusive a regard, and do not lay sufficient stress upon the other beauties of character which go towards making a human being loveable or admirable, this may be admitted. Utilitarians who have cultivated their moral feelings, but not their sympathies nor their artistic perceptions, do fall into this mistake; and so do all other moralists under the same conditions. What can be said in excuse for other moralists is equally available for them, namely, that if there is to be any error, it is better that it should be on that side. As a matter of fact, we may affirm that among utilitarians as among adherents of other systems, there is every imaginable degree of rigidity and of laxity in the application of their standard: some are even puritanically rigorous, while others are as indulgent as can possibly be desired by sinner or by sentimentalist. But on the whole, a doctrine which brings prominently forward the interest that mankind have in the repression and prevention of conduct which violates the moral law, is likely to be inferior to no other in turning the sanctions of opinion against such violations. It is true the question What does violate the moral law? is one on which those who recognize different standards of morality are likely now and then to differ. But difference of opinion on moral questions was not first introduced into the world by utilitarianism, while that doctrine does supply, if not always an easy, at all events a tangible and intelligible, mode of deciding such differences.

It may not be superfluous to notice a few more of the common misapprehensions of utilitarian ethics, even those which are so obvious and gross that it might appear impossible for any person of candour and intelligence to fall into them; since persons, even of considerable mental endowments, often give themselves so little trouble to understand the bearings of any opinion against which they entertain a prejudice, and men are in general so little conscious of this voluntary ignorance as a defect, that the vulgarest misunderstandings of ethical doctrines are continually met with in the deliberate writings of persons of the greatest pretensions both to high principle and to philosophy.

We not uncommonly hear the doctrine of utility inveighed against as a *godless* doctrine. If it be necessary to say anything at all against so mere an assumption, we may say that the question depends upon what idea we have formed of the moral character of the Deity. If it be a true belief that God desires, above all things, the happiness of His creatures, and that this was His purpose in their creation, utility is not only not a godless doctrine, but more profoundly religious than any other. If it be meant that utilitarianism does not recognize the revealed will of God as the supreme law of morals, I answer that a utilitarian who believes in the perfect goodness and wisdom of God necessarily believes that whatever God has thought fit to reveal on the subject of morals must fulfil the requirements of utility in a supreme degree. But others besides utilitarians have been of opinion that the Christian revelation was intended, and is fitted, to inform the hearts and minds of mankind with a spirit which should enable them to find for themselves what is right, and incline them to do it when found, rather than to tell them, except in a very general way, what it is; and that we need a doctrine of ethics, carefully followed out, to *interpret* to us the will of God. Whether this opinion is correct or not it is superfluous here to discuss; since whatever aid religion, either natural or revealed, can afford to ethical investigation is as open to the utilitarian moralist as to any other. He can use it as the testimony of God to the usefulness or hurtfulness of any given course of action, by as good a right as others can use it for the indication of a transcendental law, having no connexion with usefulness or with happiness.

Again, Utility is often summarily stigmatized as an immoral doctrine by giving it the name of Expediency, and taking advantage of the popular use of that term to contrast it with Principle. But the Expedient, in the sense in which it is opposed to the Right, generally means that which is expedient for the particular interest of the agent himself; as when a Minister sacrifices the interests of his country to keep himself in place. When it means anything better than this, it means that which is expedient for some immediate object, some temporary purpose, but which violates a rule whose observance is expedient in a much higher degree. The Expedient, in this sense, instead of being the same thing as the useful, is a branch of the hurtful.

Thus it would often be expedient, for the purpose of getting over some momentary embarrassment, or attaining some object immediately useful to ourselves or others, to tell a lie. But inasmuch as the cultivation in ourselves of a sensitive feeling on the subject of veracity is one of the most useful, and the enfeeblement of that feeling one of the most hurtful, things to which our conduct can be instrumental; and inasmuch as any, even unintentional, deviation from truth does that much towards weakening the trustworthiness of human assertion, which is not only the principal support of all present social well-being, but the insufficiency of which does more than any one thing that can be named to keep back civilization, virtue, everything on which human happiness on the largest scale depends; we feel that the violation, for a present advantage, of a rule of such transcendant expediency, is not expedient, and that he who, for the sake of a convenience to himself or to some other individual, does what depends on him to deprive mankind of the good, and inflict upon them the evil, involved in the greater or less reliance which they can place in each other's word, acts the part of one of their worst enemies.

Yet that even this rule, sacred as it is, admits of possible exceptions, is acknowledged by all moralists; the chief of which is when the withholding of some fact (as of information from a malefactor, or of bad news from a person dangerously ill) would save an individual (especially an individual other than oneself) from great and unmerited evil, and when the withholding can only be effected by denial. But in order that the exception may not extend itself beyond the need, and may have the least possible effect in weakening reliance on veracity, it ought to be recognized, and, if possible, its limits defined; and if the principle of utility is good for anything, it must be good for weighing these conflicting utilities against one another, and marking out the region within which one or the other preponderates.

Again, defenders of utility often find themselves called upon to reply to such objections as this—that there is not time, previous to action, for calculating and weighing the effects of any line of conduct on the general happiness. This is exactly as if any one were to say that it is impossible to guide our conduct by Christianity, because there is not time, on every occasion on which anything has to be done, to read through the Old and New Testaments. The answer to the objection is that there has been ample time, namely the whole past duration of the human species. During all that time mankind have been learning by experience the tendencies of actions; on which experience all the prudence, as well as all the morality of life, are dependent. People talk as if the commencement of this course of experience had hitherto been put off, and as if, at the moment when some man feels tempted to meddle with the property or life of another, he had to begin considering for the first time whether murder and theft are injurious to human happiness. Even then I do not think that he would find the question very puzzling; but, at all events, the matter is now done to his hand. It is truly a whimsical supposition that if mankind were agreed in considering utility to be the test of morality, they would remain without any agreement as to what *is* useful, and would take no measures for having their notions on the subject taught to the young, and enforced by law and opinion. There is no difficulty in proving any ethical standard whatever to work ill, if we suppose universal idiocy to be conjoined with it; but on any hypothesis short of that mankind must by this time have acquired positive beliefs as to the effects of some actions on their happiness; and the beliefs which have thus come down are the rules of morality for the multitude, and for the philosopher until he has succeeded in finding better.

That philosophers might easily do this, even now, on many subjects; that the received code of ethics is by no means of divine right; and that mankind have still much to learn as to the effects of actions on the general happiness, I admit, or, rather, earnestly maintain. The corollaries from the principle of utility, like the precepts of every practical art, admit of indefinite improvement, and, in a progressive state of the human mind, their improvement is perpetually going on. But to consider the rules of morality as improvable, is one thing;

to pass over the intermediate generalizations entirely, and endeavour to test each individual action directly by the first principle, is another. It is a strange notion that the acknowledgment of a first principle is inconsistent with the admission of secondary ones. To inform a traveller respecting the place of his ultimate destination is not to forbid the use of landmarks and direction-posts on the way. The proposition that happiness is the end and aim of morality does not mean that no road ought to be laid down to that goal, or that persons going thither should not be advised to take one direction rather than another. Men really ought to leave off talking a kind of nonsense on this subject, which they would neither talk nor listen to on other matters of practical concernment. Nobody argues that the art of navigation is not founded on astronomy, because sailors cannot wait to calculate the Nautical Almanack. Being rational creatures, they go to sea with it ready calculated; and all rational creatures go out upon the sea of life with their minds made up on the common questions of right and wrong, as well as on many of the far more difficult questions of wise and foolish. And this, as long as foresight is a human quality, it is to be presumed they will continue to do. Whatever we adopt as the fundamental principle of morality, we require subordinate principles to apply it by; the impossibility of doing without them, being common to all systems, can afford no argument against any one in particular; but gravely to argue as if no such secondary principles could be had, and as if mankind had remained till now, and always remain, without drawing any general conclusions from the experience of human life, is as high a pitch, I think, as absurdity has ever reached in philosophical controversy.

The remainder of the stock arguments against utilitarianism mostly consist in laying to its charge the common infirmities of human nature, and the general difficulties which embarrass conscientious persons in shaping their course through life. We are told that a utilitarian will be apt to make his own particular case an exception to moral rules, and, when under temptation, will see an utility in the breach of a rule, greater than he will see in its observance. But is utility the only creed which is able to furnish us with excuses for evil doing, and means of cheating our own conscience? They are afforded in abundance by all doctrines which recognize as a fact in morals the existence of conflicting considerations; which all doctrines do, that have been believed by sane persons. It is not the fault of any creed, but of the complicated nature of human

affairs, that rules of conduct cannot be so framed as to require
no exceptions, and that hardly any kind of action can safely
be laid down as either always obligatory or always condemnable. There is no ethical creed which does not temper the
rigidity of its laws by giving a certain latitude, under the
moral responsibility of the agent, for accommodation to peculiarities of circumstances; and under every creed, at the opening thus made, self-deception and dishonest casuistry get in.
There exists no moral system under which there do not arise
unequivocal cases of conflicting obligation. These are the real
difficulties, the knotty points both in the theory of ethics, and
in the conscientious guidance of personal conduct. They are
overcome practically with greater or with less success according to the intellect and virtue of the individual; but it can
hardly be pretended that any one will be the less qualified
for dealing with them from possessing an ultimate standard
to which conflicting rights and duties can be referred. If utility
is the ultimate source of moral obligations, utility may be invoked to decide between them when their demands are incompatible. Though the application of the standard may be
difficult, it is better than none at all: while in other systems,
the moral laws all claiming independent authority, there is no
common umpire entitled to interfere between them; their
claims to precedence one over another rest on little better
than sophistry, and unless determined, as they generally are,
by the unacknowledged influence of considerations of utility,
afford a free scope for the action of personal desires and
partialities. We must remember that only in these cases of
conflict between secondary principles is it requisite that first
principles should be appealed to. There is no case of moral
obligation in which some secondary principle is not involved;
and, if only one, there can seldom be any real doubt which
one it is, in the mind of any person by whom the principle
itself is recognized.

III. OF THE ULTIMATE SANCTION OF THE PRINCIPLE OF UTILITY

THE question is often asked, and properly so, in regard to any
supposed moral standard, What is its sanction?, what are the
motives to obey it?, or, more specifically, what is the source
of its obligation?, whence does it derive its binding force? It
is a necessary part of moral philosophy to provide the answer
to this question; which, though frequently assuming the shape

of an objection to the utilitarian morality, as if it had some special applicability to that above others, really arises in regard to all standards. It arises, in fact, whenever a person is called on to *adopt* a standard, or refer morality to any basis on which he has not been accustomed to rest it. For the customary morality, that which education and opinion have consecrated, is the only one which presents itself to the mind with the feeling of being *in itself* obligatory; and when a person is asked to believe that this morality *derives* its obligation from some general principle round which custom has not thrown the same halo, the assertion is to him a paradox; the supposed corollaries seem to have a more binding force than the original theorem; the superstructure seems to stand better without, than with, what is represented as its foundation. He says to himself, I feel that I am bound not to rob or murder, betray or deceive; but why am I bound to promote the general happiness? If my own happiness lies in something else, why may I not give that the preference?

If the view adopted by the utilitarian philosophy of the nature of the moral sense be correct, this difficulty will always present itself, until the influences which form moral character have taken the same hold of the principle which they have taken of some of the consequences—until, by the improvement of education, the feeling of unity with our fellow-creatures shall be (what it cannot be denied that Christ intended it to be) as deeply rooted in our character, and to our own consciousness as completely a part of our nature, as the horror of crime is in an ordinarily well-brought-up young person. In the meantime, however, the difficulty has no peculiar application to the doctrine of utility, but is inherent in every attempt to analyze morality and reduce it to principles; which, unless the principle is already in men's minds invested with as much sacredness as any of its applications, always seems to divest them of a part of their sanctity.

The principle of utility either has, or there is no reason why it might not have, all the sanctions which belong to any other system of morals. Those sanctions are either external or internal. Of the external sanctions it is not necessary to speak at any length. They are, the hope of favour and the fear of displeasure from our fellow creatures or from the Ruler of the Universe, along with whatever we may have of sympathy or affection for them, or of love and awe of him, inclining us to do his will independently of selfish consequences. There is evidently no reason why all these motives for observance

should not attach themselves to the utilitarian morality, as
completely and as powerfully as to any other. Indeed, those
of them which refer to our fellow creatures are sure to do
so in proportion to the amount of general intelligence; for
whether there be any other ground of moral obligation than
the general happiness or not, men do desire happiness; and,
however imperfect may be their own practice, they desire
and commend all conduct in others towards themselves, by
which they think their happiness is promoted. With regard to
the religious motive, if men believe, as most profess to, in the
goodness of God, those who think that conduciveness to the
general happiness is the essence, or even only the criterion,
of good must necessarily believe that it is also that which God
approves. The whole force therefore of external reward and
punishment, whether physical or moral, and whether proceeding from God or from our fellow-men, together with all that
the capacities of human nature admit, of disinterested devotion to either, become available to enforce the utilitarian
morality, in proportion as that morality is recognized; and the
more powerfully, the more the appliances of education and
general cultivation are bent to the purpose.

So far as to external sanctions. The internal sanction of
duty, whatever our standard of duty may be, is one and the
same—a feeling in our own mind; a pain, more or less intense,
attendant on violation of duty, which in properly cultivated
moral natures rises, in the more serious cases, into shrinking
from it as an impossibility. This feeling, when disinterested,
and connecting itself with the pure idea of duty, and not
with some particular form of it, or with any of the merely
accessory circumstances, is the essence of Conscience; though
in that complex phenomenon as it actually exists the simple
fact is in general all encrusted over with collateral associations, derived from sympathy, from love, and still more from
fear; from all the forms of religious feeling; from the recollections of childhood and of all our past life; from self-esteem,
desire of the esteem of others, and occasionally even self-
abasement. This extreme complication is, I apprehend, the
origin of the sort of mystical character which, by a tendency
of the human mind of which there are many other examples,
is apt to be attributed to the idea of moral obligation, and
which leads people to believe that the idea cannot possibly
attach itself to any other objects than those which, by a supposed mysterious law, are found in our present experience to
excite it. Its binding force, however, consists in the existence

of a mass of feeling which must be broken through in order to do what violates our standard of right, and which, if we do nevertheless violate that standard, will probably have to be encountered afterwards in the form of remorse. Whatever theory we have of the nature or origin of conscience, this is what essentially constitutes it.

The ultimate sanction, therefore, of all morality (external motives apart) being a subjective feeling in our own minds, I see nothing embarrassing to those whose standard is utility in the question, what is the sanction of that particular standard? We may answer, the same as of all other moral standards —the conscientious feelings of mankind. Undoubtedly this sanction has no binding efficacy on those who do not possess the feelings it appeals to; but neither will these persons be more obedient to any other moral principle than to the utilitarian one. On them morality of any kind has no hold but through the external sanctions. Meanwhile the feelings exist, a fact in human nature, the reality of which, and the great power with which they are capable of acting on those in whom they have been duly cultivated, are proved by experience. No reason has ever been shown why they may not be cultivated to as great intensity in connexion with the utilitarian, as with any other rule of morals.

There is, I am aware, a disposition to believe that a person who sees in moral obligation a transcendental fact, an objective reality belonging to the province of 'Things in themselves' is likely to be more obedient to it than one who believes it to be entirely subjective, having its seat in human consciousness only. But whatever a person's opinion may be on this point of Ontology, the force he is really urged by is his own subjective feeling, and is exactly measured by its strength. No one's belief that Duty is an objective reality is stronger than the belief that God is so; yet the belief in God, apart from the expectation of actual reward and punishment, operates on conduct only through, and in proportion to, the subjective religious feeling. The sanction, so far as it is disinterested, is always in the mind itself; and the notion therefore of the transcendental moralists must be, that this sanction will not exist *in* the mind unless it is believed to have its root out of the mind; and that if a person is able to say to himself This which is restraining me, and which is called my conscience, is only a feeling in my own mind, he may possibly draw the conclusion that when the feeling ceases the obligation ceases, and that if he find the feeling inconvenient, he

may disregard it, and endeavour to get rid of it. But is thi
danger confined to the utilitarian morality? Does the belie
that moral obligation has its seat outside the mind make th
feeling of it too strong to be got rid of? The fact is so fa
otherwise, that all moralists admit and lament the ease with
which, in the generality of minds, conscience can be silenced
or stifled. The question Need I obey my conscience? is quite
as often put to themselves by persons who never heard of the
principle of utility as by its adherents. Those whose conscientious feelings are so weak as to allow of their asking this
question, if they answer it affirmatively, will not do so because
they believe in the transcendental theory, but because of the
external sanctions.

It is not necessary, for the present purpose, to decide
whether the feeling of duty is innate or implanted. Assuming
it to be innate, it is an open question to what objects it naturally attaches itself; for the philosophic supporters of that
theory are now agreed that the intuitive perception is of principles of morality, and not of the details. If there be anything
innate in the matter, I see no reason why the feeling which
is innate should not be that of regard to the pleasures and
pains of others. If there is any principle of morals which is
intuitively obligatory, I should say it must be that. If so, the
intuitive ethics would coincide with the utilitarian, and there
would be no further quarrel between them. Even as it is, the
intuitive moralists, though they believe that there are other
intuitive moral obligations, do already believe this to be one;
for they unanimously hold that a large *portion* of morality
turns upon the consideration due to the interests of our fellow
creatures. Therefore, if the belief in the transcendental origin
of moral obligation gives any additional efficacy to the internal
sanction, it appears to me that the utilitarian principle has
already the benefit of it.

On the other hand, if, as is my own belief, the moral feelings are not innate, but acquired, they are not for that reason
less natural. It is natural to man to speak, to reason, to build
cities, to cultivate the ground, though these are acquired
faculties. The moral feelings are not indeed a part of our
nature, in the sense of being in any perceptible degree present
in all of us; but this, unhappily, is a fact admitted by those
who believe the most strenuously in their transcendental
origin. Like the other acquired capacities above referred to,
the moral faculty, if not a part of our nature, is a natural outgrowth from it; capable, like them, in a certain small degree,

of springing up spontaneously, and susceptible of being
brought by cultivation to a high degree of development. Unhappily it is also susceptible, by a sufficient use of the external
sanctions and of the force of early impressions, of being cultivated in almost any direction: so that there is hardly anything
so absurd or so mischievous that it may not, by means of these
influences be made to act on the human mind with all the
authority of conscience. To doubt that the same potency might
be given by the same means to the principle of utility, even
if it had no foundation in human nature, would be flying in
the face of all experience.

But moral associations which are wholly of artificial creation, when intellectual culture goes on, yield by degrees to
the dissolving force of analysis; and if the feeling of duty,
when associated with utility, would appear equally arbitrary;
if there were no leading department of our nature, no powerful class of sentiments, with which that association would
harmonize, which would make us feel it congenial, and incline
us not only to foster it in others (for which we have abundant
interested motives), but also to cherish it in ourselves; if there
were not, in short, a natural basis of sentiment for utilitarian
morality, it might well happen that this association also, even
after it had been implanted by education, might be analyzed
away.

But there *is* this basis of powerful natural sentiment; and
this it is which, when once the general happiness is recognized
as the ethical standard, will constitute the strength of the
utilitarian morality. This firm foundation is that of the social
feelings of mankind; the desire to be in unity with our fellow
creatures, which is already a powerful principle in human
nature, and happily one of those which tend to become
stronger, even without express inculcation, from the influences
of advancing civilization. The social state is at once so natural,
so necessary, and so habitual to man, that, except in some
unusual circumstances or by an effort of voluntary abstraction,
he never conceives himself otherwise than as a member of a
body; and this association is riveted more and more, as mankind are further removed from the state of savage independence. Any condition, therefore, which is essential to a state
of society, becomes more and more an inseparable part of
every person's conception of the state of things which he is
born into, and which is the destiny of a human being. Now,
society between human beings, except in the relation of master and slave, is manifestly impossible on any other footing

than that the interests of all are to be consulted. Society be
tween equals can exist only on the understanding that th
interests of all are to be regarded equally. And since in a
states of civilization, every person, except an absolute mor
arch, has equals, every one is obliged to live on these term
with somebody; and in every age some advance is mad
towards a state in which it will be impossible to live perma
nently on other terms with anybody.

In this way people grow up unable to conceive as possibl
to them a state of total disregard of other people's interest:
They are under a necessity of conceiving themselves as a
least abstaining from all the grosser injuries, and (if only fo
their own protection) living in a state of constant protes
against them. They are also familiar with the fact of co
operating with others, and proposing to themselves a collec
tive, not an individual, interest as the aim (at least for th
time being) of their actions. So long as they are co-operating
their ends are identified with those of others; there is at leas
a temporary feeling that the interests of others are their ow
interests. Not only does all strengthening of social ties, and
all healthy growth of society, give to each individual
stronger personal interest in practically consulting the welfar
of others; it also leads him to identify his *feelings* more and
more with their good, or at least with an ever greater degree
of practical consideration for it. He comes, as though instinc
tively, to be conscious of himself as a being who *of course*
pays regard to others. The good of others becomes to him
thing naturally and necessarily to be attended to, like any
of the physical conditions of our existence. Now, whatever
amount of this feeling a person has, he is urged by the strong
est motives both of interest and of sympathy to demonstrate
it, and to the utmost of his power encourage it in others; and
even if he has none of it himself, he is as greatly interested
as any one else that others should have it. Consequently the
smallest germs of the feeling are laid hold of and nourished
by the contagion of sympathy and the influences of education,
and a complete web of corroborative association is woven
round it, by the powerful agency of the external sanctions.

This mode of conceiving ourselves and human life, as civili
zation goes on, is felt to be more and more natural. Every
step in political improvement renders it more so, by removing
the sources of opposition of interest, and levelling those in
equalities of legal privilege between individuals or classes,
owing to which there are large portions of mankind whose

happiness it is still practicable to disregard. In an improving state of the human mind, the influences are constantly on the increase, which tend to generate in each individual a feeling of unity with all the rest; which, if perfect, would make him never think of, or desire, any beneficial condition for himself, in the benefits of which they are not included.

If we now suppose this feeling of unity to be taught as a religion, and the whole force of education, of institutions, and of opinion, directed, as it once was in the case of religion, to make every person grow up from infancy surrounded on all sides both by the profession and the practice of it, I think that no one who can realize this conception will feel any misgiving about the sufficiency of the ultimate sanction for the Happiness morality. To any ethical student who finds the realization difficult, I recommend, as a means of facilitating it, the second of M. Comte's two principal works, the *Traité de Politique Positive*. I entertain the strongest objections to the system of politics and morals set forth in that treatise; but I think it has superabundantly shown the possibility of giving to the service of humanity, even without the aid of belief in a Providence, both the psychological power and the social efficacy of a religion; making it take hold of human life, and colour all thought, feeling, and action, in a manner of which the greatest ascendancy ever exercised by any religion may be but a type and foretaste, and of which the danger is, not that it should be insufficient, but that it should be so excessive as to interfere unduly with human freedom and individuality.

Neither is it necessary to the feeling which constitutes the binding force of the utilitarian morality on those who recognize it, to wait for those social influences which would make its obligation felt by mankind at large. In the comparatively early state of human advancement in which we now live, a person cannot indeed feel that entireness of sympathy with all others, which would make any real discordance in the general direction of their conduct in life impossible; but already a person in whom the social feeling is at all developed, cannot bring himself to think of the rest of his fellow creatures as struggling rivals with him for the means of happiness, whom he must desire to see defeated in their object in order that he may succeed in his. The deeply rooted conception which every individual even now has of himself as a social being tends to make him feel it one of his natural wants that there should be harmony between his feelings and aims and those of his fellow creatures. If differences of opinion and of mental culture make it impossible for him to share many of their actual feelings—perhaps make him denounce and defy those feelings—he still needs to be conscious that his real aim and theirs do not conflict, that he is not opposing himself to what they really wish for, namely their own good, but is, on the contrary, promoting it.

This feeling in most individuals is much inferior in strength to their selfish feelings, and is often wanting altogether. But to those who have it, it possesses all the characters of a natural feeling. It does not present itself to their minds as a super-stition of education, or a law despotically imposed by the power of society, but as an attribute which it would not be well for them to be without. This conviction is the ultimate sanction of the greatest happiness morality. This it is which makes any mind, of well-developed feelings, work with, and not against, the outward motives to care for others, afforded by what I have called the external sanctions; and when those sanctions are wanting, or act in an opposite direction, consti-tutes in itself a powerful internal binding force, in proportion to the sensitiveness and thoughtfulness of the character; since few but those whose mind is a moral blank could bear to lay out their course of life on the plan of paying no regard to others except so far as their own private interest compels.

IV. OF WHAT SORT OF PROOF THE PRINCIPLE OF UTILITY IS SUSCEPTIBLE

It has already been remarked that questions of ultimate ends do not admit of proof, in the ordinary acceptation of the term. To be incapable of proof by reasoning is common to all first principles; to the first premises of our knowledge, as well as to those of our conduct. But the former, being matters of fact, may be the subject of a direct appeal to the faculties which judge of fact—namely our senses, and our internal con-sciousness. Can an appeal be made to the same faculties on questions of practical ends? Or by what other faculty is cognizance taken of them?

Questions about ends are, in other words, questions what things are desirable. The utilitarian doctrine is, that happiness is desirable, and the only thing desirable, as an end; all other things being only desirable as means to that end. What ought to be required of this doctrine—what conditions is it requisite that the doctrine should fulfil—to make good its claim to be believed?

The only proof capable of being given that an object is visible, is that people actually see it. The only proof that a sound is audible, is that people hear it: and so of the other sources of our experience. In like manner, I apprehend, the sole evidence it is possible to produce that anything is desirable, is that people do actually desire it. If the end which the utilitarian doctrine proposes to itself were not, in theory and in practice, acknowledged to be an end, nothing could ever convince any person that it was so. No reason can be given why the general happiness is desirable, except that each person, so far as he believes it to be attainable, desires his own happiness. This, however, being a fact, we have not only all the proof which the case admits of, but all which it is possible to require, that happiness is a good: that each person's happiness is a good to that person, and the general happiness, therefore, a good to the aggregate of all persons. Happiness has made out its title as *one* of the ends of conduct, and consequently one of the criteria of morality.

But it has not, by this alone, proved itself to be the sole criterion. To do that, it would seem, by the same rule, necessary to show, not only that people desire happiness, but that they never desire anything else. Now it is palpable that they do desire things which, in common language, are decidedly distinguished from happiness. They desire, for example, virtue, and the absence of vice no less really than pleasure and the absence of pain. The desire of virtue is not as universal, but it is as authentic a fact as the desire of happiness. And hence the opponents of the utilitarian standard deem that they have a right to infer that there are other ends of human action besides happiness, and that happiness is not the standard of approbation and disapprobation.

But does the utilitarian doctrine deny that people desire virtue, or maintain that virtue is not a thing to be desired? The very reverse. It maintains not only that virtue is to be desired, but that it is to be desired disinterestedly, for itself. Whatever may be the opinion of utilitarian moralists as to the original conditions by which virtue is made virtue; however they may believe (as they do) that actions and dispositions are only virtuous because they promote another end than virtue; yet this being granted, and it having been decided, from considerations of this description, what *is* virtuous, they not only place virtue at the very head of the things which are good as means to the ultimate end, but they also recognize as a psychological fact the possibility of its being, to the individual, a good in itself, without looking to any end beyond it; and hold, that the mind is not in a right state, not in a state conformable to Utility, not in the state most conducive to the general happiness, unless it does love virtue in this manner—as a thing desirable in itself, even although, in the individual instance, it should not produce those other desirable consequences which it tends to produce, and on account of which it is held to be virtue.

This opinion is not, in the smallest degree, a departure from the Happiness principle. The ingredients of happiness are very various, and each of them is desirable in itself, and not merely when considered as swelling an aggregate. The principle of utility does not mean that any given pleasure, as music for instance, or any given exemption from pain, as for example health, are to be looked upon as means to a collective something termed happiness, and to be desired on that account. They are desired and desirable in and for themselves; besides being means, they are a part of the end. Virtue, according to the utilitarian doctrine, is not naturally and originally part of the end, but it is capable of becoming so; and in those who love it disinterestedly it has become so, and is desired and cherished, not as a means to happiness, but as a part of their happiness.

To illustrate this farther, we may remember that virtue is not the only thing, originally a means, and which, if it were not a means to anything else, would be and remain indifferent, but which, by association with what it is a means to, comes to be desired for itself, and that too with the utmost intensity. What, for example, shall we say of the love of money? There is nothing originally more desirable about money than about any heap of glittering pebbles. Its worth is solely that of the things which it will buy; the desires for other things than itself, which it is a means of gratifying. Yet the love of money is not only one of the strongest moving forces of human life, but money is, in many cases, desired in and for itself; the desire to possess it is often stronger than the desire to use it, and goes on increasing when all the desires which point to ends beyond it, to be compassed by it, are falling off. It may, then, be said truly that money is desired not for the sake of an end, but as part of the end. From being a means to happiness, it has come to be itself a principal ingredient of the individual's conception of happiness.

The same may be said of the majority of the great objects of human life—power, for example, or fame; except that to each of these there is a certain amount of immediate pleasure annexed, which has at least the semblance of being naturally inherent in them: a thing which cannot be said of money. Still, however, the strongest natural attraction, both of power and of fame, is the immense aid they give to the attainment of our other wishes; and it is the strong association thus generated between them and all our objects of desire which gives to the direct desire of them the intensity it often assumes, so as in some characters to surpass in strength all other desires.

In these cases the means have become a part of the end, and a more important part of it than any of the things which they are means to. What was once desired as an instrument for the attainment of happiness, has come to be desired for its own sake. In being desired for its own sake it is, however, desired as *part* of happiness. The person is made, or thinks he would be made, happy by its mere possession; and is made unhappy by failure to obtain it. The desire of it is not a different thing from the desire of happiness, any more than the love of music, or the desire of health. They are included in happiness. They are some of the elements of which the desire of happiness is made up. Happiness is not an abstract idea, but a concrete whole; and these are some of its parts. And the utilitarian standard sanctions and approves their being so. Life would be a poor thing, very ill provided with sources of happiness, if there were not this provision of nature, by which things, originally indifferent, but conducive to, or otherwise associated with, the satisfaction of our primitive desires, become in themselves sources of pleasure more valuable than the primitive pleasures, both in permanency, in the space of human existence that they are capable of covering, and even in intensity.

Virtue, according to the utilitarian conception, is a good of this description. There was no original desire of it, or motive to it, save its conduciveness to pleasure, and especially to protection from pain. But through the association thus formed, it may be felt a good in itself, and desired as such with as great intensity as any other good; and with this difference between it and the love of money, of power, or of fame, that all of these may and often do render the individual noxious to the other members of the society to which he belongs, whereas there is nothing which makes him so much a blessing to them as the cultivation of the disinterested love of virtue. And consequently, the utilitarian standard, while it tolerates and approves those other acquired desires, up to the point beyond which they would be more injurious to the general happiness than promotive of it, enjoins and requires the cultivation of the love of virtue up to the greatest strength possible, as being above all things important to the general happiness.

It results from the preceding considerations that there is in reality nothing desired except happiness. Whatever is desired otherwise than as a means to some end beyond itself, and ultimately to happiness, is desired as itself a part of happiness, and is not desired for itself until it has become so. Those who desire virtue for its own sake, desire it either because the consciousness of it is a pleasure, or because the consciousness of being without it is a pain, or for both reasons united; as in truth the pleasure and pain seldom exist separately, but almost always together, the same person feeling pleasure in the degree of virtue attained, and pain in not having attained more. If one of these gave him no pleasure, and the other no pain, he would not love or desire virtue, or would desire it only for the other benefits which it might produce to himself or to persons whom he cared for.

We have now, then, an answer to the question, of what sort of proof the principle of utility is susceptible. If the opinion which I have now stated is psychologically true—if human nature is so constituted as to desire nothing which is not either a part of happiness or a means of happiness, we can have no other proof, and we require no other, that these are the only things desirable. If so, happiness is the sole end of human action, and the promotion of it the test by which to judge of all human conduct; from whence it necessarily follows that it must be the criterion of morality, since a part is included in the whole.

And now to decide whether this is really so; whether mankind do desire nothing for itself but that which is a pleasure to them, or of which the absence is a pain; we have evidently arrived at a question of fact and exprience, dependent, like all similar questions, upon evidence. It can be determined only by practised self-consciousness and self-observation, assisted by observation of others. I believe that these sources of evidence, impartially consulted, will declare that desiring a thing and finding it pleasant, aversion to it and thinking of it as painful, are phenomena entirely inseparable, or rather two parts of the same phenomenon; in strictness of language, two different modes of naming the same psychological fact: that to think of an object as desirable (unless for the sake of its consequences), and to think of it as pleasant, are one and the same thing; and that to desire anything, except in proportion as the idea of it is pleasant, is a physical and metaphysical impossibility.

So obvious does this appear to me that I expect it will hardly be disputed: and the objection made will be, not that desire can possibly be directed to anything ultimately except pleasure and exemption from pain, but that the will is a different thing from desire; that a person of confirmed virtue, or any other person whose purposes are fixed, carries out his purposes without any thought of the pleasure he has in contemplating them, or expects to derive from their fulfilment; and persists in acting on them, even though these pleasures are much diminished, by changes in his character or decay of his passive sensibilities, or are outweighed by the pains which the pursuit of the purposes may bring upon him.

All this I fully admit, and have stated it elsewhere, as positively and emphatically as any one. Will, the active phenomenon, is a different thing from desire, the state of passive sensibility, and though originally an offshoot from it, may in time take root and detach itself from the parent stock; so much so, that in the case of an habitual purpose, instead of willing the thing because we desire it, we often desire it only because we will it. This, however, is but an instance of that familiar fact, the power of habit, and is nowise confined to the case of virtuous actions. Many indifferent things, which men originally did from a motive of some sort, they continue to do from habit. Sometimes this is done unconsciously, the consciousness coming only after the action: at other times with conscious volition, but volition which has become habitual, and is put in operation by the force of habit, in opposition perhaps to the deliberate preference, as often happens with those who have contracted habits of vicious or hurtful indulgence. Third and last comes the case in which the habitual act of will in the individual instance, is not in contradiction to the general intention prevailing at other times, but in fulfilment of it; as in the case of the person of confirmed virtue, and of all who pursue deliberately and consistently any determinate end. The distinction between will and desire thus understood is an authentic and highly important psychological fact; but the fact consists solely in this—that will, like all other parts of our constitution, is amenable to habit, and that we may will from habit what we no longer desire for itself, or desire only because we will it.

It is not the less true that will, in the beginning, is entirely produced by desire; including in that term the repelling influence of pain as well as the attractive one of pleasure. Let us take into consideration, no longer the person who has a confirmed will to do right, but him in whom that virtuous will is still feeble, conquerable by temptation, and not to be fully relied on; by what means can it be strengthened? How can the will to be virtuous, where it does not exist in sufficient force, be implanted or awakened? Only by making the person *desire* virtue—by making him think of it in a pleasurable light, or of its absence in a painful one. It is by associating the doing right with pleasure, or the doing wrong with pain, or by eliciting and impressing and bringing home to the person's experience the pleasure naturally involved in the one or the pain in the other, that it is possible to call forth that will to be virtuous, which, when confirmed, acts without any thought of either pleasure or pain. Will is the child of desire, and passes out of the dominion of its parent only to come under that of habit. That which is the result of habit affords no presumption of being intrinsically good; and there would be no reason for wishing that the purpose of virtue should become independent of pleasure and pain, were it not that the influence of the pleasurable and painful associations which prompt to virtue is not sufficiently to be depended on for unerring constancy of action until it has acquired the support of habit. Both in feeling and in conduct habit is the only thing which imparts certainty; and it is because of the importance to others of being able to rely absolutely on one's feelings and conduct, and to oneself of being able to rely on one's own, that the will to do right ought to be cultivated into this habitual independence. In other words, this state of the will is a means to good, not intrinsically a good; and does not contradict the doctrine that nothing is a good to human beings but in so far as it is either itself pleasurable, or a means of attaining pleasure or averting pain.

But if this doctrine be true, the principle of utility is proved. Whether it is so or not, must now be left to the consideration of the thoughtful reader.

V. ON THE CONNEXION BETWEEN JUSTICE AND UTILITY

IN all ages of speculation one of the strongest obstacles to the reception of the doctrine that Utility or Happiness is the criterion of right and wrong has been drawn from the idea of Justice. The powerful sentiment, and apparently clear perception, which that word recalls with a rapidity and certainty resembling an instinct, have seemed to the majority of thinkers to point to an inherent quality in things; to show that the Just must have an existence in Nature as something absolute, generically distinct from every variety of the Expedient, and, in idea, opposed to it, though (as is commonly acknowledged) never, in the long run, disjoined from it in fact.

In the case of this, as of our other moral sentiments, there is no necessary connexion between the question of its origin, and that of its binding force. That a feeling is bestowed on us by Nature does not necessarily legitimate all its promptings. The feeling of justice might be a peculiar instinct, and might yet require, like our other instincts, to be controlled and enlightened by a higher reason. If we have intellectual instincts, leading us to judge in a particular way, as well as animal instincts that prompt us to act in a particular way, there is no necessity that the former should be more infallible in their sphere than the latter in theirs: it may as well happen that wrong judgments are occasionally suggested by those, as wrong actions by these. But though it is one thing to believe that we have natural feelings of justice, and another to acknowledge them as an ultimate criterion of conduct, these two opinions are very closely connected in point of fact. Mankind are always predisposed to believe that any subjective feeling, not otherwise accounted for, is a revelation of some objective reality. Our present object is to determine whether the reality, to which the feeling of justice corresponds, is one which needs any such special revelation; whether the justice or injustice of an action is a thing intrinsically peculiar, and distinct from all its other qualities, or only a combination of certain of those qualities, presented under a peculiar aspect.

For the purpose of this inquiry it is practically important to consider whether the feeling itself, of justice and injustice, is *sui generis* like our sensations of colour and taste, or a derivative feeling, formed by a combination of others. And this it is the more essential to examine, as people are in general willing enough to allow, that objectively the dictates of Justice coincide with a part of the field of General Expediency; but inasmuch as the subjective mental feeling of Justice is different from that which commonly attaches to simple expediency, and, except in the extreme cases of the latter, is far more imperative in its demands, people find it difficult to see, in Justice, only a particular kind of branch of general utility, and think that its superior binding force requires a totally different origin.

To throw light upon this question it is necessary to attempt to ascertain what is the distinguishing character of justice, or of injustice: what is the quality, or whether there is any quality, attributed in common to all modes of conduct designated as unjust (for justice, like many other moral attributes, is best defined by its opposite), and distinguishing them from such modes of conduct as are disapproved, but without having that particular epithet of disapprobation applied to them. If in everything which men are accustomed to characterize as just or unjust some one common attribute or collection of attributes is always present, we may judge whether this particular attribute or combination of attributes would be capable of gathering round it a sentiment of that peculiar character and intensity by virtue of the general laws of our emotional constitution, or whether the sentiment is inexplicable, and requires to be regarded as a special provision of Nature. If we find the former to be the case, we shall, in resolving this question, have resolved also the main problem: if the latter, we shall have to seek for some other mode of investigating it.

To find the common attributes of a variety of objects it is necessary to begin by surveying the objects themselves in the concrete. Let us therefore advert successively to the various modes of action, and arrangements of human affairs, which are classed, by universal or widely spread opinion, as Just or as Unjust. The things well known to excite the sentiments associated with those names, are of a very multifarious character. I shall pass them rapidly in review, without studying any particular arrangement.

In the first place, it is mostly considered unjust to deprive any one of his personal liberty, his property, or any other thing which belongs to him by law. Here, therefore, is one instance of the application of the terms just and unjust in a perfectly definite sense, namely that it is just to respect, unjust to violate, the *legal rights* of any one. But this judgment admits of several exceptions, arising from the other forms in which the notions of justice and injustice present themselves. For example, the person who suffers the deprivation may (as the phrase is) have *forfeited* the rights which he is so deprived of: a case to which we shall return presently. But also,

Secondly: the legal rights of which he is deprived, may be

rights which *ought* not to have belonged to him; in other words, the law which confers on him these rights, may be a bad law. When it is so, or when (which is the same thing for our purpose) it is supposed to be so, opinions will differ as to the justice or injustice of infringing it. Some maintain that no law, however bad, ought to be disobeyed by an individual citizen; that his opposition to it, if shown at all, should be shown only in endeavouring to get it altered by competent authority.

This opinion (which condemns many of the most illustrious benefactors of mankind and would often protect pernicious institutions against the only weapons which, in the state of things existing at the time, have any chance of succeeding against them) is defended by those who hold it on grounds of expediency; principally on that of the importance, to the common interest of mankind, of maintaining inviolate the sentiment of submission to law. Other persons, again, hold the directly contrary opinion, that any law, judged to be bad, may blamelessly be disobeyed, even though it be not judged to be unjust, but only inexpedient; while others would confine the license of disobedience to the case of unjust laws: but again, some say, that all laws which are inexpedient are unjust; since every law imposes some restriction on the natural liberty of mankind, which restriction is an injustice, unless legitimated by tending to their good. Among these diversities of opinion, it seems to be universally admitted that there may be unjust laws, and that law, consequently, is not the ultimate criterion of justice, but may give to one person a benefit, or impose on another an evil, which justice condemns. When, however, a law is thought to be unjust, it seems always to be regarded as being so in the same way in which a breach of law is unjust, namely, by infringing somebody's right; which, as it cannot in this case be a legal right, receives a different appellation, and is called a moral right. We may say, therefore, that a second case of injustice consists in taking or withholding from any person that to which he has a *moral right*.

Thirdly: it is universally considered just that each person should obtain that (whether good or evil) which he *deserves*; and unjust that he should obtain a good, or be made to undergo an evil, which he does not deserve. This is, perhaps, the clearest and most emphatic form in which the idea of justice is conceived by the general mind. As it involves the notion of desert, the question arises, what constitutes desert? Speaking in a general way, a person is understood to deserve good

if he does right, evil if he does wrong; and in a more particular
sense, to deserve good from those to whom he does or has
done good, and evil from those to whom he does or has done
evil. The precept of returning good for evil has never been
regarded as a case of the fulfilment of justice, but as one in
which the claims of justice are waived, in obedience to other
considerations.

Fourthly: it is confessedly unjust to *break faith* with any
one: to violate an engagement, either express or implied, or
disappoint expectations raised by our own conduct, at least
if we have raised those expectations knowingly and voluntarily. Like the other obligations of justice already spoken
of, this one is not regarded as absolute, but as capable of
being overruled by a stronger obligation of justice on the other
side; or by such conduct on the part of the person concerned
as is deemed to absolve us from our obligation to him, and to
constitute a *forfeiture* of the benefit which he has been led to
expect.

Fifthly: it is, by universal admission, inconsistent with justice to be *partial*; to show favour or preference to one person
over another, in matters to which favour and preference do
not properly apply. Impartiality, however, does not seem to
be regarded as a duty in itself, but rather as instrumental to
some other duty; for it is admitted that favour and preference
are not always censurable, and indeed the cases in which
they are condemned are rather the exception than the rule. A
person would be more likely to be blamed than applauded for
giving his family or friends no superiority in good offices over
strangers, when he could do so without violating any other
duty; and no one thinks it unjust to seek one person in preference to another as a friend, connexion, or companion. Impartiality where rights are concerned, is of course obligatory,
but this is involved in the more general obligation, of giving
to every one his right. A tribunal, for example, must be impartial, because it is bound to award, without regard to any
other consideration, a disputed object to the one of two parties
who has the right to it. There are other cases in which impartiality means, being solely influenced by desert; as with those
who, in the capacity of judges, preceptors, or parents, ad-
minister reward and punishment as such. There are cases,
again, in which it means, being solely influenced by consideration for the public interest; as in making a selection among
candidates for a government employment. Impartiality, in
short, as an obligation of justice, may be said to mean, being

exclusively influenced by the considerations which it is supposed ought to influence the particular case in hand; and resisting the solicitation of any motives which prompt to conduct different from what those considerations would dictate.

Nearly allied to the idea of impartiality, is that of *equality*; which often enters as a component part both into the conception of justice and into the practice of it, and, in the eyes of many persons, constitutes its essence. But in this, still more than in any other case, the notion of justice varies in different persons, and always conforms in its variations to their notion of utility. Each person maintains that equality is the dictate of justice, except where he thinks that expediency requires inequality. The justice of giving equal protection to the rights of all, is maintained by those who support the most outrageous inequality in the rights themselves. Even in slave countries it is theoretically admitted that the rights of the slave, such as they are, ought to be as sacred as those of the master; and that a tribunal which fails to enforce them with equal strictness is wanting in justice; while, at the same time, institutions which leave to the slave scarcely any rights to enforce, are not deemed unjust, because they are not deemed inexpedient. Those who think that utility requires distinctions of rank, do not consider it unjust that riches and social privileges should be unequally dispensed; but those who think this inequality inexpedient, think it unjust also. Whoever thinks that government is necessary, sees no injustice in as much inequality as is constituted by giving to the magistrate powers not granted to other pople. Even among those who hold levelling doctrines, there are as many questions of justice as there are differences of opinion about expediency. Some Communists consider it unjust that the produce of the labour of the community should be shared on any other principle than that of exact equality; others think it just that those should receive most whose wants are greatest; while others hold that those who work harder, or who produce more, or whose services are more valuable to the community, may justly claim a larger quota in the division of the produce. And the sense of natural justice may be plausibly appealed to in behalf of every one of these opinions.

Among so many diverse applications of the term Justice, which yet is not regarded as ambiguous, it is a matter of some difficulty to seize the mental link which holds them together, and on which the moral sentiment adhering to the term essentially depends. Perhaps, in this embarrassment, some help may be derived from the history of the word, as indicated by its etymology.

In most, if not in all, languages, the etymology of the word which corresponds to Just, points distinctly to an origin connected with the ordinances of law. *Justum* is a form of *jussum*, that which has been ordered. Δίκαιον comes directly from δίκη, a suit at law. *Recht*, from which came *right* and *righteous*, is synonymous with law. The courts of justice, the administration of justice, are the courts and the administration of law. *La justice*, in French, is the established term for judicature. I am not committing the fallacy, imputed with some show of truth to Horne Tooke, of assuming that a word must still continue to mean what it originally meant. Etymology is slight evidence of what the idea now signified is, but the very best evidence of how it sprang up. There can, I think, be no doubt that the *idée mère*, the primitive element, in the formation of the notion of justice, was conformity to law. It constituted the entire idea among the Hebrews, up to the birth of Christianity; as might be expected in the case of a people whose laws attempted to embrace all subjects on which precepts were required, and who believed those laws to be a direct emanation from the Supreme Being. But other nations, and in particular the Greeks and Romans, who knew that their laws had been made originally, and still continued to be made, by men, were not afraid to admit that those men might make bad laws; might do, by law, the same things, and from the same motives, which if done by individuals without the sanction of law, would be called unjust. And hence the sentiment of injustice came to be attached, not to all violations of law, but only to violations of such laws as *ought* to exist, including such as ought to exist, but do not; and to laws themselves, if supposed to be contrary to what ought to be law. In this manner the idea of law and of its injunctions was still predominant in the notion of justice, even when the laws actually in force ceased to be accepted as the standard of it.

It is true that mankind consider the idea of justice and its obligations as applicable to many things which neither are, nor is it desired that they should be, regulated by law. Nobody desires that laws should interfere with the whole detail of private life; yet every one allows that in all daily conduct a person may and does show himself to be either just or unjust. But even here, the idea of the breach of what ought to be law, still lingers in a modified shape. It would always give us pleasure, and chime in with our feelings of fitness, that acts which we deem unjust should be punished, though we do not always think it expedient that this should be done by the tribunals. We forego that gratification on account of incidental inconveniences. We should be glad to see just conduct enforced and injustice repressed, even in the minutest details, if we were not, with reason, afraid of trusting the magistrate with so unlimited an amount of power over individuals. When we think that a person is bound in justice to do a thing, it is an ordinary form of language to say that he ought to be compelled to do it. We should be gratified to see the obligation enforced by anybody who had the power. If we see that its enforcement by law would be inexpedient, we lament the impossibility, we consider the impunity given to injustice as an evil, and strive to make amends for it by bringing a strong expression of our own and the public disapprobation to bear upon the offender. Thus the idea of legal constraint is still the generating idea of the notion of justice, though undergoing several transformations before that notion, as it exists in an advanced state of society, becomes complete.

The above is, I think, a true account, as far as it goes, of the origin and progressive growth of the idea of justice. But we must observe, that it contains, as yet, nothing to distinguish that obligation from moral obligation in general. For the truth is, that the idea of penal sanction, which is the essence of law, enters not only into the conception of injustice, but into that of any kind of wrong. We do not call anything wrong, unless we mean to imply that a person ought to be punished in some way or other for doing it; if not by law, by the opinion of his fellow creatures; if not by opinion, by the reproaches of his own conscience. This seems the real turning point of the distinction between morality and simple expediency. It is a part of the notion of Duty in every one of its forms, that a person may rightfully be compelled to fulfil it. Duty is a thing which may be *exacted* from a person, as one exacts a debt. Unless we think that it may be exacted from him, we do not call it his duty. Reasons of prudence, or the interest of other people, may militate against actually exacting it; but the person himself, it is clearly understood, would not be entitled to complain. There are other things, on the contrary, which we wish that people should do, which we like or admire them for doing, perhaps dislike or despise them for not doing, but yet admit that they are not bound to do; it is not a case of moral obligation; we do not blame them, that is, we do not think that they are proper objects of punishment. How we come by these ideas of deserving and not deserving punishment, will appear, perhaps, in the sequel; but I think there is no doubt that this distinction lies at the bottom of the notions of right and wrong; that we call any conduct wrong, or employ, instead, some other term of dislike or disparagement, according as we think that the person ought, or ought not, to be punished for it; and we say, it would be right to do so and so, or merely that it would be desirable or laudable, according as we would wish to see the person whom it concerns, compelled, or only persuaded and exhorted, to act in that manner.*

This, therefore, being the characteristic difference which marks off, not justice, but morality in general, from the remaining provinces of Expediency and Worthiness; the character is still to be sought which distinguishes justice from other branches of morality. Now it is known that ethical writers divide moral duties into two classes, denoted by the ill-chosen expressions, duties of perfect and of imperfect obligation; the latter being those in which, though the act is obligatory, the particular occasions of performing it are left to our choice; as in the case of charity or beneficence, which we are indeed bound to practise, but not towards any definite person, nor at any prescribed time. In the more precise language of philosophic jurists, duties of perfect obligation are those duties in virtue of which a correlative *right* resides in some person or persons; duties of imperfect obligation are those moral obligations which do not give birth to any right. I think it will be found that this distinction exactly coincides with that which exists between justice and the other obligations of morality.

In our survey of the various popular acceptations of justice, the term appeared generally to involve the idea of a personal right—a claim on the part of one or more individuals, like that which the law gives when it confers a proprietary or other legal right. Whether the injustice consists in depriving a person of a possession, or in breaking faith with him, or in treating him worse than he deserves, or worse than other people who have no greater claims, in each case the supposition implies two things—a wrong done, and some assignable person who is wronged. Injustice may also be done by treating

---

* See this point enforced and illustrated by Professor Bain, in an admirable chapter (entitled *The Ethical Emotions, or the Moral Sense*) of the second of the two treatises composing his elaborate and profound work on the Mind.

a person better than others; but the wrong in this case is to his competitors, who are also assignable persons. It seems to me that this feature in the case—a right in some person, correlative to the moral obligation—constitutes the specific difference between justice, and generosity or beneficence. Justice implies something which it is not only right to do, and wrong not to do, but which some individual person can claim from us as his moral right. No one has a moral right to our generosity or beneficence, because we are not morally bound to practise those virtues towards any given individual. And it will be found with respect to this as to every correct definition, that the instances which seem to conflict with it are those which most confirm it. For if a moralist attempts, as some have done, to make out that mankind generally, though not any given individual, have a right to all the good we can do them, he at once, by that thesis, includes generosity and beneficence within the category of justice. He is obliged to say that our utmost exertions are *due* to fellow creatures, thus assimilating them to a debt; or that nothing less can be a sufficient *return* for what society does for us, thus classing the case as one of gratitude; both of which are acknowledged cases of justice. Wherever there is a right, the case is one of justice, and not of the virtue of beneficence: and whoever does not place the distinction between justice and morality in general, where we have now placed it, will be found to make no distinction between them at all, but to merge all morality in justice.

Having thus endeavoured to determine the distinctive elements which enter into the composition of the idea of justice, we are ready to enter on the inquiry, whether the feeling which accompanies the idea is attached to it by a special dispensation of nature, or whether it could have grown up, by any known laws, out of the idea itself; and in particular, whether it can have originated in considerations of general expediency.

I conceive that the sentiment itself does not arise from anything which would commonly, or correctly, be termed an idea of expediency; but that, though the sentiment does not, whatever is moral in it does.

We have seen that the two essential ingredients in the sentiment of justice are the desire to punish a person who has done harm, and the knowledge or belief that there is some definite individual or individuals to whom harm has been done.

Now it appears to me, that the desire to punish a person who has done harm to some individual, is a spontaneous outgrowth from two sentiments, both in the highest degree natural, and which either are or resemble instincts; the impulse of self-defence, and the feeling of sympathy.

It is natural to resent, and to repel, or retaliate, any harm done or attempted against ourselves, or against those with whom we sympathize. The origin of this sentiment it is not necessary here to discuss. Whether it be an instinct or a result of intelligence, it is, we know, common to all animal nature; for every animal tries to hurt those who have hurt, or who it thinks are about to hurt, itself or its young. Human beings, on this point, only differ from other animals in two particulars. First, in being capable of sympathizing, not solely with their offspring, or, like some of the more noble animals, with some superior animal who is kind to them, but with all human, and even with all sentient, beings. Secondly, in having a more developed intelligence, which gives a wider range to the whole of their sentiments, whether self-regarding or sympathetic. By virtue of his superior intelligence, even apart from his superior range of sympathy, a human being is capable of apprehending a community of interest between himself and the human society of which he forms a part, such that any conduct whcih threatens the security of the society generally, is threatening to his own, and calls forth his instinct (if instinct it be) of self-defence. The same superiority of intelligence, joined to the power of sympathizing with human beings generally, enables him to attach himself to the collective idea of his tribe, his country, or mankind, in such a manner that any act hurtful to them, raises his instinct of sympathy, and urges him to resistance.

The sentiment of justice, in that one of its elements which consists of the desire to punish, is thus, I conceive, the natural feeling of retaliation or vengeance, rendered by intellect and sympathy applicable to those injuries, that is, to those hurts, which wound us through, or in common with, society at large. This sentiment, in itself, has nothing moral in it; what is moral is, the exclusive subordination of it to the social sympathies, so as to wait on and obey their call. For the natural feeling would make us resent indiscriminately whatever any one does that is disagreeable to us; but when moralized by the social feeling, it only acts in the directions conformable to the general good: just persons resenting a hurt to society, though not otherwise a hurt to themselves, and not resenting a hurt to themselves, however painful, unless it be of the kind which society has a common interest with them in the repression of.

It is no objection against this doctrine to say, that when we feel our sentiment of justice outraged, we are not thinking of society at large, or of any collective interest, but only of the individual case. It is common enough certainly, though the reverse of commendable, to feel resentment merely because we have suffered pain; but a person whose resentment is really a moral feeling, that is, who considers whether an act is blameable before he allows himself to resent it—such a person, though he may not say expressly to himself that he is standing up for the interest of society, certainly does feel that he is asserting a rule which is for the benefit of others as well as for his own. If he is not feeling this—if he is regarding the act solely as it affects him individually—he is not consciously just; he is not concerning himself about the justice of his actions. This is admitted even by anti-utilitarian moralists. When Kant (as before remarked) propounds as the fundamental principle of morals, 'So act, that thy rule of conduct might, be adopted as a law by all rational beings', he virtually acknowledges that the interest of mankind collectively, or at least of mankind indiscriminately, must be in the mind of the agent when conscientiously deciding on the morality of the act. Otherwise he uses words without a meaning: for, that a rule even of utter selfishness could not *possibly* be adopted by all rational beings—that there is any insuperable obstacle in the nature of things to its adoption—cannot be even plausibly maintained. To give any meaning to Kant's principle, the sense put upon it must be, that we ought to shape our conduct by a rule which all rational beings might adopt *with benefit to their collective interest.*

To recapitulate: the idea of justice supposes two things; a rule of conduct, and a sentiment which sanctions the rule. The first must be supposed common to all mankind, and intended for their good. The other (the sentiment) is a desire that punishment may be suffered by those who infringe the rule. There is involved, in addition, the conception of some definite person who suffers by the infringement; whose rights (to use the expression appropriated to the case) are violated by it. And the sentiment of justice appears to me to be, the animal desire to repel or retaliate a hurt or damage to oneself, or to those with whom one sympathizes, widened so as to include all persons, by the human capacity of enlarged sympathy, and the human conception of intelligent self-interest. From the latter elements, the feeling derives its morality; from the former, its peculiar impressiveness, and energy of self-assertion.

I have, throughout, treated the idea of a *right* residing in the injured person, and violated by the injury, not as a separate element in the composition of the idea and sentiment, but as one of the forms in which the other two elements clothe themselves. These elements are a hurt to some assignable person or persons on the one hand, and a demand for punishment on the other. An examination of our own minds, I think, will show that these two things include all that we mean when we speak of violation of a right. When we call anything a person's right, we mean that he has a valid claim on society to protect him in the possession of it, either by the force of law, or by that of education and opinion. If he has what we consider a sufficient claim, on whatever account, to have something guaranteed to him by society, we say that he has a right to it. If we desire to prove that anything does not belong to him by right, we think this done as soon as it is admitted that society ought not to take measures for securing it to him, but should leave him to chance, or to his own exertions. Thus, a person is said to have a right to what he can earn in fair professional competition; because society ought not to allow any other person to hinder him from endeavouring to earn in that manner as much as he can. But he has not a right to three hundred a-year, though he may happen to be earning it; because society is not called on to provide that he shall earn that sum. On the contrary, if he owns ten thousand pounds three per cent. stock, he *has* a right to three hundred a-year; because society has come under an obligation to provide him with an income of that amount.

To have a right, then, is, I conceive, to have something which society ought to defend me in the possession of. If the objector goes on to ask, why it ought? I can give him no other reason than general utility. If that expression does not seem to convey a sufficient feeling of the strength of the obligation, nor to account for the peculiar energy of the feeling, it is because there goes to the composition of the sentiment, not a rational only but also an animal element, the thirst for retaliation; and this thirst derives its intensity, as well as its moral justification, from the extraordinarily important and impressive kind of utility which is concerned. The interest involved is that of security, to every one's feelings the most vital of all interests. All other earthly benefits are needed by one person, not needed by another; and many of them can, if necessary, be cheerfully foregone, or replaced by something else; but security no human being can possibly do without; on it we depend for all our immunity from evil, and for the whole value of all and every good, beyond the passing moment; since nothing but the gratification of the instant could be of any worth to us, if we could be deprived of everything the next instant by whoever was momentarily stronger than ourselves. Now this most indispensable of all necessaries, after physical nutriment, cannot be had, unless the machinery for providing it is kept unintermittedly in active play. Our notion, therefore, of the claim we have on our fellow creatures to join in making safe for us the very groundwork of our existence, gathers feelings around it so much more intense than those concerned in any of the more common cases of utility, that the difference in degree (as is often the case in psychology) becomes a real difference in kind. The claim assumes that character of absoluteness, that apparent infinity, and incommensurability with all other considerations, which constitute the distinction between the feeling of right and wrong and that of ordinary expediency and inexpediency. The feelings concerned are so powerful, and we count so positively on finding a responsive feeling in others (all being alike interested), that *ought* and *should* grow into *must*, and recognized indispensability becomes a moral necessity, analogous to physical, and often not inferior to it in binding force.

If the preceding analysis, or something resembling it, be not the correct account of the notion of justice; if justice be totally independent of utility, and be a standard *per se*, which the mind can recognize by simple introspection of itself, it is hard to understand why that internal oracle is so ambiguous, and why so many things appear either just or unjust, according to the light in which they are regarded.

We are continually informed that Utility is an uncertain standard, which every different person interprets differently, and that there is no safety but in the immutable, ineffaceable, and unmistakable dictates of Justice, which carry their evidence in themselves, and are independent of the fluctuations of opinion. One would suppose from this that on questions of justice there could be no controversy; that if we take that for our rule, its application to any given case could leave us in as little doubt as a mathematical demonstration. So far is this from being the fact, that there is as much difference of opinion, and as much discussion, about what is just, as about what is useful to society. Not only have different nations and individuals different notions of justice, but in the mind of one and the same individual, justice is not some one rule, principle, or maxim, but many, which do not always coincide in their dictates, and in choosing between which, he is guided either by some extraneous standard, or by his own personal predilections.

For instance, there are some who say that it is unjust to punish any one for the sake of example to others; that punishment is just, only when intended for the good of the sufferer himself. Others maintain the extreme reverse, contending that to punish persons who have attained years of discretion, for their own benefit, is despotism and injustice, since if the matter at issue is solely their own good, no one has a right to control their own judgment of it; but that they may justly be punished to prevent evil to others, this being the exercise of the legitimate right of self-defence.

Mr. Owen, again, affirms that it is unjust to punish at all; for the criminal did not make his own character; his education, and the circumstances which surrounded him, have made him a criminal, and for these he is not responsible. All these opinions are extremely plausible; and, so long as the question is argued as one of justice simply, without going down to the principles which lie under justice and are the source of its authority, I am unable to see how any of these reasoners can be refuted. For in truth every one of the three builds upon rules of justice confessedly true.

The first appeals to the acknowledged injustice of singling out an individual, and making him a sacrifice, without his consent, for other people's benefit. The second relies on the acknowledged justice of self-defence, and the admitted injustice of forcing one person to conform to another's notions of what constitutes his good. The Owenite invokes the admitted principle that it is unjust to punish any one for what he cannot help. Each is triumphant so long as he is not compelled to take into consideration any other maxims of justice than the one he has selected; but as soon as their several maxims are brought face to face, each disputant seems to have exactly as much to say for himself as the others. No one of them can carry out his own notion of justice without trampling upon another equally binding. These are difficulties; they have always been felt to be such; and many devices have been invented to turn rather than to overcome them. As a refuge from the last of the three, men imagined what they called the freedom of the will; fancying that they could not justify punishing a man whose will is in a thoroughly hateful state, unless it be supposed to have come into that state through no influence of anterior circumstances. To escape from the other difficulties, a favourite contrivance has been the fiction of a contract, whereby at some unknown period all the members of society engaged to obey the laws, and consented to be punished for any disobedience to them; thereby giving to their legislators the right, which it is assumed they would not otherwise have had, of punishing them, either for their own good or for that of society.

This happy thought was considered to get rid of the whole difficulty, and to legitimate the infliction of punishment, in virtue of another received maxim of justice, *Volenti non fit injuria;* that is not unjust which is done with the consent of the person who is supposed to be hurt by it. I need hardly remark that even if the consent were not a mere fiction, this maxim is not superior in authority to the others which it is brought in to supersede. It is, on the contrary, an instructive specimen of the loose and irregular manner in which supposed principles of justice grow up. This particular one evidently came into use as a help to the coarse exigencies of courts of law, which are sometimes obliged to be content with very uncertain presumptions on account of the greater evils which would often arise from any attempt on their part to cut finer. But even courts of law are not able to adhere consistently to the maxim, for they allow voluntary engagements to be set aside on the ground of fraud, and sometimes on that of mere mistake or misinformation.

Again, when the legitimacy of inflicting punishment is admitted, how many conflicting conceptions of justice come to light in discussing the proper apportionment of punishments to offences. No rule on the subject recommends itself so strongly to the primitive and spontaneous sentiment of justice as the *lex talionis*, an eye for an eye and a tooth for a tooth. Though this principle of the Jewish and of the Mahomedan law has been generally abandoned in Europe as a practical maxim, there is, I suspect, in most minds, a secret hankering after it; and when retribution accidentally falls on an offender in that precise shape, the general feeling of satisfaction evinced, bears witness how natural is the sentiment to which this repayment in kind is acceptable. With many the

test of justice in penal infliction is that the punishment should
be proportioned to the offence; meaning that it should be
exactly measured by the moral guilt of the culprit (whatever
be their standard for measuring moral guilt): the consideration, what amount of punishment is necessary to deter from
the offence, having nothing to do with the question of justice,
in their estimation; while there are others to whom that consideration is all in all; who maintain that it is not just, at
least for man, to inflict on a fellow-creature, whatever may be
his offences, any amount of suffering beyond the least that
will suffice to prevent him from repeating, and others from
imitating, his misconduct.

To take another example from a subject already once referred to. In a co-operative industrial association is it just or
not that talent or skill should give a title to superior remuneration? On the negative side of the question it is argued that
whoever does the best he can deserves equally well, and
ought not in justice to be put in a position of inferiority for
no fault of his own; that superior abilities have already advantages more than enough, in the admiration they excite,
the personal influence they command, and the internal sources
of satisfaction attending them, without adding to these a superior share of the world's goods; and that society is bound in
justice rather to make compensation to the less favoured, for
this unmerited inequality of advantages, than to aggravate it.
On the contrary side it is contended that society receives more
from the more efficient labourer; that his services being more
useful, society owes him a larger return for them; that a
greater share of the joint result is actually his work, and not
to allow his claim to it is a kind of robbery; that if he is only
to receive as much as others, he can only be justly required
to produce as much, and to give a smaller amount of time
and exertion, proportioned to his superior efficiency. Who
shall decide between these appeals to conflicting principles of
justice? Justice has in this case two sides to it, which it is
impossible to bring into harmony, and the two disputants
have chosen opposite sides; the one looks to what it is just
that the individual should receive, the other to what it is just
that the community should give. Each from his own point of
view is unanswerable; and any choice between them, on
grounds of justice, must be perfectly arbitrary. Social utility
alone can decide the preference.

How many, again, and how irreconcileable, are the standards of justice to which reference is made in discussing the

repartition of taxation. One opinion is that payment to the State should be in numerical proportion to pecuniary means. Others think that justice dictates what they term graduated taxation; taking a higher per-centage from those who have more to spare. In point of natural justice a strong case might be made for disregarding means altogether, and taking the same absolute sum (whenever it could be got) from every one: as the subscribers to a mess, or to a club, all pay the same sum for the same privileges, whether they can all equally afford it or not. Since the protection (it might be said) of law and government is afforded to and is equally required by all, there is no injustice in making all buy it at the same price. It is reckoned justice, not injustice, that a dealer should charge to all customers the same price for the same article, not a price varying according to their means of payment. This doctrine, as applied to taxation, finds no advocates, because it conflicts so strongly with man's feelings of humanity and of social expediency; but the principle of justice which it invokes is as true and as binding as those which can be appealed to against it. Accordingly it exerts a tacit influence on the line of defence employed for other modes of assessing taxation. People feel obliged to argue that the State does more for the rich than for the poor, as a justification for its taking more from them: though this is in reality not true, for the rich would be far better able to protect themselves, in the absence of law or government, than the poor, and indeed would probably be successful in converting the poor into their slaves. Others, again, so far defer to the same conception of justice as to maintain that all should pay an equal capitation tax for the protection of their persons (these being of equal value to all), and an unequal tax for the protection of their property, which is unequal. To this others reply that the all of one man is as valuable to him as the all of another. From these confusions there is no other mode of extrication than the utilitarian.

Is, then, the difference between the Just and the Expedient a merely imaginary distinction? Have mankind been under a delusion in thinking that justice is a more sacred thing than policy, and that the latter ought only to be listened to after the former has been satisfied? By no means. The exposition we have given of the nature and origin of the sentiment, recognizes a real distinction; and no one of those who profess the most sublime contempt for the consequences of actions as an element in their morality, attaches more importance to the distinction than I do. While I dispute the pretensions of any theory which sets up an imaginary standard of justice not grounded on utility, I account the justice which is grounded on utility to be the chief part, and incomparably the most sacred and binding part, of all morality. Justice is a name for certain classes of moral rules, which concern the essentials of human well-being more nearly, and are therefore of more absolute obligation, than any other rules for the guidance of life; and the notion which we have found to be of the essence of the idea of justice, that of a right residing in an individual, implies and testifies to this more binding obligation.

The moral rules which forbid mankind to hurt one another (in which we must never forget to include wrongful interference with each other's freedom) are more vital to human well-being than any maxims, however important, which only point out the best mode of managing some department of human affairs. They have also the peculiarity, that they are the main element in determining the whole of the social feelings of mankind. It is their observance which alone preserves peace among human beings: if obedience to them were not the rule, and disobedience the exception, every one would see in every one else an enemy, against whom he must be perpetually guarding himself. What is hardly less important, these are the precepts which mankind have the strongest and the most direct inducements for impressing upon one another. By merely giving to each other prudential instruction or exhortation, they may gain, or think they gain, nothing: in inculcating on each other the duty of positive beneficence they have an unmistakable interest, but far less in degree: a person may possibly not need the benefits of others; but he always needs that they should not do him hurt.

Thus the moralities which protect every individual from being harmed by others, either directly or by being hindered in his freedom of pursuing his own good, are at once those which he himself has most at heart, and those which he has the strongest interest in publishing and enforcing by word and deed. It is by a person's observance of these that his fitness to exist as one of the fellowship of human beings is tested and decided; for on that depends his being a nuisance or not to those with whom he is in contact. Now it is these moralities primarily, which compose the obligations of justice. The most marked cases of injustice, and those which give the tone to the feeling of repugnance which characterizes the sentiment, are acts of wrongful aggression, or wrongful exercise of power over some one; the next are those which consist in wrongfully withholding from him something which is his due: in both cases, inflicting on him a positive hurt, either in the form of direct suffering, or of the privation of some good which he had reasonable ground, either of a physical or of a social kind, for counting upon.

The same powerful motives which command the observance of these primary moralities enjoin the punishment of those who violate them; and as the impulses of self-defence, of defence of others, and of vengeance, are all called forth against such persons, retribution, or evil for evil, becomes closely connected with the sentiment of justice, and is universally included in the idea. Good for good is also one of the dictates of justice; and this, though its social utility is evident, and though it carries with it a natural human feeling, has not at first sight that obvious connexion with hurt or injury, which, existing in the most elementary cases of just and unjust, is the source of the characteristic intensity of the sentiment. But the connexion, though less obvious, is not less real. He who accepts benefits, and denies a return of them when needed, inflicts a real hurt, by disappointing one of the most natural and reasonable of expectations, and one which he must at least tacitly have encouraged, otherwise the benefits would seldom have been conferred. The important rank, among human evils and wrongs, of the disappointment of expectation, is shown in the fact that it constitutes the principal criminality of two such highly immoral acts as a breach of friendship and a breach of promise. Few hurts which human beings can sustain are greater, and none wound more, than when that on which they habitually and with full assurance relied, fails them in the hour of need; and few wrongs are greater than this mere withholding of good; none excite more resentment, either in the person suffering, or in a sympathizing spectator. The principle, therefore, of giving to each what they deserve, that is, good for good as well as evil for evil, is not only included within the idea of Justice as we have defined it, but is a proper object of that intensity of sentiment, which places the Just, in human estimation, above the simply Expedient.

Most of the maxims of justice current in the world, and commonly appealed to in its transactions, are simply instrumental to carrying into effect the principles of justice which we have now spoken of. That a person is responsible only for what he has done voluntarily, or could voluntarily have avoided; that it is unjust to condemn any person unheard;

that the punishment ought to be proportioned to the offence, and the like, are maxims intended to prevent the just principle of evil for evil from being perverted to the infliction of evil without that justification. The greater part of these common maxims have come into use from the practice of courts of justice, which have been naturally led to a more complete recognition and elaboration than was likely to suggest itself to others, of the rules necessary to enable them to fulfil their double function, of inflicting punishment when due, and of awarding to each person his right.

That first of judicial virtues, impartiality, is an obligation of justice, partly for the reason last mentioned; as being a necessary condition of the fulfilment of the obligations of justice. But this is not the only source of the exalted rank, among human obligations, of those maxims of equality and impartiality, which, both in popular estimation and in that of the most enlightened, are included among the precepts of justice. In one point of view, they may be considered as corollaries from the principles already laid down. If it is a duty to do to each according to his deserts, returning good for good as well as repressing evil by evil, it necessarily follows that we should treat all equally well (when no higher duty forbids) who have deserved equally well of *us*, and that society should treat all equally well who have deserved equally well of *it*, that is, who have deserved equally well absolutely. This is the highest abstract standard of social and distributive justice; towards which all institutions, and the efforts of all virtuous citizens, should be made in the utmost possible degree to converge.

But this great moral duty rests upon a still deeper foundation, being a direct emanation from the first principle of morals, and not a mere logical corollary from secondary or derivative doctrines. It is involved in the very meaning of Utility, or the Greatest-Happiness Principle. That principle is a mere form of words without rational signification, unless one person's happiness, supposed equal in degree (with the proper allowance made for kind), is counted for exactly as much as another's. Those conditions being supplied, Bentham's dictum, 'everybody to count for one, nobody for more than one,' might be written under the principle of utility as an explanatory commentary.* The equal claim of everybody to happiness

---

* This implication, in the first principle of the utilitarian scheme, of perfect impartiality between persons, is regarded by Mr. Herbert Spencer (in his *Social Statics*) as a disproof of the pretensions of utility to be a sufficient guide to right; since (he says) the principle of utility presupposes the anterior principle, that everybody has an equal right to happiness. It may be more

in the estimation of the moralist and the legislator, involves an equal claim to all the means of happiness, except in so far as the inevitable conditions of human life, and the general interest, in which that of every individual is included, set limits to the maxim; and those limits ought to be strictly construed. As every other maxim of justice, so this, is by no means applied or held applicable, universally; on the contrary, as I have already remarked, it bends to every person's ideas of social expediency. But in whatever case it is deemed applicable at all, it is held to be the dictate of justice. All persons are deemed to have a *right* to equality of treatment, except when some recognised social expediency requires the reverse. And hence all social inequalities which have ceased to be considered expedient, assume the character not of simple inexpediency, but of injustice, and appear so tyrannical, that people are apt to wonder how they ever could have been tolerated; forgetful that they themselves perhaps tolerate other inequalities under an equally mistaken notion of expediency, the correction of which would make that which they approve, seem quite as monstrous as what they have at least learnt to condemn. The entire history of social improvement has been a series of transitions, by which one custom or institution after another, from being a supposed primary necessity of social existence, has passed into the rank of an universally stigma-

correctly described as supposing that equal amounts of happiness are equally desirable whether felt by the same or by different persons. This, however, is not a *presupposition*; not a premise needful to support the principle of utility, but the very principle itself; for what is the principle of utility, if it be not that 'happiness' and 'desirable' are synonymous terms? If there is any anterior principle implied, it can be no other than this, that the truths of arithmetic are applicable to the valuation of happiness, as of all other measurable qualities.

[Mr. Herbert Spencer, in a private communication on the subject of the preceding Note, objects to being considered an opponent of Utilitarianism, and states that he regards happiness as the ultimate end of morality; but deems that end only partially attainable by empirical generalizations from the observed results of conduct, and completely attainable only by deducing, from the laws of life and the conditions of existence, what kinds of action necessarily tend to produce happiness, and what kinds to produce unhappiness. With the exception of the word 'necessarily' I have no dissent to express from this doctrine, and (omitting that word) I am not aware that any modern advocate of utilitarianism is of a different opinion. Bentham, certainly, to whom in the *Social Statics* Mr. Spencer particularly referred, is, least of all writers, chargeable with unwillingness to deduce the effect of actions on happiness from the laws of human nature and the universal conditions of human life. The common charge against him is of relying too exclusively upon such deductions, and declining altogether to be bound by the generalizations from specific experience which Mr. Spencer thinks that utilitarians generally confine themselves to. My own opinion (and, as I collect, Mr. Spencer's) is, that in ethics, as in all other branches of scientific study, the consilience of the results of both these processes, each corroborating and verifying the other, is requisite to give to any general proposition the kind and degree of evidence which constitutes scientific proof.]

tized injustice and tyranny. So it has been with the distinctions of slaves and freemen, nobles and serfs, patricians and plebeians; and so it will be, and in part already is, with the aristocracies of colour, race, and sex.

It appears from what has been said that justice is a name for certain moral requirements, which, regarded collectively, stand higher in the scale of social utility, and are therefore of more paramount obligation, than any others; though particular cases may occur in which some other social duty is so important, as to overrule any one of the general maxims of justice. Thus, to save a life it may not only be allowable, but a duty, to steal, or take by force, the necessary food or medicine, or to kidnap, and compel to officiate, the only qualified medical practitioner. In such cases, as we do not call anything justice which is not a virtue, we usually say, not that justice must give way to some other moral principle, but that what is just in ordinary cases is, by reason of that other principle, not just in the particular case. By this useful accommodation of language, the character of indefeasibility attributed to justice is kept up, and we are saved from the necessity of maintaining that there can be laudable injustice.

The considerations which have now been adduced resolve, I conceive, the only real difficulty in the utilitarian theory of morals. It has always been evident that all cases of justice are also cases of expediency: the difference is in the peculiar sentiment which attaches to the former as contradistinguished from the latter. If this characteristic sentiment has been sufficiently accounted for; if there is no necessity to assume for it any peculiarity of origin; if it is simply the natural feeling of resentment, moralized by being made coextensive with the demands of social good; and if this feeling not only does but ought to exist in all the classes of cases to which the idea of justice corresponds; that idea no longer presents itself as a stumblingblock to the utilitarian ethics. Justice remains the appropriate name for certain social utilities which are vastly more important, and therefore more absolute and imperative, than any others are as a class (though not more so than others may be in particular cases); and which, therefore, ought to be, as well as naturally are, guarded by a sentiment not only different in degree, but also in kind; distinguished from the milder feeling which attaches to the mere idea of promoting human pleasure or convenience, at once by the more definite nature of its commands, and by the sterner character of its sanctions.

MILL regarded *On Liberty* as the one book which would outlast all the others—with the possible exception of his *Logic*. While the *Autobiography* should be substituted for the *Logic*, Mill was right on the crucial book. In the letter he wrote his wife during the black spell of his illness, it was listed as one of the themes to be treated before he died. A draft of it, as a short essay, was planned and written that same year, 1854.

The following year Mill pondered the idea of turning the essay into a full-length book. "On my way here cogitating thereon," he wrote his wife from Rome, January 15, 1855, "I came back to an idea we have talked about, & thought that the best thing to write & publish at present would be a volume on Liberty. So many things might be brought into it & nothing seems more to be needed—it is a growing need too, for opinion tends to encroach more & more on liberty, & almost all the projects of social reformers of these days are really *liberticide*—Comte's particularly so. . . ." In his *Autobiography*, Mill recalls that, after writing the essay in 1854, "it was in mounting the steps of the Capitol, in January 1855, that the thought first arose of converting it into a volume." It was published in 1859, the year after Mrs. Mill's death, with a deeply moving dedication to her.

We have Mill's repeated testimony that, of all his books, this is the one that most bears the stamp of her thought and is closest to being the product of their joint authorship. There was not a sentence of it, he wrote, which they did not go through together and weigh carefully, for thought and word. It may well be so. But Mill's letters from Italy in 1855 show that he was working on the draft of the book himself, and that he had great hopes for its reception. "The more I think of the plan of a volume on Liberty, the more likely it seems to me that it will be read & will make a sensation. The title itself with any known name to it would sell an edition."

He was reading Macaulay at the time ("he is what all cockneys are, an intellectual dwarf"), but even more he was reading Goethe ("What strikes me most in him is the grand effort of his life to make himself a Greek"). If Mill was sketching and writing his book during the next six months, which is likely, he was doing so in scenes of extraordinary beauty as he traveled from Sorrento to Naples to Palermo and Messina, from Sicily to Corfu, from there to Athens and Delphi, and from there back to Florence, Milan, and Lugano. He was delighted to be alive, after his scare of the previous year. He was witnessing a broad array of national and personality types different from the British he had known. It was in this setting that he wrote his book, whose great theme is that the purpose of liberty in human affairs is to give scope and direction for the expression "of a large variety in types of character . . . and full freedom to human nature to expand itself in innumerable and conflicting directions."

He later acknowledged Goethe as one of the sources for his thinking in the book. What struck him about Goethe was his "theory of the right and duty of self-development." It is an extraordinary combination that the two men offer. Here was Mill, a man essentially of the Reformation and the European Enlightenment, reaching out in the dazzling setting of Greek and Italian beauty to touch the hand of Goethe, the man of the Renaissance, whose views of morals and conduct in life he abhorred but whose vision of man's fulfillment he caught. The "saint of rationalism," struggling for health, grateful to be vouchsafed another stretch of life, straining to leave behind some permanent memorial of his best thought on the noblest theme on which he was capable of writing, turned to Goethe's great category of self-realization in the fullest aesthetic as well as intellectual sense.

The theory of society contained in this book is perhaps its weakest phase. Mill still saw society not as an organic whole, with a life of its own, but as a collection of individual atoms. He was influenced at the time by Joseph Warren, the American anarchist thinker, who had raised the banner of "the sovereignty of the individual." Mill came close to seeing society as a congeries of these individual sovereignties, each with complete authority over himself provided he did not hurt others.

The great strength of the book lies in its moving away from a narrow view of human freedom as an immunity from the power of the state. Mill takes two giant steps away from this, toward a broader view of freedom. One step is to see that the enemies of human freedom may be found in the attitudes of the people themselves, and that the tyranny of the majority may be as hostile to the expression of a man's life and temperament as the tyranny of the state. He saw history as a kind of circulation of creeds, each of which demanded acceptance from the individual: no sooner is one swept away, then another starts forming, and—after a period of transition in which the latitude for opinions is relatively great—the new one is established and solidified, and exercises the same "power of compression" as the other.

Mill was a pioneer in seeing, with the growth of social egalitarianism and mass culture, the shadow of "an oppressive yoke of uniformity in opinion and practice." Jacob Burckhardt in Switzerland and Lord Acton in England were to take up this theme, and Alexis de Tocqueville had already stressed it in his *Democracy in America*, which Mill had reviewed. I am convinced that Tocqueville's influence on Mill, especially in the case of *On Liberty*, was far greater than his biographers and editors have thus far recognized. The letters which J. P. Mayer, Tocqueville's editor, has recently gathered and published in the collected edition of Tocqueville's works, will bear further study from that angle.

Mill's second great step was to base his concept of liberty on the concept of a developing person. We have here more than a theory of liberty. It is a theory of personality, and of the growth, potential richness, and self-realization of the personality. Here is what liberty is about. It is what gives meaning to the martyrdoms suffered in its behalf: Mill's passages on Socrates and on Jesus have a grave eloquence which is all the more impressive because he did not really understand the Greek mind and the irrationals in it, nor was he a Christian. But he did see that the ordeals of great historic figures in the history of liberty were given additional meaning because they opened the way for other men to be themselves, whatever their heterodoxies of creed and their diversities of outlook, behavior, and personality.

To create the conditions for this expression of diversity, Mill counted upon "those who have been in advance of society in thought and feeling." This comes close to a theory of a creative elite, although Mill shrank from making it explicit. He was committed to the idea that the mass of the people would somehow rise through education. He was proud of the appeal he had to the working class, and he was willing to forgo royalties on his book, *On Liberty*, in order to have it published at a cheap price in a People's Edition. Yet he did not delude himself about the intellectual or moral level of the British workers and middle class, nor about their impact on the society as a whole. He saw the nature of the cultural homogenization that was already in process in his day—the forces which "tend to raise the low and to lower the high" in the society. In the end, he counted upon the combination of the intellectual elite and the forces of liberty to create the good society.

As for the nature of that good society, Mill had no rigid formula. He was against any reform group which believed it had a pipeline to the eternal truth, whether it be the Chinese mandarins or the Jesuits in Europe or the Comtists. In that direction, he felt, lay the forces of rigidity (the "stationary society") as against the forces of dynamism. His conception of the good society was a humane and generous one: the society in which there was the greatest freedom for the competition of ideas, whether in truth or error, and for diversity of personality and styles of life. No one since Mill has gone much farther.

CONTENTS

DEDICATION

To the beloved and deplored memory of her who was the inspirer, and in part the author, of all that is best in my writings—the friend and wife whose exalted sense of truth and right was my strongest incitement, and whose approbation was my chief reward—I dedicate this volume. Like all that I have written for many years, it belongs as much to her as to me; but the work as it stands has had, in a very insufficient degree, the inestimable advantage of her revision; some of the most important portions having been reserved for a more careful re-examination, which they are now never destined to receive. Were I but capable of interpreting to the world one half the great thoughts and noble feelings which are buried in her grave, I should be the medium of a greater benefit to it, than is ever likely to arise from anything that I can write, unprompted and unassisted by her all but unrivalled wisdom.

ON LIBERTY

[handwritten: civil, social]

[handwritten: 1. nature of limits of the power of society over individual]

I. INTRODUCTORY

The subject of this Essay is not the so-called Liberty of the Will, so unfortunately opposed to the misnamed doctrine of Philosophical Necessity; but Civil, or Social Liberty: the nature and limits of the power which can be legitimately exercised by society over the individual. A question seldom stated, and hardly ever discussed, in general terms, but which profoundly influences the practical controversies of the age by its latent presence, and is likely soon to make itself recognised as the vital question of the future. It is so far from being new, that in a certain sense, it has divided mankind, almost from the remotest ages; but in the stage of progress into which the more civilized portions of the species have now entered, it presents itself under new conditions, and requires a different and more fundamental treatment.

The struggle between Liberty and Authority is the most conspicuous feature in the portions of history with which we are earliest familiar, particularly in that of Greece, Rome, and England. But in old times this contest was between subjects, or some classes of subjects, and the government. By liberty was meant protection against the tyranny of the political rulers. The rulers were conceived (except in some of the popular governments of Greece) as in a necessarily antagonistic position to the people whom they ruled. They consisted of a governing One, or a governing tribe or caste, who derived their authority from inheritance or conquest, who, at all events, did not hold it at the pleasure of the governed, and whose supremacy men did not venture, perhaps did not desire, to contest, whatever precautions might be taken against

[handwritten margin notes: history of a struggle for Liberty; from one]

its oppressive exercise. Their power was regarded as necessary, but also as highly dangerous; as a weapon which they would attempt to use against their subjects, no less than against external enemies. To prevent the weaker members of the community from being preyed upon by innumerable vultures, it was needful that there should be an animal of prey stronger than the rest, commissioned to keep them down. But as the king of the vultures would be no less bent upon preying on the flock, than any of the minor harpies, it was indispensable to be in a perpetual attitude of defence against his beak and claws. The aim, therefore, of patriots, was to set limits to the power which the ruler should be suffered to exercise over the community; and this limitation was what they meant by liberty. It was attempted in two ways. First, by obtaining a recognition of certain immunities, called political liberties or rights, which it was to be regarded as a breach of duty in the ruler to infringe, and which if he did infringe, specific resistance, or general rebellion, was held to be justifiable. A second, and generally a later expedient, was the establishment of constitutional checks; by which the consent of the community, or of a body of some sort, supposed to represent its interests, was made a necessary condition to some of the more important acts of the governing power. To the first of these modes of limitation, the ruling power, in most European countries, was compelled, more or less, to submit. It was not so with the second; and to attain this, or when already in some degree possessed, to attain it more completely, became everywhere the principal object of the lovers of liberty. And so long as mankind were content to combat one enemy by another, and to be ruled by a master, on condition of being guaranteed more or less efficaciously against his tyranny, they did not carry their aspirations beyond this point.

A time, however, came, in the progress of human affairs, when men ceased to think it a necessity of nature that their governors should be an independent power, opposed in interest to themselves. It appeared to them much better that the various magistrates of the State should be their tenants or delegates, revocable at their pleasure. In that way alone, it seemed, could they have complete security that the powers of government would never be abused to their disadvantage. By degrees, this new demand for elective and temporary rulers became the prominent object of the exertions of the popular party, wherever any such party existed; and superseded, to a considerable extent, the previous efforts to limit the power of rulers. As the struggle proceeded for making the ruling power emanate from the periodical choice of the ruled, some persons began to think that too much importance had been attached to the limitation of the power itself. *That* (it might seem) was a resource against rulers whose interests were habitually opposed to those of the people. What was now wanted was, that the rulers should be identified with the people; that their interest and will should be the interest and will of the nation. The nation did not need to be protected against it own will. There was no fear of its tyrannizing over itself. Let the rulers be effectually responsible to it, promptly removable by it, and it could afford to trust them with power of which it could itself dictate the use to be made. Their power was but the nation's own power, concentrated, and in a form convenient for exercise. This mode of thought, or rather perhaps of feeling, was common among the last generation of European liberalism, in the Continental section of which, it still apparently predominates. Those who admit any limit to what a government may do, except in the case of such governments as they think ought not to exist, stand out as brilliant exceptions among the political thinkers of the Continent. A similar tone of sentiment might by this time have been prevalent in our own country, if the circumstances which for a time encouraged it, had continued unaltered.

But, in political and philosophical theories, as well as in persons, success discloses faults and infirmities which failure might have concealed from observation. The notion, that the people have no need to limit their power over themselves, might seem axiomatic, when popular government was a thing only dreamed about, or read of as having existed at some distant period of the past. Neither was that notion necessarily disturbed by such temporary aberrations as those of the French Revolution, the worst of which were the work of an usurping few, and which, in any case, belonged, not to the permanent working of popular institutions, but to a sudden and convulsive outbreak against monarchical and aristocratic despotism. In time, however, a democratic republic came to occupy a large portion of the earth's surface, and made itself felt as one of the most powerful members of the community of nations; and elective and responsible government became subject to the observations and criticisms which wait upon a great existing fact. It was now perceived that such phrases as 'self-government,' and 'the power of the people over themselves,' do not express the true state of the case. The 'people' who exercise the power, are not always the same people with those over whom it is exercised; and the 'self-government' spoken of, is not the government of each by himself, but of each by all the rest. The will of the people, moreover, practically means, the will of the most numerous or the most active *part* of the people; the majority, or those who succeed in making themselves accepted as the majority: the people, consequently, *may* desire to oppress a part of their number; and precautions are as much needed against this, as against any other abuse of power. The limitation, therefore, of the power of government over individuals, loses none of its importance when the holders of power are regularly accountable to the community, that is, to the strongest party therein. This view of things, recommending itself equally to the intelligence of thinkers and to the inclination of those important classes in European society to whose real or supposed interests democracy is adverse, has had no difficulty in establishing itself; and in political speculations 'the tyranny of the majority' is now generally included among the evils against which society requires to be on its guard.

Like other tyrannies, the tyranny of the majority was at first, and is still vulgarly, held in dread, chiefly as operating through the acts of the public authorities. But reflecting persons perceived that when society is itself the tyrant—society collectively, over the separate individuals who compose it—its means of tyrannizing are not restricted to the acts which it may do by the hands of its political functionaries. Society can and does execute its own mandates: and if it issues wrong mandates instead of right, or any mandates at all in things with which it ought not to meddle, it practises a social tyranny more formidable than many kinds of political oppression, since, though not usually upheld by such extreme penalties, it leaves fewer means of escape, penetrating much more deeply into the details of life, and enslaving the soul itself. Protection, therefore, against the tyranny of the magistrate is not enough: there needs protection also against the tyranny of the prevailing opinion and feeling; against the tendency of society to impose, by other means than civil penalties, its own ideas and practices as rules of conduct on those who dissent from them; to fetter the development, and, if possible, prevent the formation, of any individuality not in harmony with its ways, and compel all characters to fashion themselves upon the model of its own. There is a limit to the legitimate interference of collective opinion with individual independence:

and to find that limit and maintain it against encroachment,
is as indispensable to a good condition of human affairs, as
protection against political despotism.

But though this proposition is not likely to be contested in
general terms, the practical question, where to place the limit
—how to make the fitting adjustment between individual independence and social control—is a subject on which nearly
everything remains to be done. All that makes existence valuable to any one, depends on the enforcement of restraints
upon the actions of other people. Some rules of conduct, therefore, must be imposed, by law in the first place, and by
opinion on many things which are not fit subjects for the
operation of law. What these rules should be, is the principal
question in human affairs; but if we except a few of the most
obvious cases, it is one of those which least progress has been
made in resolving. No two ages, and scarcely any two countries, have decided it alike; and the decision of one age or
country is a wonder to another. Yet the people of any given
age and country no more suspect any difficulty in it, than if it
were a subject on which mankind had always been agreed.
The rules which obtain among themselves appear to them self-
evident and self-justifying. This all but universal illusion is
one of the examples of the magical influence of custom, which
is not only, as the proverb says, a second nature, but is continually mistaken for the first. The effect of custom, in preventing any misgiving respecting the rules of conduct which
mankind impose on one another, is all the more complete because the subject is one on which it is not generally considered necessary that reasons should be given, either by one
person to others, or by each to himself. People are accustomed
to believe, and have been encouraged in the belief by some
who aspire to the character of philosophers, that their feelings, on subjects of this nature, are better than reasons, and
render reasons unnecessary. The practical principle which
guides them to their opinions on the regulation of human conduct, is the feeling in each person's mind that everybody
should be required to act as he, and those with whom he sympathizes, would like them to act. No one, indeed, acknowledges to himself that his standard of judgment is his own
liking; but an opinion on a point of conduct, not supported
by reasons, can only count as one person's preference; and if
the reasons, when given, are a mere appeal to a similar preference felt by other people, it is still only many people's liking
instead of one. To an ordinary man, however, his own pref-

erence, thus supported, is not only a perfectly satisfactory
reason, but the only one he generally has for any of his notions of morality, taste, or propriety, which are not expressly
written in his religious creed; and his chief guide in the interpretation even of that. Men's opinions, accordingly, on what
is laudable or blameable, are affected by all the multifarious
causes which influence their wishes in regard to the conduct
of others, and which are as numerous as those which determine their wishes on any other subject. Sometimes their reason—at other times their prejudices or superstitions: often their
social affections, not seldom their antisocial ones, their envy or
jealousy, their arrogance or contemptuousness: but most commonly, their desires or fears for themselves—their legitimate
or illegitimate self-interest. Wherever there is an ascendant
class, a large portion of the morality of the country emanates
from its class interests, and its feelings of class superiority.
The morality between Spartans and Helots, between planters
and negroes, between princes and subjects, between nobles
and roturiers, between men and women, has been for the most
part the creation of these class interests and feelings: and the
sentiments thus generated, react in turn upon the moral feelings of the members of the ascendant class, in their relations
among themselves. Where, on the other hand, a class, formerly ascendant, has lost its ascendancy, or where its ascendancy is unpopular, the prevailing moral sentiments frequently
bear the impress of an impatient dislike of superiority. Another grand determining principle of the rules of conduct,
both in act and forbearance, which have been enforced by law
or opinion, has been the servility of mankind towards the supposed preferences or aversions of their temporal masters, or of
their gods. This servility, though essentially selfish, is not
hypocrisy; it gives rise to perfectly genuine sentiments of abhorrence; it made men burn magicians and heretics. Among
so many baser influences, the general and obvious interests of
society have of course had a share, and a large one, in the
direction of the moral sentiments: less, however, as a matter
of reason, and on their own account, than as a consequence
of the sympathies and antipathies which grew out of them:
and sympathies and antipathies which had little or nothing
to do with the interests of society, have made themselves felt
in the establishment of moralities with quite as great force.

The likings and dislikings of society, or of some powerful
portion of it, are thus the main thing which has practically
determined the rules laid down for general observance, under

the penalties of law or opinion. And in general, those who have been in advance of society in thought and feeling, have left this condition of things unassailed in principle, however they may have come into conflict with it in some of its details. They have occupied themselves rather in inquiring what things society ought to like or dislike, than in questioning whether its likings or dislikings should be a law to individuals. They preferred endeavouring to alter the feelings of mankind on the particular points on which they were themselves heretical, rather than make common cause in defence of freedom, with heretics generally. The only case in which the higher ground has been taken on principle and maintained with consistency, by any but an individual here and there, is that of religious belief: a case instructive in many ways, and not least so as forming a most striking instance of the fallibility of what is called the moral sense: for the *odium theologicum*, in a sincere bigot, is one of the most unequivocal cases of moral feeling. Those who first broke the yoke of what called itself the Universal Church, were in general as little willing to permit difference of religious opinion as that Church itself. But when the heat of the conflict was over, without giving a complete victory to any party, and each church or sect was reduced to limit its hopes to retaining possession of the ground it already occupied; minorities, seeing that they had no chance of becoming majorities, were under the necessity of pleading to those whom they could not convert, for permission to differ. It is accordingly on this battlefield, almost solely, that the rights of the individual against society have been asserted on broad grounds of principle, and the claim of society to exercise authority over dissentients, openly controverted. The great writers to whom the world owes what religious liberty it possesses, have mostly asserted freedom of conscience as an indefeasible right, and denied absolutely that a human being is accountable to others for his religious belief. Yet so natural to mankind is intolerance in whatever they really care about, that religious freedom has hardly anywhere been practically realized, except where religious indifference, which dislikes to have its peace disturbed by theological quarrels, has added its weight to the scale. In the minds of almost all religious persons, even in the most tolerant countries, the duty of toleration is admitted with tacit reserves. One person will bear with dissent in matters of church government, but not of dogma; another can tolerate everybody, short of a Papist or an Unitarian; another, every one who believes in revealed religion; a few extend their charity a little further, but stop at the belief in a God and in a future state. Wherever the sentiment of the majority is still genuine and intense, it is found to have abated little of its claim to be obeyed.

In England, from the peculiar circumstances of our political history, though the yoke of opinion is perhaps heavier, that of law is lighter, than in most other countries of Europe; and there is considerable jealousy of direct interference, by the legislative or the executive power, with private conduct; not so much from any just regard for the independence of the individual, as from the still subsisting habit of looking on the government as representing an opposite interest to the public. The majority have not yet learnt to feel the power of the government their power, or its opinions their opinions. When they do so, individual liberty will probably be as much exposed to invasion from the government, as it already is from public opinion. But, as yet, there is a considerable amount of feeling ready to be called forth against any attempt of the law to control individuals in things in which they have not hitherto been accustomed to be controlled by it; and this with very little discrimination as to whether the matter is, or is not, within the legitimate sphere of legal control; insomuch that the feeling, highly salutary on the whole, is perhaps quite as often misplaced as well grounded in the particular instances of its application. There is, in fact, no recognised principle by which the propriety or impropriety of government interference is customarily tested. People decide according to their personal preferences. Some, whenever they see any good to be done, or evil to be remedied, would willingly instigate the government to undertake the business; while others prefer to bear almost any amount of social evil, rather than add one to the departments of human interests amenable to governmental control. And men range themselves on one or the other side in any particular case, according to this general direction of their sentiments; or according to the degree of interest which they feel in the particular thing which it is proposed that the government should do, or according to the belief they entertain that the government would, or would not, do it in the manner they prefer; but very rarely on account of any opinion to which they consistently adhere, as to what things are fit to be done by a government. And it seems to me that in consequence of this absence of rule or principle, one side is at present as often wrong as the other; the interference of government is, with about equal frequency improperly invoked and improperly condemned.

The object of this Essay is to assert one very simple principle, as entitled to govern absolutely the dealings of society with the individual in the way of compulsion and control, whether the means used be physical force in the form of legal penalties, or the moral coercion of public opinion. That principle is, that the sole end for which mankind are warranted, individually or collectively, in interfering with the liberty of action of any of their number, is self-protection. That the only purpose for which power can be rightfully exercised over any member of a civilized community, against his will, is to prevent harm to others. His own good, either physical or moral, is not a sufficient warrant. He cannot rightfully be compelled to do or forbear because it will be better for him to do so, because it will make him happier, because, in the opinions of others, to do so would be wise, or even right. These are good reasons for remonstrating with him, or reasoning with him, or persuading him, or entreating him, but not for compelling him, or visiting him with any evil in case he do otherwise. To justify that, the conduct from which it is desired to deter him, must be calculated to produce evil to some one else. The only part of the conduct of any one, for which he is amenable to society, is that which concerns others. In the part which merely concerns himself, his independence is, of right, absolute. Over himself, over his own body and mind, the individual is sovereign.

It is, perhaps, hardly necessary to say that this doctrine is meant to apply only to human beings in the maturity of their faculties. We are not speaking of children, or of young persons below the age which the law may fix as that of manhood or womanhood. Those who are still in a state to require being taken care of by others, must be protected against their own actions as well as against external injury. For the same reason, we may leave out of consideration those backward states of society in which the race itself may be considered as in its nonage. The early difficulties in the way of spontaneous progress are so great, that there is seldom any choice of means for overcoming them; and a ruler full of the spirit of improvement is warranted in the use of any expedients that will attain an end, perhaps otherwise unattainable. Despotism is a legitimate mode of government in dealing with barbarians, provided the end be their improvement, and the means justified by actually effecting that end. Liberty, as a principle, has no application to any state of things anterior to the time when mankind have become capable of being improved by free and equal discussion. Until then, there is nothing for them but implicit obedience to an Akbar or a Charlemagne, if they are so fortunate as to find one. But as soon as mankind have attained the capacity of being guided to their own improvement by conviction or persuasion (a period long since reached in all nations with whom we need here concern ourselves), compulsion, either in the direct form or in that of pains and penalties for non-compliance, is no longer admissible as a means to their own good, and justifiable only for the security of others.

It is proper to state that I forgo any advantage which could be derived to my argument from the idea of abstract right, as a thing independent of utility. I regard utility as the ultimate appeal on all ethical questions; but it must be utility in the largest sense, grounded on the permanent interests of man as a progressive being. Those interests, I contend, authorize the subjection of individual spontaneity to external control, only in respect to those actions of each, which concern the interest of other people. If any one does an act hurtful to others, there is a *primâ facie* case for punishing him, by law, or, where legal penalties are not safely applicable, by general disapprobation. There are also many positive acts for the benefit of others, which he may rightfully be compelled to perform; such as, to give evidence in a court of justice; to bear his fair share in the common defence, or in any other joint work necessary to the interest of the society of which he enjoys the protection; and to perform certain acts of individual beneficence, such as saving a fellow creature's life, or interposing to protect the defenceless against ill-usage, things which whenever it is obviously a man's duty to do, he may rightfully be made responsible to society for not doing. A person may cause evil to others not only by his actions but by his inaction, and in either case he is justly accountable to them for the injury. The latter case, it is true, requires a much more cautious exercise of compulsion than the former. To make any one answerable for doing evil to others, is the rule; to make him answerable for not preventing evil, is, comparatively speaking, the exception. Yet there are many cases clear enough and grave enough to justify that exception. In all things which regard the external relations of the individual, he is *de jure* amenable to those whose interests are concerned, and if need be, to society as their protector. There are often good reasons for not holding him to the responsibility; but these reasons must arise from the special expediencies of the case: either because it is a kind of case in which he is on the whole likely to act better, when left to his own discretion, than when controlled in any way in which society have it in their power to control him; or because the attempt to exercise control would produce other evils, greater than those which it would prevent. When such reasons as these preclude the enforcement of responsibility, the conscience of the agent himself should step into the vacant judgment seat, and protect those interests of others which have no external protection; judging himself all the more rigidly, because the case does not admit of his being made accountable to the judgment of his fellow-creatures.

But there is a sphere of action in which society, as distinguished from the individual, has, if any, only an indirect interest; comprehending all that portion of a person's life and conduct which affects only himself, or if it also affects others, only with their free, voluntary, and undeceived consent and participation. When I say only himself, I mean directly, and in the first instance: for whatever affects himself, may affect others *through* himself; and the objection which may be grounded on this contingency, will receive consideration in the sequel. This, then, is the appropriate region of human liberty. It comprises, first, the inward domain of consciousness; demanding liberty of conscience, in the most comprehensive sense; liberty of thought and feeling; absolute freedom of opinion and sentiment on all subjects, practical or speculative, scientific, moral, or theological. The liberty of expressing and publishing opinions may seem to fall under a different principle, since it belongs to that part of the conduct of an individual which concerns other people; but, being almost of as much importance as the liberty of thought itself, and resting in great part on the same reasons, is practically inseparable from it. Secondly, the principle requires liberty of tastes and pursuits; of framing the plan of our life to suit our own character; of doing as we like, subject to such consequences as may follow: without impediment from our fellow-creatures, so long as what we do does not harm them, even though they should think our conduct foolish, perverse, or wrong. Thirdly, from this liberty of each individual, follows the liberty, within the same limits, of combination among individuals; freedom to unite, for any purpose not involving harm to others: the persons combining being supposed to be of full age, and not forced or deceived.

No society in which these liberties are not, on the whole, respected, is free, whatever may be its form of government; and none is completely free in which they do not exist absolute and unqualified. The only freedom which deserves the name, is that of pursuing our own good in our own way, so long as we do not attempt to deprive others of theirs, or impede their efforts to obtain it. Each is the proper guardian of his own health, whether bodily, or mental and spiritual. Mankind are greater gainers by suffering each other to live as seems good to themselves, than by compelling each to live as seems good to the rest.

Though this doctrine is anything but new, and, to some persons, may have the air of a truism, there is no doctrine which stands more directly opposed to the general tendency of existing opinion and practice. Society has expended fully as much effort in the attempt (according to its lights) to compel people to conform to its notions of personal, as of social excellence. The ancient commonwealths thought themselves entitled to practise, and the ancient philosophers countenanced, the regulation of every part of private conduct by public authority, on the ground that the State had a deep interest in the whole bodily and mental discipline of every one of its citizens; a mode of thinking which may have been admissible in small republics surrounded by powerful enemies, in constant peril of being subverted by foreign attack or internal commotion, and to which even a short interval of relaxed energy and self-command might so easily be fatal, that they could not afford to wait for the salutary permanent effects of freedom. In the modern world, the greater size of political communities, and above all, the separation between spiritual and temporal authority (which placed the direction of men's consciences in other hands than those which controlled their worldly affairs), prevented so great an interference by law in the details of private life; but the engines of moral repression have been wielded more strenuously against divergence from the reigning opinion in self-regarding, than even in social matters; religion, the most powerful of the elements which have entered into the formation of moral feeling, having almost always been governed either by the ambition of a hierarchy, seeking control over every department of human conduct, or by the spirit of Puritanism. And some of those modern reformers who have placed themselves in strongest opposition to the religions of the past, have been noway behind either churches or sects in their assertion of the right of spiritual domination: M. Comte, in particular, whose social system, as unfolded in his *Traité de Politique Positive*, aims at establishing (though by moral more than by legal appliances) a despotism of society over the individual, surpassing anything contemplated in the political ideal of the most rigid disciplinarian among the ancient philosophers.

Apart from the peculiar tenets of individual thinkers, there is also in the world at large an increasing inclination to stretch unduly the powers of society over the individual, both by the force of opinion and even by that of legislation: and as the tendency of all the changes taking place in the world is to strengthen society, and diminish the power of the individual, this encroachment is not one of the evils which tend spontaneously to disappear, but, on the contrary, to grow more and more formidable. The disposition of mankind, whether as rulers or as fellow-citizens, to impose their own opinions and inclinations as a rule of conduct on others, is so energetically supported by some of the best and by some of the worst feelings incident to human nature, that it is hardly ever kept under restraint by anything but want of power; and as the power is not declining, but growing, unless a strong barrier of moral conviction can be raised against the mischief, we must expect, in the present circumstances of the world, to see it increase.

It will be convenient for the argument, if, instead of at once entering upon the general thesis, we confine ourselves in the first instance to a single branch of it, on which the principle here stated is, if not fully, yet to a certain point, recognised by the current opinions. This one branch is the Liberty of Thought: from which it is impossible to separate the cognate liberty of speaking and of writing. Although these liberties, to some considerable amount, form part of the political morality of all countries which profess religious toleration and free institutions, the grounds, both philosophical and practical, on which they rest, are perhaps not so familiar to the general mind, nor so thoroughly appreciated by many even of the leaders of opinion, as might have been expected. Those grounds, when rightly understood, are of much wider application than to only one division of the subject, and a thorough consideration of this part of the question will be found the best introduction to the remainder. Those to whom nothing which I am about to say will be new, may therefore, I hope, excuse me, if on a subject which for now three centuries has been so often discussed, I venture on one discussion more.

II. OF THE LIBERTY OF THOUGHT AND DISCUSSION

THE time, it is to be hoped, is gone by, when any defence would be necessary of the 'liberty of the press' as one of the securities against corrupt or tyrannical government. No argument, we may suppose, can now be needed, against permitting a legislature or an executive, not identified in interest with the people, to prescribe opinions to them, and determine what doctrines or what arguments they shall be allowed to hear. This aspect of the question, besides, has been so often and so triumphantly enforced by preceding writers, that it needs not be specially insisted on in this place. Though the law of England, on the subject of the press, is as servile to this day as it was in the time of the Tudors, there is little danger of its being actually put in force against political discussion, except during some temporary panic, when fear of insurrection drives ministers and judges from their propriety;* and, speaking generally, it is not, in constitutional countries, to be apprehended, that the government, whether completely responsible to the people or not, will often attempt to control the expression of opinion, except when in doing so it makes itself the organ of the general intolerance of the public. Let us suppose, therefore, that the government is entirely at one with the

* These words had scarcely been written, when, as if to give them an emphatic contradiction, occurred the Government Press Prosecutions of 1858. That ill-judged interference with the liberty of public discussion has not, however, induced me to alter a single word in the text, nor has it at all weakened my conviction that, moments of panic excepted, the era of pains and penalties for political discussion has, in our own country, passed away. For, in the first place, the prosecutions were not persisted in; and, in the second, they were never, properly speaking, political prosecutions. The offence charged was not that of criticising institutions, or the acts or persons of rulers, but of circulating what was deemed an immoral doctrine, the lawfulness of Tyrannicide.

If the arguments of the present chapter are of any validity, there ought to exist the fullest liberty of professing and discussing, as a matter of ethical conviction, any doctrine, however immoral it may be considered. It would, therefore, be irrelevant and out of place to examine here, whether the doctrine of Tyrannicide deserves that title. I shall content myself with saying, that the subject has been at all times one of the open questions of morals; that the act of a private citizen in striking down a criminal, who, by raising himself above the law, has placed himself beyond the reach of legal punishment or control, has been accounted by whole nations, and by some of the best and wisest of men, not a crime, but an act of exalted virtue; and that, right or wrong, it is not of the nature of assassination, but of civil war. As such, I hold that the instigation to it, in a specific case, may be a proper subject of punishment, but only if an overt act has followed, and at least a probable connexion can be established between the act and the instigation. Even then, it is not a foreign government, but the very government assailed, which alone, in the exercise of self-defence, can legitimately punish attacks directed against its own existence.

people, and never thinks of exerting any power of coercion unless in agreement with what it conceives to be their voice. But I deny the right of the people to exercise such coercion, either by themselves or by their government. The power itself is illegitimate. The best government has no more title to it than the worst. It is as noxious, or more noxious, when exerted in accordance with public opinion, than when in opposition to it. If all mankind minus one, were of one opinion, and only one person were of the contrary opinion, mankind would be no more justified in silencing that one person, than he, if he had the power, would be justified in silencing mankind. Were an opinion a personal possession of no value except to the owner; if to be obstructed in the enjoyment of it were simply a private injury, it would make some difference whether the injury was inflicted only on a few persons or on many. But the peculiar evil of silencing the expression of an opinion is, that it is robbing the human race; posterity as well as the existing generation; those who dissent from the opinion, still more than those who hold it. If the opinion is right, they are deprived of the opportunity of exchanging error for truth: if wrong, they lose, what is almost as great a benefit, the clearer perception and livelier impression of truth, produced by its collision with error.

It is necessary to consider separately these two hypotheses, each of which has a distinct branch of the argument corresponding to it. We can never be sure that the opinion we are endeavouring to stifle is a false opinion; and if we were sure, stifling it would be an evil still.

First: the opinion which it is attempted to suppress by authority may possibly be true. Those who desire to suppress it, of course deny its truth; but they are not infallible. They have no authority to decide the question for all mankind, and exclude every other person from the means of judging. To refuse a hearing to an opinion, because they are sure that it is false, is to assume that *their* certainty is the same thing as *absolute* certainty. All silencing of discussion is an assumption of infallibility. Its condemnation may be allowed to rest on this common argument, not the worse for being common.

Unfortunately for the good sense of mankind, the fact of their fallibility is far from carrying the weight in their practical judgment, which is always allowed to it in theory; for while every one well knows himself to be fallible, few think it necessary to take any precautions against their own fallibility,

or admit the supposition that any opinion, of which they feel
very certain, may be one of the examples of the error to which
they acknowledge themselves to be liable. Absolute princes,
or others who are accustomed to unlimited deference, usually
feel this complete confidence in their own opinions on nearly
all subjects. People more happily situated, who sometimes
hear their opinions disputed, and are not wholly unused to be
set right when they are wrong, place the same unbounded
reliance only on such of their opinions as are shared by all
who surround them, or to whom they habitually defer: for in
proportion to a man's want of confidence in his own solitary
judgment, does he usually repose, with implicit trust, on the
infallibility of 'the world' in general. And the world, to each
individual, means the part of it with which he comes in contact; his party, his sect, his church, his class of society: the
man may be called, by comparison, almost liberal and large-
minded to whom it means anything so comprehensive as his
own country or his own age. Nor is his faith in this collective
authority at all shaken by his being aware that other ages,
countries, sects, churches, classes, and parties have thought,
and even now think, the exact reverse. He devolves upon his
own world the responsibility of being in the right against the
dissentient worlds of other people; and it never troubles him
that mere accident has decided which of these numerous
worlds is the object of his reliance, and that the same causes
which make him a Churchman in London, would have made
him a Buddhist or a Confucian in Pekin. Yet it is as evident
in itself, as any amount of argument can make it, that ages
are no more infallible than individuals; every age having held
many opinions which subsequent ages have deemed not only
false but absurd; and it is as certain that many opinions, now
general, will be rejected by future ages, as it is that many,
once general, are rejected by the present.

The objection likely to be made to this argument, would
probably take some such form as the following. There is no
greater assumption of infallibility in forbidding the propagation of error, than in any other thing which is done by
public authority on its own judgment and responsibility.
Judgment is given to men that they may use it. Because
it may be used erroneously, are men to be told that they
ought not to use it at all? To prohibit what they think
pernicious, is not claiming exemption from error, but fulfilling the duty incumbent on them, although fallible, of acting on their conscientious conviction. If we were never to act

on our opinions, because those opinions may be wrong, we should leave all our interests uncared for, and all our duties unperformed. An objection which applies to all conduct, can be no valid objection to any conduct in particular. It is the duty of governments, and of individuals, to form the truest opinions they can; to form them carefully, and never impose them upon others unless they are quite sure of being right. But when they are sure (such reasoners may say), it is not conscientiousness but cowardice to shrink from acting on their opinions, and allow doctrines which they honestly think dangerous to the welfare of mankind, either in this life or in another, to be scattered abroad without restraint, because other people, in less enlightened times, have persecuted opinions now believed to be true. Let us take care, it may be said, not to make the same mistake: but governments and nations have made mistakes in other things, which are not denied to be fit subjects for the exercise of authority: they have laid on bad taxes, made unjust wars. Ought we therefore to lay on no taxes, and, under whatever provocation, make no wars? Men, and governments, must act to the best of their ability. There is no such thing as absolute certainty, but there is assurance sufficient for the purposes of human life. We may, and must, assume our opinion to be true for the guidance of our own conduct: and it is assuming no more when we forbid bad men to pervert society by the propagation of opinions which we regard as false and pernicious.

I answer, that it is assuming very much more. There is the greatest difference between presuming an opinion to be true, because, with every opportunity for contesting it, it has not been refuted, and assuming its truth for the purpose of not permitting its refutation. Complete liberty of contradicting and disproving our opinion, is the very condition which justi- fies us in assuming its truth for purposes of action; and on no other terms can a being with human faculties have any ra- tional assurance of being right.

When we consider either the history of opinion, or the ordinary conduct of human life, to what is it to be ascribed that the one and the other are no worse than they are? Not certainly to the inherent force of the human understanding; for, on any matter not self-evident, there are ninety-nine per- sons totally incapable of judging of it, for one who is capable; and the capacity of the hundredth person is only compara- tive; for the majority of the eminent men of every past gen- eration held many opinions now known to be erroneous, and did or approved numerous things which no one will now justify. Why is it, then, that there is on the whole a preponderance among mankind of rational opinions and rational conduct? If there really is this preponderance—which there must be, unless human affairs are, and have always been, in an almost desperate state—it is owing to a quality of the human mind, the source of everything respectable in man either as an intellectual or as a moral being, namely, that his errors are corrigible. He is capable of rectifying his mistakes, by discussion and experience. Not by experience alone. There must be discussion, to show how experience is to be interpreted. Wrong opinions and practices gradually yield to fact and argument: but facts and arguments, to produce any effect on the mind, must be brought before it. Very few facts are able to tell their own story, without comments to bring out their meaning. The whole strength and value, then, of human judgment, depending on the one property, that it can be set right when it is wrong, reliance can be placed on it only when the means of setting it right are kept constantly at hand. In the case of any person whose judgment is really deserving of confidence, how has it become so? Because he has kept his mind open to criticism of his opinions and conduct. Because it has been his practice to listen to all that could be said against him; to profit by as much of it as was just, and expound to himself, and upon occasion to others, the fallacy of what was fallacious. Because he has felt, that the only way in which a human being can make some approach to knowing the whole of a subject, is by hearing what can be said about it by persons of every variety of opinion, and studying all modes in which it can be looked at by every character of mind. No wise man ever acquired his wisdom in any mode but this; nor is it in the nature of human intellect to become wise in any other manner. The steady habit of correcting and completing his own opinion by collating it with those of others, so far from causing doubt and hesitation in carrying it into practice, is the only stable foundation for a just reliance on it: for, being cognisant of all that can, at least obviously, be said against him, and having taken up his position against all gainsayers—knowing that he has sought for objections and difficulties, instead of avoiding them, and has shut out no light which can be thrown upon the subject from any quarter—he has a right to think his judgment better than that of any person, or any multitude, who have not gone through a similar process.

It is not too much to require that what the wisest of mankind, those who are best entitled to trust their own judgment, find necessary to warrant their relying on it, should be submitted to by that miscellaneous collection of a few wise and many foolish individuals, called the public. The most intolerant of churches, the Roman Catholic Church, even at the canonization of a saint, admits, and listens patiently to, a 'devil's advocate.' The holiest of men, it appears, cannot be admitted to posthumous honours, until all that the devil could say against him is known and weighed. If even the Newtonian philosophy were not permitted to be questioned, mankind could not feel as complete assurance of its truth as they now do. The beliefs which we have most warrant for, have no safeguard to rest on, but a standing invitation to the whole world to prove them unfounded. If the challenge is not accepted, or is accepted and the attempt fails, we are far enough from certainty still; but we have done the best that the existing state of human reason admits of; we have neglected nothing that could give the truth a chance of reaching us: if the lists are kept open, we may hope that if there be a better truth, it will be found when the human mind is capable of receiving it; and in the meantime we may rely on having attained such approach to truth, as is possible in our own day. This is the amount of certainty attainable by a fallible being, and this the sole way of attaining it.

Strange it is, that men should admit the validity of the arguments for free discussion, but object to their being 'pushed to an extreme;' not seeing that unless the reasons are good for an extreme case, they are not good for any case. Strange that they should imagine that they are not assuming infallibility, when they acknowledge that there should be free discussion on all subjects which can possibly be *doubtful*, but think that some particular principle or doctrine should be forbidden to be questioned because it is *so certain*, that is, because *they are certain* that it is certain. To call any proposition certain, while there is any one who would deny its certainty if permitted, but who is not permitted, is to assume that we ourselves, and those who agree with us, are the judges of certainty, and judges without hearing the other side.

In the present age—which has been described as 'destitute of faith, but terrified at scepticism'—in which people feel sure, not so much that their opinions are true, as that they should not know what to do without them—the claims of an opinion to be protected from public attack are rested not so much on its truth, as on its importance to society. There are, it is alleged, certain beliefs, so useful, not to say indispensable to well-being that it is as much the duty of governments to uphold those beliefs, as to protect any other of the interests of society. In a case of such necessity, and so directly in the line of their duty, something less than infallibility may, it is maintained, warrant, and even bind, governments, to act on their own opinion, confirmed by the general opinion of mankind. It is also often argued, and still oftener thought, that none but bad men would desire to weaken these salutary beliefs; and there can be nothing wrong, it is thought, in restraining bad men, and prohibiting what only such men would wish to practise. This mode of thinking makes the justification of restraints on discussion not a question of the truth of doctrines, but of their usefulness; and flatters itself by that means to escape the responsibility of claiming to be an infallible judge of opinions. But those who thus satisfy themselves, do not perceive that the assumption of infallibility is merely shifted from one point to another. The usefulness of an opinion is itself matter of opinion: as disputable, as open to discussion, and requiring discussion as much, as the opinion itself. There is the same need of an infallible judge of opinions to decide an opinion to be noxious, as to decide it to be false, unless the opinion condemned has full opportunity of defending itself. And it will not do to say that the heretic may be allowed to maintain the utility or harmlessness of his opinion, though forbidden to maintain its truth. The truth of an opinion is part of its utility. If we would know whether or not it is desirable that a proposition should be believed, is it possible to exclude the consideration of whether or not it is true? In the opinion, not of bad men, but of the best men, no belief which is contrary to truth can be really useful: and can you prevent such men from urging that plea, when they are charged with culpability for denying some doctrine which they are told is useful, but which they believe to be false? Those who are on the side of received opinions, never fail to take all possible advantage of this plea; you do not find *them* handling the question of utility as if it could be completely abstracted from that of truth: on the contrary, it is, above all, because their doctrine is 'the truth,' that the knowledge or the belief of it is held to be so indispensable. There can be no fair discussion of the question of usefulness, when an argument so vital may be employed on one side, but not on the other. And in point of fact, when law or public feeling do not permit the truth of an opinion to be disputed, they are just as little tolerant of a denial of its usefulness. The utmost they allow is an extenuation of its absolute necessity, or of the positive guilt of rejecting it.

In order more fully to illustrate the mischief of denying a hearing to opinions because we, in our own judgment, have condemned them, it will be desirable to fix down the discussion to a concrete case; and I choose, by preference, the cases which are least favourable to me—in which the argument against freedom of opinion, both on the score of truth and on that of utility, is considered the strongest. Let the opinions impugned be the belief in a God and in a future state, or any of the commonly received doctrines of morality. To fight the battle on such ground, gives a great advantage to an unfair antagonist; since he will be sure to say (and many who have no desire to be unfair will say it internally), Are these the doctrines which you do not deem sufficiently certain to be taken under the protection of law? Is the belief in a God one of the opinions, to feel sure of which, you hold to be assuming infallibility? But I must be permitted to observe, that it is not the feeling sure of a doctrine (be it what it may) which I call an assumption of infallibility. It is the undertaking to decide that question *for others*, without allowing them to hear what can be said on the contrary side. And I denounce and reprobate this pretension not the less, if put forth on the side of my most solemn convictions. However positive any one's persuasion may be, not only of the falsity, but of the pernicious consequences—not only of the pernicious consequences, but (to adopt expressions which I altogether condemn) the immorality and impiety of an opinion; yet if, in pursuance of that private judgment, though backed by the public judgment of his country or his cotemporaries, he prevents the opinion from being heard in its defence, he assumes infallibility. And so far from the assumption being less objectionable or less dangerous because the opinion is called immoral or impious, this is the case of all others in which it is most fatal. These are exactly the occasions on which the men of one generation commit those dreadful mistakes, which excite the astonishment and horror of posterity. It is among such that we find the instances memorable in history, when the arm of the law has been employed to root out the best men and the noblest doctrines; with deplorable success as to the men, though some of the doctrines have survived to be (as if in mockery) invoked, in defence of similar conduct towards those who dissent from *them*, or from their received interpretation.

Mankind can hardly be too often reminded, that there was once a man named Socrates, between whom and the legal authorities and public opinion of his time, there took place a memorable collision. Born in an age and country abounding in individual greatness, this man has been handed down to us by those who best knew both him and the age, as the most virtuous man in it; while *we* know him as the head and proto-type of all subsequent teachers of virtue, the source equally of the lofty inspiration of Plato and the judicious utilitarian-ism of Aristotle, '*i maëstri di color che sanno,*' the two head-springs of ethical as of all other philosophy. This acknowledged master of all the eminent thinkers who have since lived—whose fame, still growing after more than two thousand years, all but outweighs the whole remainder of the names which make his native city illustrious—was put to death by his countrymen, after a judicial conviction, for impiety and immorality. Impiety, in denying the gods recognised by the State; indeed his accuser asserted (see the 'Apologia') that he believed in no gods at all. Immorality, in being, by his doc-trines and instructions, a 'corruptor of youth.' Of these charges the tribunal, there is every ground for believing, honestly found him guilty, and condemned the man who probably of all then born had deserved best of mankind, to be put to death as a criminal.

To pass from this to the only other instance of judicial in-iquity, the mention of which, after the condemnation of Soc-rates, would not be an anticlimax: the event which took place on Calvary rather more than eighteen hundred years ago. The man who left on the memory of those who witnessed his life and conversation, such an impression of his moral grandeur, that eighteen subsequent centuries have done homage to him as the Almighty in person, was ignominiously put to death, as what? As a blasphemer. Men did not merely mistake their benefactor, they mistook him for the exact contrary of what he was, and treated him as that prodigy of impiety, which they themselves are now held to be, for their treatment of him. The feelings with which mankind now regard these lamentable transactions, especially the later of the two, render them extremely unjust in their judgment of the unhappy actors. These were, to all appearance, not bad men—not worse than men commonly are, but rather the contrary; men who possessed in a full, or somewhat more than a full measure, the religious, moral, and patriotic feelings of their time and people: the very kind of men who, in all times, our own included, have every chance of passing through life blameless and respected. The high-priest who rent his garments when the words were pronounced, which, according to all the ideas of his country, constituted the blackest guilt, was in all probability quite as sincere in his horror and indignation, as the generality of respectable and pious men now are in the religious and moral sentiments they profess; and most of those who now shudder at his conduct, if they had lived in his time, and been born Jews, would have acted precisely as he did. Orthodox Christians who are tempted to think that those who stoned to death the first martyrs must have been worse men than they themselves are, ought to remember that one of those persecutors was Saint Paul.

Let us add one more example, the most striking of all, if the impressiveness of an error is measured by the wisdom and virtue of him who falls into it. If ever any one, possessed of power, had grounds for thinking himself the best and most enlightened among his cotemporaries, it was the Emperor Marcus Aurelius. Absolute monarch of the whole civilized world, he preserved through life not only the most unblemished justice, but what was less to be expected from his Stoical breeding, the tenderest heart. The few failings which are attributed to him, were all on the side of indulgence: while his writings, the highest ethical product of the ancient mind, differ scarcely perceptibly, if they differ at all, from the most characteristic teachings of Christ. This man, a better Christian in all but the dogmatic sense of the word, than almost any of the ostensibly Christian sovereigns who have since reigned, persecuted Christianity. Placed at the summit of all the previous attainments of humanity, with an open, unfettered intellect, and a character which led him of himself to embody in his moral writings the Christian ideal, he yet failed to see that Christianity was to be a good and not an evil to the world, with his duties to which he was so deeply penetrated. Existing society he knew to be in a deplorable state. But such as it was, he saw, or thought he saw, that it was held together, and prevented from being worse, by belief and reverence of the received divinities. As a ruler of mankind, he deemed it his duty not to suffer society to fall in pieces; and saw not how, if its existing ties were removed, any others could be formed which could again knit it together. The new religion openly aimed at dissolving these ties: unless, therefore, it was his duty to adopt that religion, it seemed to be his duty to put it down. Inasmuch then as the theology of Christianity did not appear to him true or of divine origin; inasmuch as this strange history of a crucified God was not credible to him, and a system which purported to rest entirely upon a foundation to him so wholly unbelievable, could not be foreseen by him to be that renovating agency which, after all abatements, it has in fact proved to be; the gentlest and most amiable of philosophers and rulers, under a solemn sense of duty, authorized the persecution of Christianity. To my mind this is one of the most tragical facts in all history. It is a bitter thought, how different a thing the Christianity of the world might have been, if the Christian faith had been adopted as the religion of the empire under the auspices of Marcus Aurelius instead of those of Constantine. But it would be equally unjust to him and false to truth, to deny, that no one plea which can be urged for punishing anti-Christian teaching, was wanting to Marcus Aurelius for punishing, as he did, the propagation of Christianity. No Christian more firmly believes that Atheism is false, and tends to the dissolution of society, than Marcus Aurelius believed the same things of Christianity; he who, of all men then living, might have been thought the most capable of appreciating it. Unless any one who approves of punishment for the promulgation of opinions, flatters himself that he is a wiser and better man than Marcus Aurelius—more deeply versed in the wisdom of his time, more elevated in his intellect above it—more earnest in his search for truth, or more single-minded in his devotion to it when found;—let him abstain from that assumption of the joint infallibility of himself and the multitude, which the great Antoninus made with so unfortunate a result.

Aware of the impossibilty of defending the use of punishment for restraining irreligious opinions, by any argument which will not justify Marcus Antoninus, the enemies of religious freedom, when hard pressed, occasionally accept this consequence, and say, with Dr. Johnson, that the persecutors of Christianity were in the right; that persecution is an ordeal through which truth ought to pass, and always passes successfully, legal penalties being, in the end, powerless against truth, though sometimes beneficially effective against mischievous errors. This is a form of the argument for religious intolerance, sufficiently remarkable not to be passed without notice.

A theory which maintains that truth may justifiably be persecuted because persecution cannot possibly do it any harm, cannot be charged with being intentionally hostile to the reception of new truths; but we cannot commend the generosity of its dealing with the persons to whom mankind are indebted for them. To discover to the world something which deeply concerns it, and of which it was previously ignorant; to prove to it that it had been mistaken on some vital point of temporal or spiritual interest, is as important a service as a human being can render to his fellow-creatures, and in certain cases, as in those of the early Christians and of the Reformers, those who think with Dr. Johnson believe it to have been the most precious gift which could be bestowed on mankind. That the authors of such splendid benefits should be requited by martyrdom; that their reward should be to be dealt with as the vilest of criminals, is not, upon this theory, a deplorable error and misfortune, for which humanity should mourn in sackcloth and ashes, but the normal and justifiable state of things. The propounder of a new truth, according to this doctrine, should stand, as stood, in the legislation of the Locrians, the proposer of a new law, with a halter round his neck, to be instantly tightened if the public assembly did not, on hearing his reasons, then and there adopt his proposition. People who defend this mode of treating benefactors, cannot be supposed to set much value on the benefit; and I believe this view of the subject is mostly confined to the sort of persons who think that new truths may have been desirable once, but that we have had enough of them now.

But, indeed, the dictum that truth always triumphs over persecution, is one of those pleasant falsehoods which men repeat after one another till they pass into commonplaces, but which all experience refutes. History teems with instances of truth put down by persecution. If not suppressed for ever, it may be thrown back for centuries. To speak only of religious opinions: the Reformation broke out at least twenty times before Luther, and was put down. Arnold of Brescia was put down. Fra Dolcino was put down. Savonarola was put down. The Albigeois were put down. The Vaudois were put down. The Lollards were put down. The Hussites were put down. Even after the era of Luther, wherever persecution was persisted in, it was successful. In Spain, Italy, Flanders, the Austrian empire, Protestantism was rooted out; and, most likely, would have been so in England, had Queen Mary lived, or Queen Elizabeth died. Persecution has always succeeded, save where the heretics were too strong a party to be effectually persecuted. No reasonable person can doubt that Christianity might have been extirpated in the Roman Empire. It spread, and became predominant, because the persecutions were only occasional, lasting but a short time, and separated by long intervals of almost undisturbed propagandism. It is a piece of idle sentimentality that truth, merely as truth, has any inherent power denied to error, of prevailing against the dungeon and the stake. Men are not more zealous for truth than they often are for error, and a sufficient application of legal or even of social penalties will generally succeed in stopping the propagation of either. The real advantage which truth has, consists in this: that when an opinion is true, it may be extinguished once, twice or many times, but in the course of ages there will generally be found persons to rediscover it, until some one of its reappearances falls on a time when from favourable circumstances it escapes persecution until it has made such head as to withstand all subsequent attempts to suppress it.

It will be said, that we do not now put to death the introducers of new opinions: we are not like our fathers who slew the prophets, we even build sepulchres to them. It is true we no longer put heretics to death; and the amount of penal infliction which modern feeling would probably tolerate, even against the most obnoxious opinions, is not sufficient to extirpate them. But let us not flatter ourselves that we yet free from the stain even of legal persecution. Penalties for opinion, or at least for its expression, still exist by law; and their enforcement is not, even in these times, so unexampled as to make it at all incredible that they may some day be revived in full force. In the year 1857, at the summer assizes of the county of Cornwall, an unfortunate man,* said to be of unexceptionable conduct in all relations of life, was sentenced to twenty-one months imprisonment, for uttering, and writing on a gate, some offensive words concerning Christianity. Within a month of the same time, at the Old Bailey, two persons, on two separate occasions,† were rejected as jurymen, and one of them grossly insulted by the judge and by one of the counsel, because they honestly declared that they had no theological belief; and a third, a foreigner,‡ for the same reason, was denied justice against a thief. This refusal of redress took place in virtue of the legal doctrine, that no person can be allowed to give evidence in a court of justice, who does not

* Thomas Pooley, Bodmin Assizes, July 31, 1857. In December following, he received a free pardon from the Crown.
† George Jacob Holyoake, August 17, 1857; Edward Truelove, July, 1857.
‡ Baron de Gleichen, Marlborough Street Police Court, August 4, 1857.

profess belief in a God (any god is sufficient) and in a future
state; which is equivalent to declaring such persons to be out-
laws, excluded from the protection of the tribunals; who may
not only be robbed or assaulted with impunity, if no one but
themselves, or persons of similar opinions, be present, but any
one else may be robbed or assaulted with impunity, if the
proof of the fact depends on their evidence. The assumption
on which this is grounded, is that the oath is worthless, of a
person who does not believe in a future state; a proposition
which betokens much ignorance of history in those who assent
to it (since it is historically true that a large proportion of infidels in all ages have been persons of distinguished integrity
and honour); and would be maintained by no one who had the
smallest conception how many of the persons in greatest
repute with the world, both for virtues and for attainments,
are well known, at least to their intimates, to be unbelievers.
The rule, besides, is suicidal, and cuts away its own foundation. Under pretence that atheists must be liars, it admits the
testimony of all atheists who are willing to lie, and rejects
only those who brave the obloquy of publicly confessing a
detested creed rather than affirm a falsehood. A rule thus
self-convicted of absurdity so far as regards its professed purpose, can be kept in force only as a badge of hatred, a relic
of persecution; a persecution, too, having the peculiarity, that
the qualification for undergoing it, is the being clearly proved
not to deserve it. The rule, and the theory it implies, are
hardly less insulting to believers than to infidels. For if he who
does not believe in a future state, necessarily lies, it follows
that they who do believe are only prevented from lying, if
prevented they are, by the fear of hell. We will not do the
authors and abettors of the rule the injury of supposing, that
the conception which they have formed of Christian virtue is
drawn from their own consciousness.

These, indeed, are but rags and remnants of persecution,
and may be thought to be not so much an indication of the
wish to persecute, as an example of that very frequent infirmity of English minds, which makes them take a prepos-
terous pleasure in the assertion of a bad principle, when they
are no longer bad enough to desire to carry it really into
practice. But unhappily there is no security in the state of the
public mind, that the suspension of worse forms of legal persecution, which has lasted for about the space of a generation,
will continue. In this age the quiet surface of routine is as
often ruffled by attempts to resuscitate past evils, as to intro-

duce new benefits. What is boasted of at the present time
as the revival of religion, is always, in narrow and uncultivated minds, at least as much the revival of bigotry; and
where there is the strong permanent leaven of intolerance in
the feelings of a people, which at all times abides in the middle classes of this country, it needs but little to provoke them
into actively persecuting those whom they have never ceased
to think proper objects of persecution.* For it is this—it is the
opinions men entertain, and the feelings they cherish, respecting those who disown the beliefs they deem important, which
makes this country not a place of mental freedom. For a long
time past, the chief mischief of the legal penalties is that they
strengthen the social stigma. It is that stigma which is really
effective, and so effective is it that the profession of opinions
which are under the law of society is much less common in
England, than is, in many other countries, the avowal of those
which incur risk of judicial punishment. In respect to all persons but those whose pecuniary circumstances make them independent of the good will of other people, opinion, on this
subject, is as efficacious as law; men might as well be imprisoned, as excluded from the means of earning their bread.
Those whose bread is already secured, and who desire no
favours from men in power, or from bodies of men, or from
the public, have nothing to fear from the open avowal of any
opinions, but to be ill-thought of and ill-spoken of, and this it
ought not to require a very heroic mould to enable them to

* Ample warning may be drawn from the large infusion of the passions of
a persecutor, which mingled with the general display of the worst parts of
our national character on the occasion of the Sepoy insurrection. The ravings
of fanatics or charlatans from the pulpit may be unworthy of notice; but the
heads of the Evangelical party have announced as their principle, for the government of Hindoos and Mahomedans, that no schools be supported by public
money in which the Bible is not taught, and by necessary consequence that no
public employment be given to any but real or pretended Christians. An
Under-Secretary of State, in a speech delivered to his constituents on November 12, 1857, is reported to have said: 'Toleration of their faith' (the
faith of a hundred millions of British subjects), 'the superstition which they
called religion, by the British Government, had had the effect of retarding the
ascendancy of the British name, and preventing the salutary growth of Christianity. . . . Toleration was the great corner-stone of the religious liberties of
this country; but do not let them abuse that precious word toleration. As he
understood it, it meant the complete liberty to all, freedom of worship, *among
Christians, who worshipped upon the same foundation.* It meant toleration
of all sects and denominations of *Christians who believed in the one mediation.*' I desire to call attention to the fact—that a man who has been deemed
fit to fill a high office in the government of this country, under a liberal
Ministry, maintains the doctrine that all who do not believe in the divinity of
Christ are beyond the pale of toleration. Who, after this imbecile display, can
indulge the illusion that religious persecution has passed away, never to return?

bear. There is no room for any appeal *ad misericordiam* in
behalf of such persons. But though we do not now inflict so
much evil on those who think differently from us, as it was
formerly our custom to do, it may be that we do ourselves as
much evil as ever by our treatment of them. Socrates was put
to death, but the Socratic philosophy rose like the sun in
heaven, and spread its illumination over the whole intellectual
firmament. Christians were cast to the lions, but the Christian
church grew up a stately and spreading tree, overtopping the
older and less vigorous growths, and stifling them by its
shade. Our merely social intolerance kills no one, roots out no
opinions, but induces men to disguise them, or to abstain from
any active effort for their diffusion. With us, heretical opinions do not perceptibly gain, or even lose, ground in each
decade or generation; they never blaze out far and wide,
but continue to smoulder in the narrow circles of thinking
and studious persons among whom they originate, without
ever lighting up the general affairs of mankind with either a
true or a deceptive light. And thus is kept a state of things
very satisfactory to some minds, because, without the unpleasant process of fining or imprisoning anybody, it maintains
all prevailing opinions outwardly undisturbed, while it does
not absolutely interdict the exercise of reason by dissentients
afflicted with the malady of thought. A convenient plan for
having peace in the intellectual world, and keeping all things
going on therein very much as they do already. But the price
for this sort of intellectual pacification, is the sacrifice of the
entire moral courage of the human mind. A state of things in
which a large portion of the most active and inquiring intellects find it advisable to keep the genuine principles and
grounds of their convictions within their own breasts, and attempt, in what they address to the public, to fit as much as
they can of their own conclusions to premises which they
have internally renounced, cannot send forth the open, fear-
less characters, and logical, consistent intellects who once
adorned the thinking world. The sort of men who can be
looked for under it, are either mere conformers to commonplace, or time-servers for truth, whose arguments on all great
subjects are meant for their hearers, and are not those which
have convinced themselves. Those who avoid this alternative,
do so by narrowing their thoughts and interest to things
which can be spoken of without venturing within the region
of principles, that is, to small practical matters, which would
come right of themselves, if but the minds of mankind were

strengthened and enlarged, and which will never be made effectually right until then: while that which would strengthen and enlarge men's minds, free and daring speculation on the highest subjects, is abandoned.

Those in whose eyes this reticence on the part of heretics is no evil, should consider in the first place, that in consequence of it there is never any fair and thorough discussion of heretical opinions; and that such of them as could not stand such a discussion, though they may be prevented from spreading, do not disappear. But it is not the minds of heretics that are deteriorated most, by the ban placed on all enquiry which does not end in the orthodox conclusions. The greatest harm done is to those who are not heretics, and whose whole mental development is cramped, and their reason cowed, by the fear of heresy. Who can compute what the world loses in the multitude of promising intellects combined with timid characters, who dare not follow out any bold, vigorous, independent train of thought, lest it should land them in something which would admit of being considered irreligious or immoral? Among them we may occasionally see some man of deep conscientiousness, and subtle and refined understanding, who spends a life in sophisticating with an intellect which he cannot silence, and exhausts the resources of ingenuity in attempting to reconcile the promptings of his conscience and reason with orthodoxy, which yet he does not, perhaps, to the end succeed in doing. No one can be a great thinker who does not recognise, that as a thinker it is his first duty to follow his intellect to whatever conclusions it may lead. Truth gains more even by the errors of one who, with due study and preparation, thinks for himself, than by the true opinions of those who only hold them because they do not suffer themselves to think. Not that it is solely, or chiefly, to form great thinkers, that freedom of thinking is required. On the contrary, it is as much, and even more indispensable, to enable average human beings to attain the mental stature which they are capable of. There have been, and may again be, great individual thinkers, in a general atmosphere of mental slavery. But there never has been, nor ever will be, in that atmosphere, an intellectually active people. Where any people has made a temporary approach to such a character, it has been because the dread of heterodox speculation was for a time suspended. Where there is a tacit convention that principles are not to be disputed; where the discussion of the greatest questions which can occupy humanity is considered to be closed, we cannot

hope to find that generally high scale of mental activity which
has made some periods of history so remarkable. Never when
controversy avoided the subjects which are large and important enough to kindle enthusiasm, was the mind of a people
stirred up from its foundations, and the impulse given which
raised even persons of the most ordinary intellect to something
of the dignity of thinking beings. Of such we have had an example in the condition of Europe during the times immediately following the Reformation; another, though limited to
the Continent and to a more cultivated class, in the speculative movement of the latter half of the eighteenth century;
and a third, of still briefer duration, in the intellectual fer-
mentation of Germany during the Goethian and Fichtean
period. These periods differed widely in the particular opinions which they developed; but were alike in this, that during
all three the yoke of authority was broken. In each, an old
mental despotism had been thrown off, and no new one had
yet taken its place. The impulse given at these three periods
has made Europe what it now is. Every single improvement
which has taken place either in the human mind or in institutions, may be traced distinctly, to one or other of them. Appearances have for some time indicated that all three impulses are well nigh spent; and we can expect no fresh start,
until we again assert our mental freedom.

Let us now pass to the second division of the argument,
and dismissing the supposition that any of the received opinions may be false, let us assume them to be true, and examine
into the worth of the manner in which they are likely to be
held, when their truth is not freely and openly canvassed.
However unwillingly a person who has a strong opinion may
admit the possibility that his opinion may be false, he ought
to be moved by the consideration that however true it may
be, if it is not fully, frequently, and fearlessly discussed, it will
be held as a dead dogma, not a living truth.

There is a class of persons (happily not quite so numerous
as formerly) who think it enough if a person assents undoubt-
ingly to what they think true, though he has no knowledge
whatever of the grounds of the opinion, and could not make
a tenable defence of it against the most superficial objections.
Such persons, if they can once get their creed taught from
authority, naturally think that no good, and some harm,
comes of its being allowed to be questioned. Where their influence prevails, they make it nearly impossible for the received opinion to be rejected wisely and considerately, though

it may still be rejected rashly and ignorantly; for to shut out discussion entirely is seldom possible, and when it once gets in, beliefs not grounded on conviction are apt to give way before the slightest semblance of an argument. Waiving, however, this possibility—assuming that the true opinion abides in the mind, but abides as a prejudice, a belief independent of, and proof against, argument—this is not the way in which truth ought to be held by a rational being. This is not knowing the truth. Truth, thus held, is but one superstition the more, accidentally clinging to the words which enunciate a truth.

If the intellect and judgment of mankind ought to be cultivated, a thing which Protestants at least do not deny, on what can these faculties be more appropriately exercised by any one, than on the things which concern him so much that it is considered necessary for him to hold opinions on them? If the cultivation of the understanding consists in one thing more than in another, it is surely in learning the grounds of one's own opinions. Whatever people believe, on subjects on which it is of the first importance to believe rightly, they ought to be able to defend against at least the common objections. But, some one may say, 'Let them be *taught* the grounds of their opinions. It does not follow that opinions must be merely parroted because they are never heard controverted. Persons who learn geometry do not simply commit the theorems to memory, but understand and learn likewise the demonstrations; and it would be absurd to say that they remain ignorant of the grounds of geometrical truths, because they never hear any one deny, and attempt to disprove them.' Undoubtedly: and such teaching suffices on a subject like mathematics, where there is nothing at all to be said on the wrong side of the question. The peculiarity of the evidence of mathematical truths is, that all the argument is on one side. There are no objections, and no answers to objections. But on every subject on which difference of opinion is possible, the truth depends on a balance to be struck between two sets of conflicting reasons. Even in natural philosophy, there is always some other explanation possible of the same facts; some geocentric theory instead of heliocentric, some phlogiston instead of oxygen; and it has to be shown why that other theory cannot be the true one: and until this is shown, and until we know how it is shown, we do not understand the grounds of our opinion. But when we turn to subjects infinitely more complicated—to morals, religion, politics, social relations, and the business of life, three-fourths of the arguments for every disputed opinion consist in dispelling the appearances which favour some opinion different from it. The greatest orator, save one, of antiquity, has left it on record that he always studied his adversary's case with as great, if not with still greater, intensity than even his own. What Cicero practised as the means of forensic success, requires to be imitated by all who study any subject in order to arrive at the truth. He who knows only his own side of the case, knows little of that. His reasons may be good, and no one may have been able to refute them. But if he is equally unable to refute the reasons on the opposite side; if he does not so much as know what they are, he has no ground for preferring either opinion. The rational position for him would be suspension of judgment, and unless he contents himself with that, he is either led by authority, or adopts, like the generality of the world, the side to which he feels most inclination. Nor is it enough that he should hear the arguments of adversaries from his own teachers, presented as they state them, and accompanied by what they offer as refutations. That is not the way to do justice to the arguments, or bring them into real contact with his own mind. He must be able to hear them from persons who actually believe them; who defend them in earnest, and do their very utmost for them. He must know them in their most plausible and persuasive form; he must feel the whole force of the difficulty which the true view of the subject has to encounter and dispose of; else he will never really possess himself of the portion of truth which meets and removes that difficulty. Ninety-nine in a hundred of what are called educated men are in this condition; even of those who can argue fluently for their opinions. Their conclusion may be true, but it might be false for anything they know: they have never thrown themselves into the mental position of those who think differently from them, and considered what such persons may have to say; and consequently they do not, in any proper sense of the word, know the doctrine which they themselves profess. They do not know those parts of it which explain and justify the remainder; the considerations which show that a fact which seemingly conflicts with another is reconcilable with it, or that, of two apparently strong reasons, one and not the other ought to be preferred. All that part of the truth which turns the scale, and decides the judgment of a completely informed mind, they are strangers to; nor is it ever really known, but to those who have attended equally and impartially to both sides, and endeavoured to see the reasons of both in the strongest light. So essential is this discipline to a real understanding of moral and human subjects, that if opponents of all important truths do not exist, it is indispensable to imagine them, and supply them with the strongest arguments which the most skilful devil's advocate can conjure up.

To abate the force of these considerations, an enemy of free discussion may be supposed to say, that there is no necessity for mankind in general to know and understand all that can be said against or for their opinions by philosophers and theologians. That it is not needful for common men to be able to expose all the misstatements or fallacies of an ingenious opponent. That it is enough if there is always somebody capable of answering them, so that nothing likely to mislead uninstructed persons remains unrefuted. That simple minds, having been taught the obvious grounds of the truths inculcated on them, may trust to authority for the rest, and being aware that they have neither knowledge nor talent to resolve every difficulty which can be raised, may repose in the assurance that all those which have been raised have been or can be answered, by those who are specially trained to the task.

Conceding to this view of the subject the utmost that can be claimed for it by those most easily satisfied with the amount of understanding of truth which ought to accompany the belief of it; even so, the argument for free discussion is no way weakened. For even this doctrine acknowledges that mankind ought to have a rational assurance that all objections have been satisfactorily answered; and how are they to be answered if that which requires to be answered is not spoken? or how can the answer be known to be satisfactory, if the objectors have no opportunity of showing that it is unsatisfactory? If not the public, at least the philosophers and theologians who are to resolve the difficulties, must make themselves familiar with those difficulties in their most puzzling form; and this cannot be accomplished unless they are freely stated, and placed in the most advantageous light which they admit of. The Catholic Church has its own way of dealing with this embarrassing problem. It makes a broad separation between those who can be permitted to receive its doctrines on conviction, and those who must accept them on trust. Neither, indeed, are allowed any choice as to what they will accept; but the clergy, such at least as can be fully confided in, may admissibly and meritoriously make themselves acquainted with the arguments of opponents, in order to answer them, and may, therefore, read heretical books; the laity, not unless by special permission, hard to be obtained. This discipline recognises knowledge of the enemy's case as beneficial to the teachers, but finds means, consistent with this, of denying it to the rest of the world: thus giving to the *élite* more mental culture, though not more mental freedom, than it allows to the mass. By this device it succeeds in obtaining the kind of mental superiority which its purposes require; for though culture without freedom never made a large and liberal mind, it can make a clever *nisi prius* advocate of a cause. But in countries professing Protestantism, this resource is denied; since Protestants hold, at least in theory, that the responsibility for the choice of a religion must be borne each for himself, and cannot be thrown off upon teachers. Besides, in the present state of the world, it is practically impossible that writings which are read by the instructed can be kept from the uninstructed. If the teachers of mankind are to be cognisant of all that they ought to know, everything must be free to be written and published without restraint.

If, however, the mischievous operation of the absence of free discussion, when the received opinions are true, were confined to leaving men ignorant of the grounds of those opinions, it might be thought that this, if an intellectual, is no moral evil, and does not affect the worth of the opinions, regarded in their influence on the character. The fact, however, is, that not only the grounds of the opinion are forgotten in the absence of discussion, but too often the meaning of the opinion itself. The words which convey it, cease to suggest ideas, or suggest only a small portion of those they were originally employed to communicate. Instead of a vivid conception and a living belief, there remain only a few phrases retained by rote; or, if any part, the shell and husk only of the meaning is retained, the finer essence being lost. The great chapter in human history which this fact occupies and fills, cannot be too earnestly studied and meditated on.

It is illustrated in the experience of almost all ethical doctrines and religious creeds. They are all full of meaning and vitality to those who originate them, and to the direct disciples of the originators. Their meaning continues to be felt in undiminished strength, and is perhaps brought out into even fuller consciousness, so long as the struggle lasts to give the doctrine or creed an ascendancy over other creeds. At last it either prevails, and becomes the general opinion, or its progress stops; it keeps possession of the ground it has gained, but ceases to spread further. When either of these results has become apparent, controversy on the subject flags, and gradually dies away. The doctrine has taken its place, if not as a received opinion, as one of the admitted sects or divisions of opinion: those who hold it have generally inherited, not adopted it; and conversion from one of these doctrines to another, being now an exceptional fact, occupies little place in the thoughts of their professors. Instead of being, as at first, constantly on the alert either to defend themselves against the world, or to bring the world over to them, they have subsided into acquiescence, and neither listen, when they can help it, to arguments against their creed, nor trouble dissentients (if there be such) with arguments in its favour. From this time may usually be dated the decline in the living power of the doctrine. We often hear the teachers of all creeds lamenting the difficulty of keeping up in the minds of believers a lively apprehension of the truth which they nominally recognise, so that it may penetrate the feelings, and acquire a real mastery over the conduct. No such difficulty is complained of while the creed is still fighting for its existence: even the weaker combatants then know and feel what they are fighting for, and the difference between it and other doctrines; in that period of every creed's existence, not a few persons may be found, who have realized its fundamental principles in all the forms of thought, have weighed and considered them in all their important bearings, and have experienced the full effect on the character, which belief in that creed ought to produce in a mind thoroughly imbued with it. But when it has come to be an hereditary creed, and to be received passively not actively—when the mind is no longer compelled, in the same degree as at first, to exercise its vital powers on the questions which its belief presents to it, there is a progressive tendency to forget all of the belief except the formularies, or to give it a dull and torpid assent, as if accepting it on trust dispenses with the necessity of realizing it in consciousness, or testing it by personal experience; until it almost ceases to connect itself at all with the inner life of the human being. Then are seen the cases, so frequent in this age of the world as almost to form the majority, in which the creed remains as it were outside the mind, encrusting and petrifying it against all other influences addressed to the higher parts of our nature; manifesting its power by not suffering any fresh and living conviction to get in, but itself doing nothing for the mind or heart, except standing sentinel over them to keep them vacant.

To what an extent doctrines intrinsically fitted to make the deepest impression upon the mind may remain in it as dead beliefs, without being ever realized in the imagination, the feelings, or the understanding, is exemplified by the manner in which the majority of believers hold the doctrines of Christianity. By Christianity I here mean what is accounted such by all churches and sects—the maxims and precepts contained in the New Testament. These are considered sacred, and accepted as laws, by all professing Christians. Yet it is scarcely too much to say that not one Christian in a thousand guides or tests his individual conduct by reference to those laws. The standard to which he does refer it, is the custom of his nation, his class, or his religious profession. He has thus, on the one hand, a collection of ethical maxims, which he believes to have been vouchsafed to him by infallible wisdom as rules for his government; and on the other, a set of every-day judgments and practices, which go a certain length with some of those maxims, not so great a length with others, stand in direct opposition to some, and are, on the whole, a compromise between the Christian creed and the interests and suggestions of worldly life. To the first of these standards he gives his homage; to the other his real allegiance. All Christians believe that the blessed are the poor and humble, and those who are ill-used by the world; that it is easier for a camel to pass through the eye of a needle than for a rich man to enter the kingdom of heaven; that they should judge not, lest they should be judged; that they should swear not at all; that they should love their neighbour as themselves; that if one take their cloak, they should give him their coat also; that they should take no thought for the morrow; that if they would be perfect, they should sell all that they have and give it to the poor. They are not insincere when they say that they believe these things. They do believe them, as people believe what they have always heard lauded and never discussed. But in the sense of that living belief which regulates conduct, they believe these doctrines just up to the point to which it is usual to act upon them. The doctrines in their integrity are serviceable to pelt adversaries with; and it is understood that they are to be put forward (when possible) as the reasons for whatever people do that they think laudable. But any one who reminded them that the maxims require an infinity of things which they never even think of doing, would gain

nothing but to be classed among those very unpopular characters who affect to be better than other people. The doctrines
have no hold on ordinary believers—are not a power in their
minds. They have an habitual respect for the sound of them,
but no feeling which spreads from the words to the things
signified, and forces the mind to take *them* in, and make
them conform to the formula. Whenever conduct is concerned, they look round for Mr. A and B to direct them how
far to go in obeying Christ.

Now we may be well assured that the case was not thus,
but far otherwise, with the early Christians. Had it been thus,
Christianity never would have expanded from an obscure sect
of the despised Hebrews into the religion of the Roman empire. When their enemies said, 'See how these Christians love
one another' (a remark not likely to be made by anybody
now), they assuredly had a much livelier feeling of the meaning of their creed than they have ever had since. And to this
cause, probably, it is chiefly owing that Christianity now
makes so little progress in extending its domain, and after
eighteen centuries, is still nearly confined to Europeans and
the descendants of Europeans. Even with the strictly religious,
who are much in earnest about their doctrines, and attach a
greater amount of meaning to many of them than people in
general, it commonly happens that the part which is thus
comparatively active in their minds is that which was made
by Calvin, or Knox, or some such person much nearer in
character to themselves. The sayings of Christ coexist passively
in their minds, producing hardly any effect beyond what is
caused by mere listening to words too amiable and bland.
There are many reasons, doubtless, why doctrines which are
the badge of a sect retain more of their vitality than those
common to all recognised sects, and why more pains are
taken by teachers to keep their meaning alive; but one reason
certainly is, that the peculiar doctrines are more questioned,
and have to be oftener defended against open gainsayers.
Both teachers and learners go to sleep at their post, as soon
as there is no enemy in the field.

The same thing holds true, generally speaking, of all traditional doctrines—those of prudence and knowledge of life, as
well as of morals or religion. All languages and literatures are
full of general observations on life, both as to what it is, and
how to conduct oneself in it; observations which everybody
knows, which everybody repeats, or hears with acquiesence,
which are received as truisms, yet of which most people first

truly learn the meaning, when experience, generally of a painful kind, has made it a reality to them. How often, when smarting under some unforeseen misfortune or disappointment, does a person call to mind some proverb or common saying familiar to him all his life, the meaning of which, if he had ever before felt it as he does now, would have saved him from the calamity. There are indeed reasons for this, other than the absence of discussion: there are many truths of which the full meaning *cannot* be realized, until personal experience has brought it home. But much more of the meaning even of these would have been understood, and what was understood would have been far more deeply impressed on the mind, if the man had been accustomed to hear it argued *pro* and *con* by people who did understand it. The fatal tendency of mankind to leave off thinking about a thing when it is no longer doubtful, is the cause of half their errors. A contemporary author has well spoken of 'the deep slumber of a decided opinion.'

But what! (it may be asked) Is the absence of unanimity an indispensable condition of true knowledge? Is it necessary that some part of mankind should persist in error, to enable any to realize the truth? Does a belief cease to be real and vital as soon as it is generally received—and is a proposition never thoroughly understood and felt unless some doubt of it remains? As soon as mankind have unanimously accepted a truth, does the truth perish within them? The highest aim and best result of improved intelligence, it has hitherto been thought, is to unite mankind more and more in the acknowledgment of all important truths: and does the intelligence only last as long as it has not achieved its object? Do the fruits of conquest perish by the very completeness of the victory?

I affirm no such thing. As mankind improve, the number of doctrines which are no longer disputed or doubted will be constantly on the increase: and the well-being of mankind may almost be measured by the number and gravity of the truths which have reached the point of being uncontested. The cessation, on one question after another, of serious controversy, is one of the necessary incidents of the consolidation of opinion; a consolidation as salutary in the case of true opinions, as it is dangerous and noxious when the opinions are erroneous. But though this gradual narrowing of the bounds of diversity of opinion is necessary in both senses of the term, being at once inevitable and indispensable, we are not therefore obliged to conclude that all its consequences must be beneficial. The loss of so important an aid to the intelligent and living apprehension of a truth, as is afforded by the necessity of explaining it to, or defending it against, opponents, though not sufficient to outweigh, is no trifling drawback from, the benefit of its universal recognition. Where this advantage can no longer be had, I confess I should like to see the teachers of mankind endeavouring to provide a substitute for it; some contrivance for making the difficulties of the question as present to the learner's consciousness, as if they were pressed upon him by a dissentient champion, eager for his conversion.

But instead of seeking contrivances for this purpose, they have lost those they formerly had. The Socratic dialectics, so magnificently exemplified in the dialogues of Plato, were a contrivance of this description. They were essentially a negative discussion of the great questions of philosophy and life, directed with consummate skill to the purpose of convincing any one who had merely adopted the commonplaces of received opinion, that he did not understand the subject—that he as yet attached no definite meaning to the doctrines he professed; in order that, becoming aware of his ignorance, he might be put in the way to attain a stable belief, resting on a clear apprehension both of the meaning of doctrines and of their evidence. The school disputations of the middle ages had a somewhat similar object. They were intended to make sure that the pupil understood his own opinion, and (by necessary correlation) the opinion opposed to it, and could enforce the grounds of the one and confute those of the other. These last-mentioned contests had indeed the incurable defect, that the premisses appealed to were taken from authority, not from reason; and, as a discipline to the mind, they were in every respect inferior to the powerful dialectics which formed the intellects of the 'Socratici viri:' but the modern mind owes far more to both than it is generally willing to admit, and the present modes of education contain nothing which in the smallest degree supplies the place either of the one or of the other. A person who derives all his instruction from teachers or books, even if he escape the besetting temptation of contenting himself with cram, is under no compulsion to hear both sides; accordingly it is far from a frequent accomplishment, even among thinkers, to know both sides; and the weakest part of what everybody says in defence of his opinion, is what he intends as a reply to antagonists. It is the fashion of the present time to disparage negative logic—that which points out weaknesses in theory or errors in practice, without establishing positive truths. Such negative criticism would indeed be poor enough as an ultimate result; but as a means to attaining any positive knowledge or conviction worthy the name, it cannot be valued too highly; and until people are again systematically trained to it, there will be few great thinkers, and a low general average of intellect, in any but the mathematical and physical departments of speculation. On any other subject no one's opinions deserve the name of knowledge, except so far as he has either had forced upon him by others, or gone through of himself, the same mental process which would have been required of him in carrying on an active controversy with opponents. That, therefore, which when absent, it is so indispensable, but so difficult, to create, how worse than absurd is it to forgo, when spontaneously offering itself! If there are any persons who contest a received opinion, or who will do so if law or opinion will let them, let us thank them for it, open our minds to listen to them, and rejoice that there is some one to do for us what we otherwise ought, if we have any regard for either the certainty or the vitality of our convictions, to do with much greater labour for ourselves.

It still remains to speak of one of the principal causes which make diversity of opinion advantageous, and will continue to do so until mankind shall have entered a stage of intellectual advancement which at present seems at an incalculable distance. We have hitherto considered only two possibilities: that the received opinion may be false, and some other opinion, consequently, true; or that, the received opinion being true, a conflict with the opposite error is essential to a clear apprehension and deep feeling of its truth. But there is a commoner case than either of these; when the conflicting doctrines, instead of being one true and the other false, share the truth between them; and the nonconforming opinion is needed to supply the remainder of the truth, of which the received doctrine embodies only a part. Popular opinions, on subjects not palpable to sense, are often true, but seldom or never the whole truth. They are a part of the truth; sometimes a greater, sometimes a smaller part, but exaggerated, distorted, and disjoined from the truths by which they ought to be accompanied and limited. Heretical opinions, on the other hand, are generally some of these suppressed and neglected truths, bursting the bonds which kept them down, and either seeking reconciliation with the truth contained in the common opinion, or fronting it as enemies, and setting themselves up, with similar exclusiveness, as the whole truth. The latter case is hitherto the most frequent, as, in the human mind, one-sidedness has always been the rule, and many-sidedness the exception. Hence, even in revolutions of opinion, one part of the truth usually sets while the other rises. Even progress, which ought to superadd, for the most part only substitutes one partial and incomplete truth for another; improvement consisting chiefly in this, that the new fragment of truth is more wanted, more adapted to the needs of the time, than that which it displaces. Such being the partial character of prevailing opinions, even when resting on a true foundation; every opinion which embodies somewhat of the portion of truth which the common opinion omits, ought to be considered precious, with whatever amount of error and confusion that truth may be blended. No sober judge of human affairs will feel bound to be indignant because those who force on our notice truths which we should otherwise have overlooked, overlook some of those which we see. Rather, he will think that so long as popular truth is onesided, it is more desirable than otherwise that unpopular truth should have onesided asserters too; such being usually the most energetic, and the most likely to compel reluctant attention to the fragment of wisdom which they proclaim as if it were the whole.

Thus, in the eighteenth century, when nearly all the instructed, and all those of the uninstructed who were led by them, were lost in admiration of what is called civilization, and of the marvels of modern science, literature, and philosophy, and while greatly overrating the amount of unlikeness between the men of modern and those of ancient times, indulged the belief that the whole of the difference was in their own favour; with what a salutary shock did the paradoxes of Rousseau explode like bombshells in the midst, dislocating the compact mass of one-sided opinion, and forcing its elements to recombine in a better form and with additional ingredients. Not that the current opinions were on the whole farther from the truth than Rousseau's were; on the contrary, they were nearer to it; they contained more of positive truth, and very much less of error. Nevertheless there lay in Rousseau's doctrine, and has floated down the stream of opinion along with it, a considerable amount of exactly those truths which the popular opinion wanted; and these are the deposit which was left behind when the flood subsided. The superior worth

of simplicity of life, the enervating and demoralizing effect of
the trammels and hypocrisies of artificial society, are ideas
which have never been entirely absent from cultivated minds
since Rousseau wrote; and they will in time produce their
due effect, though at present needing to be asserted as much
as ever, and to be asserted by deeds, for words, on this subject, have nearly exhausted their power.

In politics, again, it is almost a commonplace, that a party
of order or stability, and a party of progress or reform, are
both necessary elements of a healthy state of political life;
until the one or the other shall have so enlarged its mental
grasp as to be a party equally of order and of progress, knowing and distinguishing what is fit to be preserved from what
ought to be swept away. Each of these modes of thinking
derives its utility from the deficiencies of the other; but it is
in a great measure the opposition of the other that keeps each
within the limits of reason and sanity. Unless opinions favourable to democracy and to aristocracy, to property and to
equality, to co-operation and to competition, to luxury and to
abstinence, to sociality and individuality, to liberty and discipline, and all the other standing antagonisms of practical life,
are expressed with equal freedom, and enforced and defended with equal talent and energy, there is no chance of
both elements obtaining their due; one scale is sure to go up,
and the other down. Truth, in the great practical concerns of
life, is so much a question of the reconciling and combining
of opposites, that very few have minds sufficiently capacious
and impartial to make the adjustment with an approach to
correctness, and it has to be made by the rough process of a
struggle between combatants fighting under hostile banners.
On any of the great open questions just enumerated, if either
of the two opinions has a better claim than the other, not
merely to be tolerated, but to be encouraged and countenanced, it is the one which happens at the particular time
and place to be in a minority. That is the opinion which, for
the time being, represents the neglected interests, the side of
human well-being which is in danger of obtaining less than
its share. I am aware that there is not, in this country, any
intolerance of differences of opinion on most of these topics.
They are adduced to show, by admitted and multiplied examples, the universality of the fact, that only through diversity of opinion is there, in the existing state of human intellect, a chance of fair play to all sides of the truth. When
there are persons to be found, who form an exception to the

apparent unanimity of the world on any subject, even if the world is in the right, it is always probable that dissentients have something worth hearing to say for themselves, and that truth would lose something by their silence.

It may be objected, 'But *some* received principles, especially on the highest and most vital subjects, are more than half-truths. The Christian morality, for instance, is the whole truth on that subject, and if any one teaches a morality which varies from it, he is wholly in error.' As this is of all cases the most important in practice, none can be fitter to test the general maxim. But before pronouncing what Christian morality is or is not, it would be desirable to decide what is meant by Christian morality. If it means the morality of the New Testament, I wonder that any one who derives his knowledge of this from the book itself, can suppose that it was announced, or intended, as a complete doctrine of morals. The Gospel always refers to a pre-existing morality, and confines its precepts to the particulars in which that morality was to be corrected, or superseded by a wider and higher; expressing itself, moreover, in terms most general, often impossible to be interpreted literally, and possessing rather the impressiveness of poetry or eloquence than the precision of legislation. To extract from it a body of ethical doctrine, has never been possible without eking it out from the Old Testament, that is, from a system elaborate indeed, but in many respects barbarous, and intended only for a barbarous people. St. Paul, a declared enemy to this Judaical mode of interpreting the doctrine and filling up the scheme of his Master, equally assumes a pre-existing morality, namely that of the Greeks and Romans; and his advice to Christians is in a great measure a system of accommodation to that; even to the extent of giving an apparent sanction to slavery. What is called Christian, but should rather be termed theological, morality, was not the work of Christ or the Apostles, but is of much later origin, having been gradually built up by the Catholic church of the first five centuries, and though not implicitly adopted by moderns and Protestants, has been much less modified by them than might have been expected. For the most part, indeed, they have contented themselves with cutting off the additions which had been made to it in the middle ages, each sect supplying the place by fresh additions, adapted to its own character and tendencies. That mankind owe a great debt to this morality, and to its early teachers, I should be the last person to deny; but I do not scruple to say of it, that it is, in many important points, incomplete and onesided, and that unless ideas and feelings, not sanctioned by it, had contributed to the formation of European life and character, human affairs would have been in a worse condition than they now are. Christian morality (so called) has all the characters of a reaction; it is, in great part, a protest against Paganism. Its ideal is negative rather than positive; passive rather than active; Innocence rather than Nobleness; Abstinence from Evil, rather than energetic Pursuit of Good: in its precepts (as has been well said) 'thou shalt not' predominates unduly over 'thou shalt.' In its horror of sensuality, it made an idol of asceticism, which has been gradually compromised away into one of legality. It holds out the hope of heaven and the threat of hell, as the appointed and appropriate motives to a virtuous life: in this falling far below the best of the ancients, and doing what lies in it to give to human morality an essentially selfish character, by disconnecting each man's feelings of duty from the interests of his fellow-creatures, except so far as a self-interested inducement is offered to him for consulting them. It is essentially a doctrine of passive obedience; it inculcates submission to all authorities found established; who indeed are not to be actively obeyed when they command what religion forbids, but who are not to be resisted, far less rebelled against, for any amount of wrong to ourselves. And while, in the morality of the best Pagan nations, duty to the State holds even a disproportionate place, infringing on the just liberty of the individual; in purely Christian ethics, that grand department of duty is scarcely noticed or acknowledged. It is in the Koran, not the New Testament, that we read the maxim—'A ruler who appoints any man to an office, when there is in his dominions another man better qualified for it, sins against God and against the State.' What little recognition the idea of obligation to the public obtains in modern morality, is derived from Greek and Roman sources, not from Christian; as, even in the morality of private life, whatever exists of magnanimity, highmindedness, personal dignity, even the sense of honour, is derived from the purely human, not the religious part of our education, and never could have grown out of a standard of ethics in which the only worth, professedly recognised, is that of obedience.

I am as far as any one from pretending that these defects are necessarily inherent in the Christian ethics, in every manner in which it can be conceived, or that the many requisites of a complete moral doctrine which it does not contain, do not admit of being reconciled with it. Far less would I insinuate this of the doctrines and precepts of Christ himself. I believe that the sayings of Christ are all, that I can see any evidence of their having been intended to be; that they are irreconcilable with nothing which a comprehensive morality requires; that everything which is excellent in ethics may be brought within them, with no greater violence to their language than has been done to it by all who have attempted to deduce from them any practical system of conduct whatever. But it is quite consistent with this, to believe that they contain, and were meant to contain, only a part of the truth; that many essential elements of the highest morality are among the things which are not provided for, nor intended to be provided for, in the recorded deliverances of the Founder of Christianity, and which have been entirely thrown aside in the system of ethics erected on the basis of those deliverances by the Christian Church. And this being so, I think it a great error to persist in attempting to find in the Christian doctrine that complete rule for our guidance, which its author intended it to sanction and enforce, but only partially to provide. I believe, too, that this narrow theory is becoming a grave practical evil, detracting greatly from the value of the moral training and instruction, which so many well-meaning persons are now at length exerting themselves to promote. I much fear that by attempting to form the mind and feelings on an exclusively religious type, and discarding those secular standards (as for want of a better name they may be called) which heretofore co-existed with and supplemented the Christian ethics, receiving some of its spirit, and infusing into it some of theirs, there will result, and is even now resulting, a low, abject, servile type of character, which, submit itself as it may to what it deems the Supreme Will, is incapable of rising to or sympathizing in the conception of Supreme Goodness. I believe that other ethics than any which can be evolved from exclusively Christian sources, must exist side by side with Christian ethics to produce the moral regeneration of mankind; and that the Christian system is no exception to the rule, that in an imperfect state of the human mind, the interests of truth require a diversity of opinions. It is not necessary that in ceasing to ignore the moral truths not contained in Christianity, men should ignore any of those which it does contain. Such prejudice, or oversight, when it occurs, is altogether an evil; but it is one from which we cannot hope to be always exempt, and must be regarded as the price paid for an inestimable good. The exclusive pretension made by a part of the truth to be the whole, must and ought to be protested against, and if a reactionary impulse should make the protestors unjust in their turn, this onesidedness, like the other, may be lamented, but must be tolerated. If Christians would teach infidels to be just to Christianity, they should themselves be just to infidelity. It can do truth no service to blink the fact, known to all who have the most ordinary acquaintance with literary history, that a large portion of the noblest and most valuable moral teaching has been the work, not only of men who did not know, but of men who knew and rejected, the Christian faith.

I do not pretend that the most unlimited use of the freedom of enunciating all possible opinions would put an end to the evils of religious or philosophical sectarianism. Every truth which men of narrow capacity are in earnest about, is sure to be asserted, inculcated, and in many ways even acted on, as if no other truth existed in the world, or at all events none that could limit or qualify the first. I acknowledge that the tendency of all opinions to become sectarian is not cured by the freest discussion, but is often heightened and exacerbated thereby; the truth which ought to have been, but was not, seen, being rejected all the more violently because proclaimed by persons regarded as opponents. But it is not on the impassioned partisan, it is on the calmer and more disinterested bystander, that this collision of opinions works its salutary effect. Not the violent conflict between parts of the truth, but the quiet suppression of half of it, is the formidable evil: there is always hope when people are forced to listen to both sides; it is when they attend only to one that errors harden into prejudices, and truth itself ceases to have the effect of truth, by being exaggerated into falsehood. And since there are few mental attributes more rare than that judicial faculty which can sit in intelligent judgment between two sides of a question, of which only one is represented by an advocate before it, truth has no chance but in proportion as every side of it, every opinion which embodies any fraction of the truth, not only finds advocates, but is so advocated as to be listened to.

We have now recognised the necessity to the mental wellbeing of mankind (on which all their other well-being depends) of freedom of opinion, and freedom of the expression of opinion, on four distinct grounds; which we will now briefly recapitulate.

First, if any opinion is compelled to silence, that opinion may, for aught we can certainly know, be true. To deny this is to assume our own infallibility.

Secondly, though the silenced opinion be an error, it may, and very commonly does, contain a portion of truth; and since the general or prevailing opinion on any subject is rarely or never the whole truth, it is only by the collision of adverse opinions that the remainder of the truth has any chance of being supplied.

Thirdly, even if the received opinion be not only true, but the whole truth; unless it is suffered to be, and actually is, vigorously and earnestly contested, it will, by most of those who receive it, be held in the manner of a prejudice, with little comprehension or feeling of its rational grounds. And not only this, but, fourthly, the meaning of the doctrine itself will be in danger of being lost or enfeebled, and deprived of its vital effect on the character and conduct: the dogma becoming a mere formal profession, inefficacious for good, but cumbering the ground, and preventing the growth of any real and heartfelt conviction, from reason or personal experience.

Before quitting the subject of freedom of opinion, it is fit to take some notice of those who say, that the free expression of all opinions should be permitted, on condition that the manner be temperate, and do not pass the bounds of fair discussion. Much might be said on the impossibility of fixing where these supposed bounds are to be placed; for if the test be offence to those whose opinion is attacked, I think experience testifies that this offence is given whenever the attack is telling and powerful, and that every opponent who pushes them hard, and whom they find it difficult to answer, appears to them, if he shows any strong feeling on the subject, an intemperate opponent. But this, though an important consideration in a practical point of view, merges in a more fundamental objection. Undoubtedly the manner of asserting an opinion, even though it be a true one, may be very objectionable, and may justly incur severe censure. But the principal offences of the kind are such as it is mostly impossible, unless by accidental self-betrayal, to bring home to conviction. The gravest of them is, to argue sophistically, to suppress facts or arguments, to misstate the elements of the case, or misrepresent the opposite opinion. But all this, even to the most ag-

But if he refrains from molesting others in what concerns them, and merely acts according to his own inclination and judgment in things which concern himself, the same reasons which show that opinion should be free, prove also that he should be allowed, without molestation, to carry his opinions into practice at his own cost. That mankind are not infallible; that their truths, for the most part, are only half-truths; that unity of opinion, unless resulting from the fullest and freest comparison of opposite opinions, is not desirable, and diversity not an evil, but a good, until mankind are much more capable than at present of recognising all sides of the truth, are principles applicable to men's modes of action, not less than to their opinions. As it is useful that while mankind are imperfect there should be different opinions, so it is that there should be different experiments of living; that free scope should be given to varieties of character, short of injury to others; and that the worth of different modes of life should be proved practically, when any one thinks fit to try them. It is desirable, in short, that in things which do not primarily concern others, individuality should assert itself. Where, not the person's own character, but the traditions or customs of other people are the rule of conduct, there is wanting one of the principal ingredients of human happiness, and quite the chief ingredient of individual and social progress.

In maintaining this principle, the greatest difficulty to be encountered does not lie in the appreciation of means towards an acknowledged end, but in the indifference of persons in general to the end itself. If it were felt that the free development of individuality is one of the leading essentials of well-being; that it is not only a co-ordinate element with all that is designated by the terms civilization, instruction, education, culture, but is itself a necessary part and condition of all those things; there would be no danger that liberty should be undervalued, and the adjustment of the boundaries between it and social control would present no extraordinary difficulty. But the evil is, that individual spontaneity is hardly recognized by the common modes of thinking, as having any intrinsic worth, or deserving any regard on its own account. The majority, being satisfied with the ways of mankind as they now are (for it is they who make them what they are), cannot comprehend why those ways should not be good enough for everybody; and what is more, spontaneity forms no part of the ideal of the majority of moral and social reformers, but is rather looked on with jealousy, as a troublesome and perhaps rebellious obstruction to the general acceptance of what these reformers, in their own judgment, think would be best for mankind. Few persons, out of Germany, even comprehend the meaning of the doctrine which Wilhelm Von Humboldt, so eminent both as a *savant* and as a politician, made the text of a treatise—that 'the end of man, or that which is prescribed by the eternal or immutable dictates of reason, and not suggested by vague and transient desires, is the highest and most harmonious development of his powers to a complete and consistent whole;' that, therefore, the object 'towards which every human being must ceaselessly direct his efforts, and on which especially those who design to influence their fellow-men must ever keep their eyes, is the individuality of power and development;' that for this there are two requisites, 'freedom, and a variety of situations;' and that from the union of these arise 'individual vigour and manifold diversity,' which combine themselves in 'originality.'*

Little, however, as people are accustomed to a doctrine like that of Von Humboldt, and surprising as it may be to them to find so high a value attached to individuality, the question, one must nevertheless think, can only be one of degree. No one's idea of excellence in conduct is that people should do absolutely nothing but copy one another. No one would assert that people ought not to put into their mode of life, and into the conduct of their concerns, any impress whatever of their own judgment, or of their own individual character. On the other hand, it would be absurd to pretend that people ought to live as if nothing whatever had been known in the world before they came into it; as if experience had as yet done nothing towards showing that one mode of existence, or of conduct, is preferable to another. Nobody denies that people should be so taught and trained in youth, as to know and benefit by the ascertained results of human experience. But it is the privilege and proper condition of a human being, arrived at the maturity of his faculties, to use and interpret experience in his own way. It is for him to find out what part of recorded experience is properly applicable to his own circumstances and character. The traditions and customs of other people are, to a certain extent, evidence of what their experience has taught *them*; presumptive evidence, and as such, have a claim to his deference: but, in the first place, their experience may be too narrow; or they may not have interpreted it rightly. Sec-

* *The Sphere and Duties of Government*, from the German of Baron Wilhelm von Humboldt, pp. 11-13.

ondly, their interpretation of experience may be correct, but unsuitable to him. Customs are made for customary circumstances, and customary characters: and his circumstances or his character may be uncustomary. Thirdly, though the customs be both good as customs, and suitable to him, yet to conform to custom, merely *as* custom, does not educate or develop in him any of the qualities which are the distinctive endowment of a human being. The human faculties of perception, judgment, discriminative feeling, mental activity, and even moral preference, are exercised only in making a choice. He who does anything because it is the custom, makes no choice. He gains no practice either in discerning or in desiring what is best. The mental and moral, like the muscular powers, are improved only by being used. The faculties are called into no exercise by doing a thing merely because others do it, no more than by believing a thing only because others believe it. If the grounds of an opinion are not conclusive to the person's own reason, his reason cannot be strengthened, but is likely to be weakened by his adopting it: and if the inducements to an act are not such as are consentaneous to his own feelings and character (where affection, or the rights of others, are not concerned) it is so much done towards rendering his feelings and character inert and torpid, instead of active and energetic.

He who lets the world, or his own portion of it, choose his plan of life for him, has no need of any other faculty than the ape-like one of imitation. He who chooses his plan for himself, employs all his faculties. He must use observation to see, reasoning and judgment to foresee, activity to gather materials for decision, discrimination to decide, and when he has decided, firmness and self-control to hold to his deliberate decision. And these qualities he requires and exercises exactly in proportion as the part of his conduct which he determines according to his own judgment and feelings is a large one. It is possible that he might be guided in some good path, and kept out of harm's way, without any of these things. But what will be his comparative worth as a human being? It really is of importance, not only what men do, but also what manner of men they are that do it. Among the works of man, which human life is rightly employed in perfecting and beautifying, the first in importance surely is man himself. Supposing it were possible to get houses built, corn grown, battles fought, causes tried, and even churches erected and prayers said, by machinery—by automatons in human form—it would be a considerable loss to exchange for these automatons even the men and women who at present inhabit the more civilized parts of the world, and who assuredly are but starved specimens of what nature can and will produce. Human nature is not a machine to be built after a model, and set to do exactly the work prescribed for it, but a tree, which requires to grow and develop itself on all sides, according to the tendency of the inward forces which make it a living thing.

It will probably be conceded that it is desirable people should exercise their understandings, and that an intelligent following of custom, or even occasionally an intelligent deviation from custom, is better than a blind and simply mechanical adhesion to it. To a certain extent it is admitted, that our understanding should be our own: but there is not the same willingness to admit that our desires and impulses should be our own likewise; or that to possess impulses of our own, and of any strength, is anything but a peril and a snare. Yet desires and impulses are as much a part of a perfect human being, as beliefs and restraints: and strong impulses are only perilous when not properly balanced; when one set of aims and inclinations is developed into strength, while others, which ought to co-exist with them, remain weak and inactive. It is not because men's desires are strong that they act ill; it is because their consciences are weak. There is no natural connexion between strong impulses and a weak conscience. The natural connexion is the other way. To say that one person's desires and feelings are stronger and more various than those of another, is merely to say that he has more of the raw material of human nature, and is therefore capable, perhaps of more evil, but certainly of more good. Strong impulses are but another name for energy. Energy may be turned to bad uses; but more good may always be made of an energetic nature, than of an indolent and impassive one. Those who have most natural feeling, are always those whose cultivated feelings may be made the strongest. The same strong susceptibilities which make the personal impulses vivid and powerful, are also the source from whence are generated the most passionate love of virtue, and the sternest self-control. It is through the cultivation of these, that society both does its duty and protects its interests: not by rejecting the stuff of which heroes are made, because it knows not how to make them. A person whose desires and impulses are his own—are the expression of his own nature, as it has been developed and modified by his own culture—is said to have a character. One whose desires and impulses are not his own, has no character, no more than a steam-engine has a character. If, in addition to being his own, his impulses are strong, and are under the government of a strong will, he has an energetic character. Whoever thinks that individuality of desires and impulses should not be encouraged to unfold itself, must maintain that society has no need of strong natures—is not the better for containing many persons who have much character—and that a high general average of energy is not desirable.

In some early states of society, these forces might be, and were, too much ahead of the power which society then possessed of disciplining and controlling them. There has been a time when the element of spontaneity and individuality was in excess, and the social principle had a hard struggle with it. The difficulty then was, to induce men of strong bodies or minds to pay obedience to any rules which required them to control their impulses. To overcome this difficulty, law and discipline, like the Popes struggling against the Emperors, asserted a power over the whole man, claiming to control all his life in order to control his character—which society had not found any other sufficient means of binding. But society has now fairly got the better of individuality; and the danger which threatens human nature is not the excess, but the deficiency, of personal impulses and preferences. Things are vastly changed, since the passions of those who were strong by station or by personal endowment were in a state of habitual rebellion against laws and ordinances, and required to be rigorously chained up to enable the persons within their reach to enjoy any particle of security. In our times, from the highest class of society down to the lowest, every one lives as under the eye of a hostile and dreaded censorship. Not only in what concerns others, but in what concerns only themselves, the individual, or the family, do not ask themselves—what do I prefer? or, what would suit my character and disposition? or, what would allow the best and highest in me to have fair play, and enable it to grow and thrive? They ask themselves, what is suitable to my position? what is usually done by persons of my station and pecuniary circumstances? or (worse still) what is usually done by persons of a station and circumstances superior to mine? I do not mean that they choose what is customary, in preference to what suits their own inclination. It does not occur to them to have any inclination, except for what is customary. Thus the mind itself is bowed to the yoke: even in what people do for pleasure, conformity is the first thing thought of: they like in crowds; they exercise choice only among things commonly done: peculiarity of taste, eccentricity of conduct, are shunned equally with crimes: until by dint of not following their own nature, they have no nature to follow: their human capacities are withered and starved: they become incapable of any strong wishes or native pleasures, and are generally without either opinions or feelings of home growth, or properly their own. Now is this, or is it not, the desirable condition of human nature?

It is so, on the Calvinistic theory. According to that, the one great offence of man is Self-will. All the good of which humanity is capable, is comprised in Obedience. You have no choice; thus you must do, and no otherwise: 'whatever is not a duty, is a sin.' Human nature being radically corrupt, there is no redemption for any one until human nature is killed within him. To one holding this theory of life, crushing out any of the human faculties, capacities, and susceptibilities, is no evil: man needs no capacity, but that of surrendering himself to the will of God: and if he uses any of his faculties for any other purpose but to do that supposed will more effectually, he is better without them. That is the theory of Calvinism; and it is held, in a mitigated form, by many who do not consider themselves Calvinists; the mitigation consisting in giving a less ascetic interpretation to the alleged will of God; asserting it to be his will that mankind should gratify some of their inclinations; of course not in the manner they themselves prefer, but in the way of obedience, that is, in a way prescribed to them by authority; and, therefore, by the necessary conditions of the case, the same for all.

In some such insidious form there is at present a strong tendency to this narrow theory of life, and to the pinched and hidebound type of human character which it patronizes. Many persons, no doubt, sincerely think that human beings thus cramped and dwarfed, are as their Maker designed them to be; just as many have thought that trees are a much finer thing when clipped into pollards, or cut out into figures of animals, than as nature made them. But if it be any part of religion to believe that man was made by a good being, it is more consistent with that faith to believe, that this Being gave all human faculties that they might be cultivated and unfolded, not rooted out and consumed, and that he takes delight in every nearer approach made by his creatures to the ideal conception embodied in them, every increase in any of their capabilities of comprehension, of action, or of enjoyment.

There is a different type of human excellence from the Calvinistic; a conception of humanity as having its nature bestowed on it for other purposes than merely to be abnegated. 'Pagan self-assertion' is one of the elements of human worth, as well as 'Christian self-denial.'* There is a Greek ideal of self-development, which the Platonic and Christian ideal of self-government blends with, but does not supersede. It may be better to be a John Knox than an Alcibiades, but it is better to be a Pericles than either; nor would a Pericles, if we had one in these days, be without anything good which belonged to John Knox.

It is not by wearing down into uniformity all that is individual in themselves, but by cultivating it and calling it forth, within the limits imposed by the rights and interests of others, that human beings become a noble and beautiful object of contemplation; and as the works partake the character of those who do them, by the same process human life also becomes rich, diversified, and animating, furnishing more abundant aliment to high thoughts and elevating feelings, and strengthening the tie which binds every individual to the race, by making the race infinitely better worth belonging to. In proportion to the development of his individuality, each person becomes more valuable to himself, and is therefore capable of being more valuable to others. There is a greater fulness of life about his own existence, and when there is more life in the units there is more in the mass which is composed of them. As much compression as is necessary to prevent the stronger specimens of human nature from encroaching on the rights of others, cannot be dispensed with; but for this there is ample compensation even in the point of view of human development. The means of development which the individual loses by being prevented from gratifying his inclinations to the injury of others, are chiefly obtained at the expense of the development of other people. And even to himself there is a full equivalent in the better development of the social part of his nature, rendered possible by the restraint put upon the selfish part. To be held to rigid rules of justice for the sake of others, develops the feelings and capacities which have the good of others for their object. But to be restrained in things not affecting their good, by their mere displeasure, develops nothing valuable, except such force of character as may unfold itself in resisting the restraint. If acquiesced in, it dulls and blunts the whole nature. To give any fair play to the na-

* Sterling's *Essays*.

ture of each, it is essential that different persons should be allowed to lead different lives. In proportion as this latitude has been exercised in any age, has that age been noteworthy to posterity. Even despotism does not produce its worst effects, so long as Individuality exists under it; and whatever crushes individuality is despotism, by whatever name it may be called, and whether it professes to be enforcing the will of God or the injunctions of men.

Having said that Individuality is the same thing with development, and that it is only the cultivation of individuality which produces, or can produce, well-developed human beings, I might here close the argument: for what more or better can be said of any condition of human affairs, than that it brings human beings themselves nearer to the best thing they can be? or what worse can be said of any obstruction to good, than that it prevents this? Doubtless, however, these considerations will not suffice to convince those who most need convincing; and it is necessary further to show, that these developed human beings are of some use to the undeveloped—to point out to those who do not desire liberty, and would not avail themselves of it, that they may be in some intelligible manner rewarded for allowing other people to make use of it without hindrance.

In the first place, then, I would suggest that they might possibly learn something from them. It will not be denied by anybody, that originality is a valuable element in human affairs. There is always need of persons not only to discover new truths, and point out when what were once truths are true no longer, but also to commence new practices, and set the example of more enlightened conduct, and better taste and sense in human life. This cannot well be gainsaid by anybody who does not believe that the world has already attained perfection in all its ways and practices. It is true that this benefit is not capable of being rendered by everybody alike: there are but few persons, in comparison with the whole of mankind, whose experiments, if adopted by others, would be likely to be any improvement on established practice. But these few are the salt of the earth; without them, human life would become a stagnant pool. Not only is it they who introduce good things which did not before exist; it is they who keep the life in those which already existed. If there were nothing new to be done, would human intellect cease to be necessary? Would it be a reason why those who do the old things should forget why they are done, and do them like cattle, not like human beings? There is only too great a tendency in the best beliefs and practices to degenerate into the mechanical; and unless there were a succession of persons whose ever-recurring originality prevents the grounds of those beliefs and practices from becoming merely traditional, such dead matter would not resist the smallest shock from anything really alive, and there would be no reason why civilization should not die out, as in the Byzantine Empire. Persons of genius, it is true, are, and are always likely to be, a small minority; but in order to have them, it is necessary to preserve the soil in which they grow. Genius can only breathe freely in an *atmosphere* of freedom. Persons of genius are, *ex vi termini*, more individual than any other people—less capable, consequently, of fitting themselves, without hurtful compression, into any of the small number of moulds which society provides in order to save its members the trouble of forming their own character. If from timidity they consent to be forced into one of these moulds, and to let all that part of themselves which cannot expand under the pressure remain unexpanded, society will be little the better for their genius. If they are of a strong character, and break their fetters, they become a mark for the society which has not succeeded in reducing them to commonplace, to point at with solemn warning as 'wild,' 'erratic,' and the like; much as if one should complain of the Niagara river for not flowing smoothly between its banks like a Dutch canal.

I insist thus emphatically on the importance of genius, and the necessity of allowing it to unfold itself freely both in thought and in practice, being well aware that no one will deny the position in theory, but knowing also that almost every one, in reality, is totally indifferent to it. People think genius a fine thing if it enables a man to write an exciting poem, or paint a picture. But in its true sense, that of originality in thought and action, though no one says that it is not a thing to be admired, nearly all, at heart, think that they can do very well without it. Unhappily this is too natural to be wondered at. Originality is the one thing which unoriginal minds cannot feel the use of. They cannot see what it is to do for them: how should they? If they could see what it would do for them, it would not be originality. The first service which originality has to render them, is that of opening their eyes: which being once fully done, they would have a chance of being themselves original. Meanwhile, recollecting that nothing was ever yet done which some one was not the first to do,

and that all good things which exist are the fruits of originality, let them be modest enough to believe that there is something still left for it to accomplish, and assure themselves that
they are more in need of originality, the less they are conscious
of the want.

In sober truth, whatever homage may be professed, or even
paid, to real or supposed mental superiority, the general tendency of things throughout the world is to render mediocrity
the ascendant power among mankind. In ancient history, in
the middle ages, and in a diminishing degree through the long
transition from feudality to the present time, the individual
was a power in himself; and if he had either great talents or a
high social position, he was a considerable power. At present
individuals are lost in the crowd. In politics it is almost a
triviality to say that public opinion now rules the world. The
only power deserving the name is that of masses, and of governments while they make themselves the organ of the tendencies and instincts of masses. This is as true in the moral and
social relations of private life as in public transactions. Those
whose opinions go by the name of public opinion, are not
always the same sort of public: in America they are the whole
white population; in England, chiefly the middle class. But
they are always a mass, that is to say, collective mediocrity.
And what is a still greater novelty, the mass do not now take
their opinions from dignitaries in Church or State, from ostensible leaders, or from books. Their thinking is done for them
by men much like themselves, addressing them or speaking in
their name, on the spur of the moment, through the newspapers. I am not complaining of all this. I do not assert that
anything better is compatible, as a general rule, with the
present low state of the human mind. But that does not hinder
the government of mediocrity from being mediocre government. No government by a democracy or a numerous aristocracy, either in its political acts or in the opinions, qualities,
and tone of mind which it fosters, ever did or could rise above
mediocrity, except in so far as the sovereign Many have let
themselves be guided (which in their best times they always
have done) by the counsels and influence of a more highly
gifted and instructed One or Few. The initiation of all wise or
noble things, comes and must come from individuals; generally at first from some one individual. The honour and glory
of the average man is that he is capable of following that
initiative; that he can respond internally to wise and noble
things, and be led to them with his eyes open. I am not coun-

tenancing the sort of 'hero-worship' which applauds the strong man of genius for forcibly seizing on the government of the world and making it do his bidding in spite of itself. All he can claim is, freedom to point out the way. The power of compelling others into it, is not only inconsistent with the freedom and development of all the rest, but corrupting to the strong man himself. It does seem, however, that when the opinions of masses of merely average men are everywhere become or becoming the dominant power, the counterpoise and corrective to that tendency would be, the more and more pronounced individuality of those who stand on the higher eminences of thought. It is in these circumstances most especially, that exceptional individuals, instead of being deterred, should be encouraged in acting differently from the mass. In other times there was no advantage in their doing so, unless they acted not only differently, but better. In this age the mere example of nonconformity, the mere refusal to bend the knee to custom, is itself a service. Precisely because the tyranny of opinion is such as to make eccentricity a reproach, it is desirable, in order to break through that tyranny, that people should be eccentric. Eccentricity has always abounded when and where strength of character has abounded; and the amount of eccentricity in a society has generally been proportional to the amount of genius, mental vigour, and moral courage which it contained. That so few now dare to be eccentric, marks the chief danger of the time.

I have said that it is important to give the freest scope possible to uncustomary things, in order that it may in time appear which of these are fit to be converted into customs. But independence of action, and disregard of custom are not solely deserving of encouragement for the chance they afford that better modes of action, and customs more worthy of general adoption, may be struck out; nor is it only persons of decided mental superiority who have a just claim to carry on their lives in their own way. There is no reason that all human existences should be constructed on some one, or some small number of patterns. If a person possesses any tolerable amount of common sense and experience, his own mode of laying out his existence is the best, not because it is the best in itself, but because it is his own mode. Human beings are not like sheep; and even sheep are not undistinguishably alike. A man cannot get a coat or a pair of boots to fit him, unless they are either made to his measure, or he has a whole warehouseful to choose from: and is it easier to fit him with a life than with a coat,

or are human beings more like one another in their whole
physical and spiritual conformation than in the shape of their
feet? If it were only that people have diversities of taste, that
is reason enough for not attempting to shape them all after
one model. But different persons also require different conditions for their spiritual development; and can no more exist
healthily in the same moral, than all the variety of plants can
in the same physical, atmosphere and climate. The same things
which are helps to one person towards the cultivation of his
higher nature, are hindrances to another. The same mode of
life is a healthy excitement to one, keeping all his faculties of
action and enjoyment in their best order, while to another it is
a distracting burthen, which suspends or crushes all internal
life. Such are the differences among human beings in their
sources of pleasure, their susceptibilities of pain, and the
operation on them of different physical and moral agencies,
that unless there is a corresponding diversity in their modes
of life, they neither obtain their fair share of happiness, nor
grow up to the mental, moral, and æsthetic stature of which
their nature is capable. Why then should tolerance, as far as
the public sentiment is concerned, extend only to tastes and
modes of life which extort acquiescence by the multitude of
their adherents? Nowhere (except in some monastic institutions) is diversity of taste entirely unrecognised; a person may,
without blame, either like or dislike rowing, or smoking, or
music, or athletic exercises, or chess, or cards, or study, because both those who like each of these things, and those who
dislike them, are too numerous to be put down. But the man,
and still more the woman, who can be accused either of doing 'what nobody does,' or of not doing 'what everybody
does,' is the subject of as much depreciatory remark as if he or
she had committed some grave moral delinquency. Persons
require to possess a title, or some other badge of rank, or of
the consideration of people of rank, to be able to indulge
somewhat in the luxury of doing as they like without detri-
ment to their estimation. To indulge somewhat, I repeat: for
whoever allow themselves much of that indulgence, incur the
risk of something worse than disparaging speeches—they are
in peril of a commission *de lunatico*, and of having their property taken from them and given to their relations.*

* There is something both contemptible and frightful in the sort of evidence on which, of late years, any person can be judicially declared unfit for
the management of his affairs; and after his death, his disposal of his property can be set aside, if there is enough of it to pay the expenses of litiga-
tion—which are charged on the property itself. All the minute details of his

There is one characteristic of the present direction of public opinion, peculiarly calculated to make it intolerant of any marked demonstration of individuality. The general average of mankind are not only moderate in intellect, but also moderate in inclinations: they have no tastes or wishes strong enough to incline them to do anything unusual, and they consequently do not understand those who have, and class all such with the wild and intemperate whom they are accustomed to look down upon. Now, in addition to this fact which is general, we have only to suppose that a strong movement has set in towards the improvement of morals, and it is evident what we have to expect. In these days such a movement has set in; much has actually been effected in the way of increased regularity of conduct, and discouragement of excesses; and there is a philanthropic spirit abroad, for the exercise of which there is no more inviting field than the moral and prudential improvement of our fellow-creatures. These tendencies of the times cause the public to be more disposed than at most former periods to prescribe general rules of conduct, and endeavour to make every one conform to the approved standard. And that standard, express or tacit, is to desire nothing strongly. Its ideal of character is to be without any marked character; to maim by compression, like a Chinese lady's foot, every part of human nature which stands out prominently, and tends to make the person markedly dissimilar in outline to commonplace humanity.

As is usually the case with ideals which exclude one-half of what is desirable, the present standard of approbation produces only an inferior imitation of the other half. Instead of great energies guided by vigorous reason, and strong feelings

---

daily life are pried into, and whatever is found which, seen through the medium of the perceiving and describing faculties of the lowest of the low, bears an appearance unlike absolute commonplace, is laid before the jury as evidence of insanity, and often with success; the jurors being little, if at all, less vulgar and ignorant than the witnesses; while the judges, with that extraordinary want of knowledge of human nature and life which continually astonishes us in English lawyers, often help to mislead them. These trials speak volumes as to the state of feeling and opinion among the vulgar with regard to human liberty. So far from setting any value on individuality— so far from respecting the rights of each individual to act, in things indifferent, as seems good to his own judgment and inclinations, judges and juries cannot even conceive that a person in a state of sanity can desire such freedom. In former days, when it was proposed to burn atheists, charitable people used to suggest putting them in a madhouse instead: it would be nothing surprising nowadays were we to see this done, and the doers applauding themselves, because, instead of persecuting for religion, they had adopted so humane and Christian a mode of treating these unfortunates, not without a silent satisfaction at their having thereby obtained their deserts.

strongly controlled by a conscientious will, its result is weak feelings and weak energies, which therefore can be kept in outward conformity to rule without any strength either of will or of reason. Already energetic characters on any large scale are becoming merely traditional. There is now scarcely any outlet for energy in this country except business. The energy expended in that may still be regarded as considerable. What little is left from that employment, is expended on some hobby; which may be a useful, even a philanthropic hobby, but is always some one thing, and generally a thing of small dimensions. The greatness of England is now all collective: individually small, we only appear capable of anything great by our habit of combining; and with this our moral and religious philanthropists are perfectly contented. But it was men of another stamp than this that made England what it has been; and men of another stamp will be needed to prevent its decline.

The despotism of custom is everywhere the standing hindrance to human advancement, being in unceasing antagonism to that disposition to aim at something better than customary, which is called, according to circumstances, the spirit of liberty, or that of progress or improvement. The spirit of improvement is not always a spirit of liberty, for it may aim at forcing improvements on an unwilling people; and the spirit of liberty, in so far as it resists such attempts, may ally itself locally and temporarily with the opponents of improvement; but the only unfailing and permanent source of improvement is liberty, since by it there are as many possible independent centres of improvement as there are individuals. The progressive principle, however, in either shape, whether as the love of liberty or of improvement, is antagonistic to the sway of Custom, involving at least emancipation from that yoke; and the contest between the two constitutes the chief interest of the history of mankind. The greater part of the world has, properly speaking, no history, because the despotism of Custom is complete. This is the case over the whole East. Custom is there, in all things, the final appeal; justice and right mean conformity to custom; the argument of custom no one, unless some tyrant intoxicated with power, thinks of resisting. And we see the result. Those nations must once have had originality; they did not start out of the ground populous, lettered, and versed in many of the arts of life; they made themselves all this, and were then the greatest and most powerful nations in the world. What are they now? The subjects or dependants of tribes whose forefathers wandered in the forests when theirs had magnificent palaces and gorgeous temples, but over whom custom exercised only a divided rule with liberty and progress. A people, it appears, may be progressive for a certain length of time, and then stop: when does it stop? When it ceases to possess individuality. If a similar change should befall the nations of Europe, it will not be in exactly the same shape: the despotism of custom with which these nations are threatened is not precisely stationariness. It proscribes singularity, but it does not preclude change, provided all change together. We have discarded the fixed costumes of our forefathers; every one must still dress like other people, but the fashion may change once or twice a year. We thus take care that when there is change, it shall be for change's sake, and not from any idea of beauty or convenience; for the same idea of beauty or convenience would not strike all the world at the same moment, and be simultaneously thrown aside by all at another moment. But we are progressive as well as changeable: we continually make new inventions in mechanical things, and keep them until they are again superseded by better; we are eager for improvement in politics, in education, even in morals, though in this last our idea of improvement chiefly consists in persuading or forcing other people to be as good as ourselves. It is not progress that we object to; on the contrary, we flatter ourselves that we are the most progressive people who ever lived. It is individuality that we war against: we should think we had done wonders if we had made ourselves all alike; forgetting that the unlikeness of one person to another is generally the first thing which draws the attention of either to the imperfection of his own type, and the superiority of another, or the possibility, by combining the advantages of both, of producing something better than either. We have a warning example in China—a nation of much talent, and, in some respects, even wisdom, owing to the rare good fortune of having been provided at an early period with a particularly good set of customs, the work, in some measure, of men to whom even the most enlightened European must accord, under certain limitations, the title of sages and philosophers. They are remarkable, too, in the excellence of their apparatus for impressing, as far as possible, the best wisdom they possess upon every mind in the community, and securing that those who have appropriated most of it shall occupy the posts of honour and power. Surely the people who did this have discovered the secret of human progressiveness, and

must have kept themselves steadily at the head of the movement of the world. On the contrary they have become stationary—have remained so for thousands of years; and if they
are ever to be farther improved, it must be by foreigners.
They have succeeded beyond all hope in what English philanthropists are so industriously working at—in making a people
all alike, all governing their thoughts and conduct by the same
maxims and rules; and these are the fruits. The modern *régime*
of public opinion is, in an unorganized form, what the Chinese
educational and political systems are in an organized; and unless individuality shall be able successfully to assert itself
against this yoke, Europe, notwithstanding its noble antecedents and its professed Christianity, will tend to become another China.

What is it that has hitherto preserved Europe from this lot?
What has made the European family of nations an improving,
instead of a stationary portion of mankind? Not any superior
excellence in them, which, when it exists, exists as the effect,
not as the cause; but their remarkable diversity of character
and culture. Individuals, classes, nations, have been extremely
unlike one another: they have struck out a great variety of
paths, each leading to something valuable; and although at
every period those who travelled in different paths have been
intolerant of one another, and each would have thought it an
excellent thing if all the rest could have been compelled to
travel his road, their attempts to thwart each other's development have rarely had any permanent success, and each has in
time endured to receive the good which the others have offered. Europe is, in my judgment, wholly indebted to this
plurality of paths for its progressive and many-sided development. But it already begins to possess this benefit in a considerably less degree. It is decidedly advancing towards the
Chinese ideal of making all people alike. M. de Tocqueville,
in his last important work, remarks how much more the
Frenchmen of the present day resemble one another, than did
those even of the last generation. The same remark might be
made of Englishmen in a far greater degree. In a passage
already quoted from Wilhelm von Humboldt, he points out
two things as necessary conditions of human development,
because necessary to render people unlike one another;
namely, freedom, and variety of situations. The second of
these two conditions is in this country every day diminishing.
The circumstances which surround different classes and individuals, and shape their characters, are daily becoming more

assimilated. Formerly, different ranks, different neighborhoods, different trades and professions, lived in what might be called different worlds; at present, to a great degree in the same. Comparatively speaking, they now read the same things, listen to the same things, see the same things, go to the same places, have their hopes and fears directed to the same objects, have the same rights and liberties, and the same means of asserting them. Great as are the differences of position which remain, they are nothing to those which have ceased. And the assimilation is still proceeding. All the political changes of the age promote it, since they all tend to raise the low and to lower the high. Every extension of education promotes it, because education brings people under common influences, and gives them access to the general stock of facts and sentiments. Improvements in the means of communication promote it, by bringing the inhabitants of distant places into personal contact, and keeping up a rapid flow of changes of residence between one place and another. The increase of commerce and manufactures promotes it, by diffusing more widely the advantages of easy circumstances, and opening all objects of ambition, even the highest, to general competition, whereby the desire of rising becomes no longer the character of a particular class, but of all classes. A more powerful agency than even all these, in bringing about a general similarity among mankind, is the complete establishment, in this and other free countries, of the ascendancy of public opinion in the State. As the various social eminences which enabled persons entrenched on them to disregard the opinion of the multitude, gradually become levelled; as the very idea of resisting the will of the public, when it is positively known that they have a will, disappears more and more from the minds of practical politicians; there ceases to be any social support for non-conformity—any substantive power in society, which, itself opposed to the ascendancy of numbers, is interested in taking under its protection opinions and tendencies at variance with those of the public.

The combination of all these causes forms so great a mass of influences hostile to Individuality, that it is not easy to see how it can stand its ground. It will do so with increasing difficulty, unless the intelligent part of the public can be made to feel its value—to see that it is good there should be differences, even though not for the better, even though, as it may appear to them, some should be for the worse. If the claims of Individuality are ever to be asserted, the time is now, while much is still wanting to complete the enforced assimilation. It is only in the earlier stages that any stand can be successfully made against the encroachment. The demand that all other people shall resemble ourselves, grows by what it feeds on. If resistance waits till life is reduced *nearly* to one uniform type, all deviations from that type will come to be considered impious, immoral, even monstrous and contrary to nature. Mankind speedily become unable to conceive diversity, when they have been for some time unaccustomed to see it.

IV. OF THE LIMITS TO THE AUTHORITY OF SOCIETY OVER THE INDIVIDUAL

WHAT, then, is the rightful limit to the sovereignty of the individual over himself? Where does the authority of society begin? How much of human life should be assigned to individuality, and how much to society?

Each will receive its proper share, if each has that which more particularly concerns it. To individuality should belong the part of life in which it is chiefly the individual that is interested; to society, the part which chiefly interests society.

Though society is not founded on a contract, and though no good purpose is answered by inventing a contract in order to deduce social obligations from it, every one who receives the protection of society owes a return for the benefit, and the fact of living in society renders it indispensable that each should be found to observe a certain line of conduct towards the rest. This conduct consists, first, in not injuring the interests of one another; or rather certain interests, which, either by express legal provision or by tacit understanding, ought to be considered as rights; and secondly, in each person's bearing his share (to be fixed on some equitable principle) of the labours and sacrifices incurred for defending the society or its members from injury and molestation. These conditions society is justified in enforcing, at all costs to those who endeavour to withhold fulfilment. Nor is this all that society may do. The acts of an individual may be hurtful to others, or wanting in due consideration for their welfare, without going the length of violating any of their constituted rights. The offender may then be justly punished by opinion, though not by law. As soon as any part of a person's conduct affects prejudicially the interests of others, society has jurisdiction over it, and the question whether the general welfare will or will not be promoted by interfering with it, becomes open to discussion. But there is no room for entertaining any such question when a person's conduct affects the interests of no persons besides himself, or needs not affect them unless they like (all the persons concerned being of full age, and the ordinary amount of understanding). In all such cases there should be perfect freedom, legal and social, to do the action and stand the consequences.

It would be a great misunderstanding of this doctrine, to suppose that it is one of selfish indifference, which pretends that human beings have no business with each other's conduct in life, and that they should not concern themselves about the well-doing or well-being of one another, unless their own interest is involved. Instead of any diminution, there is need of a great increase of disinterested exertion to promote the good of others. But disinterested benevolence can find other instruments to persuade people to their good, than whips and scourges, either of the literal or the metaphorical sort. I am the last person to undervalue the self-regarding virtues; they are only second in importance, if even second, to the social. It is equally the business of education to cultivate both. But even education works by conviction and persuasion as well as by compulsion, and it is by the former only that, when the period of education is past, the self-regarding virtues should be inculcated. Human beings owe to each other help to distinguish the better from the worse, and encouragement to choose the former and avoid the latter. They should be for ever stimulating each other to increased exercise of their higher faculties, and increased direction of their feelings and aims towards wise instead of foolish, elevating instead of degrading, objects and contemplations. But neither one person, nor any number of persons, is warranted in saying to another human creature of ripe years, that he shall not do with his life for his own benefit what he chooses to do with it. He is the person most interested in his own well-being: the interest which any other person, except in cases of strong personal attachment, can have in it, is trifling, compared with that which he himself has; the interest which society has in him individually (except as to his conduct to others) is fractional, and altogether indirect: while, with respect to his own feelings and circumstances, the most ordinary man or woman has means of knowledge immeasurably surpassing those that can be possessed by any one else. The interference of society to overrule his judgment and purposes in what only regards himself, must be grounded on general presumptions: which may be altogether wrong, and even if right, are as likely as not to be misapplied to individual cases, by persons no better acquainted with the circumstances of such cases than those are who look at them merely from without. In this department, therefore, of human affairs, Individuality has its proper field of action. In the conduct of human beings towards one another, it is necessary that general rules should for the most part be observed, in order that people may know what they have to expect; but in each person's own concerns, his individual spontaneity is entitled to free exercise. Considerations to aid his judgment, exhortations to strengthen his will, may be offered to him, even obtruded on him, by others; but he himself is the final judge. All errors which he is likely to commit against advice and warning, are far outweighed by the evil of allowing others to constrain him to what they deem his good.

I do not mean that the feelings with which a person is regarded by others, ought not to be in any way affected by his self-regarding qualities or deficiencies. This is neither possible nor desirable. If he is eminent in any of the qualities which conduce to his own good, he is, so far, a proper object of admiration. He is so much the nearer to the ideal perfection of human nature. If he is grossly deficient in those qualities, a sentiment the opposite of admiration will follow. There is a degree of folly, and a degree of what may be called (though the phrase is not unobjectionable) lowness or depravation of taste, which, though it cannot justify doing harm to the person who manifests it, renders him necessarily and properly a subject of distaste, or, in extreme cases, even of contempt: a person could not have the opposite qualities in due strength without entertaining these feelings. Though doing no wrong to any one, a person may so act as to compel us to judge him, and feel to him, as a fool, or as a being of an inferior order: and since this judgment and feeling are a fact which he would prefer to avoid, it is doing him a service to warn him of it beforehand, as of any other disagreeable consequence to which he exposes himself. It would be well, indeed, if this good office were much more freely rendered than the common notions of politeness at present permit, and if one person could honestly point out to another that he thinks him in fault, without being considered unmannerly or presuming. We have a right, also, in various ways, to act upon our unfavourable opinion of any one, not to the oppression of his individuality, but in the exercise of ours. We are not bound, for example, to seek his society; we have a right to avoid it (though not to parade the avoidance), for we have a right to choose the society most acceptable to us. We have a right, and it may be our duty, to caution others against him, if we think his example or conversation likely to have a pernicious effect on those with whom he associates. We may give others a preference over him in optional good offices, except those which tend to his improvement. In these various modes a person may suffer very severe penalties at the hands of others, for faults which directly concern only himself; but he suffers these penalties only in so far as they are the natural and, as it were, the spontaneous consequences of the faults themselves, not because they are purposely inflicted on him for the sake of punishment. A person who shows rashness, obstinacy, self-conceit—who cannot live within moderate means—who cannot restrain himself from hurtful indulgences—who pursues animal pleasures at the expense of those of feeling and intellect—must expect to be lowered in the opinion of others, and to have a less share of their favourable sentiments; but of this he has no right to complain, unless he has merited their favour by special excellence in his social relations, and has thus established a title to their good offices, which is not affected by his demerits towards himself.

What I contend for is, that the inconveniences which are strictly inseparable from the unfavourable judgment of others, are the only ones to which a person should ever be subjected for that portion of his conduct and character which concerns his own good, but which does not affect the interests of others in their relations with him. Acts injurious to others require a totally different treatment. Encroachment on their rights; infliction on them of any loss or damage not justified by his own rights; falsehood or duplicity in dealing with them; unfair or ungenerous use of advantages over them; even selfish abstinence from defending them against injury—these are fit objects of moral reprobation, and, in grave cases, of moral retribution and punishment. And not only these acts, but the dispositions which lead to them, are properly immoral, and fit subjects of disapprobation which may rise to abhorrence. Cruelty of disposition; malice and ill-nature; that most anti-social and odious of all passions, envy; dissimulation and insincerity; irascibility on insufficient cause, and resentment disproportioned to the provocation; the love of domineering over others; the desire to engross more than one's share of advantages (the πλεονεξία of the Greeks); the pride which derives gratification from the abasement of others; the egotism which thinks self and its concerns more important than everything else, and decides all doubtful questions in its own favour;—these are moral vices, and constitute a bad and odious moral character: unlike the self-regarding faults previously mentioned which are not properly immoralities, and to whatever pitch they may be carried, do not constitute wickedness. They may be proofs of any amount of folly, or want of personal dignity and self-respect; but they are only a subject of moral reprobation when they involve a breach of duty to others, for whose sake the individual is bound to have care for himself. What are called duties to ourselves are not socially obligatory, unless circumstances render them at the same time duties to others. The term duty to oneself, when it means anything more than prudence, means self-respect or self-development; and for none of these is any one accountable to his fellow creatures, because for none of them is it for the good of mankind that he be held accountable to them.

The distinction between the loss of consideration which a person may rightly incur by defect of prudence or of personal dignity, and the reprobation which is due to him for an offence against the rights of others, is not a merely nominal distinction. It makes a vast difference both in our feelings and in our conduct towards him, whether he displeases us in things in which we think we have a right to control him, or in things in which we know that we have not. If he displeases us, we may express our distaste, and we may stand aloof from a person as well as from a thing that displeases us; but we shall not therefore feel called on to make his life uncomfortable. We shall reflect that he already bears, or will bear, the whole penalty of his error; if he spoils his life by mismanagement, we shall not, for that reason, desire to spoil it still further: instead of wishing to punish him, we shall rather endeavour to alleviate his punishment, by showing him how he may avoid or cure the evils his conduct tends to bring upon him. He may be to us an object of pity, perhaps of dislike, but not of anger or resentment: we shall not treat him like an enemy of society: the worst we shall think ourselves justified in doing is leaving him to himself, if we do not interfere benevolently by showing interest or concern for him. It is far otherwise if he has infringed the rules necessary for the protection of his fellow-creatures, individually or collectively. The evil consequences of his acts do not then fall on himself, but on others; and society, as the protector of all its members, must retaliate on him; must inflict pain on him for the express

purpose of punishment, and must take care that it be sufficiently severe. In the one case, he is an offender at our bar,
and we are called on not only to sit in judgment on him, but,
in one shape or another, to execute our own sentence: in the
other case, it is not our part to inflict any suffering on him,
except what may incidentally follow from our using the same
liberty in the regulation of our own affairs, which we allow
to him in his.

The distinction here pointed out between the part of a
person's life which concerns only himself, and that which concerns others, many persons will refuse to admit. How (it may
be asked) can any part of the conduct of a member of society
be a matter of indifference to the other members? No person
is an entirely isolated being; it is impossible for a person to
do anything seriously or permanently hurtful to himself, without mischief reaching at least to his near connexions, and
often far beyond them. If he injures his property, he does
harm to those who directly or indirectly derived support from
it, and usually diminishes, by a greater or less amount, the
general resources of the community. If he deteriorates his
bodily or mental faculties, he not only brings evil upon all
who depended on him for any portion of their happiness, but
disqualifies himself for rendering the services which he owes
to his fellow creatures generally; perhaps becomes a burthen
on their affection or benevolence; and if such conduct were
very frequent, hardly any offence that is committed would
detract more from the general sum of good. Finally, if by his
vices or follies a person does no direct harm to others, he is
nevertheless (it may be said) injurious by his example; and
ought to be compelled to control himself, for the sake of
those whom the sight or knowledge of his conduct might corrupt or mislead.

And even (it will be added) if the consequences of misconduct could be confined to the vicious or thoughtless individual,
ought society to abandon to their own guidance those who
are manifestly unfit for it? If protection against themselves is
confessedly due to children and persons under age, is not
society equally bound to afford it to persons of mature years
who are equally incapable of self-government? If gambling,
or drunkenness, or incontinence, or idleness, or uncleanliness,
are as injurious to happiness, and as great a hindrance to
improvement, as many or most of the acts prohibited by law,
why (it may be asked) should not law, so far as is consistent
with practicability and social convenience, endeavour to re-

press these also? And as a supplement to the unavoidable imperfections of law, ought not opinion at least to organize a powerful police against these vices, and visit rigidly with social penalties those who are known to practise them? There is no question here (it may be said) about restricting individuality, or impeding the trial of new and original experiments in living. The only things it is sought to prevent are things which have been tried and condemned from the beginning of the world until now; things which experience has shown not to be useful or suitable to any person's individuality. There must be some length of time and amount of experience, after which a moral or prudential truth may be regarded as established: and it is merely desired to prevent generation after generation from falling over the same precipice which has been fatal to their predecessors.

I fully admit that the mischief which a person does to himself, may seriously affect, both through their sympathies and their interests, those nearly connected with him, and in a minor degree, society at large. When, by conduct of this sort, a person is led to violate a distinct and assignable obligation to any other person or persons, the case is taken out of the self-regarding class, and becomes amenable to moral disapprobation in the proper sense of the term. If, for example, a man, through intemperance or extravagance, becomes unable to pay his debts, or, having undertaken the moral responsibility of a family, becomes from the same cause incapable of supporting or educating them, he is deservedly reprobated, and might be justly punished; but it is for the breach of duty to his family or creditors, not for the extravagance. If the resources which ought to have been devoted to them, had been diverted from them for the most prudent investment, the moral culpability would have been the same. George Barnwell murdered his uncle to get money for his mistress, but if he had done it to set himself up in business, he would equally have been hanged. Again, in the frequent case of a man who causes grief to his family by addiction to bad habits, he deserves reproach for his unkindness or ingratitude; but so he may for cultivating habits not in themselves vicious, if they are painful to those with whom he passes his life, or who from personal ties are dependent on him for their comfort. Whoever fails in the consideration generally due to the interests and feelings of others, not being compelled by some more imperative duty, or justified by allowable self-preference, is a subject of moral disapprobation for that failure, but not for the cause of it, nor for the errors, merely personal to himself, which may have remotely led to it. In like manner, when a person disables himself, by conduct purely self-regarding, from the performance of some definite duty incumbent on him to the public, he is guilty of a social offence. No person ought to be punished simply for being drunk; but a soldier or a policeman should be punished for being drunk on duty. Whenever, in short, there is a definite damage, or a definite risk of damage, either to an individual or to the public, the case is taken out of the province of liberty, and placed in that of morality or law.

But with regard to the merely contingent, or, as it may be called, constructive injury which a person causes to society, by conduct which neither violates any specific duty to the public, nor occasions perceptible hurt to any assignable individual except himself; the inconvenience is one which society can afford to bear, for the sake of the greater good of human freedom. If grown persons are to be punished for not taking proper care of themselves, I would rather it were for their own sake, than under pretence of preventing them from impairing their capacity of rendering to society benefits which society does not pretend it has a right to exact. But I cannot consent to argue the point as if society had no means of bringing its weaker members up to its ordinary standard of rational conduct, except waiting till they do something irrational, and then punishing them, legally or morally, for it. Society has had absolute power over them during all the early portion of their existence: it has had the whole period of childhood and nonage in which to try whether it could make them capable of rational conduct in life. The existing generation is master both of the training and the entire circumstances of the generation to come; it cannot indeed make them perfectly wise and good, because it is itself so lamentably deficient in goodness and wisdom; and its best efforts are not always, in individual cases, its most successful ones; but it is perfectly well able to make the rising generation, as a whole, as good as, and a little better than, itself. If society lets any considerable number of its members grow up mere children, incapable of being acted on by rational consideration of distant motives, society has itself to blame for the consequences. Armed not only with all the powers of education, but with the ascendancy which the authority of a received opinion always exercises over the minds who are least fitted to judge for themselves; and aided by the *natural* penalties which cannot be prevented from falling on those who incur the distaste or the contempt of those who know them; let not society pretend that it needs, besides all this, the power to issue commands and enforce obedience in the personal concerns of individuals, in which, on all principles of justice and policy, the decision ought to rest with those who are to abide the consequences. Nor is there anything which tends more to discredit and frustrate the better means of influencing conduct, than a resort to the worse. If there be among those whom it is attempted to coerce into prudence or temperance, any of the material of which vigorous and independent characters are made, they will infallibly rebel against the yoke. No such person will ever feel that others have a right to control him in his concerns, such as they have to prevent him from injuring them in theirs; and it easily comes to be considered a mark of spirit and courage to fly in the face of such usurped authority, and do with ostentation the exact opposite of what it enjoins; as in the fashion of grossness which succeeded, in the time of Charles II., to the fanatical moral intolerance of the Puritans. With respect to what is said of the necessity of protecting society from the bad example set to others by the vicious or the self-indulgent; it is true that bad example may have a pernicious effect, especially the example of doing wrong to others with impunity to the wrong-doer. But we are now speaking of conduct which, while it does no wrong to others, is supposed to do great harm to the agent himself; and I do not see how those who believe this, can think otherwise than that the example, on the whole, must be more salutary than hurtful, since, if it displays the misconduct, it displays also the painful or degrading consequences which, if the conduct is justly censured, must be supposed to be in all or most cases attendant on it.

But the strongest of all the arguments against the interference of the public with purely personal conduct, is that when it does interfere, the odds are that it interferes wrongly, and in the wrong place. On questions of social morality, of duty to others, the opinion of the public, that is, of an overruling majority, though often wrong, is likely to be still oftener right; because on such questions they are only required to judge of their own interests; of the manner in which some mode of conduct, if allowed to be practised, would affect themselves. But the opinion of a similar majority, imposed as a law on the minority, on questions of self-regarding conduct, is quite as likely to be wrong as right; for in these cases public opinion means, at the best, some people's opinion of what is good or bad for other people; while very often it does not even mean that; the public, with the most perfect indifference, passing over the pleasure or convenience of those whose conduct they censure, and considering only their own preference. There are many who consider as an injury to themselves any conduct which they have a distaste for, and resent it as an outrage to their feelings; as a religious bigot, when charged with disregarding the religious feelings of others, has been known to retort that they disregard his feelings, by persisting in their abominable worship or creed. But there is no parity between the feeling of a person for his own opinion, and the feeling of another who is offended at his holding it; no more than between the desire of a thief to take a purse, and the desire of the right owner to keep it. And a person's taste is as much his own peculiar concern as his opinion or his purse. It is easy for any one to imagine an ideal public, which leaves the freedom and choice of individuals in all uncertain matters undisturbed, and only requires them to abstain from modes of conduct which universal experience has condemned. But where has there been seen a public which set any such limit to its censorship? or when does the public trouble itself about universal experience? In its interferences with personal conduct it is seldom thinking of anything but the enormity of acting or feeling differently from itself; and this standard of judgment, thinly disguised, is held up to mankind as the dictate of religion and philosophy, by nine-tenths of all moralists and speculative writers. These teach that things are right because they are right; because we feel them to be so. They tell us to search in our own minds and hearts for laws of conduct binding on ourselves and on all others. What can the poor public do but apply these instructions, and make their own personal feelings of good and evil, if they are tolerably unanimous in them, obligatory on all the world?

The evil here pointed out is not one which exists only in theory; and it may perhaps be expected that I should specify the instances in which the public of this age and country improperly invests its own preferences with the character of moral laws. I am not writing an essay on the aberrations of existing moral feeling. That is too weighty a subject to be discussed parenthetically, and by way of illustration. Yet examples are necessary, to show that the principle I maintain is of serious and practical moment, and that I am not endeavouring to erect a barrier against imaginary evils. And it is not difficult to show, by abundant instances, that to extend the bounds of what may be called moral police, until it encroaches on the most unquestionably legitimate liberty of the individual, is one of the most universal of all human propensities.

As a first instance, consider the antipathies which men cherish on no better grounds than that persons whose religious opinions are different from theirs, do not practise their religious observances, especially their religious abstinences. To cite a rather trivial example, nothing in the creed or practice of Christians does more to envenom the hatred of Mahomedans against them, than the fact of their eating pork. There are few acts which Christians and Europeans regard with more unaffected disgust, than Mussulmans regard this particular mode of satisfying hunger. It is, in the first place, an offence against their religion; but this circumstance by no means explains either the degree or the kind of their repugnance; for wine also is forbidden by their religion, and to partake of it is by all Mussulmans accounted wrong, but not disgusting. Their aversion to the flesh of the 'unclean beast' is, on the contrary, of that peculiar character, resembling an instinctive antipathy, which the idea of uncleanness, when once it thoroughly sinks into the feelings, seems always to excite even in those whose personal habits are anything but scrupulously clean, and of which the sentiment of religious impurity, so intense in the Hindoos, is a remarkable example. Suppose now that in a people, of whom the majority were Mussulmans, that majority should insist upon not permitting pork to be eaten within the limits of the country. This would be nothing new in Mahomedan countries.* Would it be a legitimate exercise of the moral authority of public opinion? and if not, why not? The practice is really revolting to such a public. They also sincerely think that it is forbidden and abhorred by the Deity. Neither could the prohibition be censured as religious persecution. It might be religious in its origin, but it would not be persecution for religion, since no-

---

* The case of the Bombay Parsees is a curious instance in point. When this industrious and enterprising tribe, the descendants of the Persion fire-worshippers, flying from their native country before the Caliphs, arrived in Western India, they were admitted to toleration by the Hindoo sovereigns, on condition of not eating beef. When those regions afterwards fell under the dominion of Mahomedan conquerors, the Parsees obtained from them a continuance of indulgence, on condition of refraining from pork. What was at first obedience to authority became a second nature, and the Parsees to this day abstain both from beef and pork. Though not required by their religion, the double abstinence has had time to grow into a custom of their tribe; and custom, in the East, is a religion.

body's religion makes it a duty to eat pork. The only tenable ground of condemnation would be, that with the personal tastes and self-regarding concerns of individuals the public has no business to interfere.

To come somewhat nearer home: the majority of Spaniards consider it a gross impiety, offensive in the highest degree to the Supreme Being, to worship him in any other manner than the Roman Catholic; and no other public worship is lawful on Spanish soil. The people of all Southern Europe look upon a married clergy as not only irreligious, but unchaste, indecent, gross, disgusting. What do Protestants think of these perfectly sincere feelings, and of the attempt to enforce them against non-Catholics? Yet, if mankind are justified in interfering with each other's liberty in things which do not concern the interests of others, on what principle is it possible consistently to exclude these cases? or who can blame people for desiring to suppress what they regard as a scandal in the sight of God and man? No stronger case can be shown for prohibiting anything which is regarded as a personal immorality, than is made out for suppressing these practices in the eyes of those who regard them as impieties; and unless we are willing to adopt the logic of persecutors, and to say that we may persecute others because we are right, and that they must not persecute us because they are wrong, we must beware of admitting a principle of which we should resent as a gross injustice the application to ourselves.

The preceding instances may be objected to, although unreasonably, as drawn from contingencies impossible among us: opinion, in this country, not being likely to enforce abstinence from meats, or to interfere with people for worshipping, and for either marrying or not marrying, according to their creed or inclination. The next example, however, shall be taken from an interference with liberty which we have by no means passed all danger of. Wherever the Puritans have been sufficiently powerful, as in New England, and in Great Britain at the time of the Commonwealth, they have endeavoured, with considerable success, to put down all public, and nearly all private, amusements: especially music, dancing, public games, or other assemblages for purposes of diversion, and the theatre. There are still in this country large bodies of persons by whose notions of morality and religion these recreations are condemned; and those persons belonging chiefly to the middle class, who are the ascendant power in the present social and political condition of the kingdom, it is by no means impossible that persons of these sentiments may at some time or other command a majority in Parliament. How will the remaining portion of the community like to have the amusements that shall be permitted to them regulated by the religious and moral sentiments of the stricter Calvinists and Methodists? Would they not, with considerable peremptoriness, desire these intrusively pious members of society to mind their own business? This is precisely what should be said to every government and every public, who have the pretension that no person shall enjoy any pleasure which they think wrong. But if the principle of the pretension be admitted, no one can reasonably object to its being acted on in the sense of the majority, or other preponderating power in the country; and all persons must be ready to conform to the idea of a Christian commonwealth, as understood by the early settlers in New England, if a religious profession similar to theirs should ever succeed in regaining its lost ground, as religions supposed to be declining have so often been known to do.

To imagine another contingency, perhaps more likely to be realized than the one last mentioned. There is confessedly a strong tendency in the modern world towards a democratic constitution of society, accompanied or not by popular political institutions. It is affirmed that in the country where this tendency is most completely realized—where both society and the government are most democratic—the United States—the feeling of the majority, to whom any appearance of a more showy or costly style of living than they can hope to rival is disagreeable, operates as a tolerably effectual sumptuary law, and that in many parts of the Union it is really difficult for a person possessing a very large income, to find any mode of spending it, which will not incur popular disapprobation. Though such statements as these are doubtless much exaggerated as a representation of existing facts, the state of things they describe is not only a conceivable and possible, but a probable result of democratic feeling, combined with the notion that the public has a right to a veto on the manner in which individuals shall spend their incomes. We have only further to suppose a considerable diffusion of Socialist opinions, and it may become infamous in the eyes of the majority to possess more property than some very small amount, or any income not earned by manual labour. Opinions similar in principle to these already prevail widely among the artizan class, and weigh oppressively on those who are amenable to the opinion chiefly of that class, namely, its own members. It is known that the bad workmen who form the majority of the operatives in many branches of industry, are decidedly of opinion that bad workmen ought to receive the same wages as good, and that no one ought to be allowed, through piece-work or otherwise, to earn by superior skill or industry more than others can without it. And they employ a moral police, which occasionally becomes a physical one, to deter skilful workmen from receiving, and employers from giving, a larger remuneration for a more useful service. If the public have any jurisdiction over private concerns, I cannot see that these people are in fault, or that any individual's particular public can be blamed for asserting the same authority over his individual conduct, which the general public asserts over people in general.

But, without dwelling upon supposititious cases, there are, in our own day, gross usurpations upon the liberty of private life actually practised, and still greater ones threatened with some expectation of success, and opinions proposed which assert an unlimited right in the public not only to prohibit by law everything which it thinks wrong, but in order to get at what it thinks wrong, to prohibit any number of things which it admits to be innocent.

Under the name of preventing intemperance, the people of one English colony, and of nearly half the United States, have been interdicted by law from making any use whatever of fermented drinks, except for medical purposes: for prohibition of their sale is in fact, as it is intended to be, prohibition of their use. And though the impracticability of executing the law has caused its repeal in several of the States which had adopted it, including the one from which it derives its name, an attempt has notwithstanding been commenced, and is prosecuted with considerable zeal by many of the professed philanthropists, to agitate for a similar law in this country. The association, or 'Alliance' as it terms itself, which has been formed for this purpose, has acquired some notoriety through the publicity given to a correspondence between its Secretary and one of the very few English public men who hold that a politician's opinions ought to be founded on principles. Lord Stanley's share in this correspondence is calculated to strengthen the hopes already built on him, by those who know how rare such qualities as are manifested in some of his public appearances, unhappily are among those who figure in political life. The organ of the Alliance, who would 'deeply deplore the recognition of any principle which could be wrested to justify bigotry and persecution,' undertakes to point out the 'broad and impassable barrier' which divides such principles from those of the association. 'All matters relating to thought, opinion, conscience, appear to me,' he says, 'to be without the sphere of legislation; all pertaining to social act, habit, relation, subject only to a discretionary power vested in the State itself, and not in the individual, to be within it.' No mention is made of a third class, different from either of these, viz. acts and habits which are not social, but individual; although it is to this class, surely, that the act of drinking fermented liquors belongs. Selling fermented liquors, however, is trading, and trading is a social act. But the infringement complained of is not on the liberty of the seller, but on that of the buyer and consumer; since the State might just as well forbid him to drink wine, as purposely make it impossible for him to obtain it. The Secretary, however, says, 'I claim, as a citizen, a right to legislate whenever my social rights are invaded by the social act of another.' And now for the definition of these 'social rights.' 'If anything invades my social rights, certainly the traffic in strong drink does. It destroys my primary right of security, by constantly creating and stimulating social disorder. It invades my right of equality, by deriving a profit from the creation of a misery, I am taxed to support. It impedes my right to free moral and intellectual development, by surrounding my path with dangers, and by weakening and demoralizing society, from which I have a right to claim mutual aid and intercourse.' A theory of 'social rights,' the like of which probably never before found its way into distinct language—being nothing short of this—that it is the absolute social right of every individual, that every other individual shall act in every respect exactly as he ought; that whosoever fails thereof in the smallest particular, violates my social right, and entitles me to demand from the legislature the removal of the grievance. So monstrous a principle is far more dangerous than any single interference with liberty; there is no violation of liberty which it would not justify; it acknowledges no right to any freedom whatever, except perhaps to that of holding opinions in secret, without ever disclosing them: for the moment an opinion which I consider noxious, passes any one's lips, it invades all the 'social rights' attributed to me by the Alliance. The doctrine ascribes to all mankind a vested interest in each other's moral, intellectual, and even physical perfection to be defined by each claimant according to his own standard.

Another important example of illegitimate interference with the rightful liberty of the individual, not simply threatened, but long since carried into triumphant effect, is Sabbatarian legislation. Without doubt, abstinence on one day in the week, so far as the exigencies of life permit, from the usual daily occupation, though in no respect religiously binding on any except Jews, is a highly beneficial custom. And inasmuch as this custom cannot be observed without a general consent to that effect among the industrious classes, therefore, in so far as some persons by working may impose the same necessity on others, it may be allowable and right that the law should guarantee to each, the observance by others of the custom, by suspending the greater operations of industry on a particular day. But this justification, grounded on the direct interest which others have in each individual's observance of the practice, does not apply to the self-chosen occupations in which a person may think fit to employ his leisure; nor does it hold good, in the smallest degree, for legal restrictions on amusements. It is true that the amusement of some is the day's work of others; but the pleasure, not to say the useful recreation, of many, is worth the labour of a few, provided the occupation is freely chosen, and can be freely resigned. The operatives are perfectly right in thinking that if all worked on Sunday, seven days' work would have to be given for six days' wages: but so long as the great mass of employments are suspended, the small number who for the enjoyment of others must still work, obtain a proportional increase of earnings; and they are not obliged to follow those occupations, if they prefer leisure to emolument. If a further remedy is sought, it might be found in the establishment by custom of a holiday on some other day of the week, for those particular classes of persons. The only ground, therefore, on which restrictions on Sunday amusements can be defended, must be that they are religiously wrong; a motive of legislation which never can be too earnestly protested against. 'Deorum injuriæ Diis curæ.' It remains to be proved that society or any of its officers holds a commission from on high to avenge any supposed offence to Omnipotence, which is not also a wrong to our fellow creatures. The notion that it is one man's duty that another should be religious, was the foundation of all the religious persecutions ever perpetrated, and if admitted, would fully justify them. Though the feeling which breaks out in the repeated attempts to stop railway travelling on Sunday, in the resistance to the opening of Museums, and the like, has not the cruelty of the old persecutors, the state of mind indicated by it is fundamentally the same. It is a determination not to tolerate others in doing what is permitted by their religion, because it is not permitted by the persecutor's religion. It is a belief that God not only abominates the act of the misbeliever, but will not hold us guiltless if we leave him unmolested.

I cannot refrain from adding to these examples of the little account commonly made of human liberty, the language of downright persecution which breaks out from the press of this country, whenever it feels called on to notice the remarkable phenomenon of Mormonism. Much might be said on the unexpected and instructive fact, that an alleged new revelation, and a religion founded on it, the product of palpable imposture, not even supported by the *prestige* of extraordinary qualities in its founder, is believed by hundreds of thousands, and has been made the foundation of a society, in the age of newspapers, railways, and the electric telegraph. What here concerns us is, that this religion, like other and better religions, has its martyrs; that its prophet and founder was, for his teaching, put to death by a mob; that others of its adherents lost their lives by the same lawless violence; that they were forcibly expelled, in a body, from the country in which they first grew up; while, now that they have been chased into a solitary recess in the midst of a desert, many in this country openly declare that it would be right (only that it is not convenient) to send an expedition against them, and compel them by force to conform to the opinions of other people. The article of the Mormonite doctrine which is the chief provocative to the antipathy which thus breaks through the ordinary restraints of religious tolerance, is its sanction of polygamy; which, though permitted to Mahomedans, and Hindoos, and Chinese, seems to excite unquenchable animosity when practised by persons who speak English, and profess to be a kind of Christians. No one has a deeper disapprobation than I have of this Mormon institution; both for other reasons, and because, far from being in any way countenanced by the principle of liberty, it is a direct infraction of that principle, being a mere riveting of the chains of one half of the community, and an emancipation of the other from reciprocity of obligation towards them. Still, it must be remembered that this relation is as much voluntary on the part of the women concerned in it, and who may be deemed the sufferers by it, as is the case with any other form of the marriage institution;

and however surprising this fact may appear, it has its explanation in the common ideas and customs of the world, which, teaching women to think marriage the one thing needful, make it intelligible that many a woman should prefer being one of several wives, to not being a wife at all. Other countries are not asked to recognise such unions, or release any portion of their inhabitants from their own laws on the score of Mormonite opinions. But when the dissentients have conceded to the hostile sentiments of others, far more than could justly be demanded; when they have left the countries to which their doctrines were unacceptable, and established themselves in a remote corner of the earth, which they have been the first to render habitable to human beings; it is difficult to see on what principles but those of tyranny they can be prevented from living there under what laws they please, provided they commit no aggression on other nations, and allow perfect freedom of departure to those who are dissatisfied with their ways. A recent writer, in some respects of considerable merit, proposes (to use his own words,) not a crusade, but a *civilizade*, against this polygamous community, to put an end to what seems to him a retrograde step in civilization. It also appears so to me, but I am not aware that any community has a right to force another to be civilized. So long as the sufferers by the bad law do not invoke assistance from other communities, I cannot admit that persons entirely unconnected with them ought to step in and require that a condition of things with which all who are directly interested appear to be satisfied, should be put an end to because it is a scandal to persons some thousands of miles distant, who have no part or concern in it. Let them send missionaries, if they please, to preach against it; and let them, by any fair means (of which silencing the teachers is not one) oppose the progress of similar doctrines among their own people. If civilization has got the better of barbarism when barbarism had the world to itself, it is too much to profess to be afraid lest barbarism, after having been fairly got under, should revive and conquer civilization. A civilization that can thus succumb to its vanquished enemy, must first have become so degenerate, that neither its appointed priests and teachers, nor anybody else, has the capacity, or will take the trouble, to stand up for it. If this be so, the sooner such a civilization receives notice to quit, the better. It can only go on from bad to worse, until destroyed and regenerated (like the Western Empire) by energetic barbarians.

V. APPLICATIONS

THE principles asserted in these pages must be more generally admitted as the basis for discussion of details, before a consistent application of them to all the various departments of government and morals can be attempted with any prospect of advantage. The few observations I propose to make on questions of detail, are designed to illustrate the principles, rather than to follow them out to their consequences. I offer, not so much applications, as specimens of application; which may serve to bring into greater clearness the meaning and limits of the two maxims which together form the entire doctrine of this Essay, and to assist the judgment in holding the balance between them, in the cases where it appears doubtful which of them is applicable to the case.

The maxims are, first, that the individual is not accountable to society for his actions, in so far as these concern the interests of no person but himself. Advice, instruction, persuasion, and avoidance by other people if thought necessary by them for their own good, are the only measures by which society can justifiably express its dislike or disapprobation of his conduct. Secondly, that for such actions as are prejudicial to the interests of others, the individual is accountable, and may be subjected either to social or to legal punishments, if society is of opinion that the one or the other is requisite for its protection.

In the first place, it must by no means be supposed, because damage, or probability of damage, to the interests of others, can alone justify the interference of society, that therefore it always does justify such interference. In many cases, an individual, in pursuing a legitimate object, necessarily and therefore legitimately causes pain or loss to others, or intercepts a good which they had a reasonable hope of obtaining. Such oppositions of interest between individuals often arise from bad social institutions, but are unavoidable while those institutions last; and some would be unavoidable under any institutions. Whoever succeeds in an overcrowded profession, or in a competitive examination; whoever is preferred to another in any contest for an object which both desire, reaps benefit from the loss of others, from their wasted exertion and their disappointment. But it is, by common admission, better for the general interest of mankind, that persons should pursue their objects undeterred by this sort of consequences. In other words, society admits no right, either legal or moral, in the disappointed competitors, to immunity from this kind of suffering; and feels called on to interfere, only when means of success have been employed which it is contrary to the general interest to permit—namely, fraud or treachery, and force.

Again, trade is a social act. Whoever undertakes to sell any description of goods to the public, does what affects the interest of other persons, and of society in general; and thus his conduct, in principle, comes within the jurisdiction of society: accordingly, it was once held to be the duty of governments, in all cases which were considered of importance, to fix prices, and regulate the processes of manufacture. But it is now recognised, though not till after a long struggle, that both the cheapness and the good quality of commodities are most effectually provided for by leaving the producers and sellers perfectly free, under the sole check of equal freedom to the buyers for supplying themselves elsewhere. This is the so-called doctrine of Free Trade, which rests on grounds different from, though equally solid with, the principle of individual liberty asserted in this Essay. Restrictions on trade, or on production for purposes of trade, are indeed restraints; and all restraint, *quâ* restraint, is an evil: but the restraints in question affect only that part of conduct which society is competent to restrain, and are wrong solely because they do not really produce the results which it is desired to produce by them. As the principle of individual liberty is not involved in the doctrine of Free Trade, so neither is it in most of the questions which arise respecting the limits of that doctrine: as for example, what amount of public control is admissible for the prevention of fraud by adulteration; how far sanitary precautions, or arrangements to protect workpeople employed in dangerous occupations, should be enforced on employers. Such questions involve considerations of liberty, only in so far as leaving people to themselves is always better, *cæteris paribus*, than controlling them: but that they may be legitimately controlled for these ends, is in principle undeniable. On the other hand, there are questions relating to interference with trade, which are essentially questions of liberty; such as the Maine Law, already touched upon; the prohibition of the importation of opium into China; the restriction of the sale of poisons; all cases, in short, where the object of the interference is to make it impossible or difficult to obtain a particular commodity. These interferences are objectionable, not as infringements on the liberty of the producer or seller, but on that of the buyer.

One of these examples, that of the sale of poisons, opens a new question; the proper limits of what may be called the functions of police; how far liberty may legitimately be invaded for the prevention of crime, or of accident. It is one of the undisputed functions of government to take precautions against crime before it has been committed, as well as to detect and punish it afterwards. The preventive function of government, however, is far more liable to be abused, to the prejudice of liberty, than the punitory function; for there is hardly any part of the legitimate freedom of action of a human being which would not admit of being represented, and fairly too, as increasing the facilities for some form or other of delinquency. Nevertheless, if a public authority, or even a private person, sees any one evidently preparing to commit a crime, they are not bound to look on inactive until the crime is committed, but may interfere to prevent it. If poisons were never bought or used for any purpose except the commission of murder, it would be right to prohibit their manufacture and sale. They may, however, be wanted not only for innocent but for useful purposes, and restrictions cannot be imposed in the one case without operating in the other. Again it is a proper office of public authority to guard against accidents. If either a public officer or any one else saw a person attempting to cross a bridge which had been ascertained to be unsafe, and there were no time to warn him of his danger, they might seize him and turn him back, without any real infringement of his liberty: for liberty consists in doing what one desires, and he does not desire to fall into the river. Nevertheless, when there is not a certainty, but only a danger of mischief, no one but the person himself can judge of the sufficiency of the motive which may prompt him to incur the risk: in this case, therefore, (unless he is a child, or delirious, or in some state of excitement or absorption incompatible with the full use of the reflecting faculty), he ought, I conceive, to be only warned of the danger; not forcibly prevented from exposing himself to it. Similar considerations, applied to such a question as the sale of poisons, may enable us to decide which among the possible modes of regulation are or are not contrary to principle. Such a precaution, for example, as that of labelling the drug with some word expressive of its dangerous character, may be enforced without violation of liberty: the buyer cannot wish not to know that the thing he possesses has poisonous qualities. But to require in all cases the certificate of a medical practitioner, would make it sometimes impossible, always expensive, to obtain the article for legitimate uses. The only mode apparent to me, in which difficulties may be thrown in the way of crime committed through this means, without any infringement, worth taking into account, upon the liberty of those who desire the poisonous substance for other purposes, consists in providing what, in the apt language of Bentham, is called 'preappointed evidence.' This provision is familiar to every one in the case of contracts. It is usual and right that the law, when a contract is entered into, should require as the condition of its enforcing performance, that certain formalities should be observed, such as signatures, attestation of witnesses, and the like, in order that in case of subsequent dispute, there may be evidence to prove that the contract was really entered into, and that there was nothing in the circumstances to render it legally invalid: the effect being, to throw great obstacles in the way of fictitious contracts, or contracts made in circumstances which, if known, would destroy their validity. Precautions of a similar nature might be enforced in the sale of articles adapted to be instruments of crime. The seller, for example, might be required to enter in a register the exact time of the transaction, the name and address of the buyer, the precise quality and quantity sold: to ask the purpose for which it was wanted, and record the answer he received. When there was no medical prescription, the presence of some third person might be required to bring home the fact to the purchaser, in case there should afterwards be reason to believe that the article had been applied to criminal purposes. Such regulations would in general be no material impediment to obtaining the article, but a very considerable one to making an improper use of it without detection.

The right inherent in society, to ward off crimes against itself by antecedent precautions, suggests the obvious limitations to the maxim, that purely self-regarding misconduct cannot properly be meddled with in the way of prevention or punishment. Drunkenness, for example, in ordinary cases, is not a fit subject for legislative interference; but I should deem it perfectly legitimate that a person, who had once been convicted of any act of violence to others under the influence of drink, should be placed under a special legal restriction, personal to himself; that if he were afterwards found drunk, he should be liable to a penalty, and that if when in that state he committed another offence, the punishment to which he would be liable for that other offence should be increased in severity. The making himself drunk, in a person whom drunkenness excites to do harm to others, is a crime against others. So, again, idleness, except in a person receiving support from the public, or except when it constitutes a breach of contract, cannot without tyranny be made a subject of legal punishment: but if either from idleness or from any other avoidable cause, a man fails to perform his legal duties to others, as for instance to support his children, it is no tyranny to force him to fulfil that obligation, by compulsory labour, if no other means are available.

Again, there are many acts which, being directly injurious only to the agents themselves, ought not to be legally interdicted, but which, if done publicly, are a violation of good manners, and coming thus within the category of offences against others, may rightfully be prohibited. Of this kind are offences against decency; on which it is unnecessary to dwell, the rather as they are only connected indirectly with our subject, the objection to publicity being equally strong in the case of many actions not in themselves condemnable, nor supposed to be so.

There is another question to which an answer must be found, consistent with the principles which have been laid down. In cases of personal conduct supposed to be blameable but which respect for liberty precludes society from preventing or punishing, because the evil directly resulting falls wholly on the agent; what the agent is free to do, ought other persons to be equally free to counsel or instigate? This question is not free from difficulty. The case of a person who solicits another to do an act, is not strictly a case of self-regarding conduct. To give advice or offer inducements to any one, is a social act, and may therefore, like actions in general which effect others, be supposed amenable to social control. But a little reflection corrects the first impression, by showing that if the case is not strictly within the definition of individual liberty, yet the reasons on which the principle of individual liberty is grounded, are applicable to it. If people must be allowed, in whatever concerns only themselves, to act as seems best to themselves at their own peril, they must equally be free to consult with one another about what is fit to be so done; to exchange opinions, and give and receive suggestions. Whatever it is permitted to do, it must be permitted to advise to do. The question is doubtful, only when the instigator derives a personal benefit from his advice; when he makes it his occupation, for subsistence or pecuniary gain, to promote

what society and the State consider to be an evil. Then, indeed, a new element of complication is introduced; namely,
the existence of classes of persons with an interest opposed
to what is considered as the public weal, and whose mode of
living is grounded on the counteraction of it. Ought this to
be interfered with, or not? Fornication, for example, must be
tolerated, and so must gambling; but should a person be free
to be a pimp, or to keep a gambling-house? The case is one
of those which lie on the exact boundary line between two
principles, and it is not at once apparent to which of the two
it properly belongs. There are arguments on both sides. On
the side of toleration it may be said, that the fact of following
anything as an occupation, and living or profiting by the practice of it, cannot make that criminal which would otherwise
be admissible; that the act should either be consistently permitted or consistently prohibited; that if the principles which
we have hitherto defended are true, society has no business,
as society, to decide anything to be wrong which concerns
only the individual: that it cannot go beyond dissuasion, and
that one person should be as free to persuade, as another to
dissuade. In opposition to this it may be contended, that although the public, or the State, are not warranted in authorita-
tively deciding, for purposes of repression or punishment, that
such or such conduct affecting only the interests of the individual is good or bad, they are fully justified in assuming, if they
regard it as bad, that its being so or not is at least a disputable question. That, this being supposed, they cannot be acting
wrongly in endeavouring to exclude the influence of solicitations which are not disinterested, of instigators who cannot
possibly be impartial—who have a direct personal interest on
one side, and that side the one which the State believes to
be wrong, and who confessedly promote it for personal objects
only. There can surely, it may be urged, be nothing lost, no
sacrifice of good, by so ordering matters that persons shall
make their election, either wisely or foolishly, on their own
prompting, as free as possible from the arts of persons who
stimulate their inclinations for interested purposes of their
own. Thus (it may be said) though the statutes respecting
unlawful games are utterly indefensible—though all persons
should be free to gamble in their own or each other's houses,
or in any place of meeting established by their own subscriptions, and open only to the members and their visitors—yet
public gambling-houses should not be permitted. It is true
that the prohibition is never effectual, and that whatever

amount of tyrannical power is given to the police, gambling-houses can always be maintained under other pretences; but they may be compelled to conduct their operations with a certain degree of secrecy and mystery, so that nobody knows anything about them but those who seek them; and more than this, society ought not to aim at. There is considerable force in these arguments. I will not venture to decide whether they are sufficient to justify the moral anomaly of punishing the accessory, when the principal is (and must be) allowed to go free; of fining or imprisoning the procurer, but not the fornicator, the gambling-house keeper, but not the gambler. Still less ought the common operations of buying and selling to be interfered with on analogous grounds. Almost every article which is bought and sold may be used in excess, and the sellers have a pecuniary interest in encouraging that excess; but no argument can be founded on this, in favour, for instance, of the Maine Law; because the class of dealers in strong drinks, though interested in their abuse, are indispensably required for the sake of their legitimate use. The interest, however, of these dealers in promoting intemperance is a real evil, and justifies the State in imposing restrictions and requiring guarantees, which but for that justification would be infringements of legitimate liberty.

A further question is, whether the State, while it permits, should nevertheless indirectly discourage conduct which it deems contrary to the best interests of the agent; whether, for example, it should take measures to render the means of drunkenness more costly, or add to the difficulty of procuring them, by limiting the number of the places of sale. On this as on most other practical questions, many distinctions require to be made. To tax stimulants for the sole purpose of making them more difficult to be obtained, is a measure differing only in degree from their entire prohibition; and would be justifiable only if that were justifiable. Every increase of cost is a prohibition, to those whose means do not come up to the augmented price; and to those who do, it is a penalty laid on them for gratifying a particular taste. Their choice of pleasures, and their mode of expending their income, after satisfying their legal and moral obligations to the State and to individuals, are their own concern, and must rest with their own judgment. These considerations may seem at first sight to condemn the selection of stimulants as special subjects of taxation for purposes of revenue. But it must be remembered that taxation for fiscal purposes is absolutely inevitable; that in most countries it is necessary that a considerable part of that taxation should be indirect; that the State, therefore, cannot help imposing penalties, which to some persons may be prohibitory, on the use of some articles of consumption. It is hence the duty of the State to consider, in the imposition of taxes, what commodities the consumers can best spare; and *à fortiori*, to select in preference those of which it deems the use, beyond a very moderate quantity, to be positively injurious. Taxation, therefore, of stimulants, up to the point which produces the largest amount of revenue (supposing that the State needs all the revenue which it yields) is not only admissible, but to be approved of.

The question of making the sale of these commodities a more or less exclusive privilege, must be answered differently, according to the purposes to which the restriction is intended to be subservient. All places of public resort require the restraint of a police, and places of this kind peculiarly, because offences against society are especially apt to originate there. It is, therefore, fit to confine the power of selling these commodities (at least for consumption on the spot) to persons of known or vouched-for respectability of conduct; to make such regulations respecting hours of opening and closing as may be requisite for public surveillance, and to withdraw the licence if breaches of the peace repeatedly take place through the connivance or incapacity of the keeper of the house, or if it bcomes a rendezvous for concocting and preparing offences against the law. Any further restriction I do not conceive to be, in principle, justifiable. The limitation in number, for instance, of beer and spirit-houses, for the express purpose of rendering them more difficult of access, and diminishing the occasions of temptations, not only exposes all to an inconvenience because there are some by whom the facility would be abused, but is suited only to a state of society in which the labouring classes are avowedly treated as children or savages, and placed under an education of restraint, to fit them for future admission to the privileges of freedom. This is not the principle on which the labouring classes are professedly governed in any free country; and no person who sets due value on freedom will give his adhesion to their being so governed, unless after all efforts have been exhausted to educate them for freedom and govern them as freemen, and it has been definitely proved that they can only be governed as children. The bare statement of the alternative shows the absurdity of supposing that such efforts have been made in any case which needs be considered here. It is only because the institutions of this country are a mass of inconsistencies, that things find admittance into our practice which belong to the system of despotic, or what is called paternal, government, while the general freedom of our institutions precludes the exercise of the amount of control necessary to render the restraint of any real efficacy as a moral education.

It was pointed out in an early part of this Essay, that the liberty of the individual, in things wherein the individual is alone concerned, implies a corresponding liberty in any number of individuals to regulate by mutual agreement such things as regard them jointly, and regard no persons but themselves. This question presents no difficulty, so long as the will of all the persons implicated remains unaltered; but since that will may change, it is often necessary, even in things in which they alone are concerned, that they should enter into engagements with one another; and when they do, it is fit, as a general rule, that those engagements should be kept. Yet in the laws, probably, of every country, this general rule has some exceptions. Not only persons are not held to engagements which violate the rights of third parties, but it is sometimes considered a sufficient reason for releasing them from an engagement, that it is injurious to themselves. In this and most other civilized countries, for example, an engagement by which a person should sell himself, or allow himself to be sold, as a slave, would be null and void; neither enforced by law nor by opinion. The ground for thus limiting his power of voluntarily disposing of his own lot in life, is apparent, and is very clearly seen in this extreme case. The reason for not interfering, unless for the sake of others, with a person's voluntary acts, is consideration for his liberty. His voluntary choice is evidence that what he so chooses is desirable, or at the least endurable, to him, and his good is on the whole best provided for by allowing him to take his own means of pursuing it. But by selling himself for a slave, he abdicates his liberty; he forgoes any future use of it, beyond that single act. He therefore defeats, in his own case, the very purpose which is the justification of allowing him to dispose of himself. He is no longer free; but is thenceforth in a position which has no longer the presumption in its favour, that would be afforded by his voluntarily remaining in it. The principle of freedom cannot require that he should be free not to be free. It is not freedom, to be allowed to alienate his freedom. These reasons, the force of which is so conspicuous in this peculiar case, are evidently of far wider application; yet a limit is everywhere set to them by the necessities of life, which continually require, not indeed that we should resign our freedom, but that we should consent to this and the other limitation of it. The principle, however, which demands uncontrolled freedom of action in all that concerns only the agents themselves, requires that those who have become bound to one another, in things which concern no third party, should be able to release one another from the engagement: and even without such voluntary release, there are perhaps no contracts or engagements, except those that relate to money or money's worth, of which one can venture to say that there ought to be no liberty whatever of retractation. Baron Wilhelm von Humboldt, in the excellent essay from which I have already quoted, states it as his conviction, that engagements which involve personal relations or services should never be legally binding beyond a limited duration of time; and that the most important of these engagements, marriage, having the peculiarity that its objects are frustrated unless the feelings of both the parties are in harmony with it, should require nothing more than the declared will of either party to dissolve it. This subject is too important, and too complicated, to be discussed in a parenthesis, and I touch on it only so far as is necessary for purposes of illustration. If the conciseness and generality of Baron Humboldt's dissertation had not obliged him in this instance to content himself with enunciating his conclusion without discussing the premises, he would doubtless have recognised that the question cannot be decided on grounds so simple as those to which he confines himself. When a person, either by express promise or by conduct, has encouraged another to rely upon his continuing to act in a certain way—to build expectations and calculations, and stake any part of his plan of life upon that supposition, a new series of moral obligations arises on his part towards that person, which may possibly be overruled, but cannot be ignored. And again, if the relation between two contracting parties has been followed by consequences to others; if it has placed third parties in any peculiar position, or, as in the case of marriage, has even called third parties into existence, obligations arise on the part of both the contracting parties towards those third persons, the fulfilment of which, or at all events the mode of fulfilment, must be greatly affected by the continuance or disruption of the relation between the original parties to the contract. It does not follow, nor can I admit, that these obligations extend to requiring the fulfilment of the contract at all costs to the happiness of the reluctant party; but they are a necessary element in the question; and even if, as Von Humboldt maintains, they ought to make no difference in the *legal* freedom of the parties to release themselves from the engagement (and I also hold that they ought not to make *much* difference), they necessarily make a great difference in the *moral* freedom. A person is bound to take all these circumstances into account, before resolving on a step which may affect such important interests of others; and if he does not allow proper weight to those interests, he is morally responsible for the wrong. I have made these obvious remarks for the better illustration of the general principle of liberty, and not because they are at all needed on the particular question, which, on the contrary, is usually discussed as if the interest of children was everything, and that of grown persons nothing.

I have already observed that, owing to the absence of any recognised general principles, liberty is often granted where it should be withheld, as well as withheld where it should be granted; and one of the cases in which, in the modern European world, the sentiment of liberty is the strongest, is a case where, in my view, it is altogether misplaced. A person should be free to do as he likes in his own concerns; but he ought not to be free to do as he likes in acting for another under the pretext that the affairs of another are his own affairs. The State, while it respects the liberty of each in what specially regards himself, is bound to maintain a vigilant control over his exercise of any power which it allows him to possess over others. This obligation is almost entirely disregarded in the case of the family relations, a case, in its direct influence on human happiness, more important than all others taken together. The almost despotic power of husbands over wives needs not be enlarged upon here, because nothing more is needed for the complete removal of the evil, than that wives should have the same rights, and should receive the protection of law in the same manner, as all other persons; and because, on this subject, the defenders of established injustice do not avail themselves of the plea of liberty, but stand forth openly as the champions of power. It is in the case of children, that misapplied notions of liberty are a real obstacle to the fulfilment by the State of its duties. One would almost think that a man's children were supposed to be literally, and not metaphorically, a part of himself, so jealous is opinion of the smallest interference of law with his absolute and exclusive control over them; more jealous than of almost any interference with his own freedom of action; so much less do the generality of mankind value liberty than power. Consider, for example, the case of education. Is it not almost a self-evident axiom, that the State should require and compel the education, up to a certain standard, of every human being who is born its citizen? Yet who is there that is not afraid to recognise and assert this truth? Hardly any one indeed will deny that it is one of the most sacred duties of the parents (or, as law and usage now stand, the father), after summoning a human being into the world, to give to that being an education fitting him to perform his part well in life towards others and towards himself. But while this is unanimously declared to be the father's duty, scarcely anybody, in this country, will bear to hear of obliging him to perform it. Instead of his being required to make any exertion or sacrifice for securing education to the child, it is left to his choice to accept it or not when it is provided gratis! It still remains unrecognised, that to bring a child into existence without a fair prospect of being able, not only to provide food for its body, but instruction and training for its mind, is a moral crime, both against the unfortunate offspring and against society; and that if the parent does not fulfil this obligation, the State ought to see it fulfilled at the charge, as far as possible, of the parent.

Were the duty of enforcing universal education once admitted, there would be an end to the difficulties about what the State should teach, and how it should teach, which now convert the subject into a mere battle-field for sects and parties, causing time and labour which should have been spent in educating, to be wasted in quarrelling about education. If the government would make up its minds to *require* for every child a good education, it might save itself the trouble of *providing* one. It might leave to parents to obtain the education where and how they pleased, and content itself with helping to pay the school fees of the poorer classes of children, and defraying the entire school expenses of those who have no one else to pay for them. The objections which are urged with reason against State education, do not apply to the enforcement of education by the State, but to the State's taking upon itself to direct that education: which is a totally different thing. That the whole or any large part of the education of the people should be in State hands, I go as far as any one in deprecating. All that has been said of the importance of individuality of character, and diversity in opinions and modes of conduct, involves, as of the same unspeakable importance, diversity of education. A general State education is a mere contrivance for moulding people to be exactly like one another: and as the mould in which it casts them is that which pleases the predominant power in the government, whether this be a monarch, a priesthood, an aristocracy, or the majority of the existing generation, in proportion as it is efficient and successful, it establishes a despotism over the mind, leading by natural tendency to one over the body. An education established and controlled by the State, should only exist, if it exist at all, as one among many competing experiments, carried on for the purpose of example and stimulus, to keep the others up to a certain standard of excellence. Unless, indeed, when society in general is in so backward a state that it could not or would not provide for itself any proper institutions of education, unless the government undertook the task; then, indeed, the government may, as the less of two great evils, take upon itself the business of schools and universities, as it may that of joint stock companies, when private enterprise, in a shape fitted for undertaking great works of industry, does not exist in the country. But in general, if the country contains a sufficient number of persons qualified to provide education under government auspices, the same persons would be able and willing to give an equally good education on the voluntary principle, under the assurance of remuneration afforded by a law rendering education compulsory, combined with State aid to those unable to defray the expense.

The instrument for enforcing the law could be no other than public examinations, extending to all children, and beginning at an early age. An age might be fixed at which every child must be examined, to ascertain if he (or she) is able to read. If a child proves unable, the father, unless he has some sufficient ground of excuse, might be subjected to a moderate fine, to be worked out, if necessary, by his labour, and the child might be put to school at his expense. Once in every year the examination should be renewed, with a gradually extending range of subjects, so as to make the universal acquisition, and what is more, retention, of a certain minimum of general knowledge, virtually compulsory. Beyond that minimum, there should be voluntary examinations on all subjects, at which all who came up to a certain standard of proficiency might claim a certificate. To prevent the State from exercising through these arrangements, an improper influence over opinion, the knowledge required for passing an examination (beyond the merely instrumental parts of knowledge, such as languages and their use) should, even in the higher class of examinations, be confined to facts and positive science exclusively. The examinations on religion, politics, or other disputed topics, should not turn on the truth or falsehood of opinions, but on the matter of fact that such and such an opinion is held, on such grounds, by such authors, or schools, or churches. Under this system, the rising generation would be no worse off in regard to all disputed truths, than they are at present; they would be brought up either churchmen or dissenters as they are now, the State merely taking care that they should be instructed churchmen, or instructed dissenters. There would be nothing to hinder them from being taught religion, if their parents chose, at the same schools where they were taught other things. All attempts by the State to bias the conclusions of its citizens on disputed subjects, are evil; but it may very properly offer to ascertain and certify that a person possesses the knowledge, requisite to make his conclusions, on any given subject, worth attending to. A student of philosophy would be the better for being able to stand an examination both in Locke and in Kant, whichever of the two he takes up with, or even if with neither: and there is no reasonable objection to examining an atheist in the evidences of Christianity, provided he is not required to profess a belief in them. The examinations, however, in the higher branches of knowledge should, I conceive, be entirely voluntary. It would be giving too dangerous a power to governments, were they allowed to exclude any one from professions, even from the profession of teacher, for alleged deficiency of qualifications: and I think, with Wilhelm von Humboldt, that degrees, or other public certificates of scientific or professional acquirements, should be given to all who present themselves for examination, and stand the test; but that such certificates should confer no advantage over competitors, other than the weight which may be attached to their testimony by public opinion.

It is not in the matter of education only, that misplaced notions of liberty prevent moral obligations on the part of parents from being recognised, and legal obligations from being imposed, where there are the strongest grounds for the former always, and in many cases for the latter also. The fact itself, of causing the existence of a human being, is one of the most responsible actions in the range of human life. To undertake this responsibility—to bestow a life which may be either a curse or a blessing—unless the being on whom it is to be bestowed will have at least the ordinary chances of a desirable existence, is a crime against that being. And in a country either over-peopled, or threatened with being so, to produce children, beyond a very small number, with the effect of reducing the reward of labour by their competition, is a serious offence against all who live by the remuneration of their labour. The laws which, in many countries on the Continent, forbid marriage unless the parties can show that they have the means of supporting a family, do not exceed the legitimate powers of the State: and whether such laws be expedient or not (a question mainly dependent on local circumstances and feelings), they are not objectionable as violations of liberty. Such laws are interferences of the State to prohibit a mischievous act—an act injurious to others, which ought to be a subject of reprobation, and social stigma, even when it is not deemed expedient to superadd legal punishment. Yet the current ideas of liberty, which bend so easily to real infringements of the individual, in things which concern only himself, would repel the attempt to put any restraint upon his inclinations when the consequence of their indulgence is a life, or lives, of wretchedness and depravity to the offspring, with manifold evils to those sufficiently within reach to be in any way affected by their actions. When we compare the strange respect of mankind for liberty, with their strange want of respect for it, we might imagine that a man had an indispensable right to do harm to others, and no right at all to please himself without giving pain to any one.

I have reserved for the last place a large class of questions respecting the limits of government interference, which, though closely connected with the subject of this Essay, do not, in strictness, belong to it. These are cases in which the reasons against interference do not turn upon the principle of liberty: the question is not about restraining the actions of individuals, but about helping them: it is asked whether the government should do, or cause to be done, something for their benefit, instead of leaving it to be done by themselves, individually, or in voluntary combination.

The objections to government interference, when it is not such as to involve infringement of liberty, may be of three kinds.

The first is, when the thing to be done is likely to be better done by individuals than by the government. Speaking generally, there is no one so fit to conduct any business, or to determine how or by whom it shall be conducted as those who are personally interested in it. This principle condemns the interferences, once so common, of the legislature, or the officers of government, with the ordinary processes of industry. But this part of the subject has been sufficiently enlarged upon by political economists, and is not particularly related to the principles of this Essay.

The second objection is more nearly allied to our subject. In many cases, though individuals may not do the particular thing so well, on the average, as the officers of government, it is nevertheless desirable that it should be done by them, rather than by the government, as a means to their own mental education—a mode of strengthening their active faculties, exercising their judgment, and giving them a familiar knowledge of the subjects with which they are thus left to deal. This is a principal, though not the sole, recommendation of jury trial (in cases not political); of free and popular local and municipal institutions; of the conduct of industrial and philanthropic enterprises by voluntary associations. These are not questions of liberty, and are connected with that subject only by remote tendencies; but they are questions of development. It belongs to a different occasion from the present to dwell on these things as parts of national education; as being, in truth, the peculiar training of a citizen, the practical part of the political education of a free people, taking them out of the narrow circle of personal and family selfishness, and accustoming them to the comprehension of joint interests, the management of joint concerns—habituating them to act from public or semi-public motives, and guide their conduct by aims which unite instead of isolating them from one another. Without these habits and powers, a free constitution can neither be worked nor preserved, as is exemplified by the too-often transitory nature of political freedom in countries where it does not rest upon a sufficient basis of local liberties. The management of purely local business by the localities, and of the great enterprises of industry by the union of those who voluntarily supply the pecuniary means, is further recommended by all the advantages which have been set forth in this Essay as belonging to individuality of development, and diversity of modes of action. Government operations tend to be everywhere alike. With individuals and voluntary associations, on the contrary, there are varied experiments, and endless diversity of experience. What the State can usefully do, is to make itself a central depository, and active circulator and diffuser, of the experience resulting from many trials. Its business is to enable each experimentalist to benefit by the experiments of others, instead of tolerating no experiments but its own.

The third, and most cogent reason for restricting the interference of government, is the great evil of adding unnecessarily to its power. Every function superadded to those already exercised by the government, causes its influence over hopes and fears to be more widely diffused, and converts, more and more, the active and ambitious part of the public into hangers-on of the government, or of some party which aims at becoming the government. If the roads, the railways, the banks, the insurance offices, the great joint-stock companies, the universities, and the public charities, were all of them branches of the government; if, in addition, the municipal corporations and local boards, with all that now devolves on them, became departments of the central administration; if the employés of all these different enterprises were appointed and paid by the government, and looked to the government for every rise in life; not all the freedom of the press and popular constitution of the legislature would make this or any other country free otherwise than in name. And the evil would be greater, the more efficiently and scientifically the administrative machinery was constructed—the more skilful the arrangements for obtaining the best qualified hands and heads with which to work it. In England it has of late been proposed that all the members of the civil service of government should be selected by competitive examination, to obtain for those employments the most intelligent and instructed persons procurable; and much has been said and written for and against this proposal. One of the arguments most insisted on by its opponents, is that the occupation of a permanent official servant of the State does not hold out sufficient prospects of emolument and importance to attract the highest talents, which will always be able to find a more inviting career in the professions, or in the service of companies and other public bodies. One would not have been surprised if this argument had been used by the friends of the proposition, as an answer to its principal difficulty. Coming from the opponents it is strange enough. What is urged as an objection is the safety valve of the proposed system. If indeed all the high talent of the country *could* be drawn into the service of the government, a proposal tending to bring about that result might well inspire uneasiness. If every part of the business of society which required organized concert, or large and comprehensive views, were in the hands of the government, and if government offices were universally filled by the ablest men, all the enlarged culture and practised intelligence in the country, except the purely speculative, would be concentrated in a numerous bureaucracy, to whom alone the rest of the community would look for all things: the multitude for direction and dictation in all they had to do; the able and aspiring for personal advancement. To be admitted into the ranks of this bureaucracy, and when admitted, to rise therein, would be the sole objects of ambition. Under this régime, not only is the outside public ill-qualified, for want of practical experience, to criticize or check the mode of operation of the bureaucracy, but even if the accidents of despotic or the natural working of popular institutions occasionally raise to the summit a ruler or rulers of reforming inclinations, no reform can be effected which is contrary to the interest of the bureaucracy. Such is the melancholy condition of the Russian empire, as is shown in the accounts of those who have had sufficient opportunity of observation. The Czar himself is powerless against the bureaucratic body; he can send any one of them to Siberia, but he cannot govern without them, or against their will. On every decree of his they have a tacit veto, by merely refraining from carrying it into effect. In countries of more advanced civilization and of a more insurrectionary spirit, the public, accustomed to expect everything to be done for them by the State, or at least to do nothing for themselves without asking from the State not only leave to do it, but even how it is to be done, naturally hold the State responsible for all evil which befalls them, and when the evil exceeds their amount of patience, they rise against the government and make what is called a revolution; whereupon somebody else, with or without legitimate authority from the nation, vaults into the seat, issues his orders to the bureaucracy, and everything goes on much as it did before; the bureaucracy being unchanged, and nobody else being capable of taking their place.

A very different spectacle is exhibited among a people accustomed to transact their own business. In France, a large part of the people having been engaged in military service, many of whom have held at least the rank of non-commissioned officers, there are in every popular insurrection several persons competent to take the lead, and improvise some tolerable plan of action. What the French are in military affairs, the Americans are in every kind of civil business; let them be left without a government, every body of Americans is able to improvise one, and to carry on that or any other public business with a sufficient amount of intelligence, order, and decision. This is what every free people ought to be: and a people capable of this is certain to be free; it will never let itself be enslaved by any man or body of men because these are able to seize and pull the reins of the central administration. No bureaucracy can hope to make such a people as this do or undergo anything that they do not like. But when everything is done through the bureaucracy, nothing to which the bureaucracy is really adverse can be done at all. The constitution of such countries is an organization of the experience and practical ability of the nation, into a disciplined body for the purpose of governing the rest; and the more perfect that organization is in itself, the more successful in drawing to itself and educating for itself the persons of greatest capacity from all ranks of the community, the more complete is the bondage of all, the members of the bureaucracy included. For the governors are as much the slaves of their organization and discipline, as the governed are of the governors. A Chinese mandarin is as much the tool and creature of a despotism as the humblest cultivator. An individual Jesuit is to the utmost degree of abasement the slave of his order, though the order itself exists for the collective power and importance of its members.

It is not, also, to be forgotten, that the absorption of all the principal ability of the country into the governing body is fatal, sooner or later, to the mental activity and progressiveness of the body itself. Banded together as they are—working a system which, like all systems, necessarily proceeds in a great measure by fixed rules—the official body are under the constant temptation of sinking into indolent routine, or, if they now and then desert that mill-horse round, of rushing into some half-examined crudity which has struck the fancy of some leading member of the corps: and the sole check to these closely allied, though seemingly opposite, tendencies, the only stimulus which can keep the ability of the body itself up to a high standard, is liability to the watchful criticism of equal ability outside the body. It is indispensable, therefore, that the means should exist, independently of the government, of forming such ability, and furnishing it with the opportunities and experience necessary for a correct judgment of great practical affairs. If we would possess permanently a skilful and efficient body of functionaries—above all, a body able to originate and willing to adopt improvements; if we would not have our bureaucracy degenerate into a pedantocracy, this body must not engross all the occupations which form and cultivate the faculties required for the government of mankind.

To determine the point at which evils, so formidable to human freedom and advancement, begin, or rather at which they begin to predominate over the benefits attending the collective application of the force of society, under its recognised chiefs, for the removal of the obstacles which stand in the way of its well-being; to secure as much of the advantages of centralized power and intelligence, as can be had without turning into governmental channels too great a proportion of the general activity, is one of the most difficult and complicated questions in the art of government. It is, in a great measure, a question of detail, in which many and various considerations must be kept in view, and no absolute rule can be laid down. But I believe that the practical principle in which safety resides, the ideal to be kept in view, the standard by which to test all arrangements intended for overcoming the difficulty, may be conveyed in these words: the greatest dissemination of power consistent with efficiency; but the greatest possible centralization of information, and diffusion of it from the centre. Thus, in municipal administration, there would be, as in the New England States, a very minute division among separate officers, chosen by the localities, of all business which is not better left to the persons directly interested; but besides this, there would be, in each department of local affairs, a central superintendence, forming a branch of the general government. The organ of this superintendence would concentrate, as in a focus, the variety of information and experience derived from the conduct of that branch of public business in all the localities, from everything analogous which is done in foreign countries, and from the general principles of political science. This central organ should have a right to know all that is done, and its special duty should be that of making the knowledge acquired in one place available for others. Emancipated from the petty prejudices and narrow views of a locality by its elevated position and comprehensive sphere of observation, its advice would naturally carry much authority; but its actual power, as a permanent institution, should, I conceive, be limited to compelling the local officers to obey the laws laid down for their guidance. In all things not provided for by general rules, those officers should be left to their own judgment, under responsibility to their constituents. For the violation of rules, they

should be responsible to law, and the rules themselves should
be laid down by the legislature; the central administrative
authority only watching over their execution, and if they were
not properly carried into effect, appealing, according to the
nature of the case, to the tribunal to enforce the law, or to the
constituencies to dismiss the functionaries who had not executed it according to its spirit. Such, in its general conception,
is the central superintendence which the Poor Law Board is
intended to exercise over the administrators of the Poor Rate
throughout the country. Whatever powers the Board exercises
beyond this limit, were right and necessary in that peculiar
case, for the curse of rooted habits of maladministration in
matters deeply affecting not the localities merely, but the
whole community; since no locality has a moral right to make
itself by mismanagement a nest of pauperism, necessarily
overflowing into other localities, and impairing the moral and
physical condition of the whole labouring community. The
powers of administrative coercion and subordinate legislation
possessed by the Poor Law Board (but which, owing to the
state of opinion on the subject, are very scantily exercised by
them), though perfectly justifiable in a case of first-rate national interest, would be wholly out of place in the superintendence of interests purely local. But a central organ of
information and instruction for all the localities, would be
equally valuable in all departments of administration. A government cannot have too much of the kind of activity which
does not impede, but aids and stimulates, individual exertion
and development. The mischief begins when, instead of calling
forth the activity and powers of individuals and bodies, it
substitutes its own activity for theirs; when, instead of informing, advising, and, upon occasion, denouncing, it makes them
work in fetters, or bids them stand aside and does their work
instead of them. The worth of a State, in the long run, is the
worth of the individuals composing it; and a State which post-
pones the interests of *their* mental expansion and elevation, to
a little more of administrative skill, or of that semblance of it
which practice gives, in the details of business; a State which
dwarfs its men, in order that they may be more docile instruments in its hands even for beneficial purposes, will find that
with small men no great thing can really be accomplished;
and that the perfection of machinery to which it has sacrificed
everything, will in the end avail it nothing, for want of the
vital power which, in order that the machine might work more
smoothly, it has preferred to banish.

MILL had his three essays on religion practically finished by the 1860's, yet he did not publish them at that time. They were not published until 1874, after his death, in a volume called *Nature, The Utility of Religion, Theism*. Although his heterodox views on religion were well known, he was unwilling to live with the shock they were bound to produce on his contemporaries. One is reminded of David Hume, an earlier British thinker with not very dissimilar views on religion, who locked his thoughts on that theme in his desk until after his death.

Not that Mill lacked the courage to face social ostracism by his age. He had shown such a courage in his unconventional relations with Harriet Taylor, and in his merciless pursuit of Captain Eyre in the case of the brutalities of the Jamaican colonial administration. My guess is that he was unwilling to have the other causes for which he was working victimized because of the inevitable scandal that the publication of his religious views would involve. As it happened, when there was a move after Mill's death to have a public memorial established for him, the Church of England clerics demurred on the ground of Mill's youthful Malthusian activities, and Prime Minister Gladstone quashed the idea.

Of the two essays on religion reprinted here, the one on *Nature* was written early. In fact, Mill started to rewrite the first part of it in August 1853, and had finished that portion by September, when he and his wife—both very ill with tuberculosis—left England for the South of France. He came back at the beginning of 1854, leaving her in France, but sending her a stream of letters about his writing plans. "I have been reading the Essay on Nature," he wrote her on January 20, 1854, "as I rewrote the first part of it before we left & I think it very much improved & altogether very passable. I think I could finish it equally well."

It is important to remember two facts about the period during which Mill was setting down his ideas on religion. One was his illness and that of his wife, and his sense that their days might be numbered. This was, then, no abstract essay on religious metaphysics by a closet philosopher. Here was a man facing his own death and that of the only woman—the only person—he had ever loved, and sweating out an agonized debate between what he might have wished to believe and what his intellect told him was credible.

The second fact flowed from the first. Since the time remaining to them might be so short (actually Harriet died of the dread disease in four years, but Mill recovered and outlived her by fifteen years), Mill felt the urgency of getting his major ideas on every crucial subject into one or two volumes of Essays, which he would leave behind along with the *Autobiography*. First on the list of these essays was the one on Nature:

"The first thing to be done & which I can do immediately . . . (he wrote on January 29, 1854) is to finish the paper on Nature, & this I mean to set about to-day. . . . That paper . . . seems to me on reading it to contain a great deal which we want said, said quite well enough for the volume though not so well as we shall make it when we have time. I hope to be able in two or three weeks to finish it equally well. . . ." Then, in a letter on February 7, 1854: "I finished the 'Nature' on Sunday as I expected. I am quite puzzled what to attempt next. . . ." And then follows his famous list of subjects still to be done. Among them are "Religion de l'Avenir," and then "Utility of religion."

In her formidable letter dated February 14 and 15, 1854, from which I have quoted her instructions about how to deal with their personal relationship in his *Autobiography*, Harriet also turned to his essays on religion:

"About the Essays dear, would not religion, the Utility of Religion, be one of the subjects you would have most to say on—there is no account for the existence nearly universal of some religion (superstition) by the instincts of fear, hope and mystery etc., and throwing over all doctrines and theories, called religion, and devices for power, to show how religion and poetry fill the same want, the craving after higher objects, the consolation of suffering, the hope of heaven for the selfish, love of God for the tender and grateful—how all this must be superseded by morality deriving its power from sympathies and benevolence and its reward from the approbation of those we respect."

Mill gave this his entire approbation. "Your program of an essay on religion," he replied on February 20, 1854, "is beautiful, but it requires you to fill it up—I can try but a few paragraphs will bring me to the end of all I have got to say on the subject. What would be the use of my outliving you! I could write nothing worth keeping alive for except with your prompting."

As it turned out, her "prompting" proved productive, and the essay on the Utility of Religion followed in essence the outline she had jotted down for it. Yet one could easily argue too much from this. Harriet's mind was Mill's product more than his mind was hers. When she met him, as a young matron of 23, the world of ideas was just bursting in on her. When she wrote this letter she had been his star pupil for almost a quarter-century, just as he had been his father's star pupil for a quarter-century before that meeting. Her paragraph had a boldness of outline because she could be both inside Mill's mind and yet stand aside from it and give it the lead he thought he wanted.

I use the phrase "thought he wanted" because the Essay on Nature, despite Mill's use of "we" when writing to Harriet about it, seems to have been primarily his own product. True, he inserted in it three sentences from one of her letters, but the rest would probably have been written even if he had never known her. I suspect that this was true of the other two essays on religion as well. What she did was to re-enforce his views, give them sharpness of outline, and give him the moral bolstering to go on in the direction he had already planned.

This was the direction, one must also add, toward which his father's teaching had inclined him in his early years. There is a notable passage in the *Autobiography* on James Mill's views on religion. He had started as a Presbyterian, but on reading Butler's *Analogy* he found it convincing against both the believers in Christian revelation and against the Deists who believed in a "natural religion" common to all religious creeds. "He found it impossible to believe," Mill writes about his father in his *Autobiography*, "that a world so full of evil was the work of an Author combining infinite power with perfect goodness and righteousness. . . . Think (he used to say) of a being who would make a Hell—who would create the human race with the infallible foreknowledge . . . that the great majority of them were to be consigned to horrible and everlasting torment. . . . Multitudes have held the undoubting belief in an Omnipotent Author of Hell, and have nevertheless identified that being with the best conception they were able to form of perfect goodness. Their worship was not paid to the demon which such a Being as they imagined would really be, but to their own ideal of excellence."

When writing thus about his father's creed, Mill was in reality writing about his own as well. His intellectual break from his father was on other grounds, mainly on the question of whether one could fashion institutions for society that would operate though the majority will and make men happy by the simple psychology of the Benthamite pleasure calculus. He also broke from his father's fear of feeling of any sort. "For passionate emotions of all sorts . . . he professed the greatest contempt. He regarded them as a form of madness." Mill had himself been the victim of his father's exclusion of all emotion from his education. But on the issue of religion the break was not nearly as sharp. Mill reported with some sympathy his father's friendliness to the idea of Manichaeism—the sect belief that God and the Devil are at constant war for the world and that the Devil is, if anything, winning. He also reports his father's agnosticism about the mystery of the origin of life and the universe.

As for his own views, while he seems to have been an agnostic, he was not a Manichaean—although some commentators, like Crane Brinton, have seen this strain in him. I should think that the Manichaean view, which is a deeply tragic view of life, was beyond him. The book which influenced him most on religion, and which he read as a young man, was Philip Beauchamp's (the name was a pseudonym for a member of the Benthamite group) *Analysis of the Influence of Natural Religion on the Temporal Happiness of Mankind*. It made him reject all forms of deism, all belief in a benevolent Nature and its "natural laws," and all philosophies of design in the Universe. The reader of the two essays on religion in the present volume will recognize all these ideas which Mill carried over from the Benthamite book, as well as from his father.

Mill believed it was his duty to make his views on religion known. "The time appears to me to have come," he wrote in the *Autobiography*, "when it is the duty of all . . . who . . . have satisfied themselves that the current opinions are not only false but hurtful, to make their dissent known. . . . The world would be astonished if it knew how great a proportion of its brightest ornaments . . . are complete sceptics in religion. . . . Of unbelievers . . . as well as of believers, there are many species. . . . But the best among them . . . are more genuinely religious, in the best sense of the word religion, than those who exclusively arrogate to themselves the title." And he goes on to speak of "an ideal conception of a Perfect Being, to which they habitually refer as the guide of their conscience." It was with this "ideal of the Good" that Mill himself ended, in his essays on religion, as in his *Autobiography*. It was as far as his mind could go toward religion, and as far as his wife went in her letter from which I have quoted.

It should be noted that this passage about speaking out on religion came in a book which Mill probably knew would not be published until after his death; the same was true of his essays on religion. This gives us some measure of the distance, in point of religious tolerance, between the intellectual climate of Victorian England and our own.

The "utility of religion" turned out to be, in effect, the religion of social utility, and the "idea of the Good" was the idea of the social good. Not only did Mill and his wife exclude from their approved religious views the idea of revealed religion, natural religion, and natural laws, but they also excluded the deep sense of the mystery of the Universe as embodied in poetry and in philosophical mysticism. The reason for the exclusion was that these were matters that could neither be proved nor disproved. They were in the realm of the non-rational, and you could not base a moral code on the non-rational. Thus the whole range of feelings and ideas which Jung later subsumed under the "oceanic sense" were summarily rejected, along with revealed and natural religion.

What remained was the idea of "morality deriving its power from sympathies and benevolence and its reward from the approbation of those we respect," as Mrs. Mill had put it in her letter. It was social utilitarianism given the name of religious utility.

I have already dealt, in the general Introduction, with a critique of it. I add here that Mill could not have been wholly satisfied with utilitarianism—at least as religion—had he not himself been held in the grip of his iron intellectuality. There are tantalizing hints, in the diary he kept during his crucial illness, that he had glimpsed something else. "When we see and feel," he wrote on March 17, 1854, "that human beings can take the deepest interest in what will befall their country or mankind long after they are dead . . . we cannot doubt that if this and similar feelings were cultivated in the same manner and degree as religion they would become a religion." This is essentially the view in the Essays, yet one must ask what "the same manner and degree" mean if they do not mean the sense of reverence and worship which take the matter out of social utility into the realm of the non-rational.

On March 25 Mill had moved another, and dangerous, step toward non-rational feeling. "The only change I find in myself from a near view of probable death is that it makes me instinctively conservative. It makes me feel, not as I am accustomed—oh, for something better!—but oh, that we could be going on as we were before. Oh, that those I love could be spared the shock of great change! And this feeling goes with me into politics and all other human affairs, when my reason does not studiously contend against and repress it."

There you have it—a cry, not from reason and the mind, but *de profundis* from the heart, the cry to the Universe as good, to "be going on as we were before." It is Faust's cry to Helen, "Ah, linger still, you are so beautiful." This was the non-rational Life Force in Mill, brought out by his confrontation of death. On it, more than moral codes are based. It is the stuff on which aesthetic systems and religions are built. But Mill's reason won out in the contest, and the result is in these Essays.

NATURE

NATURE, natural, and the group of words derived from them, or allied to them in etymology, have at all times filled a great place in the thoughts and taken a strong hold on the feelings of mankind. That they should have done so is not surprising when we consider what the words, in their primitive and most obvious signification, represent; but it is unfortunate that a set of terms which play so great a part in moral and metaphysical speculation should have acquired many meanings different from the primary one, yet sufficiently allied to it to admit of confusion. The words have thus become entangled in so many foreign associations, mostly of a very powerful and tenacious character, that they have come to excite, and to be the symbols of, feelings which their original meaning will by no means justify; and which have made them one of the most copious sources of false taste, false philosophy, false morality, and even bad law.

The most important application of the Socratic *elenchus*, as exhibited and improved by Plato, consists in dissecting large abstractions of this description, fixing down to a precise definition the meaning which as popularly used they merely shadow forth, and questioning and testing the common maxims and opinions in which they bear a part. It is to be regretted that among the instructive specimens of this kind of investigation which Plato has left, and to which subsequent times have been so much indebted for whatever intellectual clearness they have attained, he has not enriched posterity with a dialogue *Of Nature*. If the idea denoted by the word had been subjected to his searching analysis, and the popular commonplaces in which it figures had been submitted to the ordeal of his powerful dialectics, his successors probably would not have rushed, as they speedily did, into modes of thinking and reasoning of which the fallacious use of that word formed the cornerstone—a kind of fallacy from which he was himself singularly free.

According to the Platonic method, which is still the best type of such investigations, the first thing to be done with so vague a term is to ascertain precisely what it means. It is also a rule of the same method, that the meaning of an abstraction is best sought for in the concrete—of a universal in the particular. Adopting this course with the word Nature, the first question must be, what is meant by the "nature" of a particular object—as of fire, of water, or of some individual plant or animal? Evidently the ensemble or aggregate of its powers or properties: the modes in which it acts on other things (counting among those things the senses of the observer) and the modes in which other things act upon it; to which, in the case of a sentient being, must be added its own capacities of feeling or being conscious. The nature of the thing means all this, means its entire capacity of exhibiting phenomena. And since the phenomena which a thing exhibits, however much they vary in different circumstances, are always the same in the same circumstances, they admit of being described in general forms of words, which are called the *laws* of the thing's nature. Thus it is a law of the nature of water that, under the mean pressure of the atmosphere at the level of the sea, it boils at 212° Fahrenheit.

As the nature of any given thing is the aggregate of its powers and properties, so Nature in the abstract is the aggregate of the powers and properties of all things. Nature means the sum of all phenomena together with the causes which produce them, including not only all that happens but all that is capable of happening, the unused capabilities of causes being as much a part of the idea of nature as those which take effect. Since all phenomena which have been sufficiently examined are found to take place with regularity, each having certain fixed conditions, positive and negative, on the occurrence of which it invariably happens, mankind have been able to ascertain, either by direct observation or by reasoning processes grounded on it, the conditions of the occurrence of many phenomena; and the progress of science mainly consists in ascertaining those conditions. When discovered, they can be expressed in general propositions, which are called laws of the particular phenomenon and also, more generally, laws of nature. Thus the truth that all material objects tend toward one another with a force directly as their masses and inversely as the square of their distance is a law of nature. The proposition that air and food are necessary to animal life, if it be, as we have good reason to believe, true without exception, is also a law of nature, though the phenomenon of which it is the law is special and not, like gravitation, universal.

Nature, then, in this its simplest acceptation, is a collective name for all facts, actual and possible, or (to speak more accurately) a name for the mode, partly known to us and partly unknown, in which all things take place. For the word suggests not so much the multitudinous detail of the phenomena as the conception which might be formed of their manner of existence as a mental whole by a mind possessing a complete knowledge of them: to which conception it is the aim of science to raise itself by successive steps of generalization from experience.

Such, then, is a correct definition of the word nature. But this definition corresponds only to one of the senses of that ambiguous term. It is evidently inapplicable to some of the modes in which the word is familiarly employed. For example, it entirely conflicts with the common form of speech by which nature is opposed to art, and natural to artificial. For in the sense of the word nature which has just been defined, and which is the true scientific sense, art is as much nature as anything else; and everything which is artificial is natural —art has no independent powers of its own: art is but the employment of the powers of nature for an end. Phenomena produced by human agency, no less than those which as far as we are concerned are spontaneous, depend on the properties of the elementary forces, or of the elementary substances and their compounds. The united powers of the whole human race could not create a new property of matter in general, or of any one of its species. We can only take advantage for our purposes of the properties which we find. A ship floats by the same laws of specific gravity and equilibrium as a tree uprooted by the wind and blown into the water. The corn which men raise for food grows and produces its grain by the same laws of vegetation by which the wild rose and the mountain strawberry bring forth their flowers and fruit. A house stands and holds together by the natural properties, the weight and cohesion, of the materials which compose

it. A steam engine works by the natural expansive force of
steam, exerting a pressure upon one part of a system of arrangements, which pressure, by the mechanical properties of
the lever, is transferred from that to another part where it
raises the weight or removes the obstacle brought into connection with it. In these and all other artificial operations the
office of man is, as has often been remarked, a very limited
one; it consists in moving things into certain places. We move
objects, and by doing this bring some things into contact
which were separate, or separate others which were in contact;
and, by this simple change of place, natural forces previously
dormant are called into action and produce the desired effect.
Even the volition which designs, the intelligence which con-
trives, and the muscular force which executes these movements, are themselves powers of nature.

It thus appears that we must recognize at least two principal meanings in the word nature. In one sense, it means
all the powers existing in either the outer or the inner world
and everything which takes place by means of those powers.
In another sense it means, not everything which happens, but
only what takes place without the agency, or without the
voluntary and intentional agency, of man. This distinction is
far from exhausting the ambiguities of the word; but it is the
key to most of those on which important consequences depend.

Such, then, being the two principal senses of the word
nature, in which of these is it taken, or is it taken in either,
when the word and its derivatives are used to convey ideas of
commendation, approval, and even moral obligation?

It has conveyed such ideas in all ages. *Naturam sequi* was
the fundamental principle of morals in many of the most admired schools of philosophy. Among the ancients, especially
in the declining period of ancient intellect and thought, it
was the test to which all ethical doctrines were brought. The
Stoics and the Epicureans, however irreconcilable in the rest
of their systems, agreed in holding themselves bound to prove
that their respective maxims of conduct were the dictates of
nature. Under their influence the Roman jurists, when attempting to systematize jurisprudence, placed in the front of
their exposition a certain *jus naturale*, "quod natura," as Jus-
tinian declares in the *Institutes*, "omnia animalia docuit";
and as the modern systematic writers, not only on law but
on moral philosophy, have generally taken the Roman jurists
for their models, treatises on the so-called law of nature have
abounded; and references to this law as a supreme rule and

ltimate standard have pervaded literature. The writers on
nternational law have done more than any others to give
urrency to this style of ethical speculation, inasmuch as, hav-
ng no positive law to write about and yet being anxious to
nvest the most approved opinions respecting international
morality with as much as they could of the authority of law,
hey endeavored to find such an authority in nature's imagi-
ary code. The Christian theology during the period of its
greatest ascendancy opposed some, though not a complete,
hindrance to the modes of thought which erected nature into
he criterion of morals, inasmuch as, according to the creed
f most denominations of Christians (though assuredly not of
Christ), a man is by nature wicked. But this very doctrine, by
he reaction which it provoked, has made the deistical moral-
sts almost unanimous in proclaiming the divinity of nature
nd setting up its fancied dictates as an authoritative rule of
action. A reference to that supposed standard is the predominant ingredient in the vein of thought and feeling which
was opened by Rousseau, and which has infiltrated itself
most widely into the modern mind, not excepting that portion
f it which calls itself Christian. The doctrines of Christianity
have in every age been largely accommodated to the philosophy which happened to be prevalent, and the Christianity of
ur day has borrowed a considerable part of its color and
flavor from sentimental deism. At the present time it cannot
be said that nature, or any other standard, is applied as it was
wont to be to deduce rules of action with juridical precision,
nd with an attempt to make its application coextensive with
ll human agency. The people of this generation do not commonly apply principles with any such studious exactness, nor
own such binding allegiance to any standard, but live in a
ind of confusion of many standards—a condition not propi-
ious to the formation of steady moral convictions but conveni-
nt enough to those whose moral opinions sit lightly on them,
ince it gives them a much wider range of arguments for de-
ending the doctrine of the moment. But though perhaps no
ne could now be found who, like the institutional writers of
ormer times, adopts the so-called law of nature as the founda-
ion of ethics, and endeavors consistently to reason from it,
he word and its cognates must still be counted among those
which carry great weight in moral argumentation. That any
mode of thinking, feeling, or acting, is "according to nature"
s usually accepted as a strong argument for its goodness. If it
an be said with any plausibility that "nature enjoins" any-

thing, the propriety of obeying the injunction is by most people considered to be made out; and conversely, the imputation of being contrary to nature is thought to bar the door against any pretension on the part of the thing so designated to be tolerated or excused, and the word "unnatural" has not ceased to be one of the most vituperative epithets in the language. Those who deal in these expressions may avoid making themselves responsible for any fundamental theorem respecting the standard of moral obligation, but they do not the less imply such a theorem, and one which must be the same in substance with that on which the more logical thinkers of a more laborious age grounded their systematic treatises on natural law.

Is it necessary to recognize in these forms of speech another distinct meaning of the word nature? Or can they be connected, by any rational bond of union, with either of the two meanings already treated of? At first it may seem that we have no option but to admit another ambiguity in the term. All inquiries are either into what is, or into what ought to be; science and history belonging to the first division, art, morals, and politics to the second. But the two senses of the word nature first pointed out agree in referring only to what is. In the first meaning, nature is a collective name for everything which is. In the second, it is a name for everything which is of itself, without voluntary human intervention. But the employment of the word nature as a term of ethics seems to disclose a third meaning, in which nature does not stand for what is but for what ought to be, or for the rule or standard of what ought to be. A little consideration, however, will show that this is not a case of ambiguity; there is not here a third sense of the word. Those who set up nature as a standard of action do not intend a merely verbal proposition; they do not mean that the standard, whatever it be, should be *called* nature; they think they are giving some information as to what the standard of action really is. Those who say that we ought to act according to nature do not mean the mere identical proposition that we ought to do what we ought to do. They think that the word nature affords some external criterion of what we should do; and if they lay down as a rule for what ought to be a word which in its proper signification denotes what is, they do so because they have a notion, either clearly or confusedly, that what is constitutes the rule and standard of what ought to be.

The examination of this notion is the object of the present

ssay. It is proposed to inquire into the truth of the doctrines
vhich make nature a test of right and wrong, good and evil,
r which in any mode or degree attach merit or approval to
ollowing, imitating, or obeying nature. To this inquiry the
oregoing discussion respecting the meaning of terms was an
indispensable introduction. Language is, as it were, the atmosphere of philosophical investigation, which must be made
transparent before anything can be seen through it in the true
figure and position. In the present case it is necessary to guard
against a further ambiguity, which, though abundantly obvious, has sometimes misled even sagacious minds, and of which
: is well to take distinct note before proceeding further. No
vord is more commonly associated with the word nature than
aw; and this last word has distinctly two meanings, in one
f which it denotes some definite portion of what is, in the
ther, of what ought to be. We speak of the law of gravitation,
he three laws of motion, the law of definite proportions in
chemical combination, the vital laws of organized beings. All
hese are portions of what is. We also speak of the criminal
aw, the civil law, the law of honor, the law of veracity, the
aw of justice—all of which are portions of what ought to be,
r of somebody's suppositions, feelings, or commands respect-
ng what ought to be. The first kind of laws, such as the laws
f motion and of gravitation, are neither more nor less than
he observed uniformities in the occurrence of phenomena:
partly uniformities of antecedence and sequence, partly of
concomitance. These are what in science, and even in ordinary parlance, are meant by laws of nature. Laws in the other
sense are the laws of the land, the law of nations, or moral
aws; among which, as already noticed, is dragged in by jurists
ind publicists something which they think proper to call the
aw of nature. Of the liability of these two meanings of the
vord to be confounded there can be no better example than
he first chapter of Montesquieu, where he remarks that the
material world has its laws, the inferior animals have their
aws, and man has his laws; and calls attention to the much
greater strictness with which the first two sets of laws are ob-
erved than the last; as if it were an inconsistency and a paradox that things always are what they are, but men not always
what they ought to be. A similar confusion of ideas pervades
he writings of Mr. George Combe, from whence it has over-
flowed into a large region of popular literature, and we are
now continually reading injunctions to obey the physical laws
f the universe as being obligatory in the same sense and man-

ner as the moral. The conception which the ethical use of the word nature implies, of a close relation if not absolute identity between what is and what ought to be, certainly derives part of its hold on the mind from the custom of designating what is by the expression "laws of nature," while the same word law is also used, and even more familiarly and emphatically, to express what ought to be.

When it is asserted or implied that nature, or the laws of nature, should be conformed to, is the nature which is meant nature in the first sense of the term, meaning all which is—the powers and properties of all things? But in this signification there is no need of a recommendation to act according to nature, since it is what nobody can possibly help doing, and equally whether he acts well or ill. There is no mode of acting which is not conformable to nature in this sense of the term, and all modes of acting are so in exactly the same degree. Every action is the exertion of some natural power, and its effects of all sorts are so many phenomena of nature, produced by the powers and properties of some of the objects of nature, in exact obedience to some law or laws of nature. When I voluntarily use my organs to take in food, the act and its consequences take place according to laws of nature; if instead of food I swallow poison, the case is exactly the same. To bid people conform to the laws of nature when they have no power but what the laws of nature give them, when it is a physical impossibility for them to do the smallest thing otherwise than through some law of nature, is an absurdity. The thing they need to be told is what particular law of nature they should make use of in a particular case. When, for example, a person is crossing a river by a narrow bridge to which there is no parapet, he will do well to regulate his proceedings by the laws of equilibrium in moving bodies, instead of conforming only to the law of gravitation and falling into the river.

Yet idle as it is to exhort people to do what they cannot avoid doing, and absurd as it is to prescribe as a rule of right conduct what agrees exactly as well with wrong, nevertheless a rational rule of conduct *may* be constructed out of the relation which it ought to bear to the laws of nature in this widest acceptation of the term. Man necessarily obeys the laws of nature, or, in other words, the properties of things, but he does not necessarily *guide* himself by them. Though all conduct is in conformity to laws of nature, all conduct is not grounded on knowledge of them and intelligently directed to

he attainment of purposes by means of them. Though we can-
ot emancipate ourselves from the laws of nature as a whole,
ve can escape from any particular law of nature if we are
ble to withdraw ourselves from the circumstances in which
t acts. Though we can do nothing except through laws of
ature, we can use one law to counteract another. According
o Bacon's maxim, we can obey nature in such a manner as to
ommand it. Every alteration of circumstances alters more or
ess the laws of nature under which we act; and by every
hoice which we make, either of ends or of means, we place
urselves to a greater or less extent under one set of laws of
ature instead of another. If, therefore, the useless precept to
ollow nature were changed into a precept to study nature—to
now and take heed of the properties of the things we have
o deal with, so far as these properties are capable of forward-
ng or obstructing any given purpose—we should have arrived
t the first principle of all intelligent action, or rather at the
lefinition of intelligent action itself. And a confused notion of
his true principle is, I doubt not, in the minds of many of
hose who set up the unmeaning doctrine which superficially
esembles it. They perceive that the essential difference be-
ween wise and foolish conduct consists in attending, or not
ttending, to the particular laws of nature on which some im-
ortant result depends. And they think that a person who
ttends to a law of nature in order to shape his conduct by it
nay be said to obey it, while a person who practically dis-
egards it and acts as if no such law existed may be said to
isobey it; the circumstance being overlooked that what is
hus called disobedience to a law of nature is obedience to
ome other or perhaps to the very law itself. For example,
 person who goes into a powder magazine either not know-
ng, or carelessly omitting to think of, the explosive force of
unpowder is likely to do some act which will cause him to be
lown to atoms in obedience to the very law which he has
isregarded.

But however much of its authority the *naturam sequi*
loctrine may owe to its being confounded with the rational
recept *naturam observare*, its favorers and promoters unques-
ionably intend much more by it than that precept. To acquire
nowledge of the properties of things and make use of the
nowledge for guidance is a rule of prudence for the adapta-
ion of means to ends, for giving effect to our wishes and
ntentions, whatever they may be. But the maxim of obedi-
nce to nature, or conformity to nature, is held up not as a

simply prudential but as an ethical maxim, and by those who talk of *jus naturae*, even as a law, fit to be administered by tribunals and enforced by sanctions. Right action must mean something more and other than merely intelligent action; yet no precept beyond this last can be connected with the word nature in the wider and more philosophical of its acceptations. We must try it, therefore, in the other sense, that in which nature stands distinguished from art and denotes, not the whole course of the phenomena which come under our observation, but only their spontaneous course.

Let us then consider whether we can attach any meaning to the supposed practical maxim of following nature in this second sense of the word, in which nature stands for that which takes place without human intervention. In nature as thus understood, is the spontaneous course of things when left to themselves the rule to be followed in endeavoring to adapt things to our use? But it is evident at once that the maxim, taken in this sense, is not merely, as it is in the other sense, superfluous and unmeaning, but palpably absurd and self-contradictory. For while human action cannot help conforming to nature in the one meaning of the term, the very aim and object of action is to alter and improve nature in the other meaning. If the natural course of things were perfectly right and satisfactory, to act at all would be a gratuitous meddling, which, as it could not make things better, must make them worse. Or if action at all could be justified, it would only be when in direct obedience to instincts, since these might perhaps be accounted part of the spontaneous order of nature; but to do anything with forethought and purpose would be a violation of that perfect order. If the artificial is not better than the natural, to what end are all the arts of life? To dig, to plow, to build, to wear clothes are direct infringements of the injunction to follow nature.

Accordingly it would be said by everyone, even of those most under the influence of the feelings which prompt the injunction, that to apply it to such cases as those just spoken of would be to push it too far. Everybody professes to approve and admire many great triumphs of art over nature: the junction by bridges of shores which nature had made separate, the draining of nature's marshes, the excavation of her wells, the dragging to light of what she has buried at immense depths in the earth; the turning away of her thunderbolts by lightning rods, of her inundations by embankments, of her ocean by breakwaters. But to commend these and similar feats

s to acknowledge that the ways of nature are to be conquered,
ot obeyed; that her powers are often toward man in the posi-
ion of enemies, from whom he must wrest, by force and
ngenuity, what little he can for his own use, and deserves to
e applauded when that little is rather more than might be
xpected from his physical weakness in comparison to those
igantic powers. All praise of civilization, or art, or contrivance
s so much dispraise of nature, an admission of imperfection
vhich it is man's business and merit to be always endeavoring
o correct or mitigate.

The consciousness that whatever man does to improve his
ondition is in so much a censure and a thwarting of the spon-
aneous order of nature has in all ages caused new and un-
recedented attempts at improvement to be generally at first
nder a shade of religious suspicion as being in any case un-
omplimentary, and very probably offensive, to the powerful
eings (or, when polytheism gave place to monotheism, to the
ll-powerful Being) supposed to govern the various phenom-
na of the universe, and of whose will the course of nature
vas conceived to be the expression. Any attempt to mold natu-
al phenomena to the convenience of mankind might easily
ppear an interference with the government of those superior
eings; and though life could not have been maintained, much
ess made pleasant, without perpetual interferences of the
ind, each new one was doubtless made with fear and trem-
ling until experience had shown that it could be ventured on
vithout drawing down the vengeance of the gods. The sagac-
ty of priests showed them a way to reconcile the impunity of
articular infringements with the maintenance of the general
lread of encroaching on the divine administration. This was
ffected by representing each of the principal human inven-
ions as the gift and favor of some god. The old religions also
fforded many resources for consulting the gods and obtaining
heir express permission for what would otherwise have ap-
eared a breach of their prerogative. When oracles had
eased, any religion which recognized a revelation afforded
xpedients for the same purpose. The Catholic religion had the
esource of an infallible Church, authorized to declare what
xertions of human spontaneity were permitted or forbidden;
nd in default of this the case was always open to argument
rom the Bible whether any particular practice had expressly
r by implication been sanctioned. The notion remained that
his liberty to control nature was conceded to man only by
pecial indulgence, and as far as required by his necessities;

and there was always a tendency, though a diminishing one
to regard any attempt to exercise power over nature, beyond
a certain degree and a certain admitted range, as an impious
effort to usurp divine power and dare more than was permitted to man. The lines of Horace in which the familiar art
of shipbuilding and navigation are reprobated as *vetitum
nefas* indicate even in that skeptical age a still unexhausted
vein of the old sentiment. The intensity of the corresponding
feeling in the Middle Ages is not a precise parallel, on account
of the superstition about dealing with evil spirits with which
it was complicated; but the imputation of prying into the
secrets of the Almighty long remained a powerful weapon of
attack against unpopular inquirers into nature; and the charge
of presumptuously attempting to defeat the designs of Providence still retains enough of its original force to be thrown in
as a makeweight along with other objections when there is a
desire to find fault with any new exertion of human forethought and contrivance. No one, indeed, asserts it to be the
intention of the Creator that the spontaneous order of the
creation should not be altered, or even that it should not be
altered in any new way. But there still exists a vague notion
that, though it is very proper to control this or the other natural phenomenon, the general scheme of nature is a model for
us to imitate; that with more or less liberty in details we
should on the whole be guided by the spirit and general conception of nature's own ways: that they are God's work, and
as such perfect; that man cannot rival their unapproachable
excellence, and can best show his skill and piety by attempting, in however imperfect a way, to reproduce their likeness;
and that if not the whole, yet some particular parts of the
spontaneous order of nature, selected according to the speaker's predilections, are in a peculiar sense manifestations of the
Creator's will, a sort of fingerposts pointing out the direction
which things in general, and therefore our voluntary actions,
are intended to take. Feelings of this sort, though repressed
on ordinary occasions by the contrary current of life, are ready
to break out whenever custom is silent and the native promptings of the mind have nothing opposed to them but reason;
and appeals are continually made to them by rhetoricians,
with the effect, if not of convincing opponents, at least of making those who already hold the opinion which the rhetorician
desires to recommend better satisfied with it. For in the present day it probably seldom happens that anyone is persuaded
to approve any course of action because it appears to him to

bear an analogy to the divine government of the world, though the argument tells on him with great force, and is felt by him to be a great support, in behalf of anything which he is already inclined to approve.

If this notion of imitating the ways of Providence as manifested in nature is seldom expressed plainly and downrightly as a maxim of general application, it also is seldom directly contradicted. Those who find it on their path prefer to turn the obstacle rather than to attack it, being often themselves not free from the feeling, and in my case afraid of incurring the charge of impiety by saying anything which might be held to disparage the works of the Creator's power. They therefore, for the most part, rather endeavor to show that they have as much right to the religious argument as their opponents, and that, if the course they recommend seems to conflict with some part of the ways of Providence, there is some other part with which it agrees better than what is contended for on the other side. In this mode of dealing with the great a priori fallacies, the progress of improvement clears away particular errors while the causes of errors are still left standing and very little weakened by each conflict; yet by a long series of such partial victories precedents are accumulated to which an appeal may be made against these powerful prepossessions, and which afford a growing hope that the misplaced feeling, after having so often learned to recede, may some day be compelled to an unconditional surrender. For however offensive the proposition may appear to many religious persons, they should be willing to look in the face the undeniable fact that the order of nature, in so far as unmodified by man, is such as no Being whose attributes are justice and benevolence would have made with the intention that his rational creatures should follow it as an example. If made wholly by such a Being, and not partly by beings of very different qualities, it could only be as a designedly imperfect work which man, in his limited sphere, is to exercise justice and benevolence in amending. The best persons have always held it to be the essence of religion that the paramount duty of man upon earth is to amend himself; but all except monkish quietists have annexed to this in their inmost minds (though seldom willing to enunciate the obligation with the same clearness) the additional religious duty of amending the world, and not solely the human part of it but the material, the order of physical nature.

In considering this subject it is necessary to divest ourselves of certain preconceptions which may justly be called natural prejudices, being grounded on feelings which, in themselves natural and inevitable, intrude into matters with which they ought to have no concern. One of these feelings is the astonishment, rising into awe, which is inspired (even independently of all religious sentiment) by any of the greater natural phenomena. A hurricane, a mountain precipice, the desert, the ocean either agitated or at rest, the solar system and the great cosmic forces which hold it together, the boundless firmament and to an educated mind any single star excite feelings which make all human enterprises and powers appear so insignificant that to a mind thus occupied it seems insufferable presumption in so puny a creature as man to look critically on things so far above him, or dare to measure himself against the grandeur of the universe. But a little interrogation of our own consciousness will suffice to convince us that what makes these phenomena so impressive is simply their vastness. The enormous extension in space and time, or the enormous power they exemplify, constitutes their sublimity—a feeling in all cases more allied to terror than to any moral emotion. And though the vast scale of these phenomena may well excite wonder, and sets at defiance all idea of rivalry, the feeling it inspires is of a totally different character from admiration of excellence. Those in whom awe produces admiration may be aesthetically developed, but they are morally uncultivated. It is one of the endowments of the imaginative part of our mental nature that conceptions of greatness and power, vividly realized, produce a feeling which, though in its higher degrees closely bordering on pain, we prefer to most of what are accounted pleasures. But we are equally capable of experiencing this feeling toward maleficent power; and we never experience it so strongly toward most of the powers of the universe as when we have most present to our consciousness a vivid sense of their capacity of inflicting evil. Because these natural powers have what we cannot imitate, enormous might, and overawe us by that one attribute, it would be a great error to infer that their other attributes are such as we ought to emulate, or that we should be justified in using our small powers after the example which nature sets us with her vast forces.

For how stands the fact? That next to the greatness of these cosmic forces, the quality which most forcibly strikes everyone who does not avert his eyes from it is their perfect and absolute recklessness. They go straight to their end, without regarding what or whom they crush on the road. Optimists, in their attempts to prove that "whatever is, is right," are obliged to maintain, not that nature ever turns one step from her path to avoid trampling us into destruction, but that it would be very unreasonable in us to expect that she should. Pope's "Shall gravitation cease when you go by?" may be a just rebuke to anyone who should be so silly as to expect common human morality from nature. But if the question were between two men, instead of between a man and a natural phenomenon, that triumphant apostrophe would be thought a rare piece of impudence. A man who should persist in hurling stones or firing cannon when another man "goes by," and having killed him should urge a similar plea in exculpation, would very deservedly be found guilty of murder.

In sober truth, nearly all the things which men are hanged or imprisoned for doing to one another are nature's everyday performances. Killing, the most criminal act recognized by human laws, nature does once to every being that lives, and in a large proportion of cases after protracted tortures such as only the greatest monsters whom we read of ever purposely inflicted on their living fellow creatures. If by an arbitrary reservation we refuse to account anything murder but what abridges a certain term supposed to be allotted to human life, nature also does this to all but a small percentage of lives, and does it in all the modes, violent or insidious, in which the worst human beings take the lives of one another. Nature impales men, breaks them as if on the wheel, casts them to be devoured by wild beasts, burns them to death, crushes them with stones like the first Christian martyr, starves them with hunger, freezes them with cold, poisons them by the quick or slow venom of her exhalations, and has hundreds of other hideous deaths in reserve such as the ingenious cruelty of a Nabis or a Domitian never surpassed. All this nature does with the most supercilious disregard both of mercy and of justice, emptying her shafts upon the best and noblest indifferently with the meanest and worst; upon those who are engaged in the highest and worthiest enterprises, and often as the direct consequence of the noblest acts; and it might almost be imagined as a punishment for them. She mows down those on whose existence hangs the well-being of a whole people, perhaps the prospects of the human race for generations to come, with as little compunction as those whose death is a relief to themselves or a blessing to those under their noxious influence. Such are nature's dealings with life. Even when she does not intend to kill, she inflicts the same tortures in apparent wantonness. In the clumsy provision which she has made for that perpetual renewal of animal life, rendered necessary by the prompt termination she puts to it in every individual instance, no human being ever comes into the world but another human being is literally stretched on the rack for hours or days, not unfrequently issuing in death. Next to taking life (equal to it, according to a high authority) is taking the means by which we live; and nature does this, too, on the largest scale and with the most callous indifference. A single hurricane destroys the hopes of a season; a flight of locusts, or an inundation, desolates a district; a trifling chemical change in an edible root starves a million of people. The waves of the sea, like banditti, seize and appropriate the wealth of the rich and the little all of the poor with the same accompaniments of stripping, wounding, and killing as their human antitypes. Everything, in short, which the worst men commit either against life or property is perpetrated on a larger scale by natural agents. Nature has noyades more fatal than those of Carrier; her explosions of firedamp are as destructive as human artillery; her plague and cholera far surpass the poison cups of the Borgias. Even the love of "order" which is thought to be a following of the ways of nature is in fact a contradiction of them. All which people are accustomed to deprecate as "disorder" and its consequences is precisely a counterpart of nature's ways. Anarchy and the Reign of Terror are overmatched in injustice, ruin, and death by a hurricane and a pestilence.

But, it is said, all these things are for wise and good ends. On this I must first remark that whether they are so or not is altogether beside the point. Supposing is true that, contrary to appearances, these horrors when perpetrated by nature promote good ends, still, as no one believes that good ends would be promoted by our following the example, the course of nature cannot be a proper model for us to imitate. Either it is right that we should kill because nature kills, torture because nature tortures, ruin and devastate because nature does the like, or we ought not to consider at all what nature does, but what it is good to do. If there is such a thing as a *reductio ad absurdum*, this surely amounts to one. If it is a sufficient reason for doing one thing that nature does it, why not another thing? If not all things, why any thing? The physical government of the world being full of the things which when done by men are deemed the greatest enormities, it cannot be religious or moral in us to guide our actions by the analogy of the course of nature. This proposition remains true whatever occult quality of producing good may reside in those facts of nature which to our perceptions are most noxious, and which no one considers it other than a crime to produce artificially.

But, in reality, no one consistently believes in any such occult quality. The phrases which ascribe perfection to the course of nature can only be considered as the exaggerations of poetic or devotional feeling, not intended to stand the test of a sober examination. No one, either religious or irreligious, believes that the hurtful agencies of nature, considered as a whole, promote good purposes in any other way than by inciting human rational creatures to rise up and struggle against them. If we believed that those agencies were appointed by a benevolent Providence as the means of accomplishing wise purposes which could not be compassed if they did not exist, then everything done by mankind which tends to chain up these natural agencies or to restrict their mischievous operation, from draining a pestilential marsh down to curing the toothache or putting up an umbrella, ought to be accounted impious; which assuredly nobody does account them, notwithstanding an undercurrent of sentiment setting in that direction which is occasionally perceptible. On the contrary, the improvements on which the civilized part of mankind most pride themselves consist in more successfully warding off those natural calamities which, if we really believed what most people profess to believe, we should cherish as medicines provided for our earthly state by infinite wisdom. Inasmuch, too, as each generation greatly surpasses its predecessors in the amount of natural evil which it succeeds in averting, our condition, if the theory were true, ought by this time to have become a terrible manifestation of some tremendous calamity against which the physical evils we have learned to overmaster had previously operated as a preservative. Anyone, however, who acted as if he supposed this to be the case would be more likely, I think, to be confined as a lunatic than reverenced as a saint.

It is undoubtedly a very common fact that good comes out of evil, and, when it does occur, it is far too agreeable not to find people eager to dilate on it. But in the first place, it is quite as often true of human crimes as of natural calamities. The fire of London, which is believed to have had so salutary an effect on the healthiness of the city, would have produced that effect just as much if it had been really the work of the *furor papisticus* so long commemorated on the monument.

The deaths of those whom tyrants or persecutors have made martyrs in any noble cause have done a service to mankind which would not have been obtained if they had died by accident or disease. Yet whatever incidental and unexpected benefits may result from crimes, they are crimes nevertheless. In the second place, if good frequently comes out of evil, the converse fact, evil coming out of good, is equally common. Every event, public or private, which, regretted on its occurrence, was declared providential at a later period on account of some unforeseen good consequence, might be matched by some other event, deemed fortunate at the time, but which proved calamitous or fatal to those whom it appeared to benefit. Such conflicts between the beginning and the end, or between the event and the expectation, are not only as frequent but as often held up to notice in the painful cases as in the agreeable, but there is not the same inclination to generalize on them or at all events they are not regarded by the moderns (though they were by the ancients) as similarly an indication of the divine purposes: men satisfy themselves with moralizing on the imperfect nature of our foresight, the uncertainty of events, and the vanity of human expectations. The simple fact is, human interests are so complicated, and the effects of any incident whatever so multitudinous, that if it touches mankind at all its influence on them is, in the great majority of cases, both good and bad. If the greater number of personal misfortunes have their good side, hardly any good fortune ever befell anyone which did not give either to the same or to some other person something to regret; and unhappily there are many misfortunes so overwhelming that their favorable side, if it exist, is entirely overshadowed and made insignificant, while the corresponding statement can seldom be made concerning blessings. The effects, too, of every cause depend so much on the circumstances which accidentally accompany it that many cases are sure to occur in which even the total result is markedly opposed to the predominant tendency; and thus not only evil has its good and good its evil side, but good often produces an overbalance of evil and evil an overbalance of good. This, however, is by no means the general tendency of either phenomenon. On the contrary, both good and evil naturally tend to fructify, each in its own kind, good producing good, and evil, evil. It is one of nature's general rules and part of her habitual injustice that "to him that hath shall be given, but from him that hath not shall be taken even that which he hath." The ordinary and predominant tendency of good is toward more good. Health, strength, wealth, knowledge, virtue are not only good in themselves but facilitate and promote the acquisition of good, both of the same and of other kinds. The person who can learn easily is he who already knows much; it is the strong and not the sickly person who can do everything which most conduces to health; those who find it easy to gain money are not the poor but the rich; while health, strength, knowledge, talents are all means of acquiring riches, and riches are often an indispensable means of acquiring these. Again, *e converso*, whatever may be said of evil turning into good, the general tendency of evil is toward further evil. Bodily illness renders the body more susceptible of disease; it produces incapacity of exertion, sometimes debility of mind, and often the loss of means of subsistence. All severe pain, either bodily or mental, tends to increase the susceptibilities of pain forever after. Poverty is the parent of a thousand mental and moral evils. What is still worse, to be injured or oppressed, when habitual, lowers the whole tone of the character. One bad action leads to others, both in the agent himself, in the bystanders, and in the sufferers. All bad qualities are strengthened by habit, and all vices and follies tend to spread. Intellectual defects generate moral, and moral, intellectual; and every intellectual or moral defect generates others, and so on without end.

That much-applauded class of authors, the writers on natural theology, have, I venture to think, entirely lost their way and missed the sole line of argument which could have made their speculations acceptable to anyone who can perceive when two propositions contradict one another. They have exhausted the resources of sophistry to make it appear that all the suffering in the world exists to prevent greater—that misery exists for fear lest there should be misery: a thesis which, if ever so well maintained, could only avail to explain and justify the works of limited beings, compelled to labor under conditions independent of their own will, but could have no application to a Creator assumed to be omnipotent who, if he bends to a supposed necessity, himself makes the necessity which he bends to. If the maker of the world *can* all that he will, he wills misery, and there is no escape from the conclusion. The more consistent of those who have deemed themselves qualified to "vindicate the ways of God to man" have endeavored to avoid the alternative by hardening their hearts and denying that misery is an evil. The goodness of God, they say, does not consist in willing the happiness of his creatures but their virtue; and the universe, if not a happy, is a just universe. But waiving the objections to this scheme of ethics, it does not at all get rid of the difficulty. If the Creator of mankind willed that they should all be virtuous, his designs are as completely baffled as if he had willed that they should all be happy; and the order of nature is constructed with even less regard to the requirements of justice than to those of benevolence. If the law of all creation were justice and the Creator omnipoent, then, in whatever amount suffering and happiness might be dispensed to the world, each person's share of them would be exactly proportioned to that person's good or evil deeds; no human being would have a worse lot than another without worse deserts; accident or favoritism would have no part in such a world, but every human life would be the playing out of a drama constructed like a perfect moral tale. No one is able to blind himself to the fact that the world we live in is totally different from this, insomuch that the necessity of redressing the balance has been deemed one of the strongest arguments for another life after death, which amounts to an admission that the order of things in this life is often an example of injustice, not justice. If it be said that God does not take sufficient account of pleasure and pain to make them the reward or punishment of the good or the wicked, but that virtue is itself the greatest good and vice the greatest evil, then these at least ought to be dispensed to all according to what they have done to deserve them; instead of which every kind of moral depravity is entailed upon multitudes by the fatality of their birth, through the fault of their parents, of society, or of uncontrollable circumstances, certainly through no fault of their own. Not even on the most distorted and contracted theory of good which ever was framed by religious or philosophical fanaticism can the government of nature be made to resemble the work of a being at once good and omnipotent.

The only admissible moral theory of Creation is that the Principle of Good *cannot* at once and altogether subdue the powers of evil, etiher physical or moral; could not place mankind in a world free from the necessity of an incessant struggle with the maleficent powers, or make them always victorious in that struggle, but could and did make them capable of carrying on the fight with vigor and with progressively increasing success. Of all the religious explanations of the order of nature, this alone is neither contradictory to itself nor to the facts for which it attempts to account. According to it, man's duty would consist, not in simply taking care of his own interests by obeying irresistible power, but in standing forward a not ineffectual auxiliary to a Being of perfect beneficence—a faith which seems much better adapted for nerving him to exertion than a vague and inconsistent reliance on an Author of Good who is supposed to be also the author of evil. And I venture to assert that such has really been, though often unconsciously, the faith of all who have drawn strength and support of any worthy kind from trust in a superintending Providence. There is no subject on which men's practical belief is more incorrectly indicated by the words they use to express it than religion. Many have derived a base confidence from imagining themselves to be favorites of an omnipotent but capricious and despotic Deity. But those who have been strengthened in goodness by relying on the sympathizing support of a powerful and good Governor of the world have, I am satisfied, never really believed that Governor to be, in the strict sense of the term, omnipotent. They have always saved his goodness at the expense of his power. They have believed, perhaps, that he could, if he willed, remove all the thorns from their individual path, but not without causing greater harm to someone else, or frustrating some purpose of greater importance to the general well-being. They have believed that he could do any one thing, but not any combination of things; that his government, like human government, was a system of adjustments and compromises; that the world is inevitably imperfect, contrary to his intention.* And since the exertion of all his power to make it as little imperfect as possible leaves it no better than it is, they cannot but regard that power, though vastly beyond human estimate, yet as in itself not merely finite but extremely limited. They are bound, for example, to suppose that the best he could do for his human creatures was to make an immense majority of all who have yet existed be born (without any fault of their

---

* This irresistible conviction comes out in the writings of religious philosophers in exact proportion to the general clearness of their understanding. It nowhere shines forth so distinctly as in Leibniz's famous *Théodicée*, so strangely mistaken for a system of optimism and, as such, satirized by Voltaire on grounds which do not even touch the author's argument. Leibniz does not maintain that this world is the best of all imaginable, but only of all possible worlds; which, he argues, it cannot but be inasmuch as God, who is absolute goodness, has chosen it and not another. In every page of the work he tacitly assumes an abstract possibility and impossibility, independent of the divine power; and though his pious feelings make him continue to designate that power by the word Omnipotence, he so explains that term as to make it mean power extending to all that is within the limits of that abstract possibility.

own) Patagonians, or Eskimos, or something nearly as brutal and degraded, but to give them capacities which, by being cultivated for very many centuries in toil and suffering and after many of the best specimens of the race have sacrificed their lives for the purpose, have at last enabled some chosen portions of the species to grow into something better, capable of being improved in centuries more into something really good, of which hitherto there are only to be found individual instances. It may be possible to believe with Plato that perfect goodness, limited and thwarted in every direction by the intractableness of the material, has done this because it could do no better. But that the same perfectly wise and good Being had absolute power over the material and made it, by voluntary choice, what it is—to admit this might have been supposed impossible to anyone who has the simplest notions of moral good and evil. Nor can any such person, whatever kind of religious phrases he may use, fail to believe that if Nature and Man are both the works of a Being of perfect goodness, that Being intended Nature as a scheme to be amended, not imitated, by Man.

But even though unable to believe that nature, as a whole, is a realization of the designs of perfect wisdom and benevolence, men do not willingly renounce the idea that some part of Nature, at least, must be intended as an exemplar or type; that on some portion or other of the Creator's works the image of the moral qualities which they are accustomed to ascribe to him must be impressed; that if not all which is, yet something which is, must not only be a faultless model of what ought to be, but must be intended to be our guide and standard in rectifying the rest. It does not suffice them to believe that what tends to good is to be imitated and perfected, and what tends to evil is to be corrected; they are anxious for some more definite indication of the Creator's designs, and, being persuaded that this must somewhere be met with in his works, undertake the dangerous responsibility of picking and choosing among them in quest of it—a choice which, except so far as directed by the general maxim that he intends all the good and none of the evil, must of necessity be perfectly arbitrary, and, if it leads to any conclusions other than such as can be deduced from that maxim, must be, exactly in that proportion, pernicious.

It has never been settled by any accredited doctrine what particular departments of the order of nature shall be reputed to be designed for our moral instruction and guidance; and accordingly each person's individual predilections, or momentary convenience, have decided to what parts of the divine government the practical conclusions that he was desirous of establishing should be recommended to approval as being analogous. One such recommendation must be as fallacious as another, for it is impossible to decide that certain of the Creator's works are more truly expressions of his character than the rest; and the only selection which does not lead to immoral results is the selection of those which most conduce to the general good—in other words, of those which point to an end which, if the entire scheme is the expression of a single omnipotent and consistent will, is evidently not the end intended by it.

There is, however, one particular element in the construction of the world which, to minds on the lookout for special indication of the Creator's will, has appeared, not without plausibility, peculiarly fitted to afford them: viz., the active impulses of human and other animated beings. One can imagine such persons arguing that when the Author of Nature only made circumstances, he may not have meant to indicate the manner in which his rational creatures were to adjust themselves to those circumstances; but that when he implanted positive stimuli in the creatures themselves, stirring them up to a particular kind of action, it is impossible to doubt that he intended that sort of action to be practiced by them. This reasoning, followed out consistently, would lead to the conclusion that the Deity intended, and approves, whatever human beings do; since all that they do being the consequence of some of the impulses with which their Creator must have endowed them, all must equally be considered as done in obedience to his will. As this practical conclusion was shrunk from, it was necessary to draw a distinction and to pronounce that not the whole, but only parts of the active nature of mankind point to a special intention of the Creator in respect to their conduct. These parts, it seemed natural to suppose, must be those in which the Creator's hand is manifested rather than the man's own, and hence the frequent antithesis between man as God made him and man as he has made himself. Since what is done with deliberation seems more the man's own act, and he is held more completely responsible for it than for what he does from sudden impulse, the considerate part of human conduct is apt to be set down as man's share in the business and the inconsiderate as God's. The result is the vein of sentiment so common in the modern

world (though unknown to the philosophic ancients) which
exalts instinct at the expense of reason, an aberration rendered
still more mischievous by the opinion commonly held in conjunction with it that every, or almost every, feeling or impulse
which acts promptly without waiting to ask questions is an
instinct. Thus almost every variety of unreflecting and un-
calculating impulse receives a kind of consecration except
those which, though unreflecting at the moment, owe their
origin to previous habits of reflection; these, being evidently
not instinctive, do not meet with the favor accorded to the
rest, so that all unreflecting impulses are invested with authority over reason except the only ones which are most probably
right. I do not mean, of course, that this mode of judgment
is even pretended to be consistently carried out; life could
not go on if it were not admitted that impulses must be controlled, and that reason ought to govern our actions. The pretension is not to drive reason from the helm but rather to
bind her by articles to steer only in a particular way. Instinct
is not to govern, but reason is to practice some vague and
unassignable amount of deference to instinct. Though the
impression in favor of instinct as being a peculiar manifestation of the divine purposes has not been cast into the form
of a consistent general theory, it remains a standing prejudice, capable of being stirred up into hostility to reason in
any case in which the dictate of the rational faculty has not
acquired the authority of prescription.

I shall not here enter into the difficult psychological question, what are or are not instincts; the subject would require
a volume to itself. Without touching upon any disputed theoretical points, it is possible to judge how little worthy is the
instinctive part of human nature to be held up as its chief
excellence—as the part in which the hand of infinite goodness
and wisdom is peculiarly visible. Allowing everything to be an
instinct which anybody has ever asserted to be one, it remains
true that nearly every respectable attribute of humanity is the
result, not of instinct, but of a victory over instinct; and that
there is hardly anything valuable in the natural man except
capacities—a whole world of possibilities, all of them dependent upon eminently artificial discipline for being realized.

It is only in a highly artificialized condition of human nature
that the notion grew up, or, I believe, ever could have grown
up, that goodness was natural; because only after a long
course of artificial education did good sentiments become so
habitual, and so predominant over bad, as to arise unprompted

when occasion called for them. In the times when mankind were nearer to their natural state, cultivated observers regarded the natural man as a sort of wild animal, distinguished chiefly by being craftier than the other beasts of the field; and all worth of character was deemed the result of a sort of taming, a phrase often applied by the ancient philosophers to the appropriate discipline of human beings. The truth is that there is hardly a single point of excellence belonging to human character which is not decidedly repugnant to the untutored feelings of human nature.

If there be a virtue which more than any other we expect to find, and really do find, in an uncivilized state, it is the virtue of courage. Yet this is from first to last a victory achieved over one of the most powerful emotions of human nature. If there is any one feeling or attribute more natural than all others to human beings it is fear; and no greater proof can be given of the power of artificial discipline than the conquest which it has at all times and places shown itself capable of achieving over so mighty and so universal a sentiment. The widest difference no doubt exists between one human being and another in the facility or difficulty with which they acquire this virtue. There is hardly any department of human excellence in which difference of original temperament goes so far. But it may fairly be questioned if any human being is naturally courageous. Many are naturally pugnacious, or irascible, or enthusiastic, and these passions when strongly excited may render them insensible to fear. But take away the conflicting emotion, and fear reasserts its dominion; consistent courage is always the effect of cultivation. The courage which is occasionally, though by no means generally, found among tribes of savages is as much the result of education as that of the Spartans or Romans. In all such tribes there is a most emphatic direction of the public sentiment into every channel of expression through which honor can be paid to courage and cowardice held up to contempt and derision. It will perhaps be said that, as the expression of a sentiment implies the sentiment itself, the training of the young to courage presupposes an originally courageous people. It presupposes only what all good customs presuppose—that there must have been individuals better than the rest who set the customs going. Some individuals who, like other people, had fears to conquer must have had strength of mind and will to conquer them for themselves. These would obtain the influence belonging to heroes, for that which is at once astonishing and obviously useful never fails to be admired; and partly through this admiration, partly through the fear they themselves excite, they would obtain the power of legislators and could establish whatever customs they pleased.

Let us next consider a quality which forms the most visible and one of the most radical of the moral distinctions between human beings and most of the lower animals, that of which the absence, more than of anything else, renders men bestial —the quality of cleanliness. Can anything be more entirely artificial? Children, and the lower classes of most countries, seem to be actually fond of dirt; the vast majority of the human race are indifferent to it; whole nations of otherwise civilized and cultivated human beings tolerate it in some of its worst forms, and only a very small minority are consistently offended by it. Indeed, the universal law of the subject appears to be that uncleanliness offends only those to whom it is unfamiliar, so that those who have lived in so artificial a state as to be unused to it in any form are the sole persons whom it disgusts in all forms. Of all virtues this is the most evidently not instinctive, but a triumph over instinct. Assuredly neither cleanliness nor the love of cleanliness is natural to man, but only the capacity of acquiring a love of cleanliness.

Our examples have thus far been taken from the personal or, as they are called by Bentham, the self-regarding virtues, because these, if any, might be supposed to be congenial even to the uncultivated mind. Of the social virtues it is almost superfluous to speak, so completely is it the verdict of all experience that selfishness is natural. By this I do not in any wise mean to deny—that sympathy is natural also; I believe, on the contrary, that on that important fact rests the possibility of any cultivation of goodness and nobleness, and the hope of their ultimate entire ascendancy. But sympathetic characters, left uncultivated and given up to their sympathetic instincts, are as selfish as others. The difference is in the *kind* of selfishness: theirs is not solitary but sympathetic selfishness —*l'egoisme à deux, à trois*, or *à quatre*—and they may be very amiable and delightful to those with whom they sympathize, and grossly unjust and unfeeling to the rest of the world. Indeed, the finer nervous organizations which are most capable of and most require sympathy have, from their fineness, so much stronger impulses of all sorts that they often furnish the most striking examples of selfishness, though of a less repulsive kind than that of colder natures. Whether there ever was a person in whom, apart from all teaching of instructors, friends, or books, and from all intentional self-modeling according to an ideal, natural benevolence was a more powerful attribute than selfishness in any of its forms may remain undecided. That such cases are extremely rare everyone must admit, and this is enough for the argument.

But (to speak no further of self-control for the benefit of others) the commonest self-control for one's own benefit—that power of sacrificing a present desire to a distant object or a general purpose which is indispensable for making the actions of the individual accord with his own notions of his individual good—even this is most unnatural to the undisciplined human being, as may be seen by the long apprenticeship which children serve to it, the very imperfect manner in which it is acquired by persons born to power whose will is seldom resisted, and by all who have been early and much indulged; and the marked absence of the quality in savages, in soldiers and sailors, and in a somewhat less degree in nearly the whole of the poorer classes in this and many other countries. The principal difference on the point under consideration between this virtue and others is that, although, like them, it requires a course of teaching, it is more susceptible than most of them of being self-taught. The axiom is trite that self-control is only learned by experience; and this endowment is only thus much nearer to being natural than the others we have spoken of, inasmuch as personal experience, without external inculcation, has a certain tendency to engender it. Nature does not of herself bestow this, any more than other virtues; but nature often administers the rewards and punishments which cultivate it, and which in other cases have to be created artificially for the express purpose.

Veracity might seem, of all virtues, to have the most plausible claim to being natural, since in the absence of motives to the contrary speech usually conforms to, or at least does not intentionally deviate from, fact. Accordingly this is the virtue with which writers like Rousseau delight in decorating savage life and setting it in advantageous contrast with the treachery and trickery of civilization. Unfortunately this is a mere fancy picture, contradicted by all the realities of savage life. Savages are always liars. They have not the faintest notion of truth as a virtue. They have a notion of not betraying to their hurt, as of not hurting in any other way, persons to whom they are bound by some special tie of obligation: their chief, their guest, perhaps, or their friend—these feelings of obligation being the taught morality of the savage state, growing out of its characteristic circumstances. But of any point of honor respecting truth for truth's sake they have not the remotest idea, no more than the whole East and the greater part of Europe; and, in the few countries which are sufficiently improved to have such a point of honor, it is confined to a small minority who alone, under any circumstances of real temptation, practice it.

From the general use of the expression "natural justice" it must be presumed that justice is a virtue generally thought to be directly implanted by nature. I believe, however, that the sentiment of justice is entirely of artificial origin, the idea of natural justice not preceding but following that of conventional justice. The farther we look back into the early modes of thinking of the human race, whether we consider ancient times (including those of the Old Testament) or the portions of mankind who are still in no more advanced a condition than that of ancient times, the more completely do we find men's notions of justice defined and bounded by the express appointment of law. A man's just rights meant the rights which the law gave him; a just man was he who never infringed, or sought to infringe, the legal property or other legal rights of others. The notion of a higher justice, to which laws themselves are amenable and by which the conscience is bound without a positive prescription of law, is a later extension of the idea suggested by and following the analogy of legal justice, to which it maintains a parallel direction through all the shades and varieties of the sentiment, and from which it borrows nearly the whole of its phraseology. The very words *justus* and *justitia* are derived from *jus*, law. Courts of justice, administration of justice, always mean the tribunals.

If it be said that there must be the germs of all these virtues in human nature, otherwise mankind would be incapable of acquiring them, I am ready, with a certain amount of explanation, to admit the fact. But the weeds that dispute the ground with these beneficent germs are themselves not germs but rankly luxuriant growths and would, in all but some one case in a thousand, entirely stifle and destroy the former, were it not so strongly the interest of mankind to cherish the good germs in one another that they always do so in as far as their degree of intelligence (in this as in other respects still very imperfect) allows. It is through such fostering, commenced early and not counteracted by unfavorable influences, that, in some happily circumstanced specimens of the human race, the most elevated sentiments of which humanity is capable become a second nature, stronger than the first, and not so much subduing the original nature as merging it into itself. Even those gifted organizations which have attained the like excellence by self-culture owe it essentially to the same cause; for what self-culture would be possible without aid from the general sentiment of mankind delivered through books, and from the contemplation of exalted characters real or ideal? This artificially created or at least artificially perfected nature of the best and noblest human beings is the only nature which it is ever commendable to follow. It is almost superfluous to say that even this cannot be erected into a standard of conduct, since it is itself the fruit of a training and culture the choice of which, if rational and not accidental, must have been determined by a standard already chosen.

This brief survey is amply sufficient to prove that the duty of man is the same in respect to his own nature as in respect to the nature of all other things, namely, not to follow but to amend it. Some people, however, who do not attempt to deny that instinct ought to be subordinate to reason, pay deference to nature so far as to maintain that every natural inclination must have some sphere of action granted to it, some opening left for its gratification. All natural wishes, they say, must have been implanted for a purpose; and this argument is carried so far that we often hear it maintained that every wish which it is supposed to be natural to entertain must have a corresponding provision in the order of the universe for its gratification; insomuch (for instance) that the desire of an indefinite prolongation of existence is believed by many to be in itself a sufficient proof of the reality of a future life.

I conceive that there is a radical absurdity in all these attempts to discover, in detail, what are the designs of Providence, in order when they are discovered to help Providence in bringing them about. Those who argue, from particular indications, that Providence intends this or that, either believe that the Creator can do all that he will or that he cannot. If the first supposition is adopted—if Providence is omnipotent—Providence intends whatever happens, and the fact of its happening proves that Providence intended it. If so, everything which a human being can do is predestined by Providence and is a fulfillment of its designs. But if, as is the more religious theory, Providence intends not all which happens, but only what is good, then indeed man has it in his power, by his voluntary actions, to aid the intentions of Providence; but he can only learn those intentions by considering what tends to promote the general good, and not what man has a natural inclination to; for, limited as, on this showing, the divine power must be by inscrutable but insurmountable obstacles, who knows that man *could* have been created without desires which never are to be, and even which never ought to be, fulfilled? The inclinations with which man has been endowed, as well as any of the other contrivances which we observe in nature, may be the expression, not of the divine will, but of the fetters which impede its free action; and to take hints from these for the guidance of our own conduct may be falling into a trap laid by the enemy. The assumption that everything which infinite goodness can desire actually comes to pass in this universe, or at least that we must never say or suppose that it does not, is worthy only of those whose slavish fears make them offer the homage of lies to a Being who, they profess to think, is incapable of being deceived and holds all falsehood in abomination.

With regard to this particular hypothesis, that all natural impulses, all propensities sufficiently universal and sufficiently spontaneous to be capable of passing for instincts, must exist for good ends and ought to be only regulated, not repressed —this is of course true of the majority of them, for the species could not have continued to exist unless most of its inclinations had been directed to things needful or useful for its preservation. But unless the instincts can be reduced to a very small number indeed, it must be allowed that we have also bad instincts which it should be the aim of education not simply to regulate but to extirpate, or rather (what can be done even to an instinct) to starve them by disuse. Those who are inclined to multiply the number of instincts usually include among them one which they call destructiveness, an instinct to destroy for destruction's sake. I can conceive no good reason for preserving this, no more than another propensity which if not an instinct is very like one, what has been called the instinct of domination, a delight in exercising despotism, in holding other beings in subjection to our will. The man who takes pleasure in the mere exertion of authority, apart from the purpose for which it is to be employed, is the last person in whose hands one would willingly entrust it. Again, there are persons who are cruel by character, or, as the phrase is, naturally cruel, who have a real pleasure in inflicting or seeing the infliction of pain. This kind of cruelty is not mere hardheartedness, absence of pity or remorse; it is a positive thing, a particular kind of voluptuous excitement. The East and southern Europe have afforded, and probably still afford, abundant examples of this hateful propensity. I suppose it will be granted that this is not one of the natural inclinations which it would be wrong to suppress. The only question would be whether it is not a duty to suppress the man himself along with it.

But even if it were true that every one of the elementary impulses of human nature has its good side and may by a sufficient amount of artificial training be made more useful than hurtful, how little would this amount to when it must in any case be admitted that, without such training, all of them, even those which are necessary to our preservation, would fill the world with misery, making human life an exaggerated likeness of the odious scene of violence and tyranny which is exhibited by the rest of the animal kingdom, except in so far as tamed and disciplined by man. There, indeed, those who flatter themselves with the notion of reading the purposes of the Creator in his works ought in consistency to have seen grounds for inferences from which they have shrunk. If there are any marks at all of special design in creation, one of the things most evidently designed is that a large proportion of all animals should pass their existence in tormenting and devouring other animals. They have been lavishly fitted out with the instruments necessary for that purpose; their strongest instincts impel them to it, and many of them seem to have been constructed incapable of supporting themselves by any other food. If a tenth part of the pains which have been expended in finding benevolent adaptations in all nature had been employed in collecting evidence to blacken the character of the Creator, what scope for comment would not have been found in the entire existence of the lower animals, divided with scarcely an exception into devourers and devoured, and a prey to a thousand ills from which they are denied the faculties necessary for protecting themselves! If we are not obliged to believe the animal creation to be the work of a demon it is because we need not suppose it to have been made by a Being of infinite power. But if imitation of the Creator's will as revealed in nature were applied as a rule of action in this case, the most atrocious enormities of the worst men would be more than justified by the apparent intention of Providence that throughout all animated nature the strong should prey upon the weak.

The preceding observations are far from having exhausted

the almost infinite variety of modes and occasions in which the idea of conformity to nature is introduced as an element into the ethical appreciation of actions and dispositions. The same favorable prejudgment follows the word nature through the numerous acceptations in which it is employed as a distinctive term for certain parts of the constitution of humanity as contrasted with other parts. We have hitherto confined ourselves to one of these acceptations, in which it stands as a general designation for those parts of our mental and moral constitution which are supposed to be innate, in contradistinction to those which are acquired: as when nature is contrasted with education; or when a savage state, without laws, arts, or knowledge, is called a state of nature; or when the question is asked whether benevolence, or the moral sentiment, is natural or acquired; or whether some persons are poets or orators by nature and others not. But in another and a more lax sense, any manifestations by human beings are often termed natural when it is merely intended to say that they are not studied or designedly assumed in the particular case, as when a person is said to move or speak with natural grace, or when it is said that a person's natural manner or character is so and so, meaning that it is so when he does not attempt to control or disguise it. In a still looser acceptation, a person is said to be naturally that which he was until some special cause had acted upon him, or which it is supposed he would be if some such cause were withdrawn. Thus a person is said to be naturally dull but to have made himself intelligent by study and perseverance; to be naturally cheerful but soured by misfortune; naturally ambitious but kept down by want of opportunity. Finally, the word natural, applied to feelings or conduct, often seems to mean no more than that they are such as are ordinarily found in human beings: as when it is said that a person acted on some particular occasion as it was natural to do; or that to be affected in a particular way by some sight, or sound, or thought, or incident in life is perfectly natural.

In all these senses of the term the quality called natural is very often confessedly a worse quality than the one contrasted with it; but whenever its being so is not too obvious to be questioned the idea seems to be entertained that by describing it as natural something has been said amounting to a considerable presumption in its favor. For my part I can perceive only one sense in which nature, or naturalness, in a human being are really terms of praise, and then the praise is only negative, namely, when used to denote the absence of affectation. Affectation may be defined the effort to appear what one is not, when the motive or the occasion is not such as either to excuse the attempt or to stamp it with the more odious name of hypocrisy. It must be added that the deception is often attempted to be practiced on the deceiver himself as well as on others; he imitates the external signs of qualities which he would like to have, in hopes to persuade himself that he has them. Whether in the form of deception or of self-deception, or of something hovering between the two, affectation is very rightly accounted a reproach, and naturalness, understood as the reverse of affectation, a merit. But a more proper term by which to express this estimable quality would be sincerity, a term which has fallen from its original elevated meaning and popularly denotes only a subordinate branch of the cardinal virtue it once designated as a whole.

Sometimes also, in cases where the term affectation would be inappropriate, since the conduct or demeanor spoken of is really praiseworthy, people say in disparagement of the person concerned that such conduct or demeanor is not natural to him, and make uncomplimentary comparisons between him and some other person to whom it is natural, meaning that what in the one seemed excellent was the effect of temporary excitement, or of a great victory over himself, while in the other it is the result to be expected from the habitual character. This mode of speech is not open to censure, since nature is here simply a term for the person's ordinary disposition, and if he is praised it is not for being natural but for being naturally good.

Conformity to nature has no connection whatever with right and wrong. The idea can never be fitly introduced into ethical discussions at all, except occasionally and partially into the question of degrees of culpability. To illustrate this point let us consider the phrase by which the greatest intensity of condemnatory feeling is conveyed in connection with the idea of nature—the word unnatural. That a thing is unnatural, in any precise meaning which can be attached to the word, is no argument for its being blamable, since the most criminal actions are, to a being like man, not more unnatural than most of the virtues. The acquisition of virtue has in all ages been accounted a work of labor and difficulty, while the *descensus Averni* on the contrary is of proverbial facility; and it assuredly requires in most persons a greater conquest over a greater number of natural inclinations to become eminently virtuous than transcendently vicious. But if an action or an inclination has been decided on other grounds to be blamable, it may be a circumstance in aggravation that it is unnatural, that is, repugnant to some strong feeling usually found in human beings; since the bad propensity, whatever it be, has afforded evidence of being both strong and deeply rooted by having overcome that repugnance. This presumption, of course, fails if the individual never had the repugnance, and the argument, therefore, is not fit to be urged unless the feeling which is violated by the act is not only justifiable and reasonable but is one which it is blamable to be without.

The corresponding plea in extenuation of a culpable act because it was natural, or because it was prompted by a natural feeling, never, I think, ought to be admitted. There is hardly a bad action ever perpetrated which is not perfectly natural, and the motives to which are not perfectly natural feelings. In the eye of reason, therefore, this is no excuse, but it is quite "natural" that it should be so in the eyes of the multitude because the meaning of the expression is that they have a fellow feeling with the offender. When they say that something which they cannot help admitting to be blamable is nevertheless natural, they mean that they can imagine the possibility of their being themselves tempted to commit it. Most people have a considerable amount of indulgence toward all acts of which they feel a possible source within themselves, reserving their rigor for those which, though perhaps really less bad, they cannot in any way understand how it is possible to commit. If an action convinces them (which it often does on very inadequate grounds) that the person who does it must be a being totally unlike themselves, they are seldom particular in examining the precise degree of blame due to it, or even if blame is properly due to it at all. They measure the degree of guilt by the strength of their antipathy; and hence differences of opinion, and even differences of tastes, have been objects of as intense moral abhorrence as the most atrocious crimes.

It will be useful to sum up in a few words the leading conclusions of this essay.

The word Nature has two principal meanings: it either denotes the entire system of things, with the aggregate of all their properties, or it denotes things as they would be, apart from human intervention.

In the first of these senses, the doctrine that man ought to follow nature is unmeaning, since man has no power to do anything else than follow nature; all his actions are done through and in obedience to some one or many of nature's physical or mental laws.

In the other sense of the term, the doctrine that men ought to follow nature or, in other words, ought to make the spontaneous course of things the model of his voluntary actions is equally irrational and immoral:

Irrational, because all human action whatever consists in altering, and all useful action in improving, the spontaneous course of nature:

Immoral, because the course of natural phenomena being replete with everything which when committed by human beings is most worthy of abhorrence, anyone who endeavored in his actions to imitate the natural course of things would be universally seen and acknowledged to be the wickedest of men.

The scheme of nature regarded in its whole extent cannot have had, for its sole or even principal object, the good of human or other sentient beings. What good it brings to them is mostly the result of their own exertions. Whatsoever in nature gives indication of beneficent design proves this beneficence to be armed only with limited power; and the duty of man is to co-operate with the beneficent powers, not by imitating but by perpetually striving to amend the course of nature—and bringing that part of it over which we can exercise control more nearly into conformity with a high standard of justice and goodness.

UTILITY OF RELIGION

It has sometimes been remarked how much has been written, both by friends and enemies, concerning the truth of religion, and how little, at least in the way of discussion or controversy, concerning its usefulness. This, however, might have been expected; for the truth, in matters which so deeply affect us, is our first concernment. If religion, or any particular form of it, is true, its usefulness follows without other proof. If to know authentically in what order of things, under what government of the universe, it is our destiny to live were not useful, it is difficult to imagine what could be considered so. Whether a person is in a pleasant or in an unpleasant place, a palace or a prison, it cannot be otherwise than useful to him to know where he is. So long, therefore, as men accepted the teachings of their religion as positive facts, no more a matter of doubt than their own existence or the existence of the objects around them, to ask the use of believing it could not possibly occur to them. The utility of religion did not need to be asserted until the arguments for its truth had in a great measure ceased to convince. People must either have ceased to believe, or have ceased to rely on the belief of others, before they could take that inferior ground of defense without a consciousness of lowering what they were endeavoring to raise. An argument for the utility of religion is an appeal to unbelievers to induce them to practice a well-meant hypocrisy, or to semibelievers to make them avert their eyes from what might possibly shake their unstable belief, or, finally, to persons in general to abstain from expressing any doubts they may feel, since a fabric of immense importance to mankind is so insecure at its foundations that men must hold their breath in its neighborhood for fear of blowing it down.

In the present period of history, however, we seem to have arrived at a time when, among the arguments for and against religion, those which relate to its usefulness assume an important place. We are in an age of weak beliefs, in which such belief as men have is much more determined by their wish to believe than by any mental appreciation of evidence. The wish to believe does not arise only from selfish but often from the most disinterested feelings; and though it cannot produce the unwavering and perfect reliance which once existed, it fences round all that remains of the impressions of early education; it often causes direct misgivings to fade away by disuse; and, above all, it induces people to continue laying out their lives according to doctrines which have lost part of their hold on the mind, and to maintain toward the world the same or a rather more demonstrative attitude of belief than they thought it necessary to exhibit when their personal conviction was more complete.

If religious belief be indeed so necessary to mankind as we are continually assured that it is, there is great reason to lament that the intellectual grounds of it should require to be backed by moral bribery or subornation of the understanding. Such a state of things is most uncomfortable even for those who may, without actual insincerity, describe themselves as believers, and still worse as regards those who, having consciously ceased to find the evidences of religion convincing, are withheld from saying so lest they should aid in doing an irreparable injury to mankind. It is a most painful position to a conscientious and cultivated mind to be drawn in contrary directions by the two noblest of all objects of pursuit—truth and the general good. Such a conflict must inevitably produce a growing indifference to one or other of these objects, most probably to both. Many who could render giant's service both to truth and to mankind if they believed that they could serve the one without loss to the other are either totally paralyzed or led to confine their exertions to matters of minor detail by the apprehension that any real freedom of speculation, or any considerable strengthening or enlargement of the thinking faculties of mankind at large, might, by making them unbelievers, be the surest way to render them vicious and miserable. Many, again, having observed in others or experienced in themselves elevated feelings which they imagine incapable of emanating from any other source than religion, have an

honest aversion to anything tending, as they think, to dry u
the fountain of such feelings. They, therefore, either dislik
and disparage all philosophy or addict themselves with in
tolerant zeal to those forms of it in which intuition usurps th
place of evidence and internal feeling is made the test of ob
jective truth. The whole of the prevalent metaphysics of th
present century is one tissue of suborned evidence in favo
of religion, often of deism only, but in any case involving
misapplication of noble impulses and speculative capacitie
among the most deplorable of those wretched wastes of huma
faculties which make us wonder that enough is left to kee
mankind progressive, at however slow a pace. It is time t
consider, more impartially and therefore more deliberatel
than is usually done, whether all this straining to prop u
beliefs which require so great an expense of intellectual to
and ingenuity to keep them standing yields any sufficient re
turn in human well-being; and whether that end would no
be better served by a frank recognition that certain subject
are inaccessible to our faculties, and by the application of th
same mental powers to the strengthening and enlargement o
those other sources of virtue and happiness which stand in n
need of the support or sanction of supernatural beliefs an
inducements.

Neither, on the other hand, can the difficulties of the ques
tion be so promptly disposed of as skeptical philosophers ar
sometimes inclined to believe. It is not enough to aver, i
general terms, that there never can be any conflict betwee
truth and utility, that if religion be false nothing but goo
can be the consequence of rejecting it. For, though the knowl
edge of every positive truth is a useful acquisition, this doc
trine cannot without reservation be applied to negative truth
When the only truth ascertainable is that nothing can b
known, we do not by this knowledge gain any new fact b
which to guide ourselves; we are, at best, only disabused o
our trust in some former guidemark which, though itself fal
lacious, may have pointed in the same direction with the bes
indications we have, and if it happens to be more conspicuou
and legible, may have kept us right when they might hav
been overlooked. It is, in short, perfectly conceivable tha
religion may be morally useful without being intellectuall
sustainable; and it would be a proof of great prejudice in an
unbeliever to deny that there have been ages, and that ther
are still both nations and individuals, with regard to whom
this is actually the case. Whether it is the case generally, an

with reference to the future, it is the object of this paper to examine. We propose to inquire whether the belief in religion, considered as a mere persuasion apart from the question of its truth, is really indispensable to the temporal welfare of mankind; whether the usefulness of the belief is intrinsic and universal, or local, temporary and, in some sense, accidental; and whether the benefits which it yields might not be obtained otherwise, without the very large alloy of evil by which, even in the best form of the belief, those benefits are qualified.

With the arguments on one side of the question we all are familiar: religious writers have not neglected to celebrate to the utmost the advantages both of religion in general and of their own religious faith in particular. But those who have held the contrary opinion have generally contented themselves with insisting on the more obvious and flagrant of the positive evils which have been engendered by past and present forms of religious belief. And, in truth, mankind have been so unremittingly occupied in doing evil to one another in the name of religion, from the sacrifice of Iphigenia to the dragonnades of Louis XIV (not to descend lower), that for any immediate purpose there was little need to seek arguments further off. These odious consequences, however, do not belong to religion in itself, but to particular forms of it, and afford no argument against the usefulness of any religions except those by which such enormities are encouraged. Moreover, the worst of these evils are already in a great measure extirpated from the more improved forms of religion; and as mankind advance in ideas and in feelings, this process of extirpation continually goes on: the immoral or otherwise mischievous consequences which have been drawn from religion are, one by one, abandoned and, after having been long fought for as of its very essence, are discovered to be easily separable from it. These mischiefs, indeed, after they are past, though no longer arguments against religion, remain valid as large abatements from its beneficial influence by showing that some of the greatest improvements ever made in the moral sentiments of mankind have taken place without it and in spite of it, and that what we are taught to regard as the chief of all improving influences has in practice fallen so far short of such a character that one of the hardest burdens laid upon the other good influences of human nature has been that of improving religion itself. The improvement, however, has taken place; it is still proceeding, and for the sake of fairness it should be assumed to be complete. We ought to suppose religion to have accepted the best human morality which reason and goodness can work out, from philosophical, Christian, or any other elements. When it has thus freed itself from the pernicious consequences which result from its identification with any bad moral doctrine, the ground is clear for considering whether its useful properties are exclusively inherent in it, or their benefits can be obtained without it.

This essential portion of the inquiry into the temporal usefulness of religion is the subject of the present essay. It is a part which has been little treated of by skeptical writers. The only direct discussion of it with which I am acquainted is in a short treatise, understood to have been partly compiled from manuscripts of Mr. Bentham* and abounding in just and profound views; but which, as it appears to me, presses many parts of the argument too hard. This treatise, and the incidental remarks scattered through the writings of M. Comte, are the only sources known to me from which anything very pertinent to the subject can be made available for the skeptical side of the argument. I shall use both of them freely in the sequel of the present discourse.

The inquiry divides itself into two parts, corresponding to the double aspect of the subject: its social and its individual aspect. What does religion do for society, and what for the individual? What amount of benefit to social interests, in the ordinary sense of the phrase, arises from religious belief? And what influence has it in improving and ennobling individual human nature?

The first question is interesting to everybody, the latter only to the best; but to them it is, if there be any difference, the more important of the two. We shall begin with the former as being that which best admits of being easily brought to a precise issue.

To speak first, then, of religious belief as an instrument of social good. We must commence by drawing a distinction most commonly overlooked. It is usual to credit religion *as such* with the whole of the power inherent in *any* system of moral duties inculcated by education and enforced by opinion. Undoubtedly mankind would be in a deplorable state if no principles or precepts of justice, veracity, beneficence were taught publicly or privately, and if these virtues were not encouraged and the opposite vices repressed by the praise and blame, the favorable and unfavorable sentiments, of mankind.

* "Analysis of the Influence of Natural Religion on the Temporal Happiness of Mankind," by Philip Beauchamp.

And since nearly everything of this sort which does take place takes place in the name of religion, since almost all who are taught any morality whatever have it taught to them *as* religion and inculcated on them through life principally in that character, the effect which the teaching produces as teaching it is supposed to produce as religious teaching, and religion receives the credit of all the influence in human affairs which belongs to any generally accepted system of rules for the guidance and government of human life.

Few persons have sufficiently considered how great an influence this is, what vast efficacy belongs naturally to any doctrine received with tolerable unanimity as true and impressed on the mind from the earliest childhood as duty. A little reflection will, I think, lead us to the conclusion that it is this which is the great moral power in human affairs, and that religion only seems so powerful because this mighty power has been under its command.

Consider first the enormous influence of authority on the human mind. I am now speaking of involuntary influence—effect on men's conviction, on their persuasion, on their involuntary sentiments. Authority is the evidence on which the mass of mankind believe everything which they are said to know, except facts of which their own senses have taken cognizance. It is the evidence on which even the wisest receive all those truths of science, or facts in history or in life, of which they have not personally examined the proofs. Over the immense majority of human beings the general concurrence of mankind, in any matter of opinion, is all powerful. Whatever is thus certified to them they believe with a fullness of assurance which they do not accord even to the evidence of their senses when the general opinion of mankind stands in opposition to it. When, therefore, any rule of life and duty, whether grounded or not on religion, has conspicuously received the general assent, it obtains a hold on the belief of every individual stronger than it would have even if he had arrived at it by the inherent force of his own understanding. If Novalis could say, not without a real meaning, "My belief has gained infinitely to me from the moment when one other human being has begun to believe the same," how much more when it is not one other person but all the human beings whom one knows of. Some may urge it as an objection that no scheme of morality has this universal assent and that none, therefore, can be indebted to this source for whatever power it possesses over the mind. So far as relates to the present age the assertion is true, and strengthens the argument which it might at first seem to controvert; for exactly in proportion as the received systems of belief have been contested, and it has become known that they have many dissentients, their hold on the general belief has been loosened, and their practical influence on conduct has declined; and since this has happened to them notwithstanding the religious sanction which attached to them, there can be no stronger evidence that they were powerful, not as religion, but as beliefs generally accepted by mankind. To find people who believe their religion as a person believes that fire will burn his hand when thrust into it, we must seek them in those Oriental countries where Europeans do not yet predominate, or in the European world when it was still universally Catholic. Men often disobeyed their religion in those times because their human passions and appetites were too strong for it, or because the religion itself afforded means of indulgence to breaches of its obligations; but though they disobeyed, they for the most part did not doubt. There was in those days an absolute and unquestioning completeness of belief never since general in Europe.

Such being the empire exercised over mankind by simple authority, the mere belief and testimony of their fellow creatures, consider next how tremendous is the power of education, how unspeakable is the effect of bringing people up from infancy in a belief and in habits founded on it. Consider also that in all countries, and from the earliest ages down to the present, not merely those who are called, in a restricted sense of the term, the educated, but all or nearly all who have been brought up by parents, or by anyone interested in them, have been taught from their earliest years some kind of religious belief, and some precepts as the commands of the heavenly powers to them and to mankind. And as it cannot be imagined that the commands of God are to young children anything more than the commands of their parents, it is reasonable to think that any system of social duty which mankind might adopt, even though divorced from religion, would have the same advantage of being inculcated from childhood, and would have it hereafter much more perfectly than any doctrine has it at present, society being far more disposed than formerly to take pains for the moral tuition of those numerous classes whose education it has hitherto left very much to chance. Now it is especially characteristic of the impressions of early education that they possess what it is so much more difficult for later convictions to obtain—command over the feelings. We see daily how powerful a hold these first impressions retain over the feelings even of those who have given up the opinions which they were early taught. While, on the other hand, it is only persons of a much higher degree of natural sensibility and intellect combined than it is at all common to meet with whose feelings entwine themselves with anything like the same force around opinions which they have adopted from their own investigations later in life; and even when they do, we may say with truth that it is because the strong sense of moral duty, the sincerity, courage, and self-devotion which enabled them to do so, were themselves the fruits of early impressions.

The power of education is almost boundless; there is not one natural inclination which it is not strong enough to coerce and, if needful, to destroy by disuse. In the greatest recorded victory which education has ever achieved over a whole host of natural inclinations in an entire people—the maintenance through centuries of the institutions of Lycurgus—it was very little, if even at all, indebted to religion: for the gods of the Spartans were the same as those of other Greek states; and though, no doubt, every state of Greece believed that its particular polity had at its first establishment some sort of divine sanction (mostly that of the Delphian oracle), there was seldom any difficulty in obtaining the same or an equally powerful sanction for a change. It was not religion which formed the strength of the Spartan institutions; the root of the system was devotion to Sparta, to the ideal of the country or state, which, transformed into ideal devotion to a greater country, the world, would be equal to that and far nobler achievements. Among the Greeks generally, social morality was extremely independent of religion. The inverse relation was rather that which existed between them; the worship of the gods was inculcated chiefly as a social duty, inasmuch as if they were neglected or insulted it was believed that their displeasure would fall not more upon the offending individual than upon the state or community which bred and tolerated him. Such moral teaching as existed in Greece had very little to do with religion. The gods were not supposed to concern themselves much with men's conduct to one another, except when men had contrived to make the gods themselves an interested party by placing an assertion or an engagement under the sanction of a solemn appeal to them by oath or vow. I grant that the sophists and philosophers, and even popular orators, did their best to press religion into the service of their special objects, and to make it be thought that the sentiments of whatever kind which they were engaged in inculcating were particularly acceptable to the gods, but this never seems the primary consideration in any case save those of direct offense to the dignity of the gods themselves. For the enforcement of human moralities secular inducements were almost exclusively relied on. The case of Greece is, I believe, the only one in which any teaching other than religious has had the unspeakable advantage of forming the basis of education; and though much may be said against the quality of some part of the teaching, very little can be said against its effectiveness. The most memorable example of the power of education over conduct is afforded (as I have just remarked) by this exceptional case, constituting a strong presumption that in other cases early religious teaching has owed its power over mankind rather to its being early than to its being religious.

We have now considered two powers, that of authority and that of early education, which operate through men's involuntary beliefs, feelings, and desires, and which religion has hitherto held as its almost exclusive appanage. Let us now consider a third power which operates directly on their actions, whether their involuntary sentiments are carried with it or not. This is the power of public opinion, of the praise and blame, the favor and disfavor, of their fellow creatures; and is a source of strength inherent in any system of moral belief which is generally adopted, whether connected with religion or not.

Men are so much accustomed to give the motives that decide their actions more flattering names than justly belong to them, that they are generally quite unconscious how much those parts of their conduct which they most pride themselves on (as well as some which they are ashamed of) are determined by the motive of public opinion. Of course public opinion for the most part enjoins the same things which are enjoined by the received social morality, that morality being, in truth, the summary of the conduct which each one of the multitude, whether he himself observes it with any strictness or not, desires that others should observe toward him. People are therefore easily able to flatter themselves that they are acting from the motive of conscience when they are doing in obedience to the inferior motive things which their conscience approves. We continually see how great is the power of opinion in opposition to conscience, how men "follow a multitude to do evil," how often opinion induces them to do what their conscience disapproves and still oftener prevents them from doing what it commands. But when the motive of public opinion acts in the same direction with conscience, which, since it has usually itself made the conscience in the first instance, it for the most part naturally does, it is then, of all motives which operate on the bulk of mankind, the most over-powering.

The names of all the strongest passions (except the merely animal ones) manifested by human nature are each of them a name for some one part only of the motive derived from what I here call public opinion. The love of glory, the love of praise, the love of admiration, the love of respect and deference, even the love of sympathy, are portions of its attractive power. Vanity is a vituperative name for its attractive influence generally, when considered excessive in degree. The fear of shame, the dread of ill repute or of being disliked or hated are the direct and simple forms of its deterring power. But the deterring force of the unfavorable sentiments of mankind does not consist solely in the painfulness of knowing oneself to be the object of those sentiments; it includes all the penalties which they can inflict: exclusion from social intercourse and from the innumerable good offices which human beings require from one another; the forfeiture of all that is called success in life; often the great diminution or total loss of means of subsistence; positive ill offices of various kinds, sufficient to render life miserable and reaching in some states of society as far as actual persecution to death. And again the attractive or impelling influence of public opinion includes the whole range of what is commonly meant by ambition; for, except in times of lawless military violence, the objects of social ambition can only be attained by means of the good opinion and favorable disposition of our fellow creatures; nor, in nine cases out of ten, would those objects be even desired were it not for the power they confer over the sentiments of mankind. Even the pleasure of self-approbation, in the great majority, is mainly dependent on the opinion of others. Such is the involuntary influence of authority on ordinary minds that persons must be of a better than ordinary mold to be capable of a full assurance that they are in the right when the world —that is, when *their* world—thinks them wrong; nor is there, to most men, any proof so demonstrative of their own virtue or talent as that people in general seem to believe in it. Through all departments of human affairs, regard for the sentiments of our fellow creatures is in one shape or other, in nearly all characters, the pervading motive. And we ought to note that this motive is naturally strongest in the most sensitive natures, which are the most promising material for the formation of great virtues. How far its power reaches is known by too familiar experience to require either proof or illustration here. When once the means of living have been obtained, the far greater part of the remaining labor and effort which takes place on the earth has for its object to acquire the respect or the favorable regard of mankind, to be looked up to, or at all events not to be looked down upon by them. The industrial and commercial activity which advance civilization, the frivolity, prodigality, and selfish thirst of aggrandizement which retard it, flow equally from that source. While as an instance of the power exercised by the terrors derived from public opinion, we know how many murders have been committed merely to remove a witness who knew and was likely to disclose some secret that would bring disgrace upon his murderer.

Anyone who fairly and impartially considers the subject will see reason to believe that those great effects on human conduct which are commonly ascribed to motives derived directly from religion have mostly for their proximate cause the influence of human opinion. Religion has been powerful, not by its intrinsic force, but because it has wielded that additional and more mighty power. The effect of religion has been immense in giving a direction to public opinion, which has, in many most important respects, been wholly determined by it. But without the sanctions superadded by public opinion, its own proper sanctions have never, save in exceptional characters or in peculiar moods of mind, exercised a very potent influence, after the times had gone by in which divine agency was supposed habitually to employ temporal rewards and punishments. When a man firmly believed that if he violated the sacredness of a particular sanctuary he would be struck dead on the spot or smitten suddenly with a mortal disease, he doubtless took care not to incur the penalty; but when anyone had had the courage to defy the danger and escaped with impunity, the spell was broken. If ever any people were taught that they were under a divine government and that unfaithfulness to their religion and law would be visited from above with temporal chastisements, the Jews were so. Yet their history was a mere succession of lapses into paganism. Their prophets and historians, who held fast to the ancient beliefs (though they gave them so liberal an interpretation as to think it a sufficient manifestation of God's displeasure toward a king if any evil happened to his great-grandson), never ceased to complain that their countrymen turned a deaf ear to their vaticinations; and hence, with the faith they held in a divine government operating by temporal penalties, they could not fail to anticipate (as Mirabeau's father without such prompting was able to do on the eve of the French Revolution) *la culbute générale*, an expectation which, luckily for the credit of their prophetic powers, was fulfilled—unlike that of the Apostle John who, in the only intelligible prophecy in the Revelations, foretold to the city of the seven hills a fate like that of Nineveh and Babylon, which prediction remains to this hour unaccomplished. Unquestionably the conviction which experience in time forced on all but very ignorant, that divine punishments were not to be confidently expected in a temporal form, contributed much to the downfall of the old religions and the general adoption of one which, without absolutely excluding providential interferences in this life for the punishment of guilt or the reward of merit, removed the principal scene of divine retribution to a world after death. But rewards and punishments postponed to that distance of time, and never seen by the eye, are not calculated, even when infinite and eternal, to have on ordinary minds a very powerful effect in opposition to strong temptation. Their remoteness alone is a prodigious deduction from their efficacy on such minds as those which most require the restraint of punishment. A still greater abatement is their uncertainty, which belongs to them from the very nature of the case; for rewards and punishments administered after death must be awarded not definitely to particular actions but on a general survey of the person's whole life, and he easily persuades himself that, whatever may have been his peccadilloes, there will be a balance in his favor at the last. All positive religions aid this self-delusion. Bad religions teach that divine vengeance may be bought off, by offerings or personal abasement; the better religions, not to drive sinners to despair, dwell so much on the divine mercy that hardly anyone is compelled to think himself irrevocably condemned. The sole quality in these punishments which might seem calculated to make them efficacious, their overpowering magnitude, is itself a reason why nobody (except a hypochondriac here and there) ever really believes that he is in any very serious danger of incurring them. Even the worst malefactor is hardly able to think that any crime he

has had it in his power to commit, any evil he can have inflicted in this short space of existence, can have deserved torture extending through an eternity. Accordingly religious
writers and preachers are never tired of complaining how little
effect religious motives have on men's lives and conduct, notwithstanding the tremendous penalties denounced.

Mr. Bentham, whom I have already mentioned as one of the
few authors who have written anything to the purpose on the
efficacy of the religious sanction, adduces several cases to
prove that religious obligation, when not enforced by public
opinion, produces scarcely any effect on conduct. His first example is that of oaths. The oaths taken in courts of justice, and
any others which, from the manifest importance to society of
their being kept, public opinion rigidly enforces, are felt as
real and binding obligations. But university oaths and customhouse oaths, though in a religious point of view equally obligatory, are in practice utterly disregarded even by men in other
respects honorable. The university oath to obey the statutes
has been for centuries, with universal acquiescence, set at
nought; and utterly false statements are (or used to be) daily
and unblushingly sworn to at the customhouse by persons as
attentive as other people to all the ordinary obligations of life.
The explanation being that veracity in these cases was not
enforced by public opinion. The second case which Bentham
cites is dueling, a practice now, in this country, obsolete, but
in full vigor in several other Christian countries; deemed and
admitted to be a sin by almost all who, nevertheless, in obedience to opinion and to escape from personal humiliation, are
guilty of it. The third case is that of illicit sexual intercourse,
which in both sexes stands in the very highest rank of religious
sins; yet, not being severely censured by opinion in the male
sex, they have in general very little scruple in committing it;
while in the case of women, though the religious obligation
is not stronger, yet, being backed in real earnest by public
opinion, it is commonly effectual.

Some objection may doubtless be taken to Bentham's instances, considered as crucial experiments on the power of the
religious sanction; for (it may be said) people do not really believe that in these cases they shall be punished by God any
more than by man. And this is certainly true in the case of
those university and other oaths which are habitually taken
without any intention of keeping them. The oath, in these
cases, is regarded as a mere formality, destitute of any serious
meaning in the sight of the Deity; and the most scrupulous

person, even if he does reproach himself for having taken an oath which nobody deems fit to be kept, does not in his conscience tax himself with the guilt of perjury, but only with the profanation of a ceremony. This, therefore, is not a good example of the weakness of the religious motive when divorced from that of human opinion. The point which it illustrates is rather the tendency of the one motive to come and go with the other, so that where the penalties of public opinion cease, the religious motive ceases also. The same criticism, however, is not equally applicable to Bentham's other examples, dueling and sexual irregularities. Those who do these acts, the first by the command of public opinion, the latter with its indulgence, really do in most cases believe that they are offending God. Doubtless they do not think that they are offending him in such a degree as very seriously to endanger their salvation. Their reliance on his mercy prevails over their dread of his resentment, affording an exemplification of the remark already made, that the unavoidable uncertainty of religious penalties makes them feeble as a deterring motive. They are so even in the case of acts which human opinion condemns, much more with those to which it is indulgent. What mankind think venial it is hardly ever supposed that God looks upon in a serious light, at least by those who feel in themselves any inclination to practice it.

I do not for a moment think of denying that there are states of mind in which the idea of religious punishment acts with the most overwhelming force. In hypochondriacal disease, and in those with whom, from great disappointments or other moral causes, the thoughts and imagination have assumed a habitually melancholy complexion, that topic, falling in with the pre-existing tendency of the mind, supplies images well fitted to drive the unfortunate sufferer even to madness. Often, during a temporary state of depression, these ideas take such a hold of the mind as to give a permanent turn to the character, being the most common cause of what, in sectarian phraseology, is called conversion. But if the depressed state ceases after the conversion, as it commonly does, and the convert does not relapse but perseveres in his new course of life, the principal difference between it and the old is usually found to be that the man now guides his life by the public opinion of his religious associates, as he before guided it by that of the profane world. At all events, there is one clear proof how little the generality of mankind, either religious or worldly, really dread eternal punishments when we see how, even at the approach of death, when the remoteness which took so much from their effect has been exchanged for the closest proximity, almost all persons who have not been guilty of some enormous crime (and many who have) are quite free from uneasiness as to their prospects in another world, and never for a moment seem to think themselves in any real danger of eternal punishment.

With regard to the cruel deaths and bodily tortures which confessors and martyrs have so often undergone for the sake of religion, I would not depreciate them by attributing any part of this admirable courage and constancy to the influence of human opinion. Human opinion indeed has shown itself quite equal to the production of similar firmness in persons not otherwise distinguished by moral excellence, such as the North American Indian at the stake. But if it was not the thought of glory in the eyes of their fellow religionists which upheld these heroic sufferers in their agony, as little do I believe that it was, generally speaking, that of the pleasures of heaven or the pains of hell. Their impulse was a divine enthusiasm—a self-forgetting devotion to an idea: a state of exalted feeling by no means peculiar to religion, but which it is the privilege of every great cause to inspire, a phenomenon belonging to the critical moments of existence, not to the ordinary play of human motives, and from which nothing can be inferred as to the efficacy of the ideas which it sprung from, whether religious or any other, in overcoming ordinary temptations and regulating the course of daily life.

We may now have done with this branch of the subject, which is, after all, the vulgarest part of it. The value of religion as a supplement to human laws, a more cunning sort of police, an auxiliary to the thief-catcher and the hangman, is not that part of its claims which the more high-minded of its votaries are fondest of insisting on; and they would probably be as ready as anyone to admit that, if the nobler offices of religion in the soul could be dispensed with, a substitute might be found for so coarse and selfish a social instrument as the fear of hell. In their view of the matter, the best of mankind absolutely require religion for the perfection of their own character, even though the coercion of the worst might possibly be accomplished without its aid.

Even in the social point of view, however, under its most elevated aspect, these nobler spirits generally assert the necessity of religion, as a teacher, if not as an enforcer, of social morality. They say that religion alone can teach us what morality is; that all the high morality ever recognized by mankind was learned from religion; that the greatest uninspired philosophers in their sublimest flights stopped far short of the Christian morality, and, whatever inferior morality they may have attained to (by the assistance, as many think, of dim traditions derived from the Hebrew books, or from a primeval revelation), they never could induce the common mass of their fellow citizens to accept it from them. That only when a morality is understood to come from the gods do men in general adopt it, rally round it, and lend their human sanctions for its enforcement. That granting the sufficiency of human motives to make the rule obeyed, were it not for the religious idea we should not have had the rule itself.

There is truth in much of this, considered as matter of history. Ancient peoples have generally, if not always, received their morals, their laws, their intellectual beliefs, and even their practical arts of life—all, in short, which tended either to guide or to discipline them—as revelations from the superior powers, and in any other way could not easily have been induced to accept them. This was partly the effect of their hopes and fears from those powers, which were of much greater and more universal potency in early times when the agency of the gods was seen in the daily events of life, experience not having yet disclosed the fixed laws according to which physical phenomena succeed one another. Independently, too, of personal hopes and fears, the involuntary deference felt by these rude minds for power superior to their own, and the tendency to suppose that beings of superhuman power must also be of superhuman knowledge and wisdom, made them disinterestedly desire to conform their conduct to the presumed preferences of these powerful beings, and to adopt no new practice without their authorization either spontaneously given or solicited and obtained.

But because when men were still savages they would not have received either moral or scientific truths unless they had supposed them to be supernaturally imparted, does it follow that they would now give up moral truths any more than scientific because they believed them to have no higher origin than wise and noble human hearts? Are not moral truths strong enough in their own evidence at all events to retain the belief of mankind when once they have acquired it? I grant that some of the precepts of Christ as exhibited in the Gospels—rising far above Paulism, which is the foundation of ordinary Christianity—carry some kinds of moral goodness to a greater height than had ever been attained before, though much even of what is supposed to be peculiar to them is equaled in the Meditations of Marcus Antoninus, which we have no ground for believing to have been in any way indebted to Christianity. But this benefit, whatever it amounts to, has been gained. Mankind have entered into the possession of it. It has become the property of humanity, and cannot now be lost by anything short of a return to primeval barbarism. The "new commandment to love one another";* the recognition that the greatest are those who serve, not who are served by, others; the reverence for the weak and humble, which is the foundation of chivalry, they and not the strong being pointed out as having the first place in God's regard and the first claim on their fellow men; the lesson of the parable of the Good Samaritan; that of "he that is without sin let him throw the first stone"; the precept of doing as we would be done by; and such other noble moralities as are to be found, mixed with some poetical exaggerations and some maxims of which it is difficult to ascertain the precise object, in the authentic sayings of Jesus of Nazareth: these are surely in sufficient harmony with the intellect and feelings of every good man or woman to be in no danger of being let go, after having been once acknowledged as the creed of the best and foremost portion of our species. There will be, as there have been, shortcomings enough for a long time to come in acting on them; but that they should be forgotten, or cease to be operative on the human conscience, while human beings remain cultivated or civilized, may be pronounced, once for all, impossible.

On the other hand, there is a very real evil consequent on ascribing a supernatural origin to the received maxims of morality. That origin consecrates the whole of them and protects them from being discussed or criticized. So that if among the moral doctrines received as a part of religion there be any which are imperfect—which were either erroneous from the first, or not properly limited and guarded in the expression, or which, unexceptionable once, are no longer suited to the changes that have taken place in human relations (and it is my firm belief that in so-called Christian morality instances of all these kinds are to be found)—these doctrines are considered

* Not, however, a new commandment. In justice to the great Hebrew lawgiver, it should always be remembered that the precept to love thy neighbor as thyself already existed in the Pentateuch; and very surprising it is to find it there.

equally binding on the conscience with the noblest, most permanent, and most universal precepts of Christ. Wherever morality is supposed to be of supernatural origin, morality is stereotyped; as law is, for the same reason, among believers in the Koran.

Belief, then, in the supernatural, great as are the services which it rendered in the early stages of human development, cannot be considered to be any longer required, either for enabling us to know what is right and wrong in social morality, or for supplying us with motives to do right and to abstain from wrong. Such belief, therefore, is not necessary for social purposes, at least in the coarse way in which these can be considered apart from the character of the individual human being. That more elevated branch of the subject now remains to be considered. If supernatural beliefs are indeed necessary to the perfection of the individual character, they are necessary also to the highest excellence in social conduct—necessary in a far higher sense than that vulgar one which constitutes it the great support of morality in common eyes.

Let us then consider what it is in human nature which causes it to require a religion, what wants of the human mind religion supplies, and what qualities it develops. When we have understood this, we shall be better able to judge how far these wants can be otherwise supplied and those qualities, or qualities equivalent to them, unfolded and brought to perfection by other means.

The old saying, *Primus in orbe Deos fecit timor*, I hold to be untrue or to contain, at most, only a small amount of truth. Belief in gods had, I conceive, even in the rudest minds a more honorable origin. Its universality has been very rationally explained from the spontaneous tendency of the mind to attribute life and volition similar to what it feels in itself to all natural objects and phenomena which appear to be self-moving. This was a plausible fancy, and no better theory could be formed at first. It was naturally persisted in so long as the motions and operations of these objects seemed to be arbitrary and incapable of being accounted for but by the free choice of the Power itself. At first, no doubt, the objects themselves were supposed to be alive, and this belief still subsists among African fetish worshipers. But as it must soon have appeared absured that things which could do so much more than man could not or would not do what man does, as for example to speak, the transition was made to supposing that the object present to the senses was inanimate, but was the creature and instrument of an invisible being with a form and organs similar to the human.

These beings having first been believed in, fear of them necessarily followed; since they were thought able to inflict at pleasure on human beings great evils which the sufferers neither knew how to avert nor to foresee, but were left dependent, for their chances of doing either, upon solicitations addressed to the deities themselves. It is true, therefore, that fear had much to do with religion; but belief in the gods evidently preceded, and did not arise from, fear; though the fear, when established, was a strong support to the belief, nothing being conceived to be so great an offense to the divinities as any doubt of their existence.

It is unnecessary to prosecute further the natural history of religion, as we have not here to account for its origin in rude minds, but for its persistency in the cultivated. A sufficient explanation of this will, I conceive, be found in the small limits of man's certain knowledge, and the boundlessness of his desire to know. Human existence is girt round with mystery: the narrow region of our experience is a small island in the midst of a boundless sea, which at once awes our feelings and stimulates our imagination by its vastness and its obscurity. To add to the mystery, the domain of our earthly existence is not only an island in infinite space but also in infinite time. The past and the future are alike shrouded from us; we neither know the origin of anything which is, nor its final destination. If we feel deeply interested in knowing that there are myriads of worlds at an immeasurable and, to our faculties, inconceivable distance from us in space; if we are eager to discover what little we can about these worlds, and when we cannot know what they are can never satiate ourselves with speculating on what they may be: is it not a matter of far deeper interest to us to learn, or even to conjecture, from whence came this nearer world which we inhabit, what cause or agency made it what it is, and on what powers depend its future fate? Who would not desire this more ardently than any other conceivable knowledge, so long as there appeared the slightest hope of attaining it? What would not one give for any credible tidings from that mysterious region, any glimpse into it which might enable us to see the smallest light through its darkness, especially any theory of it which we could believe, and which represented it as tenanted by a benignant and not a hostile influence? But since we are able to penetrate into that region with the imagination only, assisted by specious but inconclusive analogies derived from human agency and design, imagination is free to fill up the vacancy with the imagery most congenial to itself—sublime and elevating if it be a lofty imagination, low and mean if it be a groveling one.

Religion and poetry address themselves, at least in one of their aspects, to the same part of the human constitution; they both supply the same want, that of ideal conceptions grander and more beautiful than we see realized in the prose of human life. Religion, as distinguished from poetry, is the product of the craving to know whether these imaginative conceptions have realities answering to them in some other world than ours. The mind, in this state, eagerly catches at any rumors respecting other worlds, especially when delivered by persons whom it deems wiser than itself. To the poetry of the supernatural comes to be thus added a positive belief and expectation which unpoetical minds can share with the poetical. Belief in a god or gods and in a life after death becomes the canvas which every mind, according to its capacity, covers with such ideal pictures as it can either invent or copy. In that other life each hopes to find the good which he has failed to find on earth, or the better which is suggested to him by the good which on earth he has partially seen and known. More especially, this belief supplies the finer minds with material for conceptions of beings more awful than they *can* have known on earth, and more excellent than they probably *have* known. So long as human life is insufficient to satisfy human aspirations, so long there will be a craving for higher things, which finds its most obvious satisfaction in religion. So long as earthly life is full of sufferings, so long there will be need of consolations, which the hope of heaven affords to the selfish, the love of God to the tender and grateful.

The value, therefore, of religion to the individual, both in the past and present, as a source of personal satisfaction and of elevated feelings is not to be disputed. But it has still to be considered whether in order to obtain this good it is necessary to travel beyond the boundaries of the world which we inhabit, or whether the idealization of our earthly life, the cultivation of a high conception of what *it* may be made, is not capable of supplying a poetry and, in the best sense of the word, a religion equally fitted to exalt the feelings and (with the same aid from education) still better calculated to ennoble the conduct than any belief respecting the unseen powers.

At the bare suggestion of such a possibility many will exclaim that the short duration, the smallness and insignificance of life, if there is no prolongation of it beyond what we see, makes it impossible that great and elevated feelings can connect themselves with anything laid out on so small a scale; that such a conception of life can match with nothing higher than Epicurean feelings, and the Epicurean doctrine, "Let us eat and drink, for tomorrow we die."

Unquestionably, within certain limits the maxim of the Epicureans is sound, and applicable to much higher things than eating and drinking. To make the most of the present for all good purposes, those of enjoyment among the rest; to keep under control those mental dispositions which lead to undue sacrifice of present good for a future which may never arrive; to cultivate the habit of deriving pleasure from things within our reach rather than from the too eager pursuit of objects at a distance; to think all time wasted which is not spent either in personal pleasure or in doing things useful to oneself or others: these are wise maxims, and the *carpe diem* doctrine carried thus far is a rational and legitimate corollary from the shortness of life. But that because life is short we should care for nothing beyond it is not a legitimate conclusion; and the supposition that human beings in general are not capable of feeling deep and even the deepest interest in things which they will never live to see is a view of human nature as false as it is abject. Let it be remembered that if individual life is short, the life of the human species is not short; its indefinite duration is practically equivalent to endlessness; and, being combined with indefinite capability of improvement, it offers to the imagination and sympathies a large enough object to satisfy any reasonable demand for grandeur of aspiration. If such an object appears small to a mind accustomed to dream of infinite and eternal beatitudes, it will expand into far other dimensions when those baseless fancies shall have receded into the past.

Nor let it be thought that only the more eminent of our species, in mind and heart, are capable of identifying their feelings with the entire life of the human race. This noble capability implies indeed a certain cultivation, but not superior to that which might be, and certainly will be if human improvement continues, the lot of all. Objects far smaller than this, and equally confined within the limits of the earth (though not within those of a single human life), have been found sufficient to inspire large masses and long successions of mankind with an enthusiasm capable of ruling the conduct and coloring the whole life. Rome was to the entire Roman people for many generations as much a religion as Jehovah was to the Jews; nay, much more, for they never fell off from their worship as the Jews did from theirs. And the Romans, otherwise a selfish people, with no very remarkable faculties of any kind except the purely practical, derived nevertheless from this one idea a certain greatness of soul which manifests itself in all their history where that idea is concerned and nowhere else, and has earned for them the large share of admiration, in other respects not at all deserved, which has been felt for them by most noble-minded persons from that time to this.

When we consider how ardent a sentiment, in favorable circumstances of education, the love of country has become, we cannot judge it impossible that the love of that larger country, the world, may be nursed into similar strength, both as a source of elevated emotion and as a principle of duty. He who needs any other lesson on this subject than the whole course of ancient history affords, let him read Cicero *De officiis*. It cannot be said that the standard of morals laid down in that celebrated treatise is a high standard. To our notions it is on many points unduly lax and admits capitulations of conscience. But on the subject of duty to our country there is no compromise. That any man with the smallest pretensions to virtue could hesitate to sacrifice life, reputation, family, everything valuable to him, to the love of country is a supposition which this eminent interpreter of Greek and Roman morality cannot entertain for a moment. If, then, persons could be trained, as we see they were, not only to believe in theory that the good of their country was an object to which all others ought to yield, but to feel this practically as the grand duty of life, so also may they be made to feel the same absolute obligation toward the universal good. A morality grounded on large and wise views of the good of the whole, neither sacrificing the individual to the aggregate nor the aggregate to the individual but giving to duty on the one hand and to freedom and spontaneity on the other their proper province, would derive its power in the superior natures from sympathy and benevolence and the passion for ideal excellence; in the inferior, from the same feelings cultivated up to the measure of their capacity, with the superadded force of shame. This exalted morality would not depend for its ascendancy on any hope of reward; but the reward which might be looked for, and the thought of which would be a consolation in suffering and a support in moments of weakness, would not be a problematical future existence but the approbation, in this, of those whom we respect, and ideally of all those, dead or living, whom we admire or venerate. For the thought that our dead parents or friends would have approved our conduct is a scarcely less powerful motive than the knowledge that our living ones do approve it; and the idea that Socrates, or Howard, or Washington, or Antoninus, or Christ would have sympathized with us, or that we are attempting to do our part in the spirit in which they did theirs, has operated on the very best minds as a strong incentive to act up to their highest feelings and convictions.

To call these sentiments by the name morality, exclusively of any other title, is claiming too little for them. They are a real religion of which, as of other religions, outward good works (the utmost meaning usually suggested by the word morality) are only a part, and are indeed rather the fruits of the religion than the religion itself. The essence of religion is the strong and earnest direction of the emotions and desires toward an ideal object, recognized as of the highest excellence, and as rightfully paramount over all selfish objects of desire. This condition is fulfilled by the Religion of Humanity in as eminent a degree and in as high a sense as by the supernatural religions even in their best manifestations, and far more so than in any of their others.

Much more might be added on this topic; but enough has been said to convince anyone who can distinguish between the intrinsic capacities of human nature and the forms in which those capacities happen to have been historically developed that the sense of unity with mankind and a deep feeling for the general good may be cultivated into a sentiment and a principle capable of fulfilling every important function of religion and itself justly entitled to the name. I will now further maintain that it is not only capable of fulfilling these functions, but would fulfill them better than any form whatever of supernaturalism. It is not only entitled to be called a religion: it is a better religion than any of those which are ordinarily called by that title.

For, in the first place, it is disinterested. It carries the thoughts and feelings out of self and fixes them on an unselfish object, loved and pursued as an end for its own sake. The religions which deal in promises and threats regarding a future life do exactly the contrary: they fasten down the thoughts to the person's own posthumous interests; they tempt him to regard the performance of his duties to others mainly as a means to his own personal salvation; and are one of the most serious obstacles to the great purpose of moral culture, the strengthening of the unselfish and weakening of the selfish element in our nature, since they hold out to the imagination selfish good and evil of such tremendous magnitude that it is difficult for anyone who fully believes in their reality to have feeling or interest to spare for any other distant and ideal object. It is true, many of the most unselfish of mankind have been believers in supernaturalism, because their minds have not dwelt on the threats and promises of their religion but chiefly on the idea of a Being to whom they looked up with a confiding love and in whose hands they willingly left all that related especially to themselves. But in its effect on common minds, what now goes by the name of religion operates mainly through the feelings of self-interest. Even the Christ of the Gospels holds out the direct promise of reward from heaven as a primary inducement to the noble and beautiful beneficence toward our fellow creatures which he so impressively inculcates. This is a radical inferiority of the best supernatural religions compared with the Religion of Humanity, since the greatest thing which moral influences can do for the amelioration of human nature is to cultivate the unselfish feelings in the only mode in which any active principle in human nature can be effectually cultivated, namely, by habitual exericse; but the habit of expecting to be rewarded in another life for our conduct in this makes even virtue itself no longer an exercise of the unselfish feelings.

Secondly, it is an immense abatement from the worth of the old religions as means of elevating and improving human character that it is nearly, if not quite, impossible for them to produce their best moral effects unless we suppose a certain torpidity, if not positive twist, in the intellectual faculties. For it is impossible that anyone who habitually thinks and who is unable to blunt his inquiring intellect by sophistry should be able, without misgiving, to go on ascribing absolute perfection to the author and ruler of so clumsily made and capriciously governed a creation as this planet and the life of its inhabitants. The adoration of such a being cannot be with the whole heart, unless the heart is first considerably sophisticated.

The worship must either be greatly overclouded by doubt, and occasionally quite darkened by it, or the moral sentiments must sink to the low level of the ordinances of nature: the worshiper must learn to think blind partiality, atrocious cruelty, and reckless injustice not blemishes in an object of worship, since all these abound to excess in the commonest phenomena of nature. It is true, the God who is worshiped is not, generally speaking, the God of nature only, but also the God of some revelation; and the character of the revelation will greatly modify and, it may be, improve the moral influences of the religion. This is emphatically true of Christianity, since the author of the Sermon on the Mount is assuredly a far more benignant being than the Author of Nature. But unfortunately, the believer in the Christian revelation is obliged to believe that the same being is the author of both. This, unless he resolutely averts his mind from the subject or practices the act of quieting his conscience by sophistry, involves him in moral perplexities without end; since the ways of his Deity in nature are on many occasions totally at variance with the precepts, as he believes, of the same Deity in the Gospel. He who comes out with least moral damage from this embarrassment is probably the one who never attempts to reconcile the two standards with one another, but confesses to himself that the purposes of Providence are mysterious, that its ways are not our ways, that its justice and goodness are not the justice and goodness which we can conceive and which it befits us to practice. When, however, this is the feeling of the believer, the worship of the Deity ceases to be the adoration of abstract moral perfection. It becomes the bowing down to a gigantic image of something not fit for us to imitate. It is the worship of power only.

I say nothing of the moral difficulties and perversions involved in revelation itself, though even in the Christianity of the Gospels, at least in its ordinary interpretation, there are some of so flagrant a character as almost to outweigh all the beauty and benignity and moral greatness which so eminently distinguish the sayings and character of Christ. The recognition, for example, of the object of highest worship in a being who could make a Hell, and who could create countless generations of human beings with the certain foreknowledge that he was creating them for this fate. Is there any moral enormity which might not be justified by imitation of such a Deity? And is it possible to adore such a one without a frightful distortion of the standard of right and wrong? Any other of the outrages to the most ordinary justice and humanity involved in the common Christian conception of the moral character of God sinks into insignificance beside this dreadful idealization of wickedness. Most of them, too, are happily not so unequivocally deducible from the very words of Christ as to be indisputably a part of Christian doctrine. It may be doubted, for instance, whether Christianity is really responsible for atonement and redemption, original sin, and vicarious punishment; and the same may be said respecting the doctrine which makes belief in the divine mission of Christ a necessary condition of salvation. It is nowhere represented that Christ himself made this statement, except in the huddled-up account of the Resurrection contained in the concluding verses of St. Mark which some critics (I believe the best) consider to be an interpolation. Again, the proposition that "the powers that be are ordained of God" and the whole series of corollaries deduced from it in the Epistles belong to St. Paul, and must stand or fall with Paulism, not with Christianity. But there is one moral contradiction inseparable from every form of Christianity which no ingenuity can resolve and no sophistry explain away. It is that so precious a gift, bestowed on a few, should have been withheld from the many, that countless millions of human beings should have been allowed to live and die, to sin and suffer, without the one thing needful, the divine remedy for sin and suffering, which it would have cost the Divine Giver as little to have vouchsafed to all as to have bestowed by special grace upon a favored minority. Add to this that the divine message, assuming it to be such, has been authenticated by credentials so insufficient that they fail to convince a large proportion of the strongest and most cultivated minds, and the tendency to disbelieve them appears to grow with the growth of scientific knowledge and critical discrimination. He who can believe these to be the intentional shortcomings of a perfectly good Being must impose silence on every prompting of the sense of goodness and justice as received among men.

It is, no doubt, possible (and there are many instances of it) to worship with the intensest devotion either deity, that of nature or of the Gospel, without any perversion of the moral sentiments; but this must be by fixing the attention exclusively on what is beautiful and beneficent in the precepts and spirit of the Gospel and in the dispensations of nature, and putting all that is the reverse as entirely aside as if it did not exist. Accordingly, this simple and innocent faith can only, as I have said, coexist with a torpid and inactive state of the speculative faculties. For a person of exercised intellect, there is no way of attaining anything equivalent to it, save by sophistication and perversion, either of the understanding or of the conscience. It may almost always be said both of sects and of individuals who derive their morality from religion that the better logicians they are, the worse moralists.

One only form of belief in the supernatural—one only theory respecting the origin and government of the universe—stands wholly clear both of intellectual contradiction and of moral obliquity. It is that which, resigning irrevocably the idea of an omnipotent creator, regards Nature and Life not as the expression throughout of the moral character and purpose of the Deity, but as the product of a struggle between contriving goodness and an intractable material, as was believed by Plato, or a Principle of Evil, as was the doctrine of the Manichaeans. A creed like this, which I have known to be devoutly held by at least one cultivated and conscientious person of our own day, allows it to be believed that all the mass of evil which exists was undesigned by, and exists, not by the appointment of, but in spite of the Being whom we are called upon to worship. A virtuous human being assumes in this theory the exalted character of a fellow laborer with the Highest, a fellow combatant in the great strife, contributing his little, which by the aggregation of many like himself becomes much, toward that progressive ascendancy and ultimately complete triumph of good over evil which history points to, and which this doctrine teaches us to regard as planned by the Being to whom we owe all the benevolent contrivance we behold in nature. Against the moral tendency of this creed no possible objection can lie; it can produce on whoever can succeed in believing it no other than an ennobling effect. The evidence for it, indeed, if evidence it can be called, is too shadowy and unsubstantial, and the promises it holds out too distant and uncertain, to admit of its being a permanent substitute for the religion of humanity; but the two may be held in conjunction; and he to whom ideal good and the progress of the world toward it are already a religion, even though the other creed may seem to him a belief not grounded on evidence, is at liberty to indulge the pleasing and encouraging thought that its truth is possible. Apart from all dogmatic belief, there is for those who need it an ample domain in the region of the imagination which may be planted with possibilities, with hypotheses which cannot be known to be false; and when there is anything in the appearances of nature to favor them, as in this case there is (for whatever force we attach to the analogies of nature with the effects of human contrivance, there is no disputing the remark of Paley that what is good in nature exhibits those analogies much oftener than what is evil), the contemplation of these possibilities is a legitimate indulgence, capable of bearing its part, with other influences, in feeding and animating the tendency of the feelings and impulses toward good.

One advantage, such as it is, the supernatural religions must always possess over the Religion of Humanity: the prospect they hold out to the individual of a life after death. For though the skepticism of the understanding does not necessarily exclude the theism of the imagination and feelings, and this, again, gives opportunity for a hope that the power which has done so much for us may be able and willing to do this also, such vague possibility must ever stop far short of a conviction. It remains then to estimate the value of this element—the prospect of a world to come—as a constituent of earthly happiness. I cannot but think that as the condition of mankind becomes improved, as they grow happier in their lives and more capable of deriving happiness from unselfish sources, they will care less and less for this flattering expectation. It is not, naturally or generally, the happy who are the most anxious either for a prolongation of the present life or for a life hereafter: it is those who never have been happy. They who have had their happiness can bear to part with existence, but it is hard to die without ever having lived. When mankind cease to need a future existence as a consolation for the sufferings of the present, it will have lost its chief value to them, for themselves. I am now speaking of the unselfish. Those who are so wrapped up in self that they are unable to identify their feelings with anything which will survive them, or to feel their life prolonged in their younger contemporaries and in all who help to carry on the progressive movement of human affairs, require the notion of another selfish life beyond the grave to enable them to keep up any interest in existence, since the present life, as its termination approaches, dwindles into something too insignificant to be worth caring about. But if the Religion of Humanity were as sedulously cultivated as the supernatural religions are (and there is no difficulty in conceiving that it might be much more so), all who had received the customary amount of moral cultivation would up to the hour of death live ideally in the life of those who are to follow them; and though doubtless they would often willingly survive as individuals for a much longer period than the present duration of life, it appears to me probable that after a length of time, different in different persons, they would have had enough of existence and would gladly lie down and take their eternal rest. Meanwhile, and without looking so far forward, we may remark that those who believe in the immortality of the soul generally quit life with fully as much, if not more, reluctance as those who have no such expectation. The mere cessation of existence is no evil to anyone: the idea is only formidable through the illusion of imagination which makes one conceive oneself as if one were alive and feeling oneself dead. What is odious in death is not death itself but the act of dying and its lugubrious accompaniments, all of which must be equally undergone by the believer in immortality. Nor can I perceive that the skeptic loses by his skepticism any real and valuable consolation except one: the hope of reunion with those dear to him who had ended their earthly life before him. That loss, indeed, is neither to be denied nor extenuated. In many cases it is beyond the reach of comparison or estimate, and will always suffice to keep alive, in the more sensitive natures, the imaginative hope of a futurity which, if there is nothing to prove, there is as little in our knowledge and experience to contradict.

History, so far as we know it, bears out the opinion that mankind can perfectly well do without the belief in a heaven. The Greeks had anything but a tempting idea of a future state. Their Elysian fields held out very little attraction to their feelings and imagination. Achilles in the Odyssey expressed a very natural and no doubt a very common sentiment when he said that he would rather be on earth the serf of a needy master than reign over the whole kingdom of the dead. And the pensive character so striking in the address of the dying emperor Hadrian to his soul gives evidence that the popular conception had not undergone much variation during that long interval. Yet we neither find that the Greeks enjoyed life less nor feared death more than other people. The Buddhist religion counts probably at this day a greater number of votaries than either the Christian or the Mohammedan. The Buddhist creed recognizes many modes of punishment in a future life, or rather lives, by the transmigration of the soul into new bodies of men or animals. But the blessing from heaven which it proposes as a reward, to be earned by perseverance in the highest order of virtuous life, is annihilation: the cessation, at least, of all conscious or separate existence. It is impossible to mistake in this religion the work of legislators and moralists endeavoring to supply supernatural motives for the conduct which they were anxious to encourage; and they could find nothing more transcendent to hold out as the capital prize to be won by the mightiest efforts of labor and self-denial than what we are so often told is the terrible idea of annihilation. Surely this is a proof that the idea is not really or naturally terrible; that not philosophers only but the common order of mankind can easily reconcile themselves to it and even consider it as a good; and that it is no unnatural part of the idea of a happy life that life itself be laid down, after the best that it can give has been fully enjoyed through a long lapse of time, when all its pleasures, even those of benevolence, are familiar and nothing untasted and unknown is left to stimulate curiosity and keep up the desire of prolonged existence. It seems to me not only possible but probable that in a higher and, above all, a happier condition of human life, not annihilation but immortality may be the burdensome idea; and that human nature, though pleased with the present and by no means impatient to quit it, would find comfort and not sadness in the thought that it is not chained through eternity to a conscious existence which it cannot be assured that it will always wish to preserve.

FURTHER READING

The two indispensable books on John Stuart Mill's life are:

F. A. Hayek, *John Stuart Mill and Harriet Taylor: Their Correspondence and Subsequent Marriage* (University of Chicago Press, 1951).

M. St. John Packe, *The Life of John Stuart Mill* (Macmillan, 1954).

The Hayek book makes available the rich material of the earlier letters and gives a balanced view of their relationship. The Packe is a model biography of a social thinker.

The older edition of Mill's letters is Hugh Elliott's *Letters of J. S. Mill* (2 vols., 1910). John Jacob Coss contributed to Mill scholarship when he published the *Autobiography* from the original manuscript, without changes or omissions (Columbia University Press, 1924).

For those who wish to study Mill primarily as a philosopher, I suggest R. P. Anschütz, *The Philosophy of J. S. Mill* (Oxford, 1953); and Karl Britton, *John Stuart Mill* (Penguin Books, 1953); also Bertrand Russell, *History of Western Philosophy* (Simon and Schuster, 1945).

For the intellectual background of Mill's England and his British philosophical predecessors, see Elie Halevy, *The Growth of Philosophic Radicalism* (Beacon, 1955), and the same author's *History of the English People* (5 vols., Peter Smith, 1949-1952). See also Leslie Stephen's *The English Utilitarians* (3 vols., London, 1900), especially vol. 3, and John Plamenatz's *The English Utilitarians* (Oxford, 1949).

For Mill's relations with other thinkers, see Emery Neff's *Carlyle and Mill* (2nd ed., Columbia, 1926); F. R. Leavis' *Mill on Bentham and Coleridge* (London, 1950); and J. P. Mayer, ed., *Oeuvres Complètes d'Alexis de Tocqueville*, vol. 6, *Correspondance Anglaise*, Part 2 (Gallimard, Paris, 1954), containing sixty-two pages of letters between Tocqueville and Mill, in both French and English.

For Mill's place in the history of political theory, see W. E. Davidson's *Political Thought in England: the Utilitarians, from Bentham to J. S. Mill* (Home University Library, Oxford, 1915). For his place as an economic theorist, see Robert L. Heilbroner's *The Worldly Philosophers* (Simon and Schuster, 1953). For his theory of religion, each of his three essays on religion—*Nature, The Utility of Religion*, and *Theism*—has been well edited with able introductions in separate volumes of the Library of Liberal Arts, under the general editorship of Oskar Piest.

There is an excellent essay by Harold Laski, as the introduction to the Worlds Classics edition of the *Autobiography* (Oxford, 1924), and the reader willing to use the detailed index will find some delightful material on Mill in the *Holmes-Laski Letters*, ed. by Mark DeWolfe Howe (2 vols., Harvard University Press, 1953).

Dorothy Fosdick's reprint of the essay *On Social Freedom* (Columbia University Press, 1941), has a useful introduction comparing it with *On Liberty*.

The major writings of John Stuart Mill, in order of first publication, are:

A System of Logic, Ratiocinative and Inductive (1843).
Essays on Some Unsettled Questions of Political Economy (1844).
Principles of Political Economy (1848).
The Enfranchisement of Women (1853).
On Liberty (1859).
Dissertations and Discussions (1859-75).
Considerations on Representative Government (1861).
Utilitarianism (1863).
Examination of Sir W. Hamilton's Philosophy (1865).
Auguste Comte and Positivism (1865).
The Subjection of Women (1869).
Autobiography (1873).
Three Essays on Religion: Nature, Utility of Religion, Theism (1874).